Mona Winks

Mona Winks

Self-Guided Tours of
Europe's Top Museums

Second Edition

Rick Steves & Gene Openshaw

John Muir Publications
Santa Fe, New Mexico

Other books by Rick Steves
Asia Through the Back Door (with John Gottberg)
Europe Through the Back Door
Europe 101: History & Art for the Traveler (with Gene Openshaw)
2 to 22 Days in Europe
2 to 22 Days in France (with Steve Smith)
2 to 22 Days in Germany, Austria & Switzerland
2 to 22 Days in Great Britain
2 to 22 Days in Italy
2 to 22 Days in Norway, Sweden & Denmark
2 to 22 Days in Spain & Portugal

Thanks to Dave Hoerlein for research help and photographs, Steve Smith, Matthew Nolan, and Eileen "Sam" Owen for research and office help, Shirley Openshaw for maternal support, Nadine Caracciolo for internal support, and Anne Steves for patience, and special thanks to all those with nuclear bombs for not using them.

John Muir Publications, P.O. Box 613, Santa Fe, NM 87504

Library of Congress Cataloging-in-Publication Data
Steves, Rick, 1955-
    Mona Winks : self-guided tours of Europe's top museums / by Rick Steves & Gene Openshaw. — 2nd ed.
        p. cm.
    Includes index.
    ISBN 1-56261-067-8
    1. Art Museums—Europe—Guidebooks.   I. Openshaw, Gene.
II. Title.
N1010.S7   1993
708.94—dc20   92-42954
                                                          CIP

Typesetting by Copygraphics
Maps by David C. Hoerlein
Mona Lisa Cover Art by Peter Aschwanden
Printed by McNaughton & Gunn
Cover Photo by Leo de Wys Inc./Eddy Van Der Veen

Distributed to the book trade by
W.W. Norton & Company
New York, New York

To
all the artists
whose works hang
in no museums —
and
to those
who appreciate them

Contents

Introduction

Even at its best, museum-going is hard work. This book attempts to tame Europe's "required" museums, making them meaningful, fun, fast and painless. Here are some tips on how to use this book to get the most out of your museum visits.

Beforehand

Do Some Background Reading
The more you know, the more you'll appreciate the art. Before your trip, take a class or read a book on art.

Rip Up This Book
Before your trip rip out, staple-bind and pack just the individual chapters you'll use. (If this really bugs you, send all the pieces and $5.00 to Europe Through The Back Door, 120 4th North, Edmonds, WA 98020 and we'll send you a new copy. Really.)

Skim Chapters
Skim the chapter the night before you visit the museum. Get a feel for the kind of art and artists you'll see.

Check the Introductory Material
Read the first page of each tour. It shows the museum hours, cost, availability of information and so forth. Many tactical problems can be avoided by planning ahead.

In The Museum

Get Oriented
Use each tour's overview map and paragraph to understand the general layout of the museum, how the art is arranged and the basic tour route.

Use The Maps And Written Directions
All featured art appears on the room maps. Maps are usually oriented so you enter from the bottom (look for the "start" arrow). Written directions reinforce the maps.

Keep The Big Picture
As you enter each room, get the *general feel*. Scan for the common characteristics of the art. Next, study the *specific example* mentioned in the text. Then *browse*, trying out what you've learned.

Use The Index
Use the index to find supplemental information on artists and styles.

Partners, Take Turns Acting As Guide
Couples can take turns being "guide."

Watch For Changes

Museums Change
Paintings can be on tour, on loan, out sick or shifted at the whims of the curator. Even museum walls are often moved. To adapt to these changes:
1) Pick up any available free floorplans as you enter.
2) Let the museum information person glance at this book's maps to confirm locations of painting.
3) If you can't find a particular painting, ask any museum worker where it is. Just point to the photograph in this book and ask, "Where?" ("Dove?" "Ou est?" "Donde?" "Wo ist?")

Museum Hours Change
Museums change their entrance hours, especially in Italy and off-season. Confirm by telephone or at the city tourist office upon arrival.

General Museum Policies (Be alert to exceptions)

Last Entry
Many museums (especially in Italy) have "last entry" thirty to sixty minutes before closing. Also, guards often start ushering people out before the official closing time.

Photography
Cameras are normally allowed, but no flashes or tripods (without special permission). Flashes damage oil paintings and distract others in the room. Video cameras are usually allowed, Even without a flash, a handheld camera with ASA 400 film and an F-2 aperture will take a fine picture. Otherwise, buy slides or cards at the museum bookstore.

Bag Checks

For security reasons museums often require that you check even small bags. Every museum has a free cloak and check room at the entrance. They're very safe. Check everything (except *Mona Winks*) and enjoy the museum.

Toilets

WCs are free and generally better and cleaner than the European average, with far and away the most entertaining graffiti.

Food

Museum-going stokes appetites. Most museums have cafeterias with reasonable prices and decent food. Check the introductory information at the beginning of each chapter for evaluations and for good places nearby.

Museum Bookstores

These have cards, prints, posters, slides and guidebooks. Thumb through a museum's biggest guidebook (or scan its index) to be sure you haven't overlooked something that is of particular interest to you.

No Apologies

This book will drive art snobs nuts. Its gross generalizations, sketchy dates, oversimplifications and shoot-from-the-hip opinions will likely irritate art highbrows.

Mona Winks isn't an art history text; it's a quick taste of Europe's fascinating but difficult museums. Use it as an introduction — not the final word.

Note

From this point on, "we" (your co-authors) will shed our respective egos and become "I". Enjoy.

Art History —
Five Millennia
in Seven Pages

Egypt (3000-1000 B.C.)

Tombs and mummies to preserve corpses and possessions for the afterlife. Statues of pharaohs were political propaganda. Stiff, unrealistic, standing-at-attention statues and paintings seem built for eternity.

* British Museum (statues, mummies, Rosetta Stone)
* Vatican Museum
* Louvre

Greece (700 B.C. to 1 A.D.)

Foundation of our "Western" civilization — science, democracy, art, and the faith that the universe is orderly and rational.

1) Archaic (700-500 B.C.)

A time of wars (think of the legendary Trojan War) and nomadism (the wandering hero Odysseus). Stiff statues reflect their search for stability and order amid chaos.

* "Kouros" statues (in Louvre and British Museum)

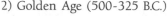

2) Golden Age (500-325 B.C.)

Athens rules a coalition of city-states in the days of Socrates, Pericles, Plato, and Aristotle. The Greek gods were portrayed as idealized human beings. Statues are realistic and natural, but their balanced poses show the order found in Nature. Nothing in extreme.

* Apollo Belvedere (Vatican Museum, see photo)
* Elgin Marbles from the Parthenon (British Museum)
* Venus de Milo (Louvre)
* Venus de' Medici (Uffizi)

3) Hellenism (325 B.C. to 1 A.D.)
Alexander the Great spreads Greek culture around the Mediterranean. Their lust for individual freedom produces restless statues of people in motion — struggling against other people, animals, and themselves. Everything in extreme.
  * Laocöon (Vatican Museum, see photo)
  * Winged Victory (Louvre)

Rome (500 B.C.-500 A.D.)
Rome conquered Greek lands and absorbed their culture and gods. The result: Greek style, but bigger is better. Romans were engineers, not artists. They built grand structures using the arch and concrete decorated with Greek columns and statues. Realistic portrait busts of the emperors reminded subjects who was in charge.
  * Colosseum, Forum, and Pantheon (Rome)
  * Greek-style statues (Vatican Museum, Louvre, British Museum)
  * Portrait busts

Byzantine (300-1300 A.D.)
The Eastern half of the Roman Empire, centered in Constantinople (Istanbul), lived on when Rome fell. Preserved arts and learning through the Dark Ages, reentering Europe via Venice.
  * St. Mark's Church — mosaics, domes, and treasures (Venice)
  * icon-style gold leaf backgrounds in medieval paintings

Medieval Europe (500-1400 A.D.)

Rome falls, plunging Europe into centuries of poverty, war, famine, and hand-me-down leotards. The church is people's refuge, and Heaven is their hope. Art serves the church — Bible scenes, Crucifixes, saints and Madonnas (Mary, the mother of Jesus) decorate churches and inspire the illiterate masses.

Art is symbolic, not realistic. Saints float in a golden, heavenly realm, far removed from life on earth. Humans are scrawny sinners living in a flat, two-dimensional world.

* Altarpieces in many museums.

Italian Renaissance (1400-1600 A.D.)

The "rebirth" of the arts and learning of ancient Greece and Rome — democracy, science and humanism. In architecture, it meant balanced structures using Greek columns and Roman domes and arches. In sculpture, 3-D realism of glorified human beings (like Greek nudes). In painting, capturing the 3-D world on a 2-D canvas using mathematical laws of perspective. They saw God in the orderliness of Nature and the beauty of the human body. Art is no longer tied to the church — art for art's sake.

1) Florence (1400-1520)

Birthplace of the Renaissance. Revived Greek-style sculpture and Roman-style architecture. Pioneered three-dimensional painting, placing statuelike people in spacious settings.

* Michelangelo's *David* (Florence's Accademia)
* Botticelli's *Birth of Venus* (Uffizi, see photo)
* Brunelleschi's church dome
* Donatello sculpture (Bargello)
* Leonardo da Vinci, Giotto, Raphael (Uffizi and other museums)

2) Roman Renaissance (1500-1550)

Grand rebuilding of the city of Rome by energetic, secular-minded Renaissance popes.

* Sistine Chapel, Michelangelo (Vatican Museum, see photo)
* St. Peter's Church, with dome by Michelangelo
* Raphael (Vatican Museum)

3) Venetian Renaissance (1500-1600)

Big, colorful, sensual paintings celebrate the Venetian good life, funded by trade with the East. Whereas Florentine painters drew their figures with heavy outlines, Venetians "built" figures out of patches of color.

* Titian (see photo)
* Veronese
* Tintoretto
* Best museums: Venice's Accademia, Prado

Northern Protestant Art (1500-1700)

Bought by middle-class merchants, not popes and kings. Everyday things painted on small canvases in a simple, realistic, unemotional style. Loving attention to detail. Portraits, landscapes, still lifes and wacky slice-of-life scenes.

* Rembrandt
* Vermeer (see photo)
* Brueghel
* Durer
* Bosch (but that's another story. . .)
* Best museums: Rijksmuseum, Alte Pinakothek, Kunsthistorisches, Prado

Baroque (1600-1700)

The style of divine-right kings (Louis XIV) and the Counter-Reformation Catholic church to overpower the common man. Big,

colorful, ornamented, though based on Renaissance balance. Exaggerated beauty and violence. Greek gods, angels, nudes and pudgy, winged babies.
* Palace of Versailles
* Rubens (many museums, see photo)

Rococo (1700-1800)

Baroque's frilly little sister. Smaller, lighter, even more ornamented; pastel colors and pudgier winged babies. In architecture, the oval

replaces the circle as the basic pattern. Aristocratic tastes were growing more refined and more out of touch with the everyday world.
* Versailles interior decoration
* Boucher (see photo), Watteau and Fragonard (Louvre)

Neo-Classical (1750-1850)

With the French Revolution, rococo became politically incorrect. Neoclassical is yet another rebirth of the Greek and Roman world. Sim-

pler and more austere than Renaissance and baroque versions of the classical style. The art of democracy and the "Age of Reason."
* J.L. David (Louvre)
* Ingres (Louvre and Orsay, see photo)

Romanticism (1800-1850)
Reaction against the overly rational Industrial Age. Return to Nature and Man's primitive roots. Dramatic, colorful art expresses the most

intense inner emotions. Both individuals and nations struggle to be free.

* Delacroix (Louvre)
* Goya (Prado, see photo)
* Blake and Turner (Tate)

Impressionism and Post-Impressionism (1850-1900)
Capturing quick "impressions" of everyday scenes (landscapes, cafes) with a fast and messy style. Thick brush strokes of bright colors laid side-by-side on the canvas blend at a distance, leaving the impres-

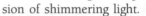

sion of shimmering light.

* Monet, Manet, Degas, and Renoir (see photo)
* Van Gogh (Van Gogh Museum)
* Gauguin, Cézanne, Rodin
* Best museums: Orsay, Tate, and National Gallery

Modern Art (1900-?)
Many styles reflect our jumbled, modern world. Let the camera tell us what things "really" look like. The artist's task now is to show life in a fresh, new way. More and more, "how" something is painted is more important than "what" is painted.

Two strains:

1) Artists continue to paint real things, but distort them to give us a new perspective (surrealism, expressionism, pop art).

2) Artists use the building blocks of painting — colors and lines — to create new and interesting patterns that hint at the non-visual aspects of the world. (abstract art, abstract expressionism). Most modern art mixes the two strains.

But what does it "mean"? Modern art offers an alternative to our normal, orderly, programmed McLives. It's a wild, chaotic jungle that you'll have to explore and tame on your own. Grrr.

* Picasso (Cubism and many other styles)
* Dali (Surrealism)
* Mondrian (Abstract)
* Warhol (Pop Art)
* Pollock (Abstract Expressionism)
* Chagall (mix of various styles)
* Best museums: Pompidou, Tate, and Stedelijk

Additional Information

If you'd like to read an entire book on art, history and culture, let me humbly recommend *Europe 101: History and Art for Travelers* by my two favorite authors, Rick Steves and Gene Openshaw. While *Mona Winks* is your on-the-spot museum manual, *Europe 101* has the necessary background information. Written in the same fun and practical style, with many of the same jokes, *Europe 101* brings Europe's churches, palaces, and statues to life.

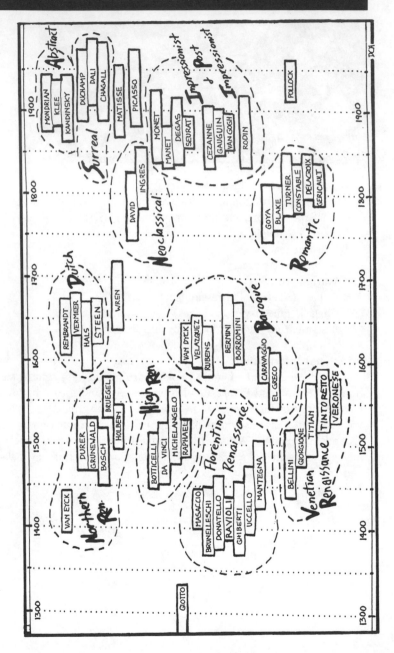

Artist Timeline (1300-1985)

Artists & Dates

Bernini (pron: bayr-NEE-nee), 1598-1680 — baroque grandeur.

Blake, William, 1757-1827 — mystical visions.

Bosch, Hieronymous (pron: bosh), 1450-1516 — crowded, bizarre scenes.

Botticelli, Sandro (pron: bah-tih-CHELL-ee), 1445-1510 — delicate Renaissance beauty.

Braque, Georges (pron: brock), 1882-1963 — Cubist pioneer.

Brunelleschi, Filippo (pron: broon-uh-LESS-key), 1377-1446) — first great Renaissance architect.

Bruegel, Pieter (pron: BROY-gull), ca.1525-1569 — Netherlands, peasant scenes.

Caravaggio (pron: car-rah-VAH-jee-oh), 1573-1610 — shocking ultra-realism.

Cézanne, Paul (pron: say-ZAH , 1839-1906 — bridged Impressionism and Cubism.

Dali, Salvador (pron: DAH-lee) 1904- ? — father of Surrealism.

Degas, Edgar (pron: day-GAH), 1834-1917 — Impressionist snapshots, dancers.

Donatello, (pron: doh-na-TELL-oh), ca. 1386-1466) — early Renaissance sculptor.

Dürer, Albrecht (pron: DEWR-er), 1471-1528 — Renaissance symmetry with German detail; "the Leonardo of the north."

El Greco (pron: el GRECK-oh), 1541-1614 — spiritual scenes, enlongated bodies.

Fra Angelico (pron: frah an-JELL-i-co), 1387-1455 — Renaissance techniques, medieval piety.

Gauguin, Paul (pron: go-GA , 1848-1903 — Primitivism, native scenes, bright colors.

Giorgione (pron: jor-JONE-ee), 1477-1510 — Venetian Renaissance, mysterious beauty.

Giotto (pron: ZHOTT-oh), 1266-1337 — proto-Renaissance painter (3-D) in medieval times.

Goya, Francisco (pron: GOY-ah), 1746-1828 — Three stages: frilly court painter, political rebel, dark stage.

Hals, Frans (pron: halls), 1581-1666 — snapshot portraits of Dutch merchants.

Ingres, Jean Auguste Dominique (pron: ANG-gruh), 1780-1867 — Neo-classical.

Leonardo Da Vinci (pron: dah VINCH-ee), 1452-1519 — a well-rounded Renaissance genius who also painted.

Manet, Edouard (pron: man-NAY), 1823-1883 — forerunner of Impressionist rebels.

Mantegna, Andrea (pron: mahn-TAYN-ya), 1431-1506 — Renaissance 3-D and "sculptural" painting.

Matisse, Henri (pron: mah-TEESS), 1869-1954 — decorative "wallpaper," bright colors.

Michelangelo (pron: mee-kell-AN-jell-oh), 1475-1564 — Earth's greatest sculptor and one of its greatest painters.

Mondrian, Piet (pron: manh-dree-ahn), 1872-1944 — abstract, geometrical canvases.

Monet, Claude (pron: moh-NAY), 1840-1926 — father of Impressionism.

Picasso, Pablo (pron: pee-KAHSS-oh), 1881-1973 — master of many modern styles, especially Cubism.

Pollock, Jackson (pron: PAHL-luck), 1912-1956 — wild drips of paint.

Raphael (pron: roff-eye-ELL), 1483-1520 — epitome of the Renaissance — balance, realism, beauty.

Rembrandt (pron: REM-brant), 1606-1669 — greatest Dutch painter, brown canvases, back-lighting.

Renoir, Auguste (pron: ren-WAH), 1841-1919 — Impressionist style, idealized beauty, pastels.

Rodin, Auguste (pron: roh-DA , 1840-1917 — rough-finish "Impressionist" sculpture.

Rubens, Peter Paul (pron: REW-buns), 1577-1640 — baroque, fleshy women, violent scenes.

Steen, Jan (pron: steen), 1626-1679 — slice-of-life everyday Dutch scenes.

Tiepolo, Giovanni Battista (pron: tee-EPP-o-lo), 1696-1770 — 3-D illusions on ceilings.

Tintoretto (pron: tin-toh-RETT-oh), 1518-1594 — Venetian Renaissance plus drama.

Titian (pron: TEESH-un), 1485-1576 — greatest Venetian Renaissance painter.

Turner, Joseph Mallord William, 1775-1851 — messy "Impressionist" scenes of nature.

Uccello, Paolo (pron: oo-CHELL-oh), 1396-1475 — early 3-D experiments.

Van Eyck, Jan (pron: van IKE), 1390-1441 — northern detail.

Van Gogh, Vincent (pron: van GO), 1853-1890 — Impressionist style plus emotion.

Velázquez, Diego (pron: vel-LAHSS-kes), 1599-1660 — objective Spanish court portraits.

Vermeer, Jan (vayr-MEER), 1632-1675 — quiet Dutch art, highlighting everyday details.

Veronese, Paolo (pron: vayr-oh-NAY-zee), 1528-1588 — huge, colorful scenes with Venetian Renaissance backgrounds.

British Museum, London

The British Museum is THE chronicle of Western civilization. It's the only place I know where you can follow the rise and fall of four great civilizations in two hours with a coffee break in the middle. And, you could come back the next day for just as many historical thrills. But in this tour I'll give you just the most exciting two hours.

British Museum and British Library

Hours: Mon.-Sat. 10:00-17:00; Sun. 2:30-18:00; closed on major holidays.
Cost: free
Tour length: Two hours
Getting there: Subway to "Tottenham Court Road" or "Holborn" and a four-block walk.
 Bus 14, 14A, 18, 24, 27, 30, 68, 73, 77, 77A.
 Taxis are reasonable if you buddy up.
Information: Main lobby information booth (English spoken).
 Daily lectures on specific subjects (check at information desk).
 Tel. 636-1555.
Misc.: Check your bags — anything left lying around that looks like a bomb will be treated as one.

Cheap and decent museum café and restaurant.

There are lots of fast, cheap and colorful cafés, pubs and markets along Great Russell Street. Since you can come and go freely, go out for a pub lunch or get a picnic for the museum colonnade.

The British Library (manuscript collection, the last part of this book's tour) is quiet in the morning when the ancient collection is stampeded.

Rainy days and Sundays are most crowded.

Starring: Gütenberg, Elgin Marbles, Magna Carta, Shakespeare, mummies, the Beatles, Charles Dickens.

Orientation

☞ *Enter the Museum and orient yourself from just inside the door.*

Everything we'll see is here on the ground floor. The ancient world is to the left, through the bookstore; the manuscripts are in the British Library to the right. Upstairs, there's much more that you absolutely must see...on your next trip.

☞ *Notice where the information booth and WCs are, then pass through the bookstore on your left. At the other end, turn right and find the two huge statues of winged lions with bearded human heads. Have a seat on the bench nearby.*

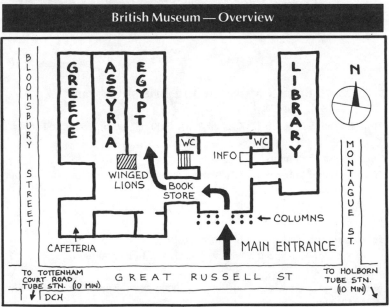

British Museum — Overview

History is a modern invention. Before about 1700 people could have cared less about crumbling statues and dusty columns. Nowadays (I hope), we see the importance of looking at past civilizations, because they tell us so much about ourselves — "Those that don't learn from history are condemned to repeat it."

We'll see artifacts from the rise and fall of three great ancient civilizations — Egypt, Assyria and Greece. Then we'll skip ahead a thousand years to manuscripts chronicling the rise (and fall?) of another great civilization — ours.

EGYPT (3000-1000 B.C.)

Egypt was one of the world's first "civilizations", that is, a group of people with a government, religion, art and written language. The Egypt we think of — pyramids, mummies, pharaohs and guys that walk funny — lasted from 3000-1000 B.C. with hardly any change in the government, religion or arts (imagine two millennia of Eisenhower). Historians divide this time up into "kingdoms", "dynasties" and so on, but we'll just stroll through and look at things typical of the whole period. The

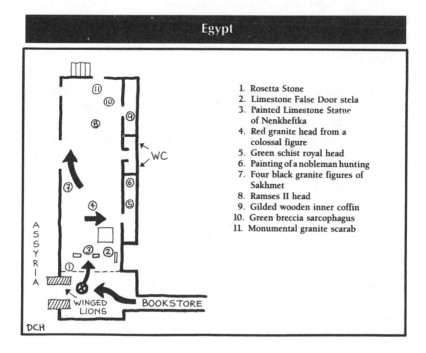

Egypt

1. Rosetta Stone
2. Limestone False Door stela
3. Painted Limestone Statue of Nenkheftka
4. Red granite head from a colossal figure
5. Green schist royal head
6. Painting of a nobleman hunting
7. Four black granite figures of Sakhmet
8. Ramses II head
9. Gilded wooden inner coffin
10. Green breccia sarcophagus
11. Monumental granite scarab

long Egyptian Gallery is laid out pretty much chronologically, oldest stuff first.

☞ *Enter the Egyptian Gallery (Room 25), walking between the two statues of pharaohs on their thrones. On your left you'll see a big black rock with writing on it.*

The Rosetta Stone, 196 B.C.

Remember that scene from *2001: A Space Odyssey* where the pack of apelike proto-humans discovers the big black monolith that raises them to their next stage of knowledge? There must have been a similar scene when this black slab, known as the Rosetta Stone, was unearthed in the Egyptian desert in 1799 — a pack of scientists screeching with amazement, dancing around it and poking curiously with their fingers. Its discovery caused a sensation in Europe and a quantum leap in the evolution of history. Finally Egyptian writing could be decoded.

Rosetta Stone — Rosetta made life very sweet for one Egyptologist. She repeated the same message in three different languages helping scholars to break the code of ancient Egyptian hieroglyphics.

For a thousand years, no one knew how to read the ancient Egyptian writing known as hieroglyphics. The Rosetta Stone allowed them to break the code. It contains a single inscription repeated in three languages. The top one is the mysterious hieroglyphics, but the other two were already known — on the bottom is plain old Greek, while the middle is the popular form of Egyptian known as "demotic". By comparing the two known languages with the one they didn't know, they figured it out. The breakthrough came by deciphering the small oval in the sixth line from the top — it turned out to be the name of the pharaoh Ptolemy.

☞ *Continue on, passing between two lion statues. On your right you'll find...*

Limestone False Door Stela from the Tomb of Bateti, c. 2400 B.C.

In ancient Egypt, you COULD take it with you. They believed that after you died your soul lived on, enjoying its earthly possessions. They built tombs to preserve what the deceased would need in the next life:

his mummified body, a resume of his accomplishments on earth and his possessions — sometimes including his servants, who might be buried alive with their master. Some tombs were built on the grand scale like the great pyramids, but most were small rectangular rooms of brick or stone.

"False Doors" like this one were slapped on the outside of the tomb. The soul of the deceased could come and go as he pleased — grave robbers couldn't. The deceased's relatives would place food outside the door to nourish the soul for the long journey to paradise. This false door has a picture of a spirit with the munchies.

☞ *Just a few steps further down the gallery, you'll run into the...*

Painted Limestone Statue of Nenkheftka, 2400 B.C.

After his snack the soul might wander through the nether lands (now part of the Benelux lands?) searching for paradise, meeting strange beings and weird situations. If things got too hairy, the soul could always find temporary refuge in statues like this one. It was always nice to have as many statues of yourself as possible to scatter around the earth, in case your soul needed a safe resting place.

This statue, like most Egyptian art, was meant to be useful, not beautiful, designed to help the soul on its journey. It's not terribly realistic — the figure is stiff, hands at the sides, left leg forward, idealized face and stylized anatomy. And talk about posture! He's got a column down his back! The sculptor cuts away the extraneous details and portrays

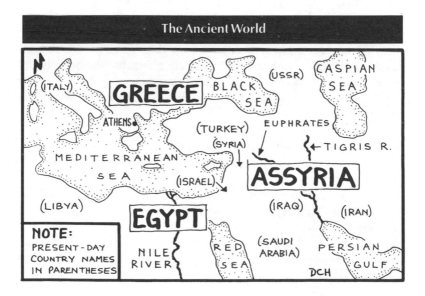

22   *British Museum, London*

only the essential features of a human being, like the simplified human figures on international traffic signs. To a soul caught in the fast lane of astral travel, this symbolic statue would be easier to spot than a detailed one.

You'll see the same rigid features in almost all the statues in the gallery.

☞ *Head to the huge head ahead a few more steps.*

Red Granite Head from a Colossal Figure of a King

Art also served as propaganda for the pharaohs, the kings who called themselves gods on earth. Put this head on top of an enormous body (which still stands in Egypt) and you have the intimidating image of an omnipotent ruler who demands servile obedience. Next to the head is, appropriately, the pharaoh's powerful fist — the long arm of the law.

Again we see symbolism taking precedence over realism. What's important here isn't a detailed portrait of the man's face, but the crown on his head. It's actually two crowns in one. The pointed upper half is the royal cap of Upper Egypt. This rests on the flat fez-like crown symbolizing Lower Egypt. A pharaoh wearing both crowns together is bragging that he rules a united Egypt.

☞ *Enter Room 25a, to the right.*

Green Schist Royal Head, c. 1490 B.C.

This pharaoh has several symbols of authority — the familiar pointed crown of Upper Egypt, the cobra-headed "hat pin" on the forehead and the stylized "chin strap" beard. This symbolism tells us clearly it's a powerful pharaoh, but which one?

Not only don't scholars know who he is, but they don't even know if he's a *he*. Is it bearded King Tuthmosis III...or the smooth-skinned Queen Hatshepsut, one of phour phemale pharaohs who actually did wear ceremonial "beards" as symbols of royal power?

☞ *Ponder the mystery of this AC/DC monarch, then turn to the painting at the end of the room.*

Painting of a Nobleman Hunting in the Marshes, 1425 B.C.

This nobleman walks like Egyptian statues look — stiff. We see his torso from the front and everything else — arms, legs, face — in profile, creating the funny walk that has become an Egyptian cliche. (You know, this is like an early version of Cubism — showing various perspectives at once...)

What strikes us about this painting is not the stiffness, but the humanness that shines through. It's a family scene. The man takes a break from

Egyptian Wall Painting — Looking as
though he were just run over by a pyramid,
this 2-D hunter is flat like most Egyptian art.

his courtly duties to go hunting. We see him standing up in a reed boat, gliding through the marshes, his arm raised ready to throw a hunting stick at some birds flying by. On the right, his wife looks on, while his daughter crouches between his legs, a symbol of fatherly protection.

Despite the two-dimensional flatness and symbolism, this is a very realistic painting. The birds above and fish below are so accurate that we can easily identify them by species. The only truly unrealistic element is the house cat (about thigh-high, in front of the man), acting as a retriever — just possibly the only cat in history that ever did anything useful.

☞ *Return to the main gallery and find four lion-headed statues.*

Four Black Granite Figures of the Goddess Sakhmet, 1400 B.C.

The Egyptian cosmos was like a big banana republic. The only way to get anywhere was by bribing the powers-that-be. So Egyptians gave offerings to the various gods to get them on their side. You could give food, animals or money to the priests for an offering, or you could build a statue of the god — like these four — as an act of devotion.

This goddess was a good one to have on your side. She looks pretty sedate here, but this lion-headed woman was a fierce mercenary warrior who fought, obviously, like a lioness against her enemies.

Throughout the gallery you'll see similar statues of animals and half-human/half-animals. Certain animals were worshipped as earthly incarnations of the Egyptian gods: the falcon was Horus, the baboon was Thoth, the jackal was Anubis, and so on.

By the way, notice the *ankh* that Sakhmet is holding. This key-shaped cross was the hieroglyph meaning "life", and was a symbol of eternal life. In later centuries it was adopted as a Christian symbol because of its cross shape and religious overtones.

☞ *Catch the happy couple to the right, seated hand in hand waiting for the Eternity Express, then continue on down the gallery. Pause at the big*

glass case in the middle with leftovers from an ancient Egyptian arts-and-crafts fair. There are WCs nearby.
End up at the big eight-foot granite head and torso further down the gallery.

Upper Half of Colossal Statue of Ramesses II of Granite, 1270 B.C.

When Moses told the king of Egypt, "Let my people go!", this was the stone-faced look he got in response. It was this pharaoh, Ramesses II (reigned c. 1290-1223 B.C.), who supposedly was in power when Moses led the Israelites out of captivity in Egypt to their homeland in Israel. According to the Bible, Moses, a former Egyptian prince himself, appealed to the pharaoh to let them go peacefully. When the pharaoh refused, Moses cursed the land with a series of plagues. Finally, the Israelites just high-tailed it out of there with the help of their God, Yahweh, who drowned the Egyptian armies in the Red Sea. Egyptian records don't exactly corroborate the tale, but this Ramesses here looks enough like Yul Brynner in *The Ten Commandments* to make me a believer.

Ramesses ruled for 67 years and went down in history as a great general for repelling an invasion of Hittites. In fact, he was a so-so general who stopped the invasion by negotiating a treaty and marrying the Hittite king's daughter.

He's also known as a great builder of temples, palaces and tombs. There are more statues of Ramesses than probably anyone in the world except Oscar. He was so concerned about achieving immortality that he even chiseled his own name over other people's statues.

This particular statue, made from two different colors of granite, is a broken-off fragment from a funeral temple in Thebes. Imagine, for a second, what the archaeologists saw when they came upon this — a colossal head and torso separated from the enormous legs, toppled into the sand, all that remained of the works of a once-great pharaoh...kings, megalomaniacs and workaholics take note.

☞   *Say, "Ooh, heavy," and climb the ramp behind Ramesses, into Room 25b. You'll come up face to face with a golden coffin.*

Gilded Wooden Inner Coffin of the Chantress of Amen-Re Henutmehit, 1290 B.C.

The Egyptians tried to cheat death by preserving their corpses. The body was needed to house the spirit when they were reunited in the next life. They'd mummify the body, place it in a coffin like this one and, often, put that coffin inside a larger one. The result is that we now have Egyptian bodies that are as well-preserved over the centuries as Dick Clark.

To mummify a body, first make sure it's quite dead, then disembowel it, fill the body cavities with pitch or other substances and dry the body with natron, a natural form of sodium carbonate (and the active ingredient, I believe, in Twinkies). Then carefully bandage it head to toe with fine linen strips. Place in a coffin, wait 2000 years, and *Voilà!* Or if you're lazy, just throw the corpse right in the ground and let the hot, dry Egyptian sand do the work — you'll get the same results.

Gilded Wooden Coffin — Corpses were dried, wrapped in linen and placed in rigid coffins like this to make sure the body — like the spirit — lasted through eternity. Relax baby, your mummy's okay.

The coffins, like this gold-painted wooden inner coffin, were decorated with the deceased's face, scenes of the deceased praising the gods, and so on. The insides were also decorated with magical spells to protect the body from evil and to act as crib notes for the confused soul in the nether lands.

Upstairs, the British Museum has a great collection of mummies, both human and animal.

☞ *Walking back down the ramp you'll see a black-green stone coffin on your right.*

Green Breccia Sarcophagus of Nectanebo II, 345 B.C.

This was the outer coffin for Egypt's last native king. After more than two millennia of pharaohs, Egypt was conquered by the Greeks under Alexander the Great in the 4th century B.C. They turned the last king's coffin into just what it looks like — a public bathtub.

☞ *Near the end of the gallery in the center of the room is a big, round stone insect.*

Monumental Granite Scarab, 200 B.C.

The ancient Egyptian culture slowly died out as the country was swallowed up first by Greece, then by Rome. Knowledge of the ancient writing died, condemning the culture to obscurity. But maybe Egyptians are immortal after all. Since the discovery of the Rosetta Stone, Egypt has come back to life and Egyptology is booming. We know more today about the ancient Egyptians than even the Romans did.

This big stone scarab is, appropriately enough, a symbol of resurrection. Don't worry, you can't get scarabs from toilet seats. They're a species of beetle with a reputation for burrowing into the ground then reappearing — like dying and rebirth. Also, the shells of Egyptian scarabs are round and bright gold — like the sun — so scarabs became a symbol of the sun god as he rises in the morning after "dying" at night.

☞   *Through the door at the end of the gallery is the staircase up to more Egyptian artifacts, if you're interested. Also, in the small room at the foot of the stairs you'll find a Dead Sea Scroll.*

Otherwise, let's head back to where we started — the Assyrian human-headed lions at the other end of the gallery. Meet you there.

ASSYRIA (1000-600 B.C.)

☞   *Have a seat again on the bench in the shadow of the winged lions.*

Assyria was the lion, the king of beasts of early civilizations. Located in the north part of the area called Mesopotamia (northern Iraq), it conquered and dominated the Middle East for over three centuries.

Mesopotamia, like Egypt, was a "cradle of civilization" nestled between two life-giving rivers, the Tigris and the Euphrates. It was the crossroads of the world, where Asia, Europe and Africa met, and this fertile ground got cultural seeds from everywhere. Assyria's southern neighbor, called Sumer, was "civilized" even before Egypt (we're talking before 3000 B.C.), with planned cities, enormous temple complexes and their greatest invention, writing.

The less-civilized Assyrians to the north were a nation of warriors — hardy, disciplined and often cruel conquistadors — whose livelihood depended on booty and slash-and-burn expansion. At its peak, Assyria consisted of parts of modern-day Iraq, Iran, Syria, Israel, and eastern Turkey.

Two Winged Lions with Human Heads, c. 870 B.C.

Assyrian art, unlike Egypt's, had a military flavor — as propaganda proclaiming great conquests or, like these lions, to intimidate enemies and defeated peoples. The lions were symbols of power, standing guard at key points in Assyrian palaces. They protected the palace from evil spirits and scared the heck out of foreign ambassadors and left-wing newspaper reporters.

Remember the four Egyptian statues of the fierce lion-headed goddess? The Assyrians took the same concept of a supernatural being with animal attributes, and expanded on it. With lion body, eagle wings and human head, these magical beasts — and therefore the Assyrian people — had the strength of a lion, the speed of an eagle, the brains of a man and the beards of the Smith Brothers cough-drop guys.

Assyrian Winged Lions — What has five legs and flies? These bearded beasts who guarded key entrances to Assyrian palaces.

Count the legs. The sculptor wanted each lion to look complete from both the front and side views.

☞ *Walk between them, glance at the large reconstructed wooden gates from an Assyrian palace, and turn right into the long narrow gallery lined with brown relief panels.*

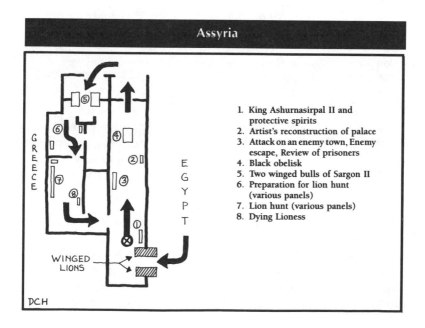

Assyria

1. King Ashurnasirpal II and protective spirits
2. Artist's reconstruction of palace
3. Attack on an enemy town, Enemy escape, Review of prisoners
4. Black obelisk
5. Two winged bulls of Sargon II
6. Preparation for lion hunt (various panels)
7. Lion hunt (various panels)
8. Dying Lioness

Nimrud Gallery

The narrow gallery here is a mini-version of the main hall of Ashurnasirpal's palace which was decorated with these pleasant sand-colored gypsum relief panels (which were, however, originally painted!). Ashurnasirpal was a conqueror's conqueror who enjoyed his reputation as a savage, merciless warrior who tortured and humiliated the vanquished. The panels chronicle his bloody career. That's him in the panel on your right with a braided beard, fez-like crown and bulging muscles, accompanied by his supernatural hawk-headed henchman.

☞   *Head toward the black obelisk in the center of the room, glancing at the plaque on the right wall showing an artist's reconstruction of the grand palace.*

On the wall opposite the plaque are battle scenes. Backtrack a few steps towards the gallery entrance and find the one labeled...

Attack on an Enemy Town

Many "nations" conquered by the Assyrians consisted of little more than a single walled city. Here, the Assyrians lay siege with the aid of a movable tower that gave them protection as they advanced to the city walls. Notice the battering ram and the king shooting arrows.

☞   *To the right you'll find...*

Enemy Escape

Though this may represent enemies fleeing the Assyrians by swimming across the Euphrates, it's more likely the Assyrians themselves with a unique amphibious invasion technique. The soldiers inflate animal skins to keep them afloat as they sneak downstream to an enemy city.

☞   *Below, you'll see...*

Review of Prisoners

The Assyrian economy depended on booty. Here a conquered nation is paraded before the Assyrian king. Above their heads the sculptor shows the rich spoils of war — elephant tusks, metal cauldrons, etc.

☞   *Now turn to the black obelisk in the center of the room.*

Black Obelisk of Shalmaneser III, c. 840 B.C.

The Assyrians demanded annual tribute from the conquered lands — or else. The obelisk shows people bringing tribute to Shalmaneser from all corners of the empire. The second band from the top shows the tribute from Israel. Parts of Israel were under Assyrian domination from the 9th century B.C. on. Old Testament prophets like Elijah and Elisha constantly warned their people of the corrupting influence of the Assyrian gods.

Also check out the parade of exotic animals on the third band, especially the missing-link monkeys.

☞ *Exit the gallery at the far end, then hang a U-turn into Room 16. More winged beasts.*

Two Winged Bulls from the Palace of Sargon II, c. 710 B.C.

These 16-ton bulls guarded the palace of Sargon II. And speaking of large amounts of bull, "Sargon" wasn't his real name. It's obvious to historians that Sargon must have been a usurper to the throne because he chose the name that meant..."True King".

☞ *Pass between these Taurean terrors and veer to the right into the small Room 17.*

Royal Lion Hunts

Lion hunting was Assyria's sport of kings. Since they prided themselves on being great warriors — kings of men — they demonstrated their power by taking on the king of beasts. Lions lived in Mesopotamia up until modern times, and it had long been the duty of kings to keep the lion population down to protect farmers and herdsmen. When this duty became a sport, the kings actually bred lions in captivity for the sole purpose of staging hunts. As we'll see, these "hunts" were far from fair fights but foregone conclusions like shooting fish in a barrel or Fascist elections. The kings of the later years of the empire had grown soft and decadent, hardly the raging warriors of Ashurnasirpal's time.

On the right wall we see horses being readied for the hunt. On the left wall, the hunting dogs. And next to them are the lions. (Beautiful, aren't they?) They rest peacefully in their leafy garden, an idyllic setting, unaware that they will shortly be rousted, stampeded and slaughtered.

☞ *Pass into the larger lion-hunt room to the right of the peaceful lions. We'll work counter-clockwise around the room, "reading" the panels like a comic strip.*

The Lion-Hunt Room

In the second panel (remember, we're moving counter-clockwise starting at the entrance) we see the lions being released from their cages. Above are soldiers on horseback. Their duty was to herd them into an enclosed arena where the king could corner them.

Next (turning the corner), the slaughter begins. Further along we see a chariot carrying King Ashurbanipal himself (reigned 688-633 B.C.), the last of Assyria's great kings. He shoots ahead while spearmen hold off lions attacking from the rear.

Moving along (to about the middle of the long wall), the fleeing lions, shot through with arrows and weighed down with fatigue, begin to fall, tragically. The lead lion carries on valiantly even while vomiting blood.

This, perhaps the low point of Assyrian cruelty, is the high point of their artistic achievement. It's a curious coincidence that, throughout history, civilizations often produce their greatest art in their declining years. Hmm.

Dying Lioness

On the opposite wall from the vomiting lion, a dying lioness roars in pain and frustration, trying to run but her body is too heavy. Her muscular hind legs, once the source of her power, are now paralyzed, a burden dragging her down. I can't help but think that the sculptor who did this sensed the coming death of his own civilization. The tragic end of these brave, fierce lions is the same as that of Assyria's once-great warrior nation. Within decades after Ashurbanipal's death, Assyria was conquered, sacked and looted by the growing Babylonian nation to the south. The mood of tragedy, of dignity, of proud struggle in a hopeless cause make this "Dying Lioness" simply one of the most beautiful of all human creations.

The Dying Lioness — Like this dying lioness, Assyria's great empire was dragging to a halt.

☞ *Return to the winged lions where we started from. To get there, just pass through the next room and you'll run into familiar territory.*

This may be a good time for a break in the cafeteria. When you're refreshed, have a seat again by the winged lions.

GREECE (600 B.C.-1 A.D.)

The history of ancient Greece is that of making order out of chaos. While Assyria dominated the Middle Eastern world, "Greece" was floundering in darkness. It was hardly a nation, just a gaggle of warring tribes roaming the Greek peninsula. But by around 700 B.C. these tribes had begun settling down, forming self-governing city-states and making ties with other city-states. Scarcely two centuries later, they would be a united community and the center of the civilized world.

Greece of the "Golden Age" (around 450-400 B.C.) set the tone for all of Western civilization to follow. Modern democracy, theater, literature, mathematics, philosophy, science, art and architecture, as we know them, were all virtually invented by a single generation of Greeks in a small town of maybe 80,000 people.

☞ *From the winged lions, trade magical Assyria for rational Greece Enter the doorway (Room 1) opposite the bookstore.*

EARLY GREECE

Cycladian Figures, c. 2500 B.C.

Let's start with Greece's primitive roots. This Room 1 has early Greek "voodoo dolls", small figures of women. These are hardly realistic, just schematic shapes with folded arms or violin-shaped bodies. As with ancient Egyptian art from the same period, these weren't beautiful but they were magical — to protect the owner from evil spirits.

☞ *Pass through the next room (with the entrances to the café and restaurant), and turn right into Room 3. Enter Room 5, which has a map on the left wall.*

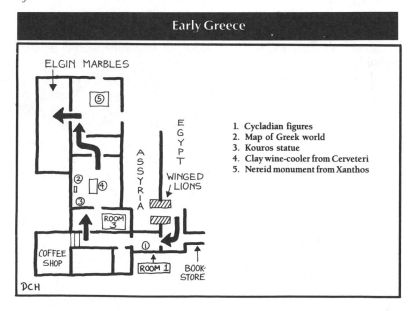

Map of Greek World
This shows the Greek and Greek-influenced world. Golden Age Greece was never really a full-fledged empire, but more a common feeling of unity among Greek-speaking peoples on the peninsula. Find Athens, the most powerful of the city-states and the center of the Greek world.

A century after the Golden Age, Greek culture was spread by conquest throughout the Mediterranean world by Alexander the Great. By 300 B.C., the "Greek" world stretched all the way to India (including most of what used to be the Assyrian Empire) and Egypt. Two hundred years later this, "Hellenistic (Greek-speaking) Empire" was then conquered by the Romans.

☞   *Look at the nude male statue to the left of the map.*

Boy (Kouros), 490 B.C.
The Egyptian influence is obvious in this male nude. He stands stiffly, arms at this side, stepping forward with one leg. The face and the anatomy show fine workmanship but they're idealized, not realistic. The Greeks were obsessed with finding the right balance of motion and stillness. This stiff is as still as the rock he's carved from, but in just a few short decades, the Greeks would cut loose and create realistic statues that seemed to move like real humans.

☞   *Look in the glass case nearby.*

Clay Wine-Cooler (psykter) from Cerveteri, 490 B.C.
The figures painted on this jar are more realistic, more three-dimensional and with more natural movements than even the literally three-dimensional *Kouros* statue. The Greeks are beginning to conquer the natural word in art.

As we walk through all this ultra-"civilized" art, it's good to keep Greece's primitive past in mind. The Greeks praised balance and moderation so much, probably because they rarely practiced it themselves. Wild Greek drinking parties ("symposia") are legendary. This clay wine-cooler, designed to float in a bowl of cooling water, is decorated with mythical beasts, called satyrs, having their own symposium. Satyrs were half-man/half-animal creatures (notice their tails) with a reputation for lewd behavior, reminding the "civilized" Greeks of their rude roots.

And speaking of balance, circle the glass case and look at the satyr on the other side of the wine-cooler — one of the most remarkable feats of balance I've ever seen.

☞   *Exit this room, veer left, and enter the large Nereid Room 7 with a Greek temple at the far end. Have a seat.*

GOLDEN AGE GREECE (500-400 B.C.)

Nereid Monument from Xanthos, c. 400 B.C.

Let's use this reconstructed Greek temple as an introduction to the nearby Elgin Marbles, the sculptural fragments from the most famous Greek temple, the Parthenon. Actually, this is only a partial reconstruction of an atypical temple (it's really a tomb in the shape of a temple), but it'll help bring the Parthenon alive. For comparison, the columns of the Parthenon are 40 feet tall.

Unlike Christian churches, which serve as meeting places for big crowds of worshippers, Greek temples like this were intended to house only the statue of a particular god or goddess. Worshippers gathered outside, so the most impressive part of the temple was always the exterior. The temple was a rectangular building surrounded by rows of columns creating a porch, topped by a slanted roof.

The triangle-shaped gable found above the columns (like the one you see here) is called the "pediment". The relief panels beneath it (that is, between the pediment and the columns) are called "metopes" (pron. MET-o-pees). Now look through the columns to the building itself. Above the doorway is another set of relief panels running around the outside of the building. We'll call these the "frieze".

☞ *Leave the British Museum. Take the Tube to Heathrow and catch a flight to Athens. In the center of the old city, on top of the high, flat hill known as the Acropolis, you'll find...*

The Parthenon

The Parthenon — the temple dedicated to Athena, goddess of wisdom and the patroness of Athens — was the crowning glory in an enormous urban renewal plan during Greece's Golden Age. After being ruined in

The Parthenon, Athens

a war with Persia, Athens, under the bold leadership of Pericles, constructed the greatest building of its day. The Parthenon was a model of balance, simplicity and harmonious elegance, the symbol of the Golden Age. Phidias, the greatest Greek sculptor, decorated the exterior with statues and relief panels.

THE ELGIN MARBLES (450 B.C.)

The so-called Elgin Marbles (technically pronounced EL-gin (hard "g"), but everyone I know says EL-jin) are the best collection of Phidias' sculptures from the Parthenon. They consist of 1) pediment sculptures; 2) metope panels; and 3) frieze panels.

They're the marble pieces named for Lord Elgin, a shrewd British ambassador who acquired them from Greece and brought them to England in the early 1800s. Elgin insisted that it was his duty to remove them from the Acropolis in order to "save" them from damage. He sold them to the British government, and here they've stayed, despite protests from the Greek government.

☞ *Enter the Elgin Marbles room through the glass door (to your left as you face the Nereid Monument).*

Look over the exhibits in the entryway and in the small room to the right — pictures of the Parthenon and the statue of Athena, a model of the Acropolis and a piece of column, giving an idea of the size of the building.

Elgin Marbles

Now enter the large hall.

The Frieze

The main hall contains 56 relief panels from the frieze that ran around the building above the inside row of columns. They depict the Panathenaic procession — Athens' "Fourth of July" parade celebrating the birth of their city — where citizens marched up the Acropolis to symbolically present a new robe to the 40-foot statue of Athena housed in the Parthenon.

☞ *Start at the first panel to your right (#134) and move counter-clock-wise around the room, ending up at the panels right in front of you on the wall opposite the entrance.*

You'll see men on horseback, chariots, musicians, animals for sacrifice and young maidens with offerings, all part of the grand parade, all heading in the same direction. Even with so many figures, there's still a sense of order and unity to the frieze — all the heads are at the same level, creating a single band around the building.

Admire the realistic musculature, the un-Egyptian bodies posed from every angle, the intricate folds in the cloaks and dresses. #111 is especially nice.

Stop at #59. The four-horse chariot, cut into marble only two inches deep, has more three-dimensionality than the Egyptians achieved in a free-standing statue.

The procession culminates in the presentation of the robe to Athena while the rest of the gods look on. In #29, that's Zeus and Hera, the king and queen of the gods, seated, enjoying the fashion show and wondering what length hemlines will be this year. The other gods spread out to the left. #35 shows the Athenians folding the robe as they present it.

☞ *Head for the right end of the hall.*

The Pediment Sculptures

These statues were nestled forming a triangle in the pediment above the columns at the Parthenon's east entrance. The peak of the triangle — which has been lost — was a group of statues showing the birth of Athena. Zeus had his head split open, allowing Athena, the goddess of wisdom, to rise from his brain fully-grown and fully-armed. ("Violence has been the sire of all the world's values"?)

The other statues slowly become aware of this amazing birth. The first to notice is the one closest to them, Hebe, the cup-bearer of the gods ("East Pediment G"). She's frightened, and turns to run to tell the others. At the far left, the reclining nude figure of Dionysus, god of wine

("East Pediment D"), is too busy bringing another glass to his lips to notice the hubbub. And to the far right of center, Aphrodite, goddess of love, leans back luxuriously into the lap of her mother, too busy posing to even look.

Since Greek gods were little more than super-humans (with exaggerated human faults as well), this birth scene became an allegory for the birth of Athena's own city, Athens. Here she rises above the lesser gods who are scared, drunk or vain — just as the city of Athens rose above her less cultured rivals.

This is amazing workmanship, light years ahead of the Egyptians for realism. Look at Dionysus with his natural, relaxed, reclining pose. Then think back on all those stiff Egyptian statues standing eternally at attention. The realism of the muscles is an amazing improvement over Egyptian art and even over the *Kouros* we saw, sculpted only 50 years earlier.

The folds of the clothes on the female figures are especially nice. Notice Hebe with her "Wet T-shirt" look and Aphrodite's rumpled robe. Sculptors would build a model of their figure first, put real clothes on it, and study how the cloth hung down before actually sculpting in marble.

These statues originally sat in a pediment 40 feet above ground. What's truly amazing is that the backs of the statues — which were never intended to be seen — are almost as detailed as the fronts. Talk about quality control.

☞ *The metopes are the panels on the walls to the left and right. Start with "South Metope XXXI" on the right wall, center.*

The Metopes

The Greeks prided themselves on creating order out of chaos. Within just a few centuries they went from nomadic barbarism to the pinnacle of early Western civilization. The metopes tell the story of this struggle between the forces of civilization and the forces of barbarism.

The human Lapiths have invited the Centaurs — wild half-man/half-horse creatures — to a wedding feast. All goes well until the brutish Centaurs, the original party animals, get too drunk and try to carry off the Lapith women. A battle ensues. In #XXXI, a Centaur grabs one of the Lapiths by the throat while the man pulls his hair.

In #XXVIII (opposite wall, center) the Centaurs get the upper hand as one rears triumphant over a fallen man. Notice in all these panels that the facial expressions are rather sketchy, always secondary to the more detailed anatomy. The Greeks expressed emotion through the pose of the body rather than the face.

Quick detour:

500 B.C. has been called the "Axial Age" — when history turned on its axis and entered a whole new era. Bold new ideas were exploding simultaneously around the world. In Greece there were Socrates and Plato; in India, Gautama Buddha; in China, Confucius. One idea they had in common was that there was a non-material, unseen order in nature. Man, too, had an unseen, non-material part to him — his rational mind or his soul. This made him separate from nature and different from the other animals. In fact, man no longer considered himself an "animal" at all.

Now, back to live action:

In #XXVII (to the left), the humans finally rally and drive off the brutish Centaurs. A Centaur, wounded in the back, tries to run, but the man grabs him by the neck and raises his right hand (missing) to deliver the final blow. This is, I think, the finest of all the panels. Notice how the Lapith's cloak drapes a rough-textured background that highlights the smooth skin of this graceful, ideal man. In the Axial Age, the Centaurs have been defeated. Civilization has triumphed over barbarism, order over chaos, and rational man over his half-animal alter-ego.

Parthenon Metope Panel — This mythical battle between humans and half-human Centaurs symbolized Greece's triumph over barbarism, chaos and uninvited wedding guests.

Why did the Elgin Marbles become so famous? Maybe because the British of the 19th century saw themselves as the new "civilized" race subduing "barbarians" in their far-flung Empire. And these rocks must have made them stop and wonder — will our great civilization also turn to rubble?

☞ *Browse through the rest of the collection, then exit the Elgin Marbles room. Now leave the Nereid Monument room through the door behind the Monument, passing into Room 9.*

Pass through several rooms, then turn right into Room 12. In the center of the room is a statue of a man.

LATER GREECE (350 B.C.-1 A.D.)

Mausoleum of Halicarnassus, c. 350 B.C.

This long-haired, mustachioed gentleman, who looks like Sgt. Pepper but is actually named Mausolus, was a Greek who would have made a great Egyptian. He built a huge Egyptian-style tomb to house his body and proclaim his greatness for eternity. In the process he also gave us our word for an elaborate tomb — Mausol-eum. His mausoleum became one of the Seven Wonders of the Ancient World to the Romans who conquered Greek lands a few centuries later. They marveled at the size and beauty of the tomb (mostly the size — the Romans were not subtle folk) and put it on their Guinness-Book-of-World-Records-type list of great structures.

On the wall near the entrance is an artist's reconstruction of this magnificent necropolis. It was built in a stepped pyramid style topped by a four-horse chariot which symbolically bore Mausolus' soul to heaven. That's one of the horses there to your right. Even with his legs broken off, he stands ten feet tall, giving an idea of the size of the whole structure.

(The most interesting and bizarre sculpture in the room for me is the lion to the left of the horse. This lion is not a glorious symbol of strength like in Egypt or Assyria, but hangs suspended in the air like a biological specimen, detached, neutered, powerless. I guess the rational Greeks

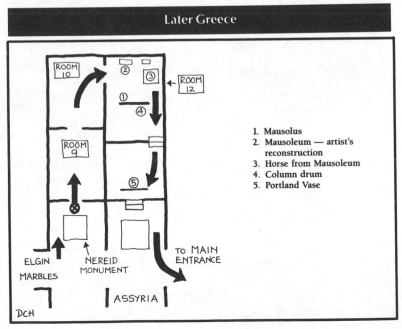

Later Greece

1. Mausolus
2. Mausoleum — artist's reconstruction
3. Horse from Mausoleum
4. Column drum
5. Portland Vase

had no place for the "barbaric" worship of animals. . .)

☞ *On the other side of the room's divider you'll find yet another Wonder of the World, the large "Column drum from the later temple of Artemis at Ephesus."*

Then climb the steps into Room 13. Near the far end, in the middle of the room. . .

The Portland Vase, c. 1 A.D.

After seeing so many rugged stones, it's refreshing to come upon the fragile beauty of this glass vase whose white figures on a cobalt-blue background seem to be eternally moonlit. The blown-glass vase was made in two layers, a blue inner layer covered with a white one. Then the white was cut away to make the cameo-like figures, a technique that became very popular in 19th-century England.

This masterpiece of Greek art is Roman. The Romans were great soldiers, administrators and engineers — but bad artists — so they simply borrowed from their Greek subjects. The craftsmanship is unparalleled, with the same 3-D realism, idealized beauty, balance and order we saw in the Elgin Marbles.

For 1800 years the vase was preserved in almost perfect condition. Then, in 1845, a madman walked into the museum and smashed the vase to bits, requiring an extensive repair job and making us wonder whether we civilized people have transcended our animal nature or merely repressed it.

☞ *Exit the vase room and you'll see the Egyptian gallery on your left. Return to the main entrance to the museum by heading back up the Egyptian Gallery, past the Assyrian winged lions, turning left and going through the bookstore. The entrance to the British Library is in the main entrance lobby, opposite the staircase.*

THE BRITISH LIBRARY

The monuments of the British Empire aren't made of stone, but paper. It's in literature that England has made her greatest contribution to the arts. The British Library contains some ten million books and hundreds of thousands of manuscripts. We'll concentrate on just a few of the documents — literary and historical — that changed the course of history. There's so much to see, so conveniently displayed, that this is one place I encourage you to stray from the book. But here are some of the highlights for me.

☞ *Enter the British Library Galleries and proceed to Room 30. Find the case — almost in the center of the room — marked "Magna Carta".*

MAGNA CARTA

How did Britain, the tiny island with a few million people, come to rule a quarter of the world? By force? No, by law. The Magna Carta was the basis for England's constitutional system of government. There are six documents in the case, including four different "Magna Cartas". Let's start with document #2.

In the year 1215, England's barons rose in revolt against the slimy King John. After they captured London, John was forced to negotiate. The barons presented him with this list of demands. John, who couldn't rule without the support of the barons, had little choice but to agree and fix his seal to it.

This was a landmark in history. In the past, kings everywhere had ruled by God-given authority. They were above the laws of men, acting however they pleased. Now for the first time there were limits — in writing — on how a king could treat his subjects. More generally, it established the idea of "due process" — that is, the government can't infringe on people's freedom without a legitimate legal reason. It was a small step, but it became the basis for all constitutional government, including that

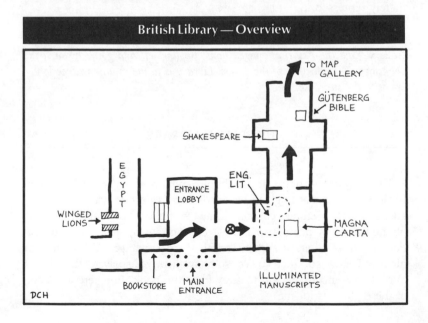

of the United States.

A few days after John agreed to this original document, it was rewritten in legal form, and some 35 copies were distributed around the kingdom. Numbers 3 and 4, in this case, are two surviving copies of this "Magna Carta", or "Great Charter". Number 6 is a slightly revised version drawn up ten years later, the version that actually passed into English law. Documents #1 and #5 are letters from the Pope at the time supporting John and annulling Magna Carta. The Pope knew what a radical principle Magna Carta represented — the questioning of church-ordained authorities by the common rabble.

So what did this radical piece of paper actually say? Not much by today's standards. Read the transcribed copy next to the case. The specific demands had to do with things like inheritance taxes, the king's duties to widows and orphans, and so on. It wasn't the specific articles that were important, but the simple fact that the king had to abide by them as law. To get an idea of how bizarre some of the Magna Carta sounds today, check out articles #7 and #8 on marriage, #10 and #11 on owing money to Jews, and #23 on building bridges.

☞ *There are many more historical documents in this room which you may want to return to — letters by Queen Elizabeth I, Isaac Newton, etc. But for now turn to the nearby case (also near the center of the room) marked "English Literature 1".*

ENGLISH LITERATURE

Four out of every five English words have been borrowed from other languages. The English language — like all of English culture — is a mix derived from foreigners who invaded the island over the centuries. Here are some of the ingredients in England's cultural stew:

1) The original Celtic tribesmen; 2) Romans (1-500 A.D.); 3) The Germanic tribes called Angles and Saxons (making English a "Germanic" language and naming the island "Angle-land" — England); 4) Vikings from Denmark (800 A.D.); and finally, 5) the French-speaking "Normans" under William the Conqueror (1066-1250).

Beowulf

This Anglo-Saxon epic poem written in Old English, the early version of our language, almost makes the hieroglyphics on the Rosetta Stone look easy. The manuscript here is from 1000 A.D., although the poem itself dates to about 750. This is the only existing manuscript of the early English legend.

In the story, the young hero Beowulf (pronounced BAY-uh-wolf) defeats two half-human monsters threatening the kingdom. Like the Greek myth of Centaurs and Lapiths, "Beowulf" symbolizes England's emergence from Dark Age chaos and barbarism.

☞ *In the same case you'll find...*

Canterbury Tales, c. 1410

Six hundred years later England was Christian but it was hardly the pious, dull, Sunday-school world we might imagine. Geoffrey Chaucer's bawdy collection of stories, told by pilgrims on their way to Canterbury, gives us the full range of life's experiences — happy, sad, silly, sexy and pious. (Late in life, Chaucer wrote an apology for those works of his "that tend toward sin".)

While most serious literature of the time was written in scholarly Latin, *The Canterbury Tales* is written in Middle English, the language that developed when the French invasion (1066) put new twists in Old English. While Old English is so foreign to us today as to be virtually another language, Middle English is more readable.

☞ *The next big step in the evolution of English language and literature was William Shakespeare, who turned the people's tongue into art. But for now let's skip ahead to a couple of centuries after Shakespeare. Look in the case marked "English Lit 6".*

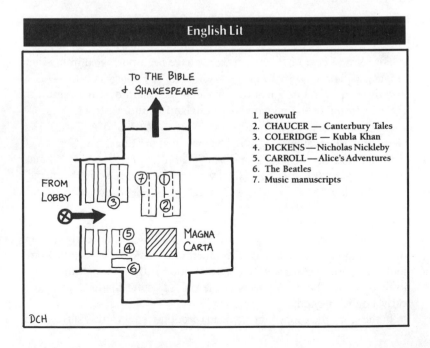

English Lit

To THE BIBLE ♦ SHAKESPEARE

FROM LOBBY

MAGNA CARTA

1. Beowulf
2. CHAUCER — Canterbury Tales
3. COLERIDGE — Kubla Khan
4. DICKENS — Nicholas Nickleby
5. CARROLL — Alice's Adventures
6. The Beatles
7. Music manuscripts

DCH

Coleridge — *Autograph Fair Copy of Kubla Khan*

One day Samuel Taylor Coleridge took opium. He fell asleep while reading about the fantastic palace of the Mongol emperor, Kubla Khan. During his three-hour drug-induced sleep, he composed in his head a poem of "from two- to three-hundred lines". When he woke up, he grabbed a pen and paper and "instantly and eagerly wrote down the lines that are here preserved". But just then, a visitor on business knocked at the door and kept Coleridge busy for an hour. When Coleridge finally kicked him out, he discovered that he'd forgotten the other couple hundred lines! The poem *Kubla Khan* is only a fragment, but it's still one of literature's masterpieces.

Coleridge (aided by his Muse-in-the-medicine-cabinet) was one of the Romantic poets. Check out his fellow Romantics, Keats, Shelley and Wordsworth, in this same case.

☞ *In the case marked "English Lit 8", you'll find...*

Dickens — *Nicholas Nickleby*

In 1400 no one but the select few could read. By 1850 in England, almost everyone could and did. Charles Dickens (1812-1870) gave them their first taste of "literature". His books were serialized in periodicals and avidly read by the increasingly-educated masses. The story is told of American fans gathering in mobs at the docks waiting for the ship from England with the latest news ("Who shot J.R.?!") of their favorite character.

Dickens also helped raise social concern for the underprivileged — of whom England had more than her share. When Dickens was 12 years old, his father was thrown into debtor's prison, and young Charles was put to work to support the family. The ordeal of poverty lasted only a few months, but it scarred him for life and gave him experiences he'd draw on later for books like *Oliver Twist* and *David Copperfield*.

☞ *Also in this case...*

Lewis Carroll — *Alice's Adventures Under Ground*

I don't know if Lewis Carroll ever dipped into Coleridge's medicine jar or not, but his series of children's books make *Kubla Khan* read like the phone book. Carroll was a stammerer, which made him uncomfortable around everyone but children. For them he created a fantasy world where grown-up rules and logic were turned upside-down.

☞ *Turn to the case marked "Beatles Loan".*

The Beatles

Future generations will have to judge whether this musical quartet ranks with artists like Shakespeare and Keats, but no one can deny its historical significance. The Beatles burst onto the scene in the early 1960s to almost unheard-of popularity. With their long hair and loud music, they brought counterculture and revolutionary ideas to the middle class, affecting the values of a whole generation.

In the case are photos of John Lennon, Paul McCartney and George Harrison before their fame (the fourth Beatle was Ringo Starr).

Most interesting are the manuscripts of song lyrics written by Lennon and McCartney, the two guiding lights of the group. "I Wanna Hold Your Hand" was the song that launched them to superstardom. John's song, "Help", was the quickly-written title song for one of the Beatles' movies. "Yesterday", by Paul, was recorded with guitar and voice backed by a string quartet — a touch of sophistication by the producer George Martin. In "Here, There and Everywhere", notice the problems Paul had deciding which word to use at the ends of verses. The manuscript for "In My Life" is especially interesting. Only the first verse here made it into the final song. The rest are some of John's memories from childhood — "Penny Lane", "The Abbey", "The Tram Sheds", and so on. Also glance at the rambling, depressed, cynical but humorous letter by John on the left. Is that a self-portrait at the bottom?

☞   *Find the case marked "Music" near the center of the room.*

Music manuscripts

Kind of an anti-climax after the Fab Four, I know, but here are manuscripts by Mozart, Beethoven, Schubert, etc.

☞   *This room contains manuscripts by almost every famous author in the English language — Donne, Milton, Boswell, Austen, Joyce, you name it. There are historical and scientific documents. Linger, or plan to return after we finish our tour.*

When you're done looking around, I'll meet you at the nearby case labeled "Sinaiticus and Alexandrinus" containing two ancient manuscripts.

THE BIBLE

My favorite excuse for not learning a foreign language is: "If English was good enough for Jesus Christ, it's good enough for me!" I don't know what that has to do with anything, but obviously Jesus didn't speak English — nor did Moses or Isaiah or Paul or any other Bible authors or characters. As a result, our present-day English Bible is not directly from the mouth and pen of these religious figures, but the product of centuries of evolution.

The Bible is not a single book; it's an anthology of books by different authors from different historical periods writing in different languages (usually Hebrew or Greek). So there are three things that editors must take into account in order to compile the most accurate Bible: 1) finding the oldest and most accurate version of each book; 2) translating it correctly; and 3) deciding which books belong in the collection we call "The Bible".

Codex Sinaiticus, c. 350 A.D.

This is the oldest complete "Bible" in existence (along with one in the Vatican), one of the first attempts to collect various books together into one authoritative anthology. It's in Greek, the language in which most of the New Testament was written. The Old Testament portions are Greek translations from the original Hebrew. This particular Bible, and the "Codex Alexandrus" next to it (425 A.D.), contain some books not included in most modern English Bibles.

☞ *In a case to the left you'll find...*

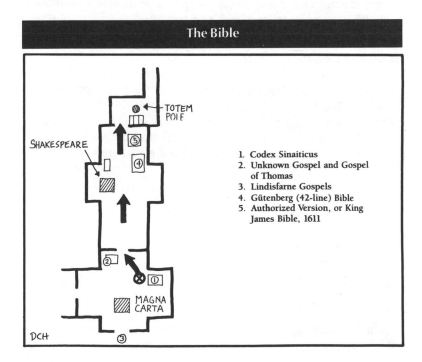

The Bible

1. Codex Sinaiticus
2. Unknown Gospel and Gospel of Thomas
3. Lindisfarne Gospels
4. Gütenberg (42-line) Bible
5. Authorized Version, or King James Bible, 1611

Fragment of an Unknown Gospel, and The Gospel of Thomas — Papyrus Fragment

Here are pieces of two such books that didn't make it into our modern Bible. The "unknown" Gospel (an account of the life of Jesus of Nazareth) is as old a manuscript as any in existence. Remember, the gospels weren't written down for a full generation after Jesus died (how good is YOUR memory?), and the oldest surviving manuscripts are from later than that. So why isn't this early version of Jesus' life part of our Bible right along with Matthew, Mark, Luke and John? Possibly because some early Bible editors didn't like the story it told about Jesus, which is not found in the four accepted Gospels — read the British Museum's translation next to it.

The "Gospel of Thomas" gives an even more radical picture of Jesus. Read the translation. This Jesus preaches enlightenment by mystical knowledge — #3 says, "The kingdom is inside you..." Jesus seems to be warning people against looking to gurus for the answers, a Christian version of "If you meet the Buddha on the road, kill him." This fragment dates from 150 A.D., more than a century after Jesus' death, but that's probably not the only reason why it's not in our Bible (after all, the Gospel of John is generally dated at 100 A.D.). Rather, the message itself, a threat to established church leaders, may have been too scary to include in the Bible — whether Jesus said it or not.

Lindisfarne Gospels, 698 A.D.

Throughout the Middle Ages Bibles had to be reproduced by hand, a painstaking process usually done by monks for a rich patron. This beautifully illustrated ("illuminated") collection of the four Gospels is the most magnificent of medieval British monk-uscripts. The text is in Latin, the language of scholars ever since the Roman empire, but the elaborate decoration mixes Irish, classical and even Byzantine forms.

Lindisfarne Gospels — In the Middle Ages all books were hand-copied and illustrated by meticulous monks.

These Gospels are a reminder that Christianity almost didn't make it in Europe. After the Fall of Rome (which had established Christianity as the official religion), much of Europe reverted to its pagan ways. This was the time of "Beowulf", with people worshipping woodland spirits and terrible Teutonic gods. It took dedicated Irish missionaries 500 years to re-establish the faith on the Continent. Lindisfarne, an obscure monastery of Irish monks on an island off the east coast of England, was one of the few beacons of light after the Fall of Rome, tending the embers of civilization through the long night of the Dark Ages.

☞ *Enter the next room, a large hall with glass cases containing manuscripts from all over the world. Pass them by. Halfway down the hall you'll come to a statue of Shakespeare. Pass him by for now. Just ahead on the right you'll find a glass case with...*

The Gütenberg (42-line) Bible, c. 1455

It looks like just another monk-made Latin manuscript, but of course it's one of the most revolutionary inventions in history. Johann Gütenberg (c. 1397-1468), a German goldsmith, figured out a convenient way to reproduce written materials quickly, neatly and cheaply — by printing with movable type. You scratch each letter onto a separate metal block, then arrange them into words, ink them up and press them onto paper. When one job was done you could re-use the same letters for a new one.

This simple idea had immediate and revolutionary consequences. For the first time, knowledge could be transmitted to a wide audience, not just the rich. Books became the "mass media" of Europe, linking people by a common set of ideas. And, as with all bad drugs, this increased supply of knowledge only created a demand for still more knowledge.

Suddenly the Bible was available for anyone to read. This was a scary thing for the church authorities, and they passed laws to prohibit the printing of bibles. They could see that putting such precious — and dangerous — ideas in the hands of the common man was like letting a kid play with matches. But it was the Church that got burned. As people read the Bible themselves, they formed their own opinions of God's message, which was often different from the version the priests had told them. The result was the Reformation, where Protestants broke away from the Catholic Church in order to follow the Bible, not the priests.

(By the way, printing was not invented by Gütenberg. Against the opposite wall is a wood-block printed version of the Buddhist "Diamond Sutra", printed in China 600 years before Gütenberg's Bible.)

☞ *Continuing down the hall you'll find the case marked "The English Bible-3." Find the Bible labeled...*

The Authorized Version, or King James Bible, 1611
Jesus spoke Aramaic, a form of Hebrew. His words were written down
in Greek. Greek manuscripts were translated into Latin, the language of
medieval monks and scholars. By 1400 there was still no English version
of the Bible, though only a small percentage of the population understood
Latin. A few brave reformers risked death to make translations into
English and print them with Gütenberg's new invention. Within two
centuries English translations were both legal and popular.

The "King James" version (done during his reign) has been the most
popular English translation since its publication. Fifty scholars worked
for four years, borrowing heavily from previous translations, to produce
the work. Its impact on the English language has been enormous, making
Elizabethan English something of the standard, even after all those "thee"s
and "thou"s fell out of fashion in everyday speech.

In our century, there have been many new translations that hope to
be both more accurate (based on better scholarship and original manuscripts) and more readable, using modern speech patterns. The King
James version is still the most popular, but you have to wonder: how
many generations, raised on the King James, grew up thinking that Jesus
spoke like a bad Shakespearean actor?

☞   *Return to Shakespeare, to the case in front of the statue of him.*

SHAKESPEARE

William Shakespeare (1564-1616) is the greatest author in any language. Period. His contribution to the English language is perhaps as
important as the King James Bible. In one fell swoop, he made the
language of everyday people as important as Latin. In the process he
gave us phrases like "one fell swoop" that we quote without knowing
it's Shakespeare.

Perhaps even more important than his language was his insight into
humanity. With his stock of great characters — Hamlet, Othello, Mac-
beth, Falstaff, Romeo and Juliet, Lear — he probed the psychology of
human beings 300 years before Freud. Even today his characters strike
a familiar chord in us.

Shakespeare's Handwriting
Supposedly this is Shakespeare's signature on the first of four labels
attached to the document. I'm sorry, but it looks like "Wm Grassfit" to me.

Shakespeare as a Collaborator
Shakespeare co-wrote this play titled "Sir Thomas More". Some schol-

ars have wondered if maybe Shakespeare had help on other plays as well. After all, they reasoned, how could a journeyman actor, with little education, have written so many masterpieces? Modern scholars, though, unanimously agree that Shakespeare did indeed write the plays ascribed to him.

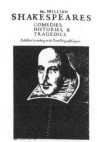

Mr. WILLIAM
SHAKESPEARES
COMEDIES,
HISTORIES, &
TRAGEDIES.
Published according to the True Originall Copies.

LONDON
Printed by Isaac Iaggard, and Ed. Blount. 1623

Shakespeare — Only with a brain the size of this could one man write so many masterpieces.

Two Hamlet Quartos

Shakespeare wrote his plays to be performed, not read. He published a few, but as his reputation grew, unauthorized "bootleg" versions also began to circulate. Some of these were written out by actors (with faulty memories) trying to recreate a play they'd been in years before. Here are two different versions of "Hamlet".

The Shakespeare First Folio

It wasn't until seven years after his death that this complete-works collection of his plays came out. The editors were two friends and fellow-actors.

The engraving of Shakespeare on the title page is one of only two likenesses done during his lifetime — all others you've ever seen, including the statue behind you with his button-bulging belly, are just "artists' conceptions". Is this what he really looked like? No one knows. The best answer probably comes from his friend and fellow-poet Ben Jonson in the introduction "To the Reader" on the facing page. He concludes: "Reader, look not on his Picture, but his book."

☞ *Continue to the end of the hall. At the door, thank the bust of Sir Hans Sloane, the father of the British Museum, for showing you a good time today. (But don't say anything about the funny part in his hair — he's real sensitive about it.)*

Exit the room and gape up the stairwell.

Totem Pole

American Indians carved totem poles to record the history of their family or clan or tribe. The wild half-animal figures are the distant ancestors, the mythical founders of the tribe. From these poles, the Indians could figure out where they came from, where they stood in the great scheme of human history...and where they as a people were headed. This marks the end of our tour through the British Museum, the totem pole of Western civilization.

National Gallery, London

The National Gallery lets you tour Europe's art without ever crossing the Channel. With so many exciting artists and styles, it's a fine overture to art if you're just starting a European trip, and a pleasant reprise if you're just finishing. Anytime, the "National Gal" is a welcome one-hour interlude from the bustle of London sightseeing.

National Gallery

Hours: Mon.-Sat. 10:00-18:00; Sun. 14:00-18:00
Cost: Free
Tour length: One hour
Getting there: It overlooks Trafalgar Square, a 15-minute walk from Big Ben. Tube to "Charing Cross".
Information: Information desk and handy floor plan brochure in lobby. The unique Micro Gallery (first floor of the Sainsbury Wing) has a dozen very user-friendly, touch-the-screen computers where you can learn more about Rembrandt's wives, rococo or chiaroscuro. Call up your favorite painting onto the high-resolution screen and get a print-out to take home. Tel. 839-3321, recorded information 839-3526.
Starring: You name it — Leonardo, Van Eyck, Raphael, Titian, Caravaggio, Rembrandt, Rubens, Velázquez, Monet, Renoir, Van Gogh.

Orientation

☞   *There are two entrances from Trafalgar Square. I'd recommend the one to the left, into the modern Sainsbury Wing, designed by an American, Robert Venturi. Pick up a current map at the information desk.*

The collection is laid out pretty much chronologically. We'll start in the Sainsbury Wing, then work clockwise around the perimeter of the museum.

The National Gallery is best seen as a quick overview of art history. Cruise like an eagle through the rooms, getting the big picture, seeing how each style progresses into the next. As you enter a room, sweep your eyes around, getting a feel for the common characteristics of all the paintings. The paintings I've singled out aren't necessarily superstar masterpieces, just good illustrations of each art style. Move quickly, and get the big picture.

This tour, like modern art history, begins in Italy in the 1400s. After the Italian Renaissance, we'll look at its Northern counterpart, then proceed century-by-century and country-by-country up to the modern world, through the styles known as baroque, rococo, Neo-classical and Impressionist. Quickly.

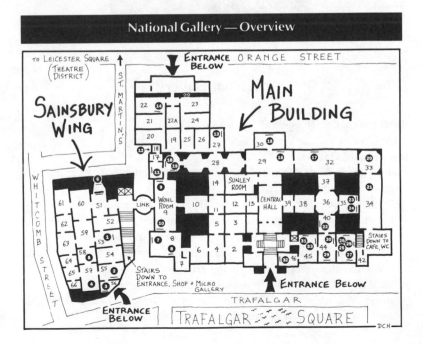

National Gallery — Overview

National Gallery

Medieval and Early Renaissance
1. Wilton Diptych
2. UCCELLO—Battle of San Romano
3. VAN EYCK—Arnolfini Marriage
4. CRIVELLI—Annunciation with St. Emidius
5. BOTTICELLI—Venus and Mars

High Renaissance
6. LEONARDO DA VINCI—Virgin and Child (cartoon)
7. MICHELANGELO—Entombment
8. RAPHAEL—Pope Julius II

Venetian Renaissance
9. TINTORETTO—Origin of the Milky Way
10. TITIAN—Bacchus and Ariadne

Northern Protestant Art
11. VERMEER—Young Woman Standing at a Virginal
12. Hoogstraten Peepshow
13. REMBRANDT—Self-portrait

Baroque
14. RUBENS—The Judgement of Paris
15. VAN DYCK—Charles I on Horseback
16. VELAZQUEZ—The Rokeby Venus
17. CARAVAGGIO—Salome Receiving the Head of John the Baptist

French and Later Italian
18. CLAUDE LORRAIN—Seaport
19. TURNER—Dido Building Carthage
20. BOUCHER—Pan and Syrinx
21. TIEPOLO

British
22. CONSTABLE—The Hay Wain
23. TURNER—The Fighting Temeraire
24. TURNER—Rain, Steam, Speed

Impressionism and Beyond
25. MONET—Gare St. Lazare
26. RENOIR—The Umbrellas
27. DEGAS—La La at the Cirque Fernando
28. MANET—The Waitress (La Servante de Bocks)
29. SEURAT—Bathers, Asnieres
30. VAN GOGH—Sunflowers
31. CEZANNE—Bathers
32. PICASSO—Bowl of Fruit, Bottle of Wine
33. MONET—Water Lilies

THE ITALIAN RENAISSANCE (1400-1550)

The Renaissance — or "rebirth" of the culture of ancient Greece and Rome — erupted in Italy and spread north. It was a cultural boom that changed people's thinking about every aspect of life. In politics, it meant democracy. In religion, a move away from Church dominance and toward the assertion of man (humanism). Science and secular learning were revived after centuries of superstition and ignorance. In architecture, it was a return to the balanced columns and arches of Greece and Rome.

In painting, the Renaissance meant realism. Artists rediscovered the beauty of Nature and the human body. Their pictures of beautiful people in harmonious surroundings expressed the optimism and confidence of the Renaissance.

☞ *We'll start in Room 53, in the Sainsbury Wing. (From the Sainsbury entrance, go to the top of the stairs and turn left.)*

MEDIEVAL AND EARLY RENAISSANCE

The Wilton Diptych — Anonymous

Our first Italian Renaissance painting is neither Italian nor Renaissance. It's French and medieval, serving as a good contrast to what we'll see later. It's not realistic. It's not three-dimensional. There's no background setting. It's not particularly beautiful or emotional. Look at the left panel — the so-called "Lamb of God" held by John the Baptist looks more like a chihuahua. In the right panel, the angels with their flame-like wings are bunched together single file across the back, rather than receding realistically into the distance. All the figures are flat and scrawny with cartoon features — far from flesh-and-blood human beings. Artists before the Renaissance hadn't yet mastered the art of putting a 3-D world onto a 2-D canvas.

The one thing the Wilton Diptych IS is religious. In the Middle Ages, the Catholic Church controlled most aspects of life, including art. Medieval paintings weren't meant to be realistic or beautiful but educational, teaching church doctrine to the illiterate masses in a picture-book, Sesame-Street way. Almost all the paintings you'll see nearby have Christian subjects — the Virgin Mary with baby Jesus, crucifixions, saints, Bible scenes, etc.

Uccello — *Battle of San Romano*

This colorful battle scene showing the victory of Florence over Siena is an early Renaissance attempt at a realistic, non-religious, three-dimensional scene. The background of farmyards, receding hedges, and tiny soldiers creates a 3-D illusion of distance. In the foreground, Uccello actually constructs a 3-D grid out of fallen lances, then places the horses

UCCELLO — Battle of San Romano. By showing horses and soldiers from every conceivable angle, Uccello pioneered a new dimension — the illusion of 3-D.

and warriors within it. Still, Uccello hasn't quite worked all the bugs out of this technique — notice the fallen soldier at left who isn't much bigger than the fallen helmet at right.

Van Eyck — *The Arnolfini Marriage*

Think back to the first painting we saw, the "Wilton Diptych". This work was painted just a few decades later, which explains its "medieval" look.

The thing that strikes us first about this simple wedding scene (set in Bruges, Belgium) is the incredible detail. No, I take that back. What strikes us first is the bride, who looks like she's about to give birth to a floorlamp.

But what strikes us next is the detail. Van Eyck has built us a medieval doll house, then invites us to linger over the finely crafted details, all with important symbolic meaning — the chandelier with its one lit candle (love), the fruit on the window sill (fertility), the whisk broom (the bride's domestic responsibilities), and the terrier (Fido — fidelity) with almost countable hairs.

JAN VAN EYCK—The Arnolfini Marriage. Like figures in a medieval dollhouse, the bride and groom are surrounded by meticulously painted knickknacks.

In fact, each object is painted at an ideal angle, with the details you'd see if you were only a foot away. And to top it off, look into the round mirror on the far wall — the whole scene is reflected backwards in miniature, showing the loving couple, the priest, and even Van Eyck himself painting the scene!

By the way, she may not be pregnant. The fashion of the day was to wear a pillow to look pregnant in hopes you'd soon get that way. At least, that's what they told their parents.

The surface detail is extraordinary, but the painting lacks depth. The tiny room looks unnaturally narrow, cramped, and claustrophobic — I hope their mother-in-law isn't moving in.

Crivelli — *The Annunciation with Saint Emidius*

This has Northern, medieval detail like Van Eyck's Shotgun Wedding (the rug and peacock) plus Italian spaciousness. We're sucked right in, accelerating through the alleyway, under the arch and off into the distance. Crivelli creates a labyrinth of rooms and walkways that we want to walk through, around, and into (or is that just a male thing?).

Renaissance Italians were interested in — some would say obsessed with — portraying 3-D space. Perhaps they focused their burning spiritual passion away from heaven, and toward the physical world. With so much restless energy, they needed lots of elbow room. Space, the final frontier.

Follow the beam of light from heaven to Mary that penetrates all of the receding planes. It's a straight line all right, but somehow this Dove makes a hard left turn along the way. The Italians still hadn't quite got this perspective thing in perspective.

Botticelli — *Venus and Mars*

Mars takes a break from war, succumbing to the delights of Love (Venus), while little satyrs play innocently with the discarded tools of death.

In the Renaissance, pagan Greek gods became symbols of human traits, virtues and vices. There was an optimistic mood in the air, the feeling that enlightened Man could solve all problems.

THE HIGH RENAISSANCE —
LEONARDO, MICHELANGELO AND RAPHAEL

With the "Big Three" of the High Renaissance — Leo, Mike and Raffi — painters had finally conquered realism. But these three Florentine artists weren't content to just copy nature, cranking out photographs-on-canvas. Like Renaissance architects (which they also were), they carefully composed their figures on the canvas, "building" them into geometrical patterns that reflected the balance and order they saw in nature.

Leonardo Da Vinci — *Virgin and Child with St. John the Baptist and St. Anne (Cartoon)*

At first glance this cartoon, or drawing, looks like a simple family snapshot of a mom, grandma and two playful kids. But looking closer we see that Leonardo has deliberately posed them into a pyramid shape, with the mothers' heads at the peak and baby Jesus squirming out from the center, creating a mood of maternal stability and serenity. The two children — both destined to suffer violent deaths — play obliviously beneath their mothers' Mona Lisa smiles.

LEONARDO — Virgin and child with St. John the Baptist and St. Anne. Leonardo surrounds baby Jesus with a pyramid of maternal security.

Follow the eyes: shadowy-eyed Anne turns toward Mary who looks tenderly down to Jesus who blesses John who gazes back dreamily. As your eyes follow theirs, you're always led back to the (literal and psychological) center of the composition — Jesus. Without the stiff symbolism of medieval art, Leonardo drives home a theological concept in a natural, human way.

☞ *Leave the Sainsbury Wing through the passageway (the "Link") that connects with the main building, entering the large Room 9. We'll return to these big, colorful canvases, but first, turn right into Room 8.*

Michelangelo — *Entombment (unfinished)*

Michelangelo, the greatest sculptor ever, proves it here in this "painted sculpture" of the crucified Jesus being carried to the tomb. The figures are almost like chiseled statues of Greek gods, especially the musclehead in red who practically ripples beneath his clothes. Christ's body is as naked as you can get — shocking to the medieval Church, but completely acceptable in the Renaissance world where classical nudes were admired as an expression of the divine.

In true Renaissance style, balance and symmetry reign. Christ is the center of the composition, flanked by two equally-leaning people who support his body with strips of cloth. They, in turn, are flanked by two more.

Where Leonardo gave us expressive faces, Michelangelo lets the bodies do the talking. The two supporters strain to hold up Christ's body, and in their tension we too feel the great weight and tragedy of their dead God. Michelangelo expresses the divine through the human form.

Raphael — *Pope Julius II*
The new worldliness of the Renaissance even reached the Church. Pope Julius II, who in his day was more a swaggering conquistador than a pious pope, set out to rebuild Rome in Renaissance style (including hiring Michelangelo to paint the Vatican's Sistine Chapel). Raphael has captured this complex man with perfect realism and psychological insight. On the one hand, the pope is an imposing pyramid of power, decked out with fancy rings and a bag of money. But at the same time, he's bent and broken, his throne backed into a corner, with an expression that seems to say, "Is this all there is?"

In fact, the great era of Florence and Rome was coming to an end. With Raphael's death in 1520, the Renaissance shifted to Venice.

☞   *Enter the long Room 9.*

VENETIAN RENAISSANCE

Big change. The canvases are bigger, the colors brighter. There are fewer Christian scenes (crucifixions, Madonnas-and-Childs, Bible stories) and more mythological and historical scenes. And there are nudes — not Michelangelo's lumps of knotted muscle — but smooth-skinned, sexy, golden centerfolds.

Venice got wealthy by trading with the luxurious and exotic East. Its happy-go-lucky art style shows a taste for the finer things in life. But despite all the flashiness and fleshiness, Venetian art still keeps a sense of Renaissance balance.

Tintoretto — *The Origin of the Milky Way*
In this Greek/Roman myth, the god Jupiter places baby Hercules at his wife Juno's breast. But the baby isn't hers and she pulls away, spilling the milk which becomes the Milky Way.

Tintoretto has carefully composed this seemingly crowded and turbulent scene into an "X" composition — Juno slants one way while Jupiter slants the other. The result is more dramatic and complex than the stable pyramids of Leonardo and Raphael. Also, notice how Jupiter appears to be flying almost directly at us. Such shocking 3-D effects hint at the baroque art we'll see later.

Titian — *Bacchus and Ariadne*
In another Greek myth, Ariadne (far left), who has been abandoned by her lover, gets cheered up by the god of Wine (leaping, with the red cape) and his motley entourage.

TITIAN — Bacchus and Ariadne. The happy-go-lucky Venetians painted sexy scenes like this Greek myth on the verge of an orgy.

Titian uses a kind of pyramid composition to balance an otherwise unbalanced scene — follow Ariadne's gaze up to the peak of Bacchus' flowing cape, then down along the snake-handler's spine to the lower right corner. Pretty nifty, huh? In addition, he "balances" the picture with harmonious colors — most everyone is dressed/undressed in greens and golds that blend into the landscape, while the two main figures stand out with matching splotches of red.

The Italian Renaissance culminates with Titian.

☞ *Exit Room 9 at the far end. You'll find Dutch art in Rooms 16-18 and the long Room 28.*

NORTHERN PROTESTANT ART (1600-1700)

Going from Venetian to Dutch is like switching from Cinemascope to a 9-inch TV — smaller canvases, subdued colors, everyday scenes, and not one single naked person.

The economic boom that hit the Low Countries produced a different kind of art than in Venice. Italy had wealthy aristocrats and the powerful Catholic Church to purchase art. But the North's patrons were middle-class hardworking, Protestant merchants. They wanted simple, cheap, no-nonsense pictures to decorate their homes and offices. Greek gods and Virgin Marys were out — ordinary people and places were in. Painted with great attention to detail, this is art meant not to wow or preach at you but to be enjoyed and lingered over. You'll find examples of the subjects popular among the Dutch middle class — portraits, landscapes, still-lifes and slice-of-life scenes. Browse around.

Vermeer — *A Young Woman Standing at a Virginal*
Here we have a simple interior of a Dutch home with a prim virgin playing a virginal. We've surprised her and she pauses to look up at us. Contrast this quiet scene with, say, Titian's bombastic, orgiastic "Bacchus and Ariadne."

VERMEER — A Young Woman Standing at a Virginal. Vermeer shows us the simple beauty of everyday things.

The Dutch even today take great pride in the orderliness of their small homes. Vermeer, by framing off such a small world to look at, forces us to appreciate the tiniest details, the beauty of everyday things — her shawl, the floor tiles, the contrasting paintings of Love in the background and, most of all, the pale diffused light that soaks in from the window at left.

☞ *Stroll down long Room 28, turning left into Room 27.*

Rembrandt — *Self-portrait, aged 63*

This is one of 60 surviving self-portraits of the greatest Dutch painter. He started out as the successful, wealthy young genius of the art world (see his confident "Self-Portrait, aged 34" nearby), but he refused to paint what others told him to. Instead of the commercial portraits, pretty landscapes and detailed still-lifes that other Dutch artists cranked out, Rembrandt painted things that he believed in but that no one would invest in — family members, down-to-earth Bible scenes and . . . himself. In this work from the year he died, Rembrandt surveyes the wreckage of his independent life. We see a disillusioned but proud old genius.

As you browse through Rembrandt, you'll notice his main painting technique—the strong contrast of light and dark. Most of the canvases are a rich, dark brown, with their few crucial details highlighted by a bright light.

☞ *Use the map to locate the baroque paintings. Start with Rubens, in the far corner of the North Wing, Room 22.*

BAROQUE

Whoa! What a change! While Protestant and democratic Europe painted simple scenes, Catholic and aristocratic countries turned to the style called "Baroque". Baroque art took what was flashy in Venetian art and made it flashier, gaudy and made it gaudier, dramatic and made it shocking.

Rubens — *The Judgement of Paris*

This whole room is full of big, colorful, emotional works by Peter Paul Rubens from Catholic Flanders (Belgium). Rubens painted anything that would raise your pulse — battles, miracles, hunts and, especially, fleshy women with dimples on all four cheeks. The painting here is little more than an excuse for a study of the female nude, showing front, back and profile all on one canvas.

Van Dyck — *Charles I on Horseback*

The grandiose baroque style was a propaganda weapon for kings and bishops, to impress the masses with their power. This portrait of England's

VAN DYCK — Charles I on Horseback.
British aristocrats loved to be painted with their possessions. Here, King Charles enjoys his head while he still has it.

Catholic, French-educated, Divine-Right king portrays him as genteel and refined, yet very much in command. All this was perfectly true...at least, until England's Civil War, when Charles' genteel head was separated from his refined body by rebels who were suddenly very much in command.

Van Dyck's portrait style set the tone for all the stuffy, boring portraits of British aristocrats who wished to be portrayed as sophisticated gentlemen — whether they were or not.

Velázquez — *The Rokeby Venus*

Spain's wealth came from its materialistadors' plunder — gold and raw materials of the New World. Her baroque art style was a strange combination of Venetian splash and religious fanaticism.

Though horny Spanish kings bought Titian-esque centerfolds by the gross, this work by the king's personal court painter is the first (and, for over a century, the only) Spanish nude. Like a Venetian model, this nude is posed diagonally across the canvas with flaring red cloth to highlight her white skin and inflame our passion. About the only concession to Spanish modesty is the false reflection in the mirror — if it really showed what the angle should show, Velázquez would have needed two mirrors...and a new job.

VELÁZQUEZ — The Rokeby Venus. While most Spanish art consisted of saints, madonnas and crucifixes, Velázquez shows us the world from the other side — Spain's first nude.

Caravaggio — *Salome Receiving the Head of John the Baptist*
Baroque took reality and exaggerated it. Most artists amplified the prettiness, but Caravaggio exaggerated its ugliness. For his Bible scenes, he shocked the public by using real, ugly, un-haloed people. His paintings look like a wet dog smells. Reality.

FRENCH

As Europe's political and economic center shifted from Italy to France, Louis XIV's court at Versailles became the cultural hub of the Continent. Every aristocrat spoke French, dressed French and bought French paintings — which were really only Italian Renaissance and baroque with an extra dash of prettiness.

**Claude Lorrain — *Seaport with the Embarkation of the Queen of Sheba*
Turner — *Dido Building Carthage***
To get an idea of luxurious, powdered-wig French tastes, compare the soft-focus harbor scene by Claude with the sober, realistic landscapes of the Dutch.
Fans of England's J.M.W. Turner will find his very-similar "Dido Building Carthage" nearby. Turner donated the painting on condition it always hang with the work of his idol.

Boucher — *Pan and Syrinx*

Rococo art is like a Rubens that got shrunk in the wash — smaller, lighter pastel colors, frillier and more delicate than the baroque style. Same dimples, though. This sensual, suggestive art was a favorite at the fabulous, decadent French court at Versailles.

LATER VENETIAN

After the Renaissance, Venice began sinking economically. She survived (as she does today) as a tourist center. Artists like Canaletto and Guardi made a living selling these small, colorful "postcard" scenes of Venice. Their style combines the pretty colors of rococo with the serenity of Dutch landscapes.

Only one artist continued in the grand Venetian tradition of big canvases, bright colors and epic themes. G.B. Tiepolo got famous painting the ceilings of Europe's greatest palaces (like Madrid's Royal Palace and the Wurzburg *Residenz*). With dramatic 3-D effects, this Rococonut created the illusion of a ceiling opening up so you could look right into heaven.

☞ *The British art is in Rooms 35-40.*

BRITISH

Constable — *The Hay Wain*

To give you an idea of how stuffy early Britain was, consider that when this simple landscape was first exhibited, it caused a scandal! Its Dutch naturalness shocked those who were used to the high-falutin', prettified baroque style pioneered by Van Dyck's portraits of King Charles I.

Turner — *The Fighting Téméraire*

Nineteenth-century England was caught up in the Industrial Revolution, when machines began to replace humans. Here a modern steamboat drags a famous masted battleship off into the sunset to be destroyed.

Turner's messy, colorful style gives us our first glimpse into the modern art world — Impressionism. (By the way, the Tate Gallery has an enormous collection of Turner's work.)

Turner — *Rain, Steam and Speed*

A train emerges from the depths of fog, rushing across a bridge towards us. The red-orange glow of the engine's furnace burns like the embers of a fire. (Turner was fascinated by how light penetrates haze.) Through the blur of paints, the outline of a bridge is visible, while in the center, shadowy figures (spirits?) head down to the river.

Turner takes an ordinary scene (like Constable), captures the play of light with messy paints (like the Impressionists), and charges it with mystery (like wow).

IMPRESSIONISM AND BEYOND (1850-1910)

For 500 years, a great artist was someone who could paint the real world with perfect accuracy. Then along came the camera and, click, the artist was replaced by a machine that could capture a perfect portrait, landscape or village scene in the blink of a shutter. But the unemployed artist didn't go looking for a straight job (God forbid). Instead, he learned from the camera.

He couldn't match the camera for painstaking detail, but he could match it — even beat it — in capturing the fleeting moment, the snapshot, the candid pose, the play of light and shadow, the quick impression a scene makes on you. A new breed of artists burst out of the stuffy confines of the studio and began to paint Nature the way they saw it. They'd set up their canvases in the open air or carry their notebooks into a crowded cafe, dashing off quick sketches in order to catch a momentary impression. They were the Impressionists.

☞   *Start with the misty Monet train station.*

Monet — *Gare St. Lazare*

Claude Monet, the father of Impressionism, was more interested in the play of light off his subject than the subject itself. Here the sun filters through the glass roof of the train station and gets filtered again through the clouds of steam.

Renoir — *The Umbrellas*

View this from about 15 feet away. It's a nice scene of many-colored umbrellas. Now move in close. The "scene" breaks up into almost random patches of bright colors.

The Impressionists used a new technique to capture the bright colors of nature. They knew that yellow and blue, for example, combine to make green. So they'd place a splotch of yellow and a splotch of blue side by side on the canvas. Viewed up close it looks like a mess, but when you back up to a proper distance, *Voilà!* a shimmering green umbrella. This kind of rough, messy brushwork (where you can actually see the brushstroke) is one of the telltale signs of Impressionism.

Degas — *La La at the Cirque Fernando*
Degas, the master of the candid snapshot, enjoyed catching everyday scenes at odd angles.

Manet — *The Waitress (La Servante de Bocks)*
Edouard Manet also captures a quick "Impression" in a cafe. Imagine how mundane (and therefore shocking!) scenes like this must have been to a public raised on Greek gods, luscious nudes and glowing Madonnas.

Seurat — *Bathers, Asnières*
Seurat took the Impressionist color technique to its logical extreme. These figures are "built," dot by dot, with small points of different colors. Only at a distance do they blend together to make a hat, a patch of "green" grass or a bather.

SEURAT — Bathers. Seurat built figures with small dots of paint.

Van Gogh — *Sunflowers*
In military terms, Van Gogh was the point-man of his culture — he went ahead of his cohorts, exploring the unknown ..and catching a bullet young. He added an emotional element to the Impressionist style, seeming to infuse his love of life even into inanimate objects. These sunflowers, painted with Van Gogh's characteristic swirling brushstrokes, seem to shimmer and writhe in either agony or ecstasy — depending on your own mood.

VAN GOGH — Sunflowers. Shortly after painting these sunflowers, the artist killed himself.

Van Gogh painted these sunflowers during his stay in southern France, a time of frenzied painting when he himself hovered between agony and ecstasy, bliss and madness. A year after painting this, he shot himself.

Soapbox time. (Skip this paragraph if you don't want to be preached to.) In his day, Van Gogh was a penniless nobody, selling only one painting in his whole career. Nowadays, a "Sunflowers" with Vincent's signature on the vase (this is one of a half dozen versions he did) sells for $40 million dollars (about $5000 a day for 70 years), and it's not even his highest-priced painting. It seems to me that if art is truly "priceless", we have to learn to value it in terms besides money — enjoy it, support it, but don't exploit it.

Cézanne — Bathers (Les Grandes Baigneuses)

Cézanne tried to link Impressionism with the classical art of the past — and in the process he brought Impressionism into the 20th century. The Impressionists (think of Seurat) "built" figures with dabs of paint. Cézanne used this technique (though his "dabs" were larger-sized "slabs"), but he aimed at making more solid, three-dimensional, geometrical figures as Leonardo or Titian had. In fact, these Bathers are arranged in strict triangles à la Leonardo — the five nudes on the left form one triangle, the seated nude on the right forms another, and even the background trees and clouds are triangular patterns of paint.

By breaking objects up into these geometrical slabs or "cubes" of paint, Cézanne inspired the most radical of modern art styles — "Cube"-ism.

Picasso — Bowl of Fruit, Bottle of Wine

Well, we made it. From the Middle Ages through the Renaissance, baroque and rococo, and finally to our century. And, in a sense, we've come full circle. Medieval artists (remember the "Wilton Dyptich") neglected realism to express their view of the world. Here, Picasso turns his back on the whole tradition of realism = beauty started in the Renaissance.

This Cubist work takes Cézanne one step further, shattering reality into shards, then putting it back together on the canvas in slightly jumbled fashion. True, this isn't a realistic work like Leonardo's "Virgin and Child" drawing. But then we live in a very different world from Leonardo's ordered, simple one. Our reality is slightly jumbled, shattered by war, conflicting ideologies, poverty and the schizophrenia of "wearing different hats" several times a day. Picasso uses a new modern style to express the wild ride of our modern world.

Monet — *Water Lilies*

Before you tumble back into the 20th-century rat race of busy London, relax for a second in Monet's garden at Giverny near Paris. Monet planned this artificial garden, re-channeled a stream, built a bridge...and planted these water lilies. He created a living work of art — a small section of order and calm in a hectic world.

Tate Gallery, London

The Tate is like two great museums in one — the world's best collection of British art, and one of the world's best overall collections of modern art. Fortunately for us, the two combine very nicely. The Tate starts us off relaxed, then slowly eases us into the wacky modern world.

Tate Gallery

Hours: Mon.-Sat. 10:00-17:50; Sun. 14:00-17:50; closed on 6 major holidays.
Cost: Free
Tour length: Two hours
Getting there: Subway to "Pimlico" or bus #88 or #77A, or 15-minute walk along Thames from Big Ben
Information: Free current map at information desk.
   Free tours (normally 11:00 — British, Noon — Impressionism, 14:00 — 20th century, 15:00 — Turner).
   Tel. 01/821-1313, recorded information 01/821-7218.
Misc.: Coffee shop, restaurant, great bookshop.
Starring: Gainsborough, Reynolds, Blake, Constable, Pre-Raphaelites, Turner, Impressionists, Henry Moore, Dali, Warhol, and Picasso.

Orientation

Orien-tate from the rotunda, near the entrance. The British collection and the modern art "classics" — the core of what we'll see — are in the left half of the museum. The more recent works (including temporary exhibits) are to the right. The Turner collection in the Clore Gallery is also to the right, through Room 18.

The gallery shop is pretty obvious, and the cafe, restaurant and W.C.'s are downstairs (staircase over your left shoulder).

The Tate rotates its huge collection of paintings, so expect changes. (The map puts an asterisk next to works lost in the most recent shuffle.) Be prepared to look for alternate paintings by the same artist.

☞   *Start in Room 1, at the far, far end of the sculpture gallery.*

Early British (Rooms 1-4)
1. Stuffy portraits
2. HOGARTH—O the Roast Beef of Old England
3. STUBBS—various horse paintings
4. GAINSBOROUGH—Giovanna Baccelli

Romanticism (Rooms 5-9)
5. FUSELI—Titania and Bottom
6. BLAKE—3 colorprints
7. BLAKE—Head of a Ghost of a Flea
8. CONSTABLE—Cloud Study
9. MARTIN—3 heavenly landscapes
10. DANBY—The Deluge
11. WARD—Gordale Scar, Yorkshire

Pre-Raphaelites (Room 9)
12. ROSSETTI—The Annunciation
13. ROSSETTI—Beata Beatrix
14. MILLAIS—The Order of Release, 1746
15. WATERHOUSE—The Lady of Shalott
16. BURNE-JONES—King Cophetua and the Beggar Maid

British Impressionism (Room 10)
17. SARGENT—Carnation, Lily, Lily, Rose
18. WHISTLER—Nocturne in Blue-Green

Impressionism and Post-Impressionism (Room 12)
19. MONET—Poplars on the Epte
20. DEGAS—Little Dancer, Aged 14 (statue)
21. VAN GOGH—Farms near Auvers

22. SEURAT—Le Bec du Hoc Grand-camp
23. GAUGUIN—Faa Iheihe
24. CÉZANNE—The Gardener

Cubism (Room 13)
25. PICASSO—Seated Nude
26. BRAQUE—Bottle and Fishes

Abstract
* MONDRIAN—Composition with Red, Yellow and Blue
* MATISSE—The Snail

Expressionism (Room 14)
27. GROSZ—Suicide

Surrealism (Room 15)
28. DALI—Lobster Telephone
29. ERNST—Celebes
30. DELVAUX—Sleeping Venus

Sculpture (central gallery)
31. RODIN—The Kiss
32. MOORE—Recumbent Figure

Postwar art
* POLLOCK—Untitled (Naked Man with Knife)
* POLLOCK—Yellow Islands
* ROTHKO
* GIACOMETTI
* ARMAN—Venus of the Shaving Brushes (statue)
* LICHTENSTEIN—Whaam!
* WARHOL—Marilyn Diptych

(* = Maybe not on display.)

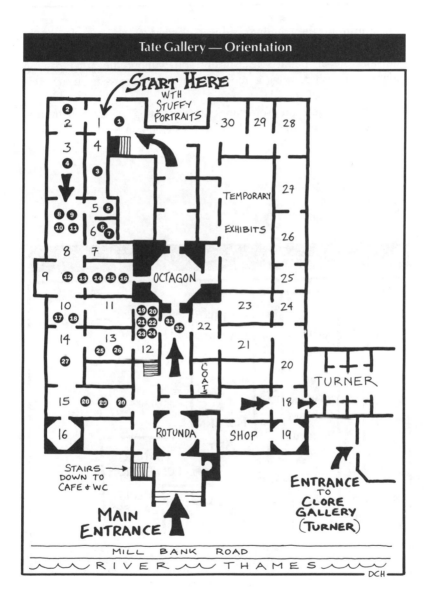

BRITISH ART

In British art, the painting's subject — what it's about — is usually more important than its style. People, horses, countrysides, scenes from daily life, are all painted realistically and without the artist passing judgment. British painting is rooted in the landscape, religion, mythology and people of the island.

Britain's painters are sometimes as interesting as their paintings. There are some genuine hoots here, so I'll spend a little more time than usual on their biographies.

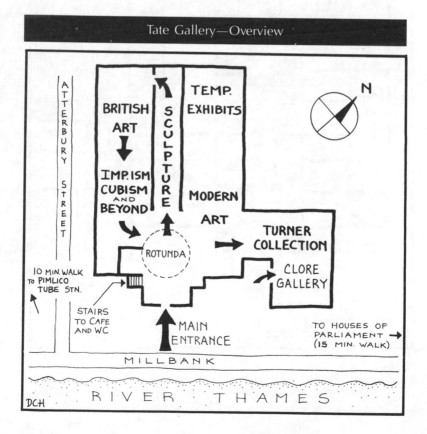

EARLY BRITISH ART (1600-1800)

Stuffy Portraits

Linger in this room just long enough to count how many pictures are NOT of people, then move on. These are flattering portraits of a beef-fed society, making uncultured people look delicate and refined. Britain's upper crust in the 1600s had little interest in art, other than as a record of themselves along with their possessions — their wives, children, clothes and guns.

Hogarth — *O the Roast Beef of Old England (The Gate of Calais)* (1748)

There was another side, a darker side, to merry olde England. And that's where you'd find William Hogarth, the Charles Dickens of the 1700s. A born Londoner, he loved every gritty aspect of the big, gut-punching city. In seedy pubs and brothels, at prizefights, cockfights, duels and public executions — that's where Hogarth would be, sketchpad in hand. With biting satire, he exposed the hypocrisy of the upper class...and exposed the upper classes to the hidden poverty of society's underbelly. Not content to paint just pretty portraits, he chose models from real life and put them into real-life scenes. "My picture is my stage," he said, "and my men and women my players."

Here we see some typical Hogarth characters. A fat-and-sassy monk drools over an enormous hunk of beef, while around him poor soldiers are dressed in rags, and beggars crouch in the shadows. A crow hunches on the top of the gate like a vulture. And, sure enough, there's Hogarth himself in the background at left, sketchbook in hand, recording the hypocrisy.

Stubbs — *Various pictures of horses*

In the 1700s, as British art came into its own, painters started doing more than just portraits. Stubbs was the Michelangelo of horses, studying their anatomy and painting them with incredible detail and realism. Normally, he'd paint the horses first on a blank canvas, then fill in the background landscape around them and between their legs.

Gainsborough — *Giovanna Baccelli (c. 1782)*

Portraits were still the bread-and-butter for painters, and Thomas Gainsborough was one of the best. His were always natural and never stuffy — notice how this famous ballerina's toes twinkle playfully. Giovanna's pink-cheeked beauty is complemented by the painting's harmonious pastel colors — the blues and pinks of her dress are matched by blue sky and pink clouds. Even the "green" trees at right have hints of reddish-pink paint that blend with her uplifted skirt. In the midst of this sea of colorful and messy brushstrokes, Giovanna's face and bosom stand out with Ivory-soap freshness.

GAINSBOROUGH — Giovanna Baccelli.
Gainsborough's portraits were never stuffy.
This ballerina is ready to boogie.

Sir Joshua Reynolds — *Three Ladies Adorning a Term of Hymen,* (1773)

Sir Joshua Reynolds, the pillar of England's art establishment, stood for all that was noble, upright, tasteful, rational, brave, clean, reverent and boring. As the influential first president of England's Royal Academy, he championed the "Grand Style" using the classical techniques of the Renaissance. According to Reynolds, art was meant to elevate the viewer, appealing to his rational nature and filling him with noble sentiment.

So Reynolds "elevated" or idealized the things he painted. In this case, he takes a simple portrait of three sisters and raises it to mythic proportions — lovely Greek nymphs in a garden paradise. Reynolds' work is meant to be appreciated on an intellectual level, and this one is full of symbolism. The woman on the right has "passed" the statue of the god Hymen — that is, she's gotten married — while her sisters are still unwed. In 18th-century England, this was the proper way to talk about s-e-x.

Since much of the art we'll see from here on was painted in the looming shadow of Reynolds, and since his technique and morals are flawless, let's dedicate a minute's silence to this painting. Fifty-nine. Fifty-eight. All right, see you in the next room.

BLAKE AND ROMANTICISM (1800-1850)

Henry Fuseli — *Titania and Bottom (1780-90)*
Have you seen the London dailies that read like the "National Enquirer"? The British, underneath their oh-so-proper exteriors, dig steamy sex, crimes of passion, madness and the dark world of human emotions. This painting is the boiling underside of Reynolds' prim and controlled uppercrust world. It's a fantasy turning Shakespeare's "Midsummer Night's Dream" into an erotic "nightmare" of S&M and female dominance. Titania, the delectably wicked fairy mistress, playfully prepares to whip Bottom's bottom, who's been given an ass's head. To the right, a seductive woman leads a tiny wizard on a leash and looks out at us triumphantly. The canvas swirls with weird half-human creatures, trolls, fairies, hooded figures, a child with a butterfly head and, in the center, a puny, naked man.

These bizarre images don't mean much on a rational level, but they pack an emotional warhead. Where Reynolds' art was intellectual, this is emotional. Where Reynolds painted "elevation", Fuseli glories in degradation, exploring the demons of the unconscious world a century before Freud. We're entering the world of Romanticism.

William Blake
At the age of four, Blake saw the face of God. A few years later, he ran across a flock of angels swinging in a tree. Twenty years later, he was living in a rundown London flat with an illiterate wife, scratching out a thin existence as an engraver. But even in this squalor, ignored by all but a few fellow artists, he still had his heavenly visitors, and he described them in poems and paintings.

One of the original space cowboys of the Western world, Blake was also a unique painter often classed with the "Romantics", because he painted in a fit of ecstatic inspiration rather than by studied technique. He painted angels, archangels, thrones and dominions rather than the dull material world. While Britain was conquering the world with guns and Nature with machines, and while his fellow Londoners were growing rich, fat and self-important, Blake turned his gaze inward, painting the glorious visions of the soul.

Blake — *Nebuchadnezzar, Newton, and Elohim Creating Adam*

Did I warn you or did I warn you? These three "mixed-media" works (colorprints finished in pen and watercolor) glow with an unearthly aura. Blake lived in a time of extraordinary progress and material wealth, but he had little confidence in science and technology. These prints illustrate the limits of rational thought and the ultimate weakness of material man.

"Nebuchadnezzar", the pagan Old Testament king, is stripped of his worldly power. Blake shows him crawling, scared, a human ape, his decaying flesh practically dripping off him. This is gross Materialism on the run.

BLAKE — Elohim Creating Adam. Blake, who hob-nobbed with the heavenly hosts, painted God creating man.

Isaac Newton, of what-goes-up fame, was the very symbol of Enlightened humanity. But this "Newton" here, despite his Greek-god anatomy, is bent over (again, like an ape), scribbling meaningless childlike figures into the dirt. For Blake, the wisdom of the world was foolishness to God.

Blake was a Christian, but his ideas are almost Eastern. He saw the material world as bad, trapping the divine spark inside each of our bodies and keeping us from true communion with God.

"Elohim [a Hebrew name for God] Creating Adam" is a pessimistic view of the Creation. Adam is born with the worm of eventual decay already wrapped around him. He lies practically crucified on our material Earth. The Old Testament God who is perpetrating this Creation is rather befuddled, open-mouthed and stupid. Blake, a famous poet as well as painter, summed up his distrust of the material world in a poem addressed to "The God of this World", Satan:

"Though thou art worshipped by the names divine
Of Jesus and Jehovah, thou art still
The son of morn in weary night's decline,
The lost traveler's dream under the hill."

Blake — *The Head of the Ghost of a Flea*

One of Blake's visions was of a flea, who told him that fleas were inhabited by the souls of bloodthirsty men. Here's one of them, the soul of an investment banker. (Read the blurb in the display case.)

☞ *Glide around the room, taking your time and finding your own favorite Blake here in this, the world's best collection of his work. Not all are so pessimistic as the four we've seen.*

John Constable

Wow, that was intense. Constable is a nice break from Blake. While Blake thought that "Nature is the work of the devil," Constable thought She was just fine. He painted the English landscape just as it is, realistically, and without idealizing it.

Explore this room chronologically (clockwise). Notice how his style becomes more "Impressionistic" near the end — messier brushwork. Stop at "Cloud Study", and appreciate the effort involved in sketching ever-changing cloud patterns for hours on end. It paid off — cloudy skies are one of his trademarks. Constable's subtle genius wasn't fully recognized in his lifetime, and the neglect caused him to tell a friend, "Can it therefore be wondered at that I paint continual storms?"

Various "Romantic" landscapes

Constable plus Blake equals these emotion-charged supernatural landscapes. Artists in the "Romantic" style saw the drama and mystery in nature as a reflection of inner emotions. God is found within Nature, and Nature is charged with the grandeur and power of God.

John Martin's three fantastic Day-Glo landscapes of Heaven (I mean, is this England, 1850 or Haight-Ashbury, 1967?!) with enormous clouds and tiny bands of angels fully express both the rapture and the terror of Judgment Day.

In "The Deluge", we see God's wrath in the fury of Nature. The earth's wicked drown in the flood, clinging to the last, highest ground as the burning sun sets on a dying world. Away in the distance, the Ark sails serenely to safety.

"Gordale Scar, Yorkshire" is a real place in England, but here it has an unreal, almost supernatural grandeur to it, with the forbidding cliff and brewing storm. Romantic artists made the natural world reflect the most intense human emotions.

PRE-RAPHAELITES (1850-1880)

You won't find Pre-Raphaelites selling flowers at the airport, but this "Brotherhood" of young British artists had a cult-like intensity. Think way back to Sir Joshua Reynolds and his Grand Style. That kind of stuffy, pompous art dominated all through the time of Blake, Constable and the Romantics. The Pre-Raphaelites finally said enough's enough.

They wanted to return to a style "Pre-Raphael" — that is, before the time of the great Renaissance artist who idealized everything he painted. "Truth to Nature" was the Pre-Raphaelite slogan. Like the Impressionists who followed, they moved their canvases out of the stuffy studio and set up outdoors, painting trees, streams and people as they really were. Their art was intended to be "medieval" in its simple, realistic style, in the melancholy mood and sometimes in subject matter.

Be prepared to suffer, unless your heart is made of stone. Despite the Pre-Raphaelite claim to paint life just as it is, this is so-beautiful-it-hurts art.

Rossetti — *Ecce Ancilla Domini! The Annunciation (1849-50)*
The Angel announces to Mary that she'll be the mother of the Messiah. This is a common medieval theme, but Rossetti paints it with a realism and "human" touch you'd never see in a medieval altarpiece. Mary is not the majestic Mother of God but a frightened little girl backed into a corner by the angel, not exactly thrilled by the whole proposition.

To the right of this work are several medieval-looking maidens painted by Rossetti that are so unnaturally beautiful (especially the misty, haloed "Beata Beatrix" in ecstatic surrender) that they violate the original Pre-Raphaelite search for ultra-realism. Rossetti often became emotionally involved with his models and practically deified them in oils, showing us the haunting, spiritual beauty of women.

ROSSETTI — The Annunciation.
Resurrecting the mystique of the Middle Ages, Pre-Raphaelites like Rossetti painted simple visions of pure beauty.

Millais — *The Order of Release, 1746* (1852-53)

The attention to detail is extraordinary, especially the skin textures, and this photographic realism gives force to what would otherwise be an overly sentimental scene. In 1746, a Scottish revolt was brutally put down by the English. The wearing of tartans was banned, and rebels were jailed. Here we see the emotion-packed reunion of a political prisoner with his loyal wife (who shows the guard the order of release) and loyal dog.

Waterhouse — *The Lady of Shalott* (1888)

Many of the works in this room combine Pre-Raphaelite realism (and "medieval" subjects) with the sentimentality of the later Victorian age. This one, looking like a scene out of Tolkien's "Lord of the Rings", is from the legends of King Arthur. The lovely maiden (and I hate to keep using meaningless adjectives like "lovely" and "beautiful", but how else can you describe the Pre-Raphaelites?), once given a castle to live in as long as she never looked out of it, broke the rules to gaze on her beloved knight Lancelot as he rode by. She lost her castle and was condemned to float down the river to her death.

WATERHOUSE — The Lady of Shalott. Enjoy this quiet boat ride while you can — the rough rapids of modern art are just around the bend.

Burne-Jones — *King Cophetua and the Beggar Maid* (1884)

The king falls in love with a beggar maid. He sits at her feet and makes goo-goo eyes, forgetting about his wealth, power and responsibilities.

Stand for awhile and enjoy the exquisite realism and human emotions of works like this, showing real people painted realistically. Get your fill, because it's the last we'll see for a while. Even as the Victorian age was coming to a close, so were old art styles. The modern world was coming, and with it, new art styles to express modern attitudes.

BRITISH IMPRESSIONISTS (1870-1900)

Sargent — *Carnation, Lily, Lily, Rose (1885-86)*
The two great British Impressionists were Americans. . .with French training. The subject of this painting — a couple of children playing in a garden — isn't nearly as interesting as the melodramatic legend of "King Cophetua and the Beggar Maid", but the style of painting is more interesting. Sargent gives us a fascinating display of light and color — the greens, whites and violets of the garden at evening and, especially, the glowing orange lanterns. This play of light and the rough, smudgy painting of the flowers make the work "Impressionistic".

Whistler — *Nocturne in Blue-Green (1871)*
Before taking a break, let's get primed for the Modern collection.
James Whistler (an American, most famous for his "Whistler's Mother") was one of the first artists concerned more with HOW he painted than WHAT he painted. The subject was of little importance — this one is a simple view across the Thames to Chelsea at evening. What was more important was the harmony of the colors (the mix of blues and greens) and the beautiful patterns they made on the canvas. (Speaking of nice patterns, notice Whistler's "butterfly" signature at the bottom.) This concern for the "how" over the "what" is the basis of modern art.
Whistler's modern style shocked the Victorian world. They found it messy, simplistic and just too darned easy. With their strong work ethic, they expected an artist to earn his pay by slaving over meticulous details the way Millais did. But most of all, they didn't like Whistler because his paintings didn't have subjects — there were no pretty maidens, handsome kings or tales of woe. One famous critic summed it up by accusing Whistler of "throwing a pot of paint in the face of the public". Welcome to the modern world.
☞ *Tea time.*

J. M. W. TURNER (1775-1851)

☞ *The Turner Collection is in the Clore Gallery, the wing that juts out to the right of the Tate. The main entrance is back outside, but you can also enter through Room 18, to the right of the rotunda.*
Britain was slow to accept the radical new Impressionist style developed in France, but you could argue that an Englishman invented it. Turner's messy use of paint to portray reflected light Chunneled its way to France to inspire Monet and ilk.

J. M. W. Turner studied at the Royal Academy, learning to paint traditional subjects in traditional ways. But his true love was nature, and he was a born hobo. Oblivious to the wealth and fame that his early paintings gave him, he set out traveling — mostly on foot — throughout England and the Continent, sketching and painting as he went.

The Tate has the world's best collection of Turners. You can trace his progression from a realistic, subject-oriented painter (seascapes, Venice scenes, historical and classical subjects) to an "Impressionist" painter of color-and-light patterns.

☞ *Start in the large square room (107) marked "High Art and the Sublime." From these early paintings, the collection runs roughly chronological as you work your way through Rooms 106, 105, and so on, back towards the Tate.*

ROOM 107 — High Art and the Sublime

Trained in the Reynolds school of grandiose epics, Turner cranked out the obligatory big canvases with big themes. Here we see great moments in history and classical themes. But Turner's classical settings don't glorify Man but Nature.

Turner — Snow Storm: Hannibal and His Army Crossing the Alps

Grey clouds drip down from above, craggy rocks point up from below, leaving a glorious sunlit-cloud view down the valley. The storm is an omen of Hannibal's coming defeat. He's in over his head, trying to conquer not merely the Romans but the Alps.

The tiny humans are secondary to the vista, drawing our attention to the grandeur of Nature and the puniness of man. They seem as stunned as we are by this awe-inspiring vision. These Alps both humble us and exalt us at the same time.

Turner could be a Romantic in the vein of Blake and Fuseli. He found the "Sublime" not in the supernatural but in the overwhelming power of Nature.

ROOM 104 — "Italy"

In his travels, Turner learned, mastered, assimilated and fused a great variety of styles — a true pan-European vision.

Turner — Rome, from the Vatican...etc.

A view of St. Peter's square, with Rome stretching in the distance. The dreamy-eyed figure in the foreground is the great Renaissance painter

Raphael. But he's badly drawn, cartoon-like, almost an afterthought. The greatest of men and the cream of Man's creations, the arches, are nothing but a setting for the blue blue sky that dwarfs all.

ROOM 103 — *"Studies"*
Turner used oils like many painters use watercolors. First he'd lay down a background (a "wash") of large patches of color, then add a few dabs of paint to suggest a figure. The final product lacked photographic clarity but showed the power of Nature. He was perhaps the most prolific painter ever, with some 2,000 finished paintings and 20,000 sketches and watercolors.

Check out his "Self-Portrait, c. 1798", and read the blurb.

ROOM 105 — *"Venice"*
I know that palazzo there is tan. But what color is it at sunset? Or after filtering through the watery haze that hangs over Venice? Can I paint the glowing haze itself? Maybe if I combine two different colors, and smudge the paint on . . . Venice titillated Turner's lust for reflected light.

This room contains finished works and unfinished sketches. Uh, which is which?

ROOM 101 — *"Later Works"*
The older he got, the messier both he and his paintings became. In his personal life, he was a very wealthy man, but he died in a rundown dive where he'd set up house with a prostitute.

His last works — whether landscape, religious or classical scene — became a blur and swirl of colors in motion, lit by the sun or a lamp burning through the mist. They're "modern" in style, with the subject secondary to the colors and form. You'll have to read the title to "get" it.

Turner — *Snow Storm: Steam-boat Off a Harbour's Mouth . . .*
Circular swirls of paint depict a storm. Turner was attracted more to the forces of nature — storms, the energy from the sun, the wild pulse of water — than to any particular features. The sea and the sky blend together, churned by the same force.

In this work, Turner doesn't use solid blocks of colors. He builds a shimmering haze with light and dark dabs of paint placed side by side — Impressionism . . .

TURNER — Snow Storm: Steam-Boat off a Harbour's Mouth. Turner's work evolved from clear realism to messy Impressionist works like this.

THE MODERN COLLECTION

☞ *Find a seat and read. Preferably, read the following.*

People who refuse to like modern art must be the same people who hunch up and squint against the rain. First off, it won't kill you, and secondly, if you'd just relax you might find you enjoy it — at least in small doses. Fortunately, the Tate collection is a light summer shower of art, a little taste of everything, giving us a quick overview of the major trends of the past century.

As we saw with Whistler's "Nocturne", artists began placing more importance on HOW something was painted than WHAT was painted. Why? Largely because the camera was taking over the artist's traditional job of capturing reality. Now the artist was called on not just to paint "what" was there like a photograph but also to give his personal version of it. More and more, the artist's individual style became important. Most modern art is a combination of "what" (realistic subjects) and "how" (the style).

Here's a viewing hint: The canvas of a realistic, subject-oriented painting is like a window that you "look through" to see the real world. But lots of modern paintings are like wallpaper, a surface on which to arrange globs of paint in colorful, interesting patterns.

IMPRESSIONISM AND POST-IMPRESSIONISM (1870-1910)

The Impressionists — a loose group of French painters working in the 1870s — were interested in reflected light. They abandoned the studio, setting up their canvases outside to paint sunny landscapes. They captured the shimmering effect of reflected light with a new technique — using rough brushstrokes and bright paints that look messy when you're up close but that blend in the eye at a distance.

The Tate has the work of the Impressionists and their followers — Post-Impressionists, Primitivists and Fauvists. Since the National Gallery on Trafalgar Square has a better collection of Impressionist works, let's just get a quick taste here.

Monet — *Poplars on the Epte (1891)*

The Impressionists thought a quick and messy "impression" of a fleeting moment was more worthwhile and realistic than a detailed work done from memory. In particular, they were interested in the changing play of light off objects at different times of day. Claude Monet, the father of Impressionism, often painted a whole series on the same subject to catch the different angles of sunlight. This is one of 23 different looks at these poplars.

Degas — *Little Dancer Aged 14 (statue)*

Degas, most famous as a painter, combines classical realism with the Impressionist interest in light effects. Notice how the rough surface of the dancer's skin reflects the light, causing the work to shimmer ever-so-slightly in the viewer's eye.

Van Gogh — *Farms Near Auvers (1890)*

Here we see the Impressionist technique of laying down thick, broad brushstrokes side by side. The eye has trouble resolving them into "building" or "sky". Instead, the colors shimmer in your eye like bright sunlight. Van Gogh's broad, swirling brushstrokes and bright colors charge his canvases with an emotion missing in Monet's sunny landscapes.

Seurat — *Le Bec du Hoc, Grandcamp (1885)*

Seurat took Impressionism to its logical, scientific extreme with his technique called "pointillism". He placed dabs ("points") of different colors side by side which, at a distance, blend in the eye to form a new color. Here, green plus white plus yellow plus pink plus blue equals. . .a grassy rock on the water's edge.

Gauguin — *Faa Iheihe (1888)*

Paul Gauguin borrowed the Impressionists' bright colors, then struck out on his own path. He rejected the entire Western tradition of art since the Renaissance, which painted everything in realistic 3-D. He also rejected the Western life-style, quitting his job as a stockbroker and moving to Tahiti to live the simple life of a native.

These naked natives, their animals and exotic plants are painted in a purposely simple and primitive style, with strong black coloring-book outlines hemming in blocks of unnaturally bright colors. There is no traditional 3-D here; we know the people at left are farther away only because they're slightly smaller. Appreciate the painting not for its depth but for its decorative patterns of bright colors.

Cézanne — *The Gardener (1906)*

Cézanne brought Impressionism into the 20th century. He learned the Impressionist style, but he didn't like the 2-D flatness it gave to a painting. He tried to use Impressionist techniques to paint more 3-D objects. Remember how Seurat used separate dabs of different colored paint to "build" a grassy rock? Cézanne "builds" this gardener with somewhat larger slabs or cubes of paint, giving a kind of 3-D chunkiness to what would otherwise be a flat scene. This technique of breaking objects down into "cubes" of color influenced one of art's most radical styles — Cubism.

CÉZANNE—The Gardener. Compare to Picasso's *Seated Nude* (p. 88).

CUBISM

Picasso — *Seated Nude (1909-10)*
Imagine a three-dimensional statue made of glass. You shatter it, then try to reconstruct it by pasting the shards onto a (two-dimensional) canvas. That's essentially what Picasso has done with this woman. In the process he gives us several different views of her at once, as though we've walked around the statue — we're looking up at the left side of her body and down at her right. Keep in mind that, bizarre as this kind of art is, we can still recognize a subject, though the subject is becoming less important than the way it gets put on the canvas.

PICASSO — Seated
Nude.
Dabs to slabs to cubes.
Cezanne's "slabs" of
paint become "cubes,"
as art enters the 20th
century.

Glance at "Bottle and Fishes" by the other pioneer of Cubism, Georges Braque. Braque virtually does away with color altogether, building his objects with geometrical planes of brown.

ABSTRACT ART

Mondrian — *Composition with Red, Yellow and Blue*
Let's face it. A painting of, say, a beautiful woman — like something by the Pre-Raphaelites, for example — is NOT a beautiful woman. It's a two-dimensional piece of canvas covered with paint. Modern artists recognize this and actually glory in it. They realize that even if their patterns of paint don't represent a real object, it can still be an interesting, orderly and even pretty painting.

Mondrian takes this to the extreme. He's boiled art down to its basic building blocks: black lines, a white canvas and the three primary colors. In the past, artists arranged these building blocks into patterns that looked like trees, water or beautiful women. But Mondrian has created his own pattern with its own rules of composition and order.

Most modern art (like the Cubism we just saw) is a mix of Abstract and "representational" art — that is, paintings that represent real objects.

Matisse — *The Snail*

As he got older, Henri Matisse, the master of color, was confined to bed. He made paper cutouts and had assistants paste them on the canvas. This work gets its name from the snail-like pattern unwinding from the green piece in the center.

EXPRESSIONISM

I've neglected to say the obvious: we live in frightening times, full of war, crime, deceit and apathy. In that kind of climate, how can we expect artists to go on producing pretty pictures and fantasies that have nothing to do with the harsh realities of life? In fact, much of the bizarre and often ugly modern art we've seen is a reflection of the world we live in.

Expressionism uses violent colors, twisted forms and mask-like faces to "express" the disgust and burn-out that settled over Europe after the horrors of World War I.

Grosz — *Suicide (1916)*

Embittered by his war experience, Grosz gives us a world populated by cynical scum. A man shoots himself and dies in the gutter. A cheap prostitute looks on apathetically. Another corpse hangs from a lamp-post. Dogs and people hurry by, not wanting to get involved. The whole scene is washed in a lurid red.

War veterans talk about the fixed faces of corpses and also about the fixed, emotionless stares of men who have seen too much death. The mask-like features in Expressionist paintings tell the whole story of a civilization watching its Victorian moral foundations collapse.

SURREALISM

The Surrealists give us photographic realism…of unreal things. They place bizarre images side by side without explanation — forcing the viewer to make his own connections. Surrealism was influenced by the psychology of Freud which said that our unconscious (and often irrational) impulses have great influence over our actions. Surrealist art explores dream-scapes — images that may seem illogical on a conscious level, but have great meaning on an emotional level.

Delvaux — *Sleeping Venus (1944)*

There's a bizarre collection of images here: a sleeping nude Venus (a symbol of Sex), a skeleton (Death), a well-dressed woman (Propriety), classical buildings (Civilization), a crescent moon in the dark night sky (Nature). On a rational level, these images aren't connected, almost contradictory. But when we find them on the same canvas we have to ask ourselves how they all connect.

DFLVAUX — Sleeping Venus. Take one mixed bag of reality, jumble in a blender, and serve on a canvas. Surrealism.

(Hmm. Remember Fuseli's "Titania and Bottom"? I'm not making a connection. Just asking.)

Dali — *Lobster Telephone*

Salvador Dali was the most famous Surrealist, combining an extraordinarily realistic technique with an extraordinarily twisted mind. Dali's dream-scape has no "correct" interpretation — at least none that Dali is aware of. He's simply assembled a set of monkey bars for your mind to play on and explore.

Ernst — *Celebes*

This elephant-like creature seems to be made of spare machine parts, with a boiler body and heating-duct trunks. It's a bionic behemoth, suggesting that our uncontrolled ragtag use of technology is both ludicrous and frightening.

MODERN SCULPTURE

Statues are the best medium for exploring the age-old question, "What is Man?" They show the human form set apart — divorced from surroundings, culture, and usually clothes—standing alone.

Rodin — *The Kiss (1901-04)*

The subject of this work — "what" it's about — is what strikes us. It's a realistic portrayal of two people kissing, and the intermingling of their arms, torsos and lips tells us more about the relationship between lovers than a whole library of Harlequin romances.

RODIN — The Kiss.

Henry Moore — *Recumbent Figure*

How did we get from the realistic "Kiss" to this pile of rocks? First, notice that there is a partially recognizable subject here — a reclining female, with a "head", a "torso", etc. But it's the stones themselves (the "how") that are really interesting. We notice their texture and graininess, feel the weight, the space they take up, and how they intermingle — much like the interpenetrating arms and legs of "The Kiss". Moore has made a kind of mini-Stonehenge that only suggests a woman's body — a hint of "what" in a pile of "how".

POST-WAR ART — Splat! Pop! Whaam!

Jackson Pollock

Start at Pollock's "Untitled (Naked Man with Knife)". If you look closely you can vaguely make out a knife fight. But you realize that Pollock could have expressed the same violent feeling without any subject matter at all — with just the swirling and ugly blacks, reds and flesh tones alone.

In his later works, he does just that, doing away with any real subject matter and expressing emotion with form alone — hence the term "Abstract Expressionism". His radical technique of slopping and throwing paint right onto the canvas earned the American Pollock the appropriate nickname "Jack the Dripper".

Mark Rothko

These big, two-tone abstract canvases are far from violent. In fact, they have an air of serenity, inviting you to get lost in contemplating them. By reducing the canvas to one basic color, Rothko makes every slight gradation in color or form significant. Which rectangle is foreground, which is background? They shift, giving us a taste of "Op (-tical illusion) Art". As you contemplate Rothko, consider the fact that a maroon canvas is every color BUT maroon, the one color it reflects.

Rothko's rectangular fields of color, some lighter than others, are like floating doors to a new reality — according to his followers.

Giacometti — *Various sculptures*
The pessimism that followed World War II is expressed in these skinny stick-figures. They reduce man to a few essential features— like primitive Easter Island statues but without their strength. In the face of technology and great historical trends, man is ultimately frail and alone.

Francis Bacon
More modern anxiety. Distorted human-like forms, isolated and alienated, can do nothing but scream in frustration and anguish, making us long for the jolly old days of Expressionism.

Arman — *Venus of the Shaving Brushes* (1969)
Pop Art uses "pop"-ular objects from our mass-produced society to create art. It makes us question what we value: if we put shaving brushes in a museum, does that make them beautiful? If so, what does that say about "real" art? Are we more concerned about household items than about objects of timeless beauty? Is Arman's statue art — or just junk?

Lichtenstein — *Whaam!* (1963)
A comic book image is blown up to absurd Sir-Joshua-Reynolds proportions. The dots (the "how") are at odds with the heroic subject matter ("what"), showing the glorification of war as a mass-produced idea.

LICHTENSTEIN — "Whaam!"
Take a comic strip, blow it up, hang it on a wall and charge a million bucks — whaam, you got Pop Art.

Andy Warhol — *Marilyn Diptych* (1962)
Warhol creates a holy modern shrine out of a cheap publicity photo.
He repeats the image in the same way television and the mass media
repeat beautiful images to sell products until the image is cheapened.

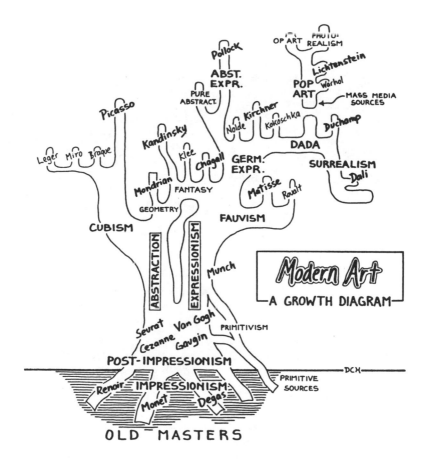

WHERE TO NOW?

Even these "modern" artists are yesterday's news by now. We're currently in what some folks call the "Post-Modern" period, a time of relative mellowness and tolerance of all styles, even traditional realism. If you get a chance, visit the Tate's temporary exhibition section (requires separate admission) to see the latest.

Enough Tate? Great. It's late.

The Louvre, Paris

Paris takes you from the beginning of art history to the present, in three world-class museums — the Louvre (Ancient world–1850), the Orsay (Impressionism, 1850-1914) and the Pompidou (20th century).

Start your art-yssey at the Louvre. The Louvre's collection — over 300,000 works of art — is a full inventory of Western civilization. To cover the entire collection in one visit is "in-Seine". We'll enjoy just three of the Louvre's specialties — Greek sculpture and French and Italian painting.

Musée du Louvre (pron: "Loove")

Hours: Daily 9:00-18:00; closed Tuesdays. Also open Wednesdays until 22:00 and Mondays (some collections) until 22:00. Last entrance 45 minutes before closing.

Apollo Gallery closed 12:30-14:00.

Cost: 31 F; under 18 — free; 18-25 and over 60 — 13 F; ticket good all day. Free on Sundays — and very crowded.

Tour length: Two hours.

Getting there: Métro to "Palais Royale/Musée du Louvre" (which is closer to the new entrance than the "Louvre" stop) leads you right into the new entrance.

Information: Busy but helpful English-speaking information booth in pyramid. Pick up free floor plan.

Best guidebook is the square Louvre book (45 F).

Ninety-minute English tours leave nearly hourly (23 F plus admission).
Since the collection is in flux, confirm location of all works on this tour at
information booth.
Tel. 40 20 53 17.
Misc.: Most services are clustered in the pyramid.
Two cafeterias in museum and plenty of cafés and snack bars on Rue de Rivoli.
Crowds worst Sunday, Monday, Wednesday, and mornings.
Starring: Leonardo, the French painters, "Vénus de Milo," "Winged Victory,"
Raphael, Titian.

Orientation — The Louvre on the Move

The Louvre is undergoing major renovation that will affect this itinerary. Be prepared for changes. As of July 1992, here's what we know:

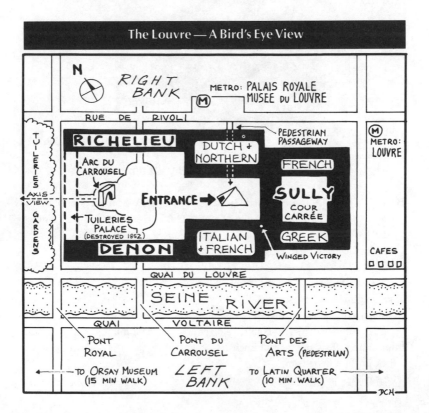

The "Grand Louvre" Project

The plan is to open all three wings of the giant U-shaped Louvre for exhibition, making the world's largest museum 80 percent larger. The north (Richelieu) wing will house Dutch and Northern art. The east (Sully) wing has the extensive French collection. Our main focus will be the southern (Denon) wing, with Italian Renaissance painting (like the "Mona Lisa") and access to ancient Greek sculpture.

I. M. PEI — New Louvre Pyramid Entrance. This glass pyramid is the latest addition to the 800-year-old building project called the Louvre. Parisians hated Pei's pyramid...almost as much as they hated Eiffel's Tower when it was new.

This itinerary will be as general as possible, with directions kept to a minimum so you can adapt if the collections are moved. If you can't find a particular work of art, just point to the photo or title in this book and ask a guard "Ou est?" (pron: "Oo-ay"). Excuse us if there are mistakes in the itinerary, but at least remember that this is the most current guidebook anywhere on the "new" Louvre. So there.

☞ *To get to the start of the tour, descend into the big glass pyramid and buy your ticket from a machine or a human. From here, you'll see signs to the three wings. Head for the Denon wing.*

Escalate up several floors, following the crowds and the signs to "Denon 3." You'll reach a staircase capped by the "Winged Victory" statue (see the photo on page 104). If you ever get lost, she'll be your beacon. We'll start downstairs, in the room on the ground floor directly beneath the "Winged Victory." Look for a pillaresque, headless statue in the middle of the room.

GREEK STATUES — 600 B.C.-1 A.D.

Every generation defines beauty differently. For the Greeks, beauty was balance. That is, when you take two opposites and combine them in the right proportions, you get something beautiful. Of course, every generation also has its own idea of what the right balance is. We'll see how the idea of beauty (as balance) evolved in ancient Greece — and then how it resurfaced in Renaissance painting 2000 years later.

EARLY GREECE

Hera of Samos (Core) — c. 570 B.C.
Auxerre Goddess (Femme debout, dite 'Dame d'Auxerre')
This statue of a woman is essentially a column with breasts. You can locate a few natural human features — the breasts, the arm across the chest, the folds of her dress, the toes poking out — but this rigid creature is better suited to propping up a building than wowing us with her feminine charms. The small "Auxerre Goddess," in the glass case behind you, is another example of this archaic stiffness.

Her grinning male counterpart ("Couros"), shown from the knees up, isn't much better. Statues like this are rigid by modern standards. The artist has sculpted a young naked athlete in an unrealistic pose — hands at his sides, facing directly to the front as if he's standing at attention, with sketchy musculature and a mask-like face.

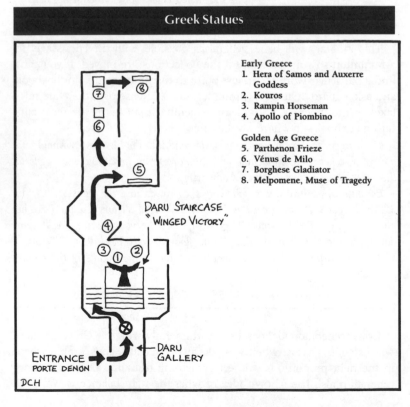

Greek Statues

Early Greece
1. Hera of Samos and Auxerre Goddess
2. Kouros
3. Rampin Horseman
4. Apollo of Piombino

Golden Age Greece
5. Parthenon Frieze
6. Vénus de Milo
7. Borghese Gladiator
8. Melpomene, Muse of Tragedy

DARU STAIRCASE
"WINGED VICTORY"

ENTRANCE
PORTE DENON

DARU
GALLERY

DCH

Hera of Samos — Typical of early Greek
art, this "column with toes" has stood at
attention for over 2500 years.

The early Greeks who admired such statues were like their legendary hero, Odysseus — wandering, war-weary and longing for the comforts of a secure home. In their art, they found stability more attractive than movement. In fact, it's the noble strength and sturdiness of these works that give them their beauty.

Note: To assess how much stability or movement there is in any particular statue, ask yourself, "If that statue came alive, and the music started playing...how would it dance?" These would look like plastic soldiers on a vibrating battlefield.

☞ *Enter the octagonal room just ahead on your left. On the way, glance at the Rampin Horseman ("Tete de Cavalier") in the glass case, whose smiling face and chin-strap beard are early attempts at human naturalism. The bits of original red paint remind us that many ancient statues were gaily painted.*

Apollo of Piombino (Apollon) — c. 475 B.C.

This small bronze god of the Sun is stepping out energetically. He's walking through the forest hunting. His hands extend out from his body, originally holding a bow and arrows. The muscles are more realistic than in the Kouros (especially in the knees and calves). This Apollo is beginning to tip the scale of balance from stability to movement.

He's more natural and relaxed than the Kouros, but he's still facing the front. Look from a three-quarters angle — he looks weird. This statue is a "cube" made of a front pose and two profiles. Seen from front, back, (check out his funky pony-tail) or the two sides, it looks pretty good, but not from three-quarters. The next step is a statue "in the round," or full 3-D.

☞ *Turn 90 degrees left from Apollo — let's call it 104 degrees for you engineers — and exit the octagonal room into the Sully Wing.*

GOLDEN AGE GREECE

In a sense, we're all Greek. Democracy, mathematics, theater, literature and science were practically invented in ancient Greece. Even the basic idea that the world is rationally ordered comes from the Greeks. Most importantly for us, the art that we'll see throughout the Louvre either came from Greece or was inspired by it.

The great Greek cultural explosion that changed the course of history happened in a fifty year stretch (around 450 B.C.) in a Greek town smaller than Muncie, Indiana. Athens, using "protection money" extracted from its weaker neighbors, set about rebuilding Athens and rewriting history — this is the Greek "Golden Age."

Parthenon Frieze (Fragment de la Frise des Panathenees) — c. 440 B.C.

The stone fragments on the wall, here, decorated the exterior of the greatest Athenian temple, the Parthenon. The reliefs show the sacred procession where the citizens marched up the hill every four years with offerings to their goddess. Here, young girls present an embroidered veil to decorate the 40-foot statue of Athena, the city's patron goddess.

The maidens, carved in less than an inch of stone, are amazingly realistic and three-dimensional — more so than any free-standing Kouros statue. Notice the realistic features — even veins — in the arm of the central figure.

Greeks of the "Golden Age" valued the "Golden Mean," that is, "balance." The ideal person was well-rounded — a balance of body and mind, an athlete and a bookworm, a bronze god and a philosopher, a realtor who plays the piano, a warrior and a poet. Their art was balanced, too. Specifically, the balance between stability and movement was what made beauty.

☞ *Exit back into the corridor. You'll see the Goddess of Love floating above a sea of worshiping tourists.*

Vénus de Milo (Aphrodite) — c. 100 B.C.

This is the epitome of Greek balance. The "Vénus de Milo" (or Goddess of Love from the Greek island of Milos) created a sensation when it was discovered in 1820. Europe was already in the grip of a classical fad, and this statue seemed to sum up all that ancient Greece stood for. (By the way, this is a rare Greek original, unlike most statues which are later Roman copies. And this "epitome of the Golden Age" was actually sculpted three centuries later, though in the style of the earlier age.)

The "Vénus de Milo" is a harmonious balance of opposites. Venus is stable, resting her weight on one leg (called *contrapposto*, or "counterpose"), yet her other leg is slightly raised as though she's about to take a step. This slight movement sets her whole body in motion...though she remains perfectly still.

Split Venus right down the middle, and see how the movement of the two halves balance each other. As she lifts her left leg, her right shoulder droops down. The other leg and shoulder counterbalance each other in the same way. And as her knee points one way, her head turns the other. The twisting pose gives an S-curve to her body (especially noticeable from the back view) that the Greeks and succeeding generations found beautiful.

Venus de Milo — For centuries, this Venus defined feminine beauty. Her pose is a combination of stability and movement. It's been said that among the warlike Greeks, Venus was the first statue to unilaterally disarm.

There are other opposites that balance as well, like the rough-cut texture of her dress that contrasts with the smooth skin of her soft and cuddly upper half. (She's actually made from two different pieces of stone plugged together at the waist.) The greatest balance, however, is between realism and ideal beauty. The face is realistic in that it looks like a woman, but it's also idealized, a goddess, too generic and too perfect to be a real person. This isn't any particular woman but Everywoman — all the idealized features that the Greeks found beautiful in women.

What were her missing arms doing? You can see several archaeologists' theories on the plaque nearby. Some say her right arm held her dress while her left arm was raised. Some say she was hugging a man statue. Some say she was leaning on a column. I say she was picking her navel.

☞ *This statue is interesting and different from every angle. Remember the view from the back — we'll see it again later. Orbit Venus. Then make your re-entry to Earth at the statue behind her.*

Borghese Gladiator (*Guerrier Combattant, dit Gladiateur Borghese*)

Don't breathe too hard, or you'll tip this guy over. We see a fighting gladiator at the peak of action. He blocks a blow with the shield that used to be on his left arm while his right hand, weighted with an early version of brass knuckles, prepares to deliver the counterpunch. His striding motion makes a diagonal line from his left foot up his leg, along the body and out the extended arm. It's a dramatic, precariously balanced pose.

This is the motion and emotion of Greece's Hellenistic Age, the time after the culture of Athens was spread around the Mediterranean by the conqueror Alexander the Great (c. 325 B.C.). We've gone from stiff and stable early Greek statues (Core) to Golden Age balance (Venus). Now Hellenistic art tips the balance from stability to movement.

The gladiator also tips the balance from placid beauty to brutal — almost ugly — realism. His rippling, knotted musculature is a far cry from "Apollo Piombino's" smooth idealized physique. Golden Age Greeks would have found this statue's off-balance pose strained, like an unfinished melody that leaves you hanging. Yet, just this sort of cliff-hanging balance is what Hellenistic Greeks found beautiful.

One final feature of Hellenistic art: artists had long been anonymous craftsmen. This work, however, is signed proudly on the tree-trunk: "Agasias of Ephesus, son of Dositheos, did this."

☞ *Return to the "Winged Victory", pausing along the way in the Roman rooms, with more statues, head-and-shoulder busts and a wonderful floor mosaic.*

The Romans were great conquerors but bad artists, who put ketchup on their escargots. So they simply copied Greek art and wrote it in capital letters — like the huge statue of Melpomene, holding the frowning mask of tragic plays.

The Romans did, however, make realistic portrait busts of their emperors, who were worshiped as gods on earth. Find Augustus and his wily wife, Livia.

Winged Victory of Samothrace (Victoire de Samothrace)

This woman with wings, poised on the prow of a ship, once stood on a hilltop to commemorate victory in a great naval battle. Her clothes are wind-blown and sea-sprayed, clinging to her body like the winner of a Wet T-shirt contest. (Notice the detail in the folds of her dress around the navel, curving down to her hips.) Originally, her right arm was stretched high celebrating the victory much like a Super Bowl champion waves his "we're-number-one" finger.

Winged Victory — Someone turned a wind machine on the Vénus de Milo. The balance between movement and stability has tipped — Hellenism.

This is the "Vénus de Milo" gone Hellenistic — a balance of opposites that produces excitement, not stability. As Victory strides forward, the wind blows her and her wings back. Her feet are firmly on the ground, but her wings (and missing arms) stretch upward. She is a pillar of vertical strength while the clothes curve and whip around her. These opposing forces create a feeling of great energy making her the lightest two-ton piece of rock in captivity.

In the glass case nearby is Victory's open right hand, discovered in 1950, a century after the statue itself was unearthed. Also in the case is Victory's finger. An archeologist saw parts of this finger in a museum in Vienna and realized who the rightful owner was. Then the French negotiated with the Turkish government, "owners" of the rest of the finger, for rights to it. Considering all the other ancient treasures French had looted from Turkey in the past, the Turks thought it only appropriate to give France the finger.

☞ *Enter the octagonal room to the left of the "Winged Victory", and bench yourself under a window.*

FRENCH HISTORY

The Louvre as a Palace

Notice the plaque under the glorious ceiling. It explains that France's Revolutionary National Assembly (the same people who brought you the guillotine) founded this museum. What could be more logical? You behead the king, inherit a great palace and the greatest collection of art in Europe. So what to do with them? Hang the art in the palace, open it to the masses and *voila!* — you've got Europe's first public museum, opened in 1793. Major supporters of the museum are listed on the walls — notice all the Rothschilds.

Look out the window. The Louvre, a former palace, was built in stages over several centuries. On your right (the Sully Wing) was the original medieval fortress, whose foundations you can visit. Next, another palace, the "Tuileries", was built 500 yards to the west — in the open area past the pyramid, past the triumphal arch. Succeeding kings tried to connect these two palaces, each one putting his mark on history by adding another section onto the skinny North and South wings. Finally, in 1852, after three centuries of building, the two palaces were connected, creating a rectangular Louvre. No sooner was it complete. . . than the Tuileries palace was burned down by rioting Parisians, leaving the U-shaped Louvre we see today.

The glass pyramid was designed by the American architect I. M. Pei (pron: pay). Many Parisians hate the pyramid. They hate it almost as much as they used to hate another new and controversial structure 100 years ago — the Eiffel Tower.

☞ *Enter the Apollo Gallery straight ahead between the two pillars.*

The Apollo Gallery (Galerie d'Apollon)

This gallery gives us a feel for the Louvre-as-glorious-palace, the original home of the French kings before Versailles was built, drenched in stucco, gold leaf, tapestries of leading Frenchmen, and paintings with mythological and symbolic themes.

In the glass case at the far end, you'll find the crown jewels, including the 137-carat Regent Diamond and the 107-carat Cote de Bretagne Ruby. Two cases away is the crown (the one with the cameos) of that great champion of democracy, Napoleon — we'll see this crown again later. Along the wall is the eagle-shaped Suger Vase made from porphyry and silver. Also find the crystal chess set where young princes learned their place in the feudal hierarchy, the inlaid tables made from marble and semi-precious stones, and many other art objects showing the wealth of France, Europe's #1 power for two centuries.

☞ *Most of the French painting collection is in the Sully wing, one floor up. It's a bit of a detour but worth it. (Art wimps have permission to skip ahead to the Italian biggies. They're just around the corner from the "Winged Victory" in the long Grand Gallery — page 113.)*

To get to the Early French art in the Sully wing, exit the Apollo Gallery and turn right (east). Then take your first left, past ancient Greek vases. You'll pass through a large hall with four white columns at each end. Exit and climb the stairs to the next floor. You're looking for "peintures françaises".

FRENCH PAINTING

The Greek ideal of beauty returned. After Europe's Dark Ages it was "reborn" in the 15th century in the Renaissance, the cultural revival of ancient art. The Renaissance began and developed in Italy but soon spread to France. French painters picked up the traditions of ancient Greece, then added a few twists of their own.

EARLY FRENCH PAINTING (1300-1650)

Before the Renaissance rediscovered the three-dimensional realism and beauty of Greek sculpture, medieval artists painted almost exclusively

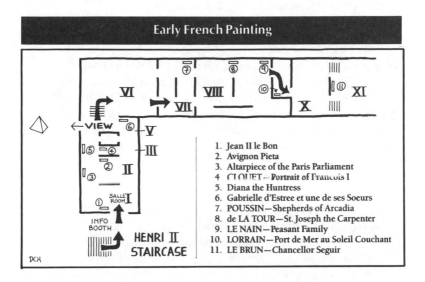

Early French Painting

1. Jean II le Bon
2. Avignon Pieta
3. Altarpiece of the Paris Parliament
4. CLOUET – Portrait of François I
5. Diana the Huntress
6. Gabrielle d'Estree et une de ses Soeurs
7. POUSSIN – Shepherds of Arcadia
8. de LA TOUR – St. Joseph the Carpenter
9. LE NAIN – Peasant Family
10. LORRAIN – Port de Mer au Soleil Couchant
11. LE BRUN – Chancellor Seguir

religious scenes. Medieval art was intended to teach church doctrine or invoke pious feelings, not necessarily to be realistic or even beautiful.

☞ *Enter "Salle 1."*

Jean II le Bon

In an age when religious paintings were the norm, this was a breakthrough — the first easel portrait of a French king ever.

☞ *Enter "Salle 2."*

Avignon Pietà (Quarton-Pietà de Villeneuve-les-Avignon)

This simple, poignant scene of Mary grieving over her crucified son is not realistic or exactly "beautiful" — but you can't deny its emotional power. In fact, it's the unrealistic distortion of Christ's body that makes it so forceful. His corpse, suffering rigor mortis, has snapped in two like

Avignon Pietà — Medieval works were religious, designed to teach or inspire the masses. In this scene, Christ's unrealistically broken body accentuates the agony.

a broken stick. The other figures melt in a sad arc around this rigid symbol of death.

Altarpiece of the Paris Parliament (*Retable du Parlement de Paris*)

There's St. Denis on the right with his head in his hands. Someone get him a Band-Aid. The fortress you see (upper left) across the Seine with the blue roofs is the Louvre in the 1400s. This is the fortress whose foundations you see in the "Louvre Medieval" downstairs.

☞   *In "Salle 3" you'll find...*

Clouet — Portrait of Francois I

Thank this man for the Louvre's collection. He was the one who first bought great Italian art, who encouraged French painters, and who invited Leonardo da Vinci to visit France. He also fostered the Renaissance spirit of humanism. Artists began painting people, not just religious subjects, like the nearby "Diana the Huntress" (Diane Chasseresse with her bow and dog), a portrait of a king's mistress as the Greek goddess Diana. Not only is the subject Greek-influenced but so is the idealized beauty. Renaissance artists gloried in the natural beauty of the human body as an expression of the divine.

☞   *Enter "Salle 5."*

CLOUET — Portrait of Francois I.
This great Renaissance king brought
Leonardo to France . . . and the Louvre's
collection to you. Merci.

École de Fontainebleu — Gabrielle d'Estrée et une de ses Soeurs

Two sisters taking a bath together, the one twisting the other's nipple. This may be idealized beauty to some, but to others it's just plain smut. Some interpret this painting as an indictment of the loose morals of the French Renaissance court. In contrast to the two sisters in the foreground is a more domestic scene in the back — the way things should be — a woman fully clothed and industriously sewing before a fire.

Others say it's about an engaged woman (with ring) concerned about her fertility, who is being reassured by a friend.

☞ *Enter "Salle 7."*

Nicolas Poussin — Shepherds of Arcadia (Les Bergers d'Arcadie)

The shepherds here are idealized humans, like Greek gods. They live in the Greek Paradise where everything is perfect. The colors are bright and the atmosphere serene. However, they've stumbled upon a tomb and the inscription worries them — there is Death even in Arcadia.

☞ *Enter "Salle 8."*

Georges de la Tour — St. Joseph the Carpenter (Saint Joseph Charpentier)

In this human look at a religious scene, the boy Jesus has joined his father in the carpentry shop and holds a candle for him while he works. Realism has been conquered here — notice the translucent glow of the candle through Jesus' hand.

Louis le Nain — Peasant Family (Famille de Paysans)

While lords and the ladies feasted and played in the rich French court, the common people continued to live the hard life. Most artists painted glorified visions of Greek gods, but this dark, drab-colored "snapshot" shows the other side — the people whom Marie-Antoinette told to eat cake. The peasants look up from their activities, staring at us like we're the rich kid who's just stumbled onto their turf.

☞ *Enter "Salle 9."*

LE NAIN — Peasant Family.
When the queen said to France's grumbling poor, "Let them eat cake," this was the look she got.

LATER FRENCH PAINTING (1600-1850)

The French loved to paint beautiful things, nudes, scenes from Greek mythology and historical events. Religious scenes are rare. I defy you to find even one crucifixion. This is colorful art designed to tickle the fancies of Louis XIV and his pleasure-seeking court at Versailles. As we move to the later Louis', it gets even frillier and prettier, as Renaissance turns to baroque and rococo.

Alongside these idealized paintings, you'll see grittier, more realistic ones. France had two worlds existing side by side — the dream world of Versailles and the hard life of the working poor

☞   *The later French painting (17th-19th centuries) unfolds chronologically as you continue on through the Sully wing.*

Claude de Lorrain (1600-1682) — *Port de Mer au Soleil Couchant*

In a typical Claude painting, the sun sets slowly on a harbor bordered by classical buildings. A boulevard of water stretches away from us, melting into an infinite sky. The tiny humans are dwarfed by both the majestic buildings and the sea and sky. A soft, proto-Impressionist haze warms the whole scene, showing the harmony of man and nature. Claude's painted fantasies became real in the landscaped gardens and canals at Versailles.

Charles le Brun — *Chancellor Seguir (Le Chacelier Seguir)*

This portrait is a frilly contrast to Le Nain's peasant family. Here a court official rides under a parasol, accompanied by wimpy attendants with ribbons on their shoes. French aristocrats were the first in Europe to develop a refined taste in clothes, manners and art. Soon feudal lords in other countries followed the French lead, leaving their farms, scraping the cow pies off their shoes and learning "cultchah".

Rigaud — *Portrait of Louis XIV, 1701*

Louis called himself the Sun King, whose radiance warmed all of France. In his youth, he was strong, handsome, witty, charming, and a pretty good hoofer — note the legs. He made France a world power and the hub of culture by centralizing the government around himself as a cult figure. Anything he did — eating, dressing, even making love — was like a ritual of state.

Here, he goes through one of those rituals, reenacting his coronation. Rigaud shows all the trappings of power: the huge fleur-de-lis robe, the canopied throne, the crown and scepter. But he also gives us a peek-a-boo glimpse of the human Louis underneath the royal robe. Louis is a bit older now, a bit weary. He poses for the obligatory photo-op. But the face that peers out from the frilly wig and pompous surroundings doesn't put on any airs. It's an honest face that seems to say, "Hey, it's my job."

Jean Antoine Watteau (1684-1721) — *Embarkation for Cythera (Pelerinage a l'Ile de Cythere)*

Louis and his successors kept the nobility from meddling in government affairs by entertaining them at the playground of Versailles. Here we see lords and ladies frolicking in a mythical landcape with anti-gravity babies. This painting was the first of many showing these jolly outings (*fêtes galantes*) where well-manicured aristocrats enjoy the delights of well-manicured Nature.

Watteau's warm, almost phosphorescent colors also set a new artistic tone. Gone is the majestic baroque grandeur of Louis XIV. Now French paintings become smaller, lighter, frillier, more intimate, more sensual.

Watteau — *Gilles*

A clown, dressed in an oversized suit that makes him look ridiculous, must perform for the amusement of the rich. The crowd is jaded and indifferent. The look on his face says, "Why am I here?" This may be a portrait of Watteau himself. . .

Francois Boucher (1703-1770) — *The Forge of Vulcan (Les Forges de Vulcain)*

In the world at Versailles, Woman (like Venus in the painting) was to rule over and civilize brutish Man (Vulcan), teaching him the indoor arts. Men wore wigs, make-up and panty-hose, while women dictated government policy. Society was changing fast, servants were challenging masters, and role-playing games were a part of the gay life.

Boucher chronicled the cult of the female body. Here, the man and woman complement each other, forming part of a stable pyramid. But there's more frills than form. Boucher's pastel pinks and blues must have been popular at Versailles baby showers.

Honore Fragonard (1732-1806) — *Women Bathing*

Guess who was teacher's pet in Boucher's class?

Fragonard takes us to the pinnacle of French rococo. Compare these puffy pastel goddesses with the clean lines of the "Venus de Milo," and you'll see how far we've come from the Greek ideal of beauty. This is sweet, cream-filled art that can only be taken, like French pastry, in small doses.

Hubert Robert — various scenes of Roman ruins in France
These overgrown Roman ruins served as inspiration for Robert when he landscaped the gardens at Versailles with designer "ruins".
The French were fascinated with earlier civilizations that had risen, dominated and declined. They were becoming aware of their own cultural mortality.

19th CENTURY - NEO-CLASSICAL AND ROMANTIC

J.L. David (1748-1825) — *various portraits of citizens (including Citizen Bonaparte)*
When the Revolution exploded, rococo became politically incorrect. The bourgeois middle class wielded power, simple dress became the fashion and painters returned to clean and sober realism.

J.A.D. Ingres (1780-1867) — *La Baioneuse (and other nudes)*
Remember the Venus de Milo, rear view? This Neo-classical nude once again preserves that backside for posterior — er, posterity.

Eugene Delacroix (1798-1863) — *Portrait of Chopin and Delacroix's Self-Portrait (Portrait de l'Artiste)*
We see the great pianist with half his face in shadow. Romantics explored the hidden world of human emotion. Chopin expressed the turmoil of his soul in flurries of notes, while Delacroix used messy patches of color.
☞ *(We'll see more 19th-century French art later. But first. . .)*
To get to the Grand Gallery and the Italian paintings from the Sully wing, backtrack downstairs to the "Winged Victory". Cross to the other side of the "Winged Victory", into Denon 4. After several rooms you'll reach the head of a long (and I mean long) hall — the Grand Gallery.
The Italian paintings are here in the Grand Gallery and in adjoining rooms, like the Salon Carre (at the head of the Gallery, in Denon 4) and the Salon des Etats (about 50 yards down the Gallery, in Denon 5).

The Grand Gallery
Built in the late 1500s to connect the old palace with the Tuileries, the Grand Gallery is a quarter-mile long, the longest hallway in the world. I hold the world's record for the Grand Gallery Heel-Toe-Fun-Run — from end to end in two minutes 56 seconds, two injured. A somewhat slower pace is advised.

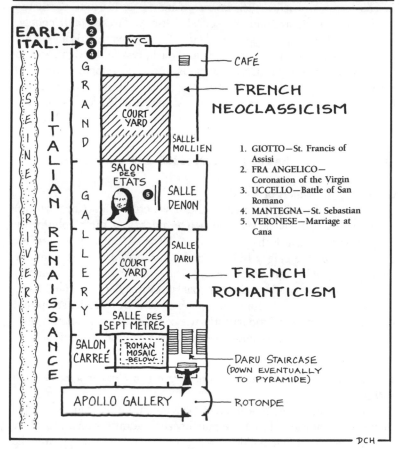

Grand Gallery — French and Early Italian Painting

EARLY ITAL. →

WC

CAFÉ

— FRENCH NEOCLASSICISM

SALLE MOLLIEN

SALON DES ETATS

SALLE DENON

SALLE DARU

— FRENCH ROMANTICISM

SALLE DES SEPT METRES

SALON CARRÉE

ROMAN MOSAIC -BELOW-

—DARU STAIRCASE (DOWN EVENTUALLY TO PYRAMIDE)

APOLLO GALLERY

— ROTONDE

— DCH —

1. GIOTTO—St. Francis of Assisi
2. FRA ANGELICO—Coronation of the Virgin
3. UCCELLO—Battle of San Romano
4. MANTEGNA—St. Sebastian
5. VERONESE—Marriage at Cana

ITALIAN PAINTING

Finally, Mona Lisa! Well, not quite. Mona stands near the peak of Italian Renaissance art, and we'll build up to that.

The revival of Greek culture began in Italy. The key to Renaissance painting was realism, and for the Italians "realism" was spelled "3-D." Painters were inspired by the realism of Greek sculpture (in Roman copies). Even when painting religious subjects, they aimed at the balanced beauty of pagan Greek art.

☞ *Start with the Early Italian works, about 150 yards down the Grand Gallery (Denon 7). Then work back to Mona and the biggies.*

Stroll down the Gallery Grandly. It's a majestic setting for this art, the cream of Western civilization. Along the way, notice some of these general features of Italian Renaissance painting: 1) Religious — there's enough Madonnas-and-children to fill heaven's daycare (and enough martyrs and saints to babysit them...). 2) Symmetrical — the Madonnas are flanked by saints, two to the left, two to the right, and so on. 3) Realistic — it's especially obvious in the occasional portrait. 4) 3-Dimensional — every scene gets a spacious setting with a distant horizon. 5) Classical — even Christian saints pose like Greek statues.

EARLY ITALIAN (1300-1500)

Giotto — *St. Francis of Assisi*

St. Francis receiving the marks of Christ's crucifixion (the *stigmata*) in his hands and feet may not look like much, but the revolutionary thing about this scene is that it is a "scene". There's a foreground (Francis), a background (the craggy hillside in the distance) and even a middle ground (the hut halfway down the hill). These simple and crude elements create the illusion of a three-dimensional landscape. Giotto (pron: ZHOT-to) has created a stage setting and peopled it with realistic, sculptural figures. This was a revolutionary advance compared with the flat, two-dimensional, unrealistic, symbolic work of his medieval contemporaries.

Fra Angelico — *Coronation of the Virgin (Le Couronnement de la Vierge)*

A century later, the "Angelic monk" expanded on this same technique to create the illusion of 3-D. He puts kneeling admirers on a tiled floor in the foreground and builds a background with the canopy over the throne. Between these borders he places figures balanced in nearly exact symmetry left and right.

Uccello — *Battle of San Romano (Bataille)*

Renaissance artists used mathematical calculations to master the illusion of 3-D. One of the most scientific was Paolo Uccello, who uses this battle scene as an excuse for painting horses, lances and soldiers from every possible angle.

Mantegna — *St. Sebastian*
No, this isn't the patron saint of porcupines. He's a Christian martyr, though he looks more like a classical Greek statue. Notice the *contrapposto* stance (weight on one leg) and the Greek ruins scattered around. His executioners look up like ignorant medieval brutes bewildered by this enlightened Renaissance man.

Italian artists learned how to create realism on the canvas. We'll now see how they used their knowledge to create beauty.

ITALIAN HIGH RENAISSANCE (1500-1600)

Renaissance art is realistic, balanced and deliberately beautiful. It takes its cue from balanced Greek sculptures like the "Venus de Milo". The two masters of Renaissance grace and balance were Raphael and Leonardo da Vinci.

Leonardo was the quintessential/consummate/archetypical (choose one) Renaissance man. Musician, sculptor, engineer, scientist and sometimes painter, he combined knowledge from all areas to create beauty. If he were alive today he'd create a Unified-Field theory in physics...and set it to music.

Leonardo was already an old man when Francois I invited him to France. He loaded up a horse with several paintings and started the long journey. One of those works was a portrait of a Lisa del Giocondo, the wife of a wealthy Florentine merchant. When he arrived, Francois immediately fell in love with the painting, making it the centerpiece of the small collection of Italian masterpieces that would, in three centuries, become the Louvre Museum. He called it "La Gioconda". We know it as a contraction of the Italian for "My lady Lisa" — Mona Lisa.

Advance Warning: You will be disappointed by Mona. There's so much hype surrounding her that there's no way she can live up to it. She's smaller than you'd expect, darker, engulfed in a huge room and hidden behind a glaring pane of glass. See her, be disillusioned and say, "So why all the hubbub, bub?"

Then look at her again. Like any lover you've got to take her for what she is, not what you'd like her to be. This is a subtle work, not a blockbuster, and there's absolutely no reason why she should be as famous as she is. Yet it's the subtlety itself that makes it a fine work of art.

☞ *Follow the crowds and the signs to "La Joconde: Mona Lisa." Fight the crowds until you can get close enough to fight the glare from the protective glass. When things get too intense, step back and watch Monamaniacs pacing back and forth watching Mona's eyes watch them.*

Leonardo Da Vinci — *Mona Lisa*

The famous smile attracts you first. Leonardo used a hazy technique called *sfumato*, where he blurred edges of whatever he painted. This is what makes Lisa's smile so mysterious — try as you might you can never quite see the corners of her mouth. Is her smile then a happy one? Sad? Tender? Or is it a softly cynical smirk? Every viewer reads it differently, projecting his own mood onto Lisa's enigmatic face. Mona is a Rorschach ink-blot...so how are you feeling?

LEONARDO DA VINCI — Mona Lisa.
Is she happy, sad . . . or smirking at the incredible fuss she's caused?

After your instant psychoanalysis, look past the smile and the eyes that really do follow you (most portraits do) to some of the subtle Renaissance elements that make this work. The body is surprisingly massive and statue-like, a perfectly balanced pyramid turned at three-quarters angle so that we can see its mass. Her arm is resting lightly on the chair's armrest almost on the level of the frame itself, making us feel as if she's sitting in a window looking out at us. The folds of her sleeves and her gently folded hands are remarkably realistic and relaxed. The typical Leonardo landscape shows distance by getting hazier and hazier.

The overall mood is one of balance and serenity, but there's also an element of mystery. Her smile and long-distance beauty are subtle and elusive, tempting — but always just out of reach like strands of a street-singer's melody drifting through the Metro tunnel. Mona doesn't knock your socks off, but she'll wink at the patient viewer.

Leonardo Da Vinci — *Virgin, Child and St. Anne (La Vierge, L'Enfant Jesus et Sainte Anne)*

Three generations — grandmother, mother and child — are arranged in a typical pyramid form (with Anne's face as the peak of the pyramid and the lamb as the lower right corner). Within this balanced structure, Leonardo gives us figures in motion. Anne's legs are pointed to our left. (Is Anne Mona? Hmm.) Her daughter Mary, sitting on her lap, reaches to the right. Jesus looks playfully to the left at her while turning away, as the lamb pulls away from him. But even with all the twisting and turning, this is still a placid scene, a perfect example of that old Greek balance of stability and movement

There's a psychological kidney-punch in this happy painting. Jesus, the picture of childish joy, is innocently playing with a lamb — the symbol of his inevitable, gruesome death.

The Louvre has the greatest collection of Leonardos in the world — all five of them. Don't miss the neighboring "Madonna of the Rocks" and "John the Baptist".

Raphael — *La Belle Jardinière*

Raphael (pron: roff-eye-ELL) perfected the style that Leonardo pioneered. This Madonna, Child and John the Baptist (holding the cross)

RAPHAEL — La Belle Jardinière. The master of grace learned a thing or two from Leonardo. Compare the pyramid composition (Mary, baby Jesus and little Johnny the Baptist) with Leonardo's Virgin, Child and St. Anne.

is also a balanced pyramid with hazy grace and beauty. Mary is a mountain of maternal tenderness (the title is known in English as "The Beautiful Kindergarten Teacher") eyeing her son with a knowing look. Jesus looks up innocently, standing *contrapposto* like a chubby Greek statue.

This painting is so beautiful that I have nothing to say about it. With Raphael, the Greek ideal of beauty reborn in the Renaissance reached its peak. His work spawned so many imitators who cranked out sickly-sweet generic Madonnas that we often take him for granted. Don't. This is the real thing.

☞ *Veronese's "Marriage at Cana" is in the Salon des Etats, the room just off the Grand Gallery, in Denon 5.*

Veronese — Marriage at Cana
Stand ten steps away from this enormous canvas to where it just fills your field of vision, and suddenly...there's a party going on around you! Step on in and pull up a glass of wine. This is the Renaissance love of beautiful things gone hog-wild. Venetian artists like Veronese painted the good life of rich, happy-go-lucky Venetian merchants.

In a spacious Renaissance architecture setting we see colorful lords and ladies decked out in their fanciest duds, feasting on a great spread of food and drink while the musicians fuel the fires of good fun. Servants prepare and serve the food, jesters play and animals wander around. Check out the guy way in the upper left poking his head out the balcony.

Believe it or not, this is a religious work showing the wedding celebration where Jesus turned water into wine. And there's Jesus, in the dead center of 130 frolicking figures, wondering if maybe wine coolers might not have been a better choice. With true Renaissance optimism, Venetians pictured Christ as a party-animal, someone who loved the created world as much as they did.

By the way, Veronese painted himself in the scene as one of the musicians, the balding guy in white with the beard bowing the viola on his lap. And on the double bass in red is the greatest Venetian painter, Titian (pron: TEESH-un). These great artists set the artistic tone for Venetians at play.

Titian — Pastoral Symphony (Le Concert Champêtre)
Venus enters the Renaissance in this colorful work by Titian (or possibly by Titian's teacher, Giorgione). The nymph turning toward the well at left is like a "Titian Reconstruction" of the "Vénus de Milo", but what a difference! Milo was cold and virginal but these babes are hot, voluptuous and sensual. The scene has balanced classical beauty (notice how the three seated figures are in a pyramid shape), but it appeals more to the senses than to the mind. The golden glow of the skin, the ample flesh and hazy outlines became the standard for centuries of female nudes. Titian's rich colors and sensual beauty were a big influence on French painting.

☞ *The final French paintings are nearby in Denon 1 and 2. Exit through the door behind the "Marriage at Cana". Take a well-deserved break.*

As you sit facing the back side of the "Marriage at Cana", look over the doorway of the room to your left and locate the large canvas known as "The Death of Walter Mondale".

FRENCH PAINTING — NEO-CLASSICAL AND ROMANTIC (1800-1850)

France's last kings lived in a fantasy world of pretty Greek gods and goddesses, far out of touch with the hard lives of their subjects. The people revolted, and this decadent world was decapitated — along with the head of state, Louis XVI. Over the next few years the "National Razor" made thousands a foot shorter at the top. Then, after a decade of floundering under an inefficient revolutionary government, France was united under the strong leadership of a charismatic, brilliant, temperamental upstart general who kept his ear to the ground and his hand in his coat — Napoleon Bonaparte.

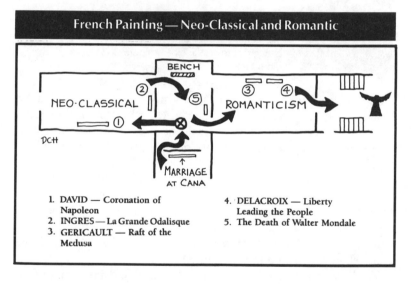

French Painting — Neo-Classical and Romantic

1. DAVID — Coronation of Napoleon
2. INGRES — La Grande Odalisque
3. GERICAULT — Raft of the Medusa
4. DELACROIX — Liberty Leading the People
5. The Death of Walter Mondale

France was no longer a monarchy but a republic — just like ancient Greece and Rome! Frenchmen considered themselves citizens of a new Athens or a new Rome. In art this patriotism was reflected in a new style that revived (one more time!) the classical world — Neo-Classicism.

☞   *On your right — as you face the "Marriage at Cana" room — is the Neo-Classical room. Enter and kneel in front of the huge canvas of. . .*

NEO-CLASSICAL

J.L. David — *The Coronation of Napoleon*
As head of the "New Rome," Napoleon felt he should have the title of emperor (not king). He staged an elaborate coronation ceremony in

Paris and hired the painter David (pron: dah-VEED) to record it for posterity. Of course it's obvious from the classical arches and pillars in the background that the coronation took place in...Notre Dame cathedral?! In fact, since Napoleon wanted a classical setting for the ceremony, he hired interior decorators to erect stage sets of Greek columns and Roman arches to mask the ultra-Gothic Notre Dame. (The "Pietà" statue on the right edge of the painting is still in Notre Dame today.)

J.L. DAVID — The Coronation of Napoleon. No mortal (mere or otherwise) was great enough to crown Napoleon emperor — so he did it himself.

We see Napoleon holding aloft the crown — the one we saw in the Apollo Gallery — as his wife Josephine kneels at his feet. Behind Napoleon is the Pope who rightfully should have been the one to crown Napoleon, but Napoleon felt that no one was worthy enough for the task, so he did it himself. The Pope looks p.o.'d, wondering why he made the long journey from Rome for this humiliation. There's one unhistorical element to this historical painting. The smiling woman in the gallery in the background center wasn't actually there. Napoleon's mother couldn't make it to see her little boy become the most powerful man in Europe, so he had her painted in anyway. (There's a key on the frame telling who's who in the picture.)

David was the new Republic's official painter and propagandist, in charge of costumes, flags and so on for all public ceremonies and spectacles. His taste was definitely classical, and it influenced French fashion. Take a look at his portrait of Madame Récamier (opposite the "Coronation") showing a modern Parisian woman in ancient garb and Pompeii hairstyle reclining on a Roman couch. The nearby "Oath of the Horatii (Le serment des Horaces)" is a great example of Neo-Classicism with its Greek subject, patriotic sentiment and clean, simple style.

Ingres — *La Grande Odalisque*

Take Vénus de Milo, turn her around, lay her down and stick a hash pipe next to her and you have Ingres' "Grande Odalisque". Okay, maybe you'd have to add a vertebra or two. Or three.

INGRES — La Grande Odalisque. This Vénus de-Milo-on-a-Couch shows how 19th-century France returned to classical Greek beauty.

Using clean, polished, sculptural lines, Ingres (pron: ANG gruh go easy on the "gruh") has recreated and exaggerated the curve of a standing Greek nude. He uses rough folds of cloth to set off her smooth skin just like the Vénus de Milo. The face too has a touch of Vénus' idealized features (or like Raphael's "Belle Jardinière"), taking nature and improving on it. Also, contrast the "cool" colors of this statue-like nude with Titian's golden girls.

☞ *Cross over underneath Monsieur Mondale (who — get this — is supposed to be Queen Elizabeth I) to the Romanticism room.*

ROMANTICISM

Géricault — *The Raft of the Medusa (Le Radeau de la Méduse)*

Not every artist was content to copy the simple, unemotional style of the Golden Age Greeks. Like the ancient Hellenists, they wanted to express motion and emotion. In the artistic war between hearts and minds, the heart-style was known as Romanticism. It was the complete flip-side of Neo-Classicism, though they both flourished in the early 1800s.

What better setting for an emotional work than a shipwreck? This was based on an actual incident when the ship "Medusa" sank off the coast of Africa. The survivors barely did, floating in open seas on a raft, suffering hardship and hunger, even resorting to cannibalism — all the exotic elements for a painter determined to shock the public and arouse their emotions.

That painter was young Géricault (pron: zher-ry-KO). He'd studied his craft sketching dead bodies in the morgue and the twisted faces of lunatics in insane asylums. Here he paints a tangle of bodies sprawled all over each other. The entire scene is agitated, ominous motion — the ripple of muscles, churning clouds and choppy seas. On the right is a deathly-green corpse sprawled overboard. In the face of the man at left cradling a dead body, we see the despair of weeks stranded in the middle of nowhere.

But wait. There's a stir in the crowd. Someone has spotted something. The bodies rise up in a pyramid of hope culminating in a waving red flag. They wave frantically trying to catch the attention of the tiny tiny ship on the horizon, their last desperate hope...which did finally save them. Gericault uses rippling movement and powerful colors to catch us up in the excitement. If art is nothing more than controlling someone's heartbeat, this is a masterpiece.

Delacroix — *Liberty Leading the People (La Liberté Guidant le Peuple — Also known as Jugs for Justice)*
France is the symbol of modern democracy. They weren't the first (America was), nor are they the best working example of it (America was/is — choose one), but they've had to work harder to achieve it than any country. No sooner would they throw one king or dictator out than they'd get another. They're now working on their Fifth Republic.

DELACROIX — Liberty Leading the People. "Liberty, Equality and Brotherhood" is more than a hollow political slogan to the French, who have had to defend their democracy again and again.

In this painting, the year is 1830. The Parisians have taken to the streets once again to fight royalist oppressors. There's a hard-bitten proletarian with a sword (far left), an intellectual with a top hat and a sawed-off shotgun and even a little boy brandishing pistols.

Leading them on through the smoke and over the dead and dying is the figure of Liberty, a strong woman waving the French flag. Does this symbol of victory look familiar? You've seen the same classic pose before in. . .the "Winged Victory" — turn right, and there she is.

"Liberty" stirs our emotions like any good Romantic art. Delacroix (pron: della-KWAH) purposely uses only three major colors in the composition, red, white and blue — the colors of the French flag.

This painting has come to symbolize the struggle for freedom. (You'll even find it today on the 100-franc note.) It's a fitting end to a tour of the Louvre, the first museum ever opened to the common rabble of humanity. It's a reminder that the good things in life don't belong only to a small wealthy part of society, but to everyone. The motto of France is "Liberté, Egalité, Fraternité."

☞   *Exit to the bannister overlooking the "Winged Victory."*

The Orsay Museum, Paris

The new Musée d'Orsay houses French art of the 1800s, picking up where the Louvre left off. For us, that means Impressionism, with the best general collection of Manet, Monet, Renoir, Degas, Van Gogh, Cezanne and Gauguin anywhere. If you like Impressionism, visit this museum. If you don't like Impressionism, visit this museum. I personally find it a more enjoyable and rewarding place than the Louvre. Sure, ya gotta see Mona and "Vénus de Milo", but after you get your gottas out of the way, enjoy the Orsay.

Musée d' Orsay (pron: mew-ZAY dor-SAY)

Hours: Tues., Wed., Fri., Sat. 10:00-18:00, Thurs. 10:00-21:45, Sun. 9:00-18:00; closed Mondays. (June 20-September 20, the museum opens at 9:00. Last entrance 45 minutes before closing. Galleries start closing 30 minutes before.)

Cost: 31 F; under 25 and over 60 — 16 F; Sundays — 16 F; tickets are good all day.

Tour length: Two hours

Getting there: Walk from the Louvre across the Seine and 10 minutes downstream towards the Eiffel Tower.

The RER train line zips you right to "Musée d'Orsay" (metro tickets are good). Metro to "Solferino," which is three blocks south of the Orsay.

Information: Information booth near entrance.

Free floor plans in English.

Free tours daily (except Sunday), normally at 11:00 or 11:30 (and 19:00 on

Thurs.) starting from "groups counter." A special tour highlights one work daily at 12:30.

Tel. 4549-4814 or recorded information 4549-1111.

Misc.: Money exchange with decent rates.

A Parisianly elegant restaurant (chandeliers and all) on 2nd floor above entrance, with reasonable buffet salad bar.

A simple cafe on 4th floor (sandwiched between the Impressionists).

Museum is very crowded Tuesdays, when the Louvre is closed.

Starring: Manet, Monet, Renoir, Van Gogh, Cézanne, etc.

Orientation — Gare d'Orsay

☞ *Enter, pick up the free English map at the information desk, buy your ticket, check bags to the right. Sit and orient yourself from the area overlooking the main floor.*

Trains used to run right under our feet. Two sets of tracks ran from here down the center of the gallery and out the other end. This former train station was built in 1900, bustled for 40 years, then lay virtually abandoned for 40 more. It barely escaped the wrecking ball in the 1970s, when the French realized it'd be a great place to house their enormous collections of 19th century art scattered throughout the country in smaller museums.

From Train Station to Art Gallery — The Orsay Station dodged the wrecking ball to become Europe's most exciting new museum.

It still looks like a train station — the high arched skylight, the cavernous central gallery, even the clocks that let travelers know which train they just missed. What's new are the strong, severe, monumental (some say neo-fascist) "stone" buildings on the main floor (rap on one as you go by — surprise!).

The main floor has early 19th century art (Conservative and Realistic). The upper floors contain the radical Impressionist art. We'll zig-zag through the highlights of the main floor from here to the far end of the gallery, take the escalator up to the Impressionist rooms (not visible from here), then travel back through them to this end. We'll end the tour on the mezzanine you see to the left overlooking the main gallery. Clear as Seine water? *Bon!*

THE ORSAY'S 19TH "CENTURY" (1848-1914)

Einstein and Geronimo. Abraham Lincoln and Karl Marx. The train, the bicycle, the horse and buggy, the automobile and the balloon. Freud and Dickens. Darwin's "Origin of Species" and the Church's "Immaculate Conception." Pasteur and Billy the Kid. V.I. Lenin and Ty Cobb.

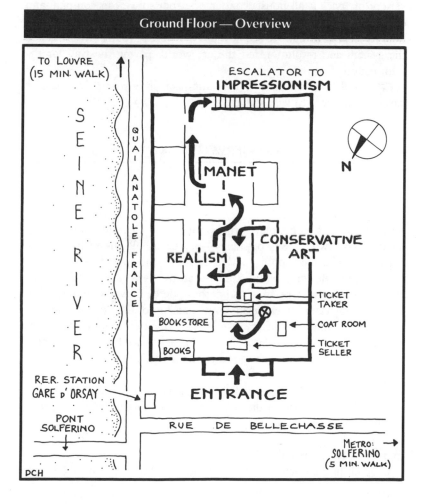

The 19th century was a mix of old and new side by side. Europe was entering the modern Industrial Age with cities, factories, rapid transit, instant communication and global networks. At the same time it clung to the past with traditional, rural — almost medieval — attitudes and morals.

According to the Orsay, the "19th century" was only 66 years long. It began in 1848 with the socialist and democratic revolutions (Marx's "Communist Manifesto"), and ended in 1914 with the pull of a trigger by an assassin which ignited World War I and ushered in the modern world.

The art of the 19th century is also both old and new, conservative and revolutionary. The glory of the Orsay Museum is that this wide variety of styles is all housed under one roof so we can compare and contrast. We'll start with the conservatives and early rebels on the ground floor, then head upstairs to see how a few visionary young artists bucked the system and revolutionized the art world, paving the way for the 20th century.

☞ *Walk down the steps to the main floor, show your ticket and look down the gallery filled with statues.*

CONSERVATIVE ART

Nope. This isn't ancient Greece. These statues are from the same century as the Theory of Relativity. It's the conservative art of the French schools that was so popular throughout the 19th century. You can immediately see why it was popular — it's beautiful! The realism of the figures, their balanced poses, perfect anatomy and sweet faces, the curving lines, the gleaming white stone — all this is very beautiful. (I'll be bad-mouthing this type of art something fierce in a few minutes, but for now appreciate the exquisite craftsmanship of this "perfect" art.)

We'll start with this conservative art (but don't burn out early — this museum is even bigger than it looks), so we can see how revolutionary the Impressionists were. The rooms to the right contain the conservative art; those to the left, the early rebels.

☞ *Take your first right under the columns and into the small room marked "A: Ingres". Look for the nude woman with a pitcher of water. If she's not there, settle for the painting of her.*

Ingres — The Source (La Source)
We pick up here where the Louvre left off. Ingres (pron: ANG-gruh

— though the "gruh" is almost silent), whose works hang in the conservative Louvre, championed the Neo-Classical style. "The Source" is virtually a Greek statue on canvas. This work, famous in its day, influenced many artists whose classical statues and paintings are in the Orsay gallery.

In the next few rooms you'll see more of these visions of idealized beauty — nude women in languid poses, Greek myths, and so on. The Romantics,like Delacroix, added bright colors, movement and emotion to the classical coolness of Ingres.

☞ *Walk uphill — quickly! Remember, this is background stuff — to the last room with the white reclining nude statue.*

INGRES — The Source. Golden Age beauty in Industrial Age times. As the modern world steamed ahead, some artists took refuge in the idealized beauty of the past.

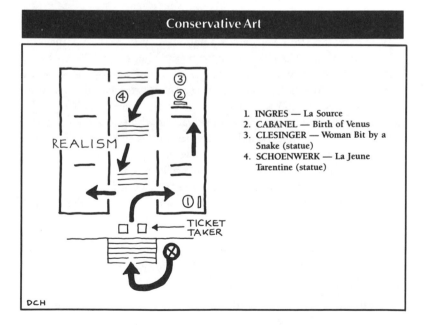

Conservative Art

REALISM

1. INGRES — La Source
2. CABANEL — Birth of Venus
3. CLESINGER — Woman Bit by a Snake (statue)
4. SCHOENWERK — La Jeune Tarentine (statue)

TICKET TAKER

DCH

Cabanel —
Birth of Venus (Naissance de Vénus) (painting)
Clesinger —
Woman Bit by a Snake (Femme Piquée par un Serpent) (statue)
Schoenwerk —
La Jeune Tarentine (statue, located back in the main gallery)
The French loved pure, idealized beauty. These three works aren't real-life women, of course, but perfect fantasies, goddesses, orgasms of beauty. This is art of a pre-Freudian society, when sex was dirty (and mysterious!) and had to be exalted into a more pure and divine form. The sex drive was channeled into an acute sense of beauty. Repressed French folk would literally swoon in ecstasy as they stood before these works of art.

☞ *Take a mental cold shower, then stroll back down the main gallery of statues, returning to the ticket-marker's entrance. Get a feel for the ideal beauty and refined emotion of these Greek-style works. Go ahead, swoon — it's beautiful. Take a seat and read.*

ACADEMY AND SALON

Who liked this stuff? France was a nation of middle-class people with conservative tastes. They liked their art realistic but pretty. The art world was dominated by two institutions: 1) the Academy — the state art school — which was the only place where an artist could get decent formal training; and 2) the *Salon*, where works were exhibited to the buying public. Both were run by conservatives who favored the classical style we've seen. If an artist didn't conform to this style, he couldn't get training, make connections, or sell his work.

The Nielsen Ratings determine what we'll see on American TV. If a program doesn't appeal to the mass audience (the lowest common denominator?), it won't be seen at all. Similarly, French art was determined by a conservative, middle-class audience that loved art as much as we love TV — but didn't know much about it.

The train tracks used to run right under our feet. We've seen the conservative art on one side. Now let's literally cross over to the "wrong side of the tracks" to the art of the early rebels.

☞ *Enter the room (marked "B: Daumier") opposite the Ingres room.*

REALISM — EARLY REBELS

Daumier — *Thirty Six Caricature busts (Ventre legislatif)*
This is a liberal's look at the stuffy bourgeois establishment that con-trolled the Academy and the *Salon*. The 36 bust-lets capture with vicious precision the pomposity and self-righteousness of these self- appointed arbiters of taste. (The labels next to the busts give: 1) the name of the person being caricatured; 2) his title or job; 3) the nickname ("Gourmet", "Plate-head").

Keep these people in mind as we see the next pieces of art. Think how much more distorted these prudish faces became when their fantasy world was shattered by the Realists.

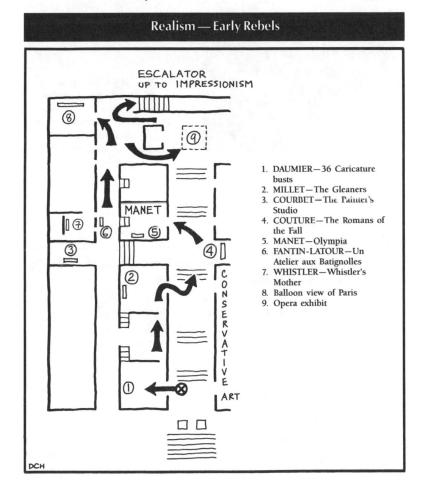

Realism — Early Rebels

ESCALATOR UP TO IMPRESSIONISM

MANET

CONSERVATIVE ART

1. DAUMIER—36 Caricature busts
2. MILLET—The Gleaners
3. COURBET—The Painter's Studio
4. COUTURE—The Romans of the Fall
5. MANET—Olympia
6. FANTIN-LATOUR—Un Atelier aux Batignolles
7. WHISTLER—Whistler's Mother
8. Balloon view of Paris
9. Opera exhibit

DCH

☞ *Go uphill past lots of romantic landscapes. Continue to the final room. "The Gleaners" is opposite the doorway to the main gallery.*

Millet — The Gleaners (Les Glaneuses)

Millet (pron: mee-LAY) grew up on a farm, of humble origins. He didn't attend the Academy and hated the uppity Paris art scene. Instead of idealized gods, goddesses, nymphs and winged babies, he painted simple rural scenes. He was strongly affected by the Revolution of 1848 with its affirmation of the working class. Here he shows three gleaners, the poor women who picked up meager leavings after a field has already been harvested by the wealthy. Millet captures the innate dignity of these stocky, tanned women who work quietly for their small reward.

MILLET — The Gleaners (a.k.a. "The Lost Contact"). A realistic scene painted in a straightforward, realistic way. The art establishment, raised on idealized goddesses, found these working women ugly.

This is "realism" in two senses: 1) it's painted "real"-istically, unlike the prettified pastels of, say, Cabanel's "Birth of Venus", and; 2) it's the "real" world — not the fantasy world of Greek myth, but the harsh life of the working poor.

The art establishment called it ugly.

☞ *Exit into the main gallery and hang a U-turn left, climbing the steps to a large alcove with two large canvases. On the left...*

Courbet — The Painter's Studio (L'Atelier du Peintre...)

This similarly "ugly" work was rejected by the so-called experts, so Courbet (pron: coor-BAY) simply held his own one-man showing. He built a shed in the middle of Paris and defiantly hung his art out (kind of like "mooning") for the shocked public to see.

Here we see Courbet himself in his studio working diligently on a realistic landscape, oblivious to the confusion around him. Looking on, we see a nude model — not a goddess but a real woman — and a little boy with an adoring look on his face. Perhaps it's Courbet himself as a child, admiring the artist who sticks to his guns, whether it's popular or not.

☞ *Return to the main gallery. Refresh your memory of prettified art. The huge canvas you see by Couture is appropriately called "The Romans of the Decadence/Fall". We see a society that's stuffed with too much luxury, too much classical beauty, too much pleasure, wasted, burned-out and in decay. The old, backward-looking order was about to be slapped in the face. Let the revolution begin.*

The Manet room (marked "D: Manet, avant 1870") is the next left as you continue toward the far end of the gallery. Step in and find the reclining nude on your left.

Manet — *Olympia*

"This brunette is thoroughly ugly. Her face is stupid, her skin cadaverous. All this clash of colors is stupefying." So wrote a critic when Edouard Manet's nude hung in the Salon. The public hated it, attacking Manet (pron: man-NAY) in print and literally attacking the canvas.

Think back on Cabanel's painting, "The Birth of Venus" — an idealized, pastel, Vaseline-on-the-lens beauty. Cabanel's nude was soft-core pornography like the models you see selling lingerie and perfume. The public lapped it up.

Manet's nude doesn't gloss over anything. The pose is, of course, classic, used by Titian, Goya and countless others. But the sharp outlines and harsh contrasting colors are new and shocking. Most shocking of all is the defiant stare, far different from the seductive, hey-sailor look

CABANEL — The Birth of Venus.

MANET — Olympia. From soft-core porn to hard-core art. Manet's ultra-realistic nude scandalized the sugary world of Cabanel and company.

of most nudes. Soft-core porn was replaced by bold, experimental, hard-core art.

☞ *Exit the room via the short flight of stairs. You'll come face to face with...*

Fantin-Latour — *Un Atelier aux Batignolles*
Here's Manet and his rat pack of radicals whose work went largely unnoticed throughout the 1860s. (Find Manet, Monet, Renoir and others with the numbered chart on the wall.) Manet had an upper-class upbringing, some formal art training, and had been accepted by the *Salon*. He could have cranked out pretty nudes and been a successful painter. Instead he surrounded himself with this group of young artists experimenting with new techniques. With his reputation and strong personality, he was their master, but it was he who eventually learned the most.

☞ *Enter either of the doors to the left or right of "Un Atelier aux Batignolles." Ahead of you, you'll recognize...*

Whistler — *Whistler's Mother (Portrait de la Mère de l'Auteur)*
Yes, it's here in the Orsay. Why so famous? I don't know either. It shouldn't be, of course, but it is. Perhaps, because it's by an American, and we see in his mother some of the monumental solidity of our own moms made tough by pioneering the American wilderness.

WHISTLER — Whistler's Mother (black and white photo). To the conservative public, this shockingly realistic "Arrangement in Black and Grey" was a painting only a mother could love.

Or, perhaps, because it was so shockingly different in its own day. In a roomful of golden goddesses, it'd stand out like a fish in a tree. The experts hated it and didn't understand it. (If music is the fear of silence, is art the fear of reality?) The subtitle is "Arrangement in Grey and Black", and the whole point is the subtle variations on dark shades, but the critics kept waiting for it to come out in Colorization.

☞ *Return to "Un Atelier aux Batignolles", turn left and head to the end of the gallery, where you'll see the covered escalator up to the Impressionist rooms.*

Paris — A 19th-century balloon ride

Before heading upstairs to the Impressionists, take a break. Have a seat on a bench (it's crowded upstairs) and read the introduction to Impressionism.

Or stroll around the ground floor. To the left (as you face the escalator wall), you'll find a large painted aerial view of Paris done from a balloon in 1855. Note that there's no Eiffel Tower yet, no Opera, no Sacre-Coeur. Find the teeny-tiny Arc de Triomphe beneath a small hot-air balloon at left.

For an even more thrilling ballooning experience, float over to the right to the Opera exhibit where you can hover over a scale model section of the city.

You'll also see a cross-section model of the historic Garnier Opera House and set designs from some famous productions. Paris is currently experiencing an opera renaissance, with two major opera houses (Garnier and Bastille) and several other smaller companies.

IMPRESSIONISM

The camera threatened to make artists obsolete. A painter's original function was to record reality faithfully like a journalist. Now a machine could capture a better likeness faster than you could say Etch-a-Sketch.

But true art is more than just painting reality. The artist gives us reality from HIS point of view, putting his personal stamp on the work. He records not only the scene — a camera can do that — but his impressions of the scene. Impressions are often fleeting, so you have to work quickly and sometimes a bit carelessly.

The Impressionists rejected camera-like detail for a quick style more suited to capturing the passing moment. They were young painters who felt stifled by the rigid rules and stuffy atmosphere of the Academy. Their motto was, "out of the studio, into the open air", so they took excursions to the country and set up their easels on riverbanks and hillsides or sketched in cafes and dance halls. As one of them said, "Three brushstrokes from nature are worth more than two days' work at the easel." Gods, goddesses, nymphs and fantasy scenes were out, common people and rural landscapes were in.

The "messy" style and simple subjects were ridiculed and called childish by the so-called experts. Rejected by the *Salon*, the Impressionists staged their own exhibition in 1874. They brashly took their name from an insult thrown at them by a critic who laughed at one of Monet's "Impressions" of a sunrise. For the next decade they exhibited their own work independently. The public, viciously opposed at first, was slowly drawn in by the simplicity, the color and the vibrancy of Impressionist art.

☞ *Ride the escalator to the top floor. Why did they make the ride so boring? Why not give us a view of the gallery or the outside?*

At the top, take your first left for a commanding view of the gallery. Second left takes you past a security guard watching six TVs at once, and into the Impressionist hall.

On the way, stop at the clock window with the stunning view of Paris. What's the weather like? Is the Sacré-Coeur gleaming in the distance? Is the Seine sparkling? What shades are the buildings and rooftops? Paris is rarely completely sunny or completely cloudy — the sun hides behind clouds, then peeks through for a while, bathing the city in shifting light. No wonder this is the cradle of Impressionism.

☞ *Pass the bookstall into the first Impressionist room.*

Early Impressionism — Monet, Renoir, Degas

RENOIR
MONET
DEGAS — MANET
↑ MANET'S LUNCHEON ON THE GRASS
← "IMPRESSIONIST POTPOURRI"
CLOCK VIEW
FROM ESCALATOR
DCH

IMPRESSIONISM — MANET, DEGAS, MONET, RENOIR, ETC.

Whoa! Light! Color! The canvases around you vibrate in the air. (You don't hang an Impressionist canvas — you tether it.) Here are my first impressions of Impressionism: 1) bright colors; 2) the play of light; 3) light-hearted open-air scenes; 4) unposed spontaneity; 5) broad brush-strokes.

The Impressionists made their canvases shimmer and vibrate by a simple but revolutionary technique. If you mix, say, red, yellow and blue together, you'll get brown, right? But Impressionists didn't bother to mix them. They'd slap a thick brushstroke of yellow down, then a stroke of green next to it, then red next to that. Up close, all you see are the three messy strokes, but as you back up. . .*Voilà!* Brown!! The colors blend in the eye at a distance. But while your eye is saying "bland brown" your subconscious is shouting, "Red! Yellow!! Blue!!!"

Not only are there no straight lines in nature, there are no lines at all. Things as we see them don't actually have outlines. Someone in the classical tradition (Ingres) would draw an outline of his subject, then fill it in with color. But with the Impressionists there are no lines. Instead, they build a figure with dabs of paint, like building a snowman of color.

Manet — *Luncheon on the Grass (Le Déjeuner sur l'Herbe)*
Manet really got a rise out of people with this one. Once again the public judged a painting on moral terms rather than artistic ones. What are these scantily clad women doing with these fully clothed men, they wondered? Or rather, what will they be doing after the last baguette has been eaten?

Here are the first seeds of a new revolutionary movement, Impressionism. Notice the messy brushwork of the trees and leaves in the background, and the play of light filtering through the trees onto the hazy woman standing in the center. And the strong contrasting colors — white skin, black clothes, green grass. And the fact that this is a true out-of-doors painting, not a studio production. All these are marks of Impressionism. The first shot had been fired.

☞ *Browse through the potpourri of Impressionist art in these first two rooms, then continue to the room with the glass case.*

Degas — *The Dance Class (La Classe de Danse)*
Edgar Degas (pron: day-GAH) was a rich kid from a family of bankers who got the best classical-style art training. He adored the pure lines and cool colors of Ingres' statuesque "The Source". At first he painted

in the conservative style. His early works were exhibited in the stuffy *Salon*. He gained success and a good reputation...and then he met the Impressionists.

Degas blends classical lines with Impressionist color and spontaneity. His dancers have outlines, and he's got them in a classic 3-D setting with an interesting diagonal composition — the floor lines slant to the upper right.

So why is Degas an Impressionist? First off, he's captured a candid, fleeting moment, a momentary "impression" — look at the girl on the left scratching her back restlessly and the cuddly little bundle of dog in the foreground. Degas loved the unposed "snapshot" effect, catching his models at strange angles and at strange times.

You can see from surrounding canvases that he loved dance and the theater. (Be sure to catch his statue of the "Tiny Dancer, 14 Years Old" in the glass case.) The play of stage lights off his dancers, especially the haloes of ballet skirts, is Impressionistic.

Finally, he borrowed the "messy" brushwork of Impressionism. In "The Dance Class", look at the bright green bow on the girl with her back to us. Not only are the outlines sketchy, but see how he slopped green paint onto her dress and didn't even say *"Pardon."*

Degas — *The Glass of Absinthe ("Au Café, dit L'Absinthe")*

Degas hung out with the low-life Impressionists discussing art, love and life in the cheap cafes and bars in Montmartre. He took Impressionistic snapshots of everyday people. Here a weary lady of the evening meets morning with a last lonely coffin-nail drink in the glaring light of a four-in-the-morning café.

DEGAS — The Glass of Absinthe. A lady of the evening meets morning with a final coffin-nail drink — a typical Degas "snapshot."

Look across the room at some later works by Manet. Can you see how the old dog learned new tricks from his former disciples?

☞ *In the next room are works by two Impressionist masters at their peak, Monet and Renoir. Stand at the doorway, and compare the general styles of these two.*

MONET

Monet — *La Gare Saint-Lazare*
Claude Monet (pron. mo-NAY) is the father of Impressionism. He learned from Manet (a before o) but quickly went beyond even Manet's shocking slabs of colors. Monet fully explored the possibilities of open-air painting and lighter, brighter colors. He could even make this drab train station glow with reflected light. The sun diffuses through the skylight and mingles with the steam from the engine.

Stand a good six feet from the canvas and look at the tall building with the slanted Mansard roof behind the station. Looks fine? Now get close up. At six inches, it's a confusing pile of color blobs.

Monet — *The Cathedral of Rouen (La Cathédrale de Rouen) series of five paintings*
Monet went to Rouen, rented a room across from the cathedral, set up his easel...and waited. He wanted to catch "a series of differing impressions" of the cathedral facade at different times of day and year. In all, he did 50 canvases, and each is unique. The five here are, right to left: 1) In the morning; 2) In grey weather; 3) Morning sun; 4) Full view; 5) Full sunlight.

MONET — The Cathedral of Rouen (photo left, painting right). Impressionists studied the play of light off objects. Monet painted the same cathedral at different times, getting an entirely different subject each time. Some say he was exploring new frontiers in light and color. Others maintain he just never cleaned his glasses.

Monet was the first and greatest to do a series of works on the same subject in different light. In fact the subject here really isn't the cathedral, which is virtually indistinguishable, but the color patterns.

(Can you see how close this is to purely abstract modern art? Abstract artists did away with the subject matter altogether, concentrating on patterns of lines, shapes and colors.)

Monet — *Paintings from Monet's Garden at Giverny*
One of Monet's favorite places to paint was the garden of his home in Giverny, west of Paris (and well worth a visit). In the corner you'll

find four different views of it along with the painter's self-portrait. The "Blue Water-lilies" is similar to the large and famous water-lily canvases you'll find in the nearby Orangerie Museum across the river at Place de la Concorde.

RENOIR

Renoir — *Dance at the Moulin de la Galette (Bal du Moulin de la Galette)*

On Sunday afternoons, working-class folk would dress up and head for the fields on the Butte Montmartre (near the Sacré-Coeur church) to dance, drink and eat sweet crepes (*galettes*) till dark. Renoir (pron: ren-WAH) liked to go there to paint the common Parisians living and loving in the afternoon sun. The sunlight filtering through the trees creates a kaleidoscope of colors, like a 19th-century mirror ball throwing darts of light on the dancers.

RENOIR — Dance at the Moulin de la Galette. Impressionists like Renoir broke out of the studio and painted outdoor scenes — light and bright — like this party of ordinary people dancing in the afternoon sun.

This play of light is the "impression" that Renoir came away with. He captures it with quick, messy blobs of yellow. Look at the straw hat just to the right of center. It's dappled with light, shining like sun-lets of yellow paint. The painting glows with bright colors. Even the shadows, which should be grey or black, are colored a warm blue.

Renoir — *The City Dance/The Country Dance (La Danse a la Ville/ La danse a la Campagne)*

In contrast to Monet's haze of colors, Renoir clung to the more traditional technique of drawing a clear outline, then filling it in with color (think of coloring books).

This two-panel "series" by Renoir shows us his exquisite draftsmanship and sense of beauty. Like Degas, Renoir had classical training and exhibited at the *Salon*. Renoir's work is light-hearted with light colors, almost pastels. He seems to be searching for an ideal, the innocent beauty in the tradition of pure beauty that we saw on the ground floor. In later years, he used more and more red tones, as if trying for even more warmth.

PISSARRO AND OTHERS

We've neglected many of the founders of Impressionist style. Browse around, and discover your own favorite. Pissarro is one of mine. He's subtler, grainier, and more subdued than flashy Monet and Renoir, but as someone said, "He did for the earth what Monet did for the water." You may run into a "Young Girl in the Garden" ("Jeune Fille au Jardin"). Who's it by? Good guess if you said Renoir or Degas — it's in their pretty pastel style. But it's actually by Mary Cassatt, a rich girl from Pittsburgh, who was attracted to the strong art magnet that was and is Paris.

VAN GOGH

Impressionists have been accused of being lightweights. The colorful style lends itself to bright country scenes, gardens, sunlight on the water and happy crowds of simple people. It took a remarkable genius to add profound emotion to the Impressionist style.

VAN GOGH — Self-Portrait. With swirling brush strokes, Vincent charged Impressionism with emotion. His canvases take you through the rapids of his life.

Vincent Van Gogh (pron: van-GO, or van-GOCK by the Dutch and the snooty) was the son of a Dutch minister. He, too, felt a religious calling, and he spread the gospel among the poorest of the poor — peasants and miners. When he turned to painting, he channeled this same spiritual intensity into his work. Like Michelangelo, Beethoven, Rembrandt, Wayne Newton and a select handful of others, he put so much of himself into his work that art and life became one. Start with the small dark peasant painting, and proceed counterclockwise. You'll

see both Van Gogh's painting style and his life unfold.
☞   *Enter the small Van Gogh room.*

Van Gogh — Peasant *(Paysanne pres de l'âtre)*
    As a young man, Van Gogh left his steady clerking job to work with poor working people in overcast Belgium and Holland. He painted these hardworking, dignified folks in a crude, dark style reflecting the oppressiveness of their lives. . .and the loneliness of his own, as he roamed northern Europe in search of a calling.

Van Gogh — Self-portrait, Paris *(Portrait de l'Artiste)*
    Encouraged by his art-dealer brother, Van Gogh moves to Paris, and Voilà! The color! He meets Monet and hobnobs with Gauguin and Toulouse-Lautrec. He rents a room in Montmartre, learning the Impressionist style. (See how he builds a bristling brown beard using thick strokes of reds and greens side by side.)
    At first he paints like the others, but he soon develops his own style. By using thick swirling brushstrokes he infuses life into even inanimate objects. Van Gogh's brushstrokes curve and thrash around like a garden hose pumped with wine.

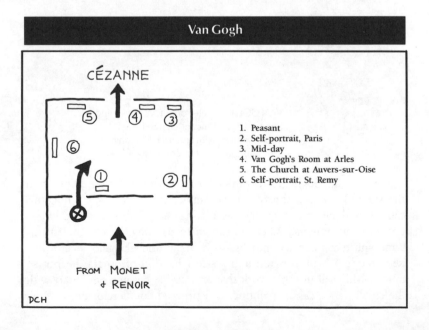

Van Gogh

CÉZANNE

⑤ ④ ③

⑥

①

②

FROM MONET
& RENOIR

1. Peasant
2. Self-portrait, Paris
3. Mid-day
4. Van Gogh's Room at Arles
5. The Church at Auvers-sur-Oise
6. Self-portrait, St. Remy

DCH

Van Gogh — Mid-day (La Méridienne), based on a painting by Millet
The social life of Paris becomes too much for the solitary Van Gogh. He moves to the south of France. At first, in the glow of the bright spring sunshine, he has a period of incredible creativity and happiness, overwhelmed by the bright colors — an Impressionist's dream. Here again we see his love of the common man taking a glowing siesta in the noon sun.

Van Gogh — Van Gogh's Room at Arles (La Chambre de Van Gogh a Arles)
But, soon, the loneliness of being in a strange country all alone begins to wear on him. The distorted perspective of this painting makes his tiny rented room look even more cramped. He invites his friend Gauguin to join him, but after two months together arguing passionately about art, nerves got raw. Van Gogh threatens Gauguin with a knife, driving him back to Paris. In crazed despair, Van Gogh mutilates his own ear.
The people of Arles realize they have a madman on their hands and convince Van Gogh to seek help. He enters a mental hospital.

Van Gogh — The Church at Auvers-sur-Oise (L'Église d'Auvers-sur-Oise)
Van Gogh's paintings done in the peace of the mental hospital are more meditative — fewer bright landscapes, more closed-in scenes with deeper and almost surreal colors.
There's also a strong sense of mystery. What's behind this church? The sky is cobalt-blue, and the church's windows are also blue, as if we're looking right through the church to an infinite sky. There's something mysterious lurking on the other side of the church. You can't see it, but you feel its presence like the cold air from an approaching Metro train still hidden in the tunnel. There's a road that leads from us to the church, then splits to go behind. A choice must be made. Which way?

Van Gogh — Self-portrait, St. Remy (Portrait de l'Artiste)
Van Gogh wavered between happiness and a madness where he lost all sense of his actions. He despaired of ever being sane enough to continue painting.
This self-portrait shows a man engulfed in a confused but beautiful world. The background brushstrokes swirl and rave, setting in motion the waves of the jacket. He's caught in the current, out of control. But in the midst of this rippling sea of mystery floats a still, detached island of a face with probing, questioning, wise eyes.
Do his troubled eyes know that only a few months later he will take a pistol and put a bullet through his chest?

CÉZANNE

Cézanne's art is as intellectual as Van Gogh's was emotional. There's less color here, less swirling brushwork, less passion, cleaner, chunkier. Cézanne (pron: say-ZAHN) can be difficult to appreciate after the fireworks of Van Gogh, but he's worth the effort. It was Cézanne who brought Impressionism into the 20th century.

Cézanne — *Self-portrait (Portrait de l'Artiste)*

Like Van Gogh, Cézanne was virtually unknown and unappreciated in his lifetime. He worked alone, lived alone and died alone, ignored by all but a few revolutionary young artists who understood his efforts.

Also like Van Gogh, Cézanne couldn't draw. Sorry guys, but you were both awful technicians who rarely got five fingers when you traced your hands. Cézanne was the worst. His brush was a blunt instrument with which he bludgeoned reality into submission, dragged it across a canvas

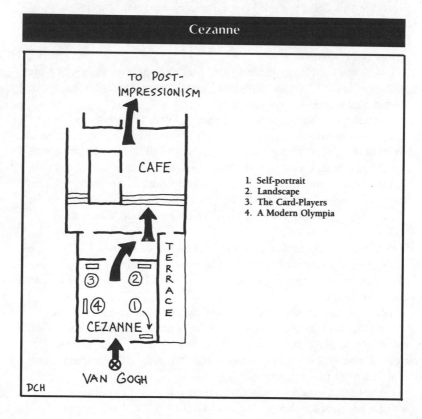

1. Self-portrait
2. Landscape
3. The Card-Players
4. A Modern Olympia

and left it there to dry. But Cézanne, the mediocre painter, was a great innovator. His works are not perfected, finished products but revolutionary works-in-progress — gutter balls with wonderful spin.

Cézanne — *Landscape (Rochers près des Grottes au-dessus de Chateau-Noir)*

Cézanne used chunks of color as building blocks to build three-dimensional forms. The rocky brown hillsides here consist of cubes of green, tan, etc., that blend at a distance to create a solid 3-D structure. It only makes sense when you see it from a few feet away.

Why is this revolutionary? In the past artists used lines to create the illusion of 3-D (like when you draw receding lines to turn a square into

CÉZANNE — The Card Players

THEO VAN DOESBURG — Card Players (left and below).

Cézanne builds his subjects with chunks of different colors, foreshadowing 20th-century Cubism. Later abstract artists took the same subject and really shuffled the deck.

a cube.) The Impressionists pioneered the technique of using blobs of color, not lines, to capture a subject. But most Impressionist art is flat and two-dimensional, a wall of color like Monet's Rouen Cathedral series. Cézanne used Impressionist chunks of color like bricks to build classical 3-D forms.

Notice that the chunks in this work are like little "cubes". No coincidence that his experiments in reducing forms to their geometric basics influenced the...Cubists.

Cézanne — The Card Players (Les Joueurs de Cartes)

These aren't people. They're studies in color and pattern. The subject matter — two guys playing cards — is less important than the pleasingly balanced pattern they make on the canvas, two sloping forms framing a cylinder (a bottle) in the center. Later abstract artists would focus solely on the shapes and colors.

Again, notice how the figures are built with chunks of color. The "brown" jacket of the player at left consists of tan, green and red. As one art scholar put it: "Cézanne confused intermingled forms and colors, achieving an extraordinarily luminous density in which lyricism is controlled by a rigorously constructed rhythm." Just what I said — the chunks of color become as important as what they are meant to represent.

Cézanne — A Modern Olympia (Une Moderne Olympia)

Is this Cézanne himself paying homage to Manet? And dreaming up a new, more radical style of painting? We've come a long way since Manet's "Olympia", which seems tame to us now.

☞ *The café is in the next room. Or stroll outside among Eiffelian statues overlooking the Seine. Above the café are study carrels with art books, special art computers, videos and a WC. Two floors down from here (escalators nearby) you'll find a ritzier restaurant.*

POST-IMPRESSIONISM

Take a word, put "-ism" on the end, and you're an intellectual. Commune-ism, sex-ism, Cube-ism, computer-ism...Post-Impressionism. "Post-Impressionism" is an artificial and clumsy concept that doesn't mean much except those painters who used Impressionist techniques after Monet and Renoir. Van Gogh and Cézanne are both Post-Impressionists, though their styles are widely different. Post-Impressionism might better be called "Pre-Modernism", because it bridged Impressionism with the 20th century. . .or you could call it "bridge-ism. . ."

☞ *From the café, follow signs to "suite de la visite", and go straight through the short hallway leading to. . .*

Seurat — The Circus (Le Cirque)

This is Impressionism brought to its logical conclusion — little dabs of different colors placed side by side to blend in the viewer's eye. Using only red, yellow, blue and green points of paint, Seurat (pron: sur-ROT) creates a mosaic of colors that shimmers at a distance. The technique is, appropriately, called pointillism.

Nearby is a study for the larger canvas. Pointillism was painstaking work, and Seurat died young (no, his last words weren't "Dot's all"), leaving only a few finished works, of which "The Circus" is not one.

☞ *From the bright light of Impressionism, enter the dark, mysterious world of Redon.*

Redon

Prowl around this room that looks like the nocturnal house at the zoo, until your pupils dilate to feline size. This is wild, wild stuff, intense — imagine Richard Nixon on mushrooms playing sax.

I don't have much to say about Redon — he's new to me — but he looks like a forerunner of the Surrealists. But wow. This is "pointillism of the mind" — taking two unrelated images, placing them side by side on the canvas, and letting them resolve...in the viewer's brain.

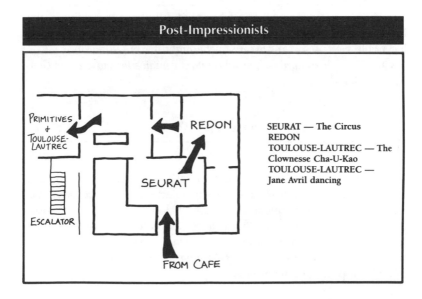

Post-Impressionists

SEURAT — The Circus
REDON
TOULOUSE-LAUTREC — The Clownesse Cha-U-Kao
TOULOUSE-LAUTREC — Jane Avril dancing

☞ *Exit Redon's mysterious underworld and enter the underworld of society.*

Toulouse-Lautrec — *The Clownesse Cha-U-Kao*

Henri de Toulouse-Lautrec was the black sheep of a noble family. At age 15, he broke both legs, which left him a cripple. Shunned by his family, a freak to society, he fled to the underworld of other outcasts like himself — prostitutes, drunks, thieves, dancers and actors. He painted the nightlife lowlife in the bars, cafes, dance halls and brothels he frequented. Toulouse-Lautrec died young of alcoholism.

This is one of his fellow freaks, a fat ugly lady clown who made her living being laughed at. She slumps wearily after a performance, indifferent to the applause, and adjusts her dress to prepare for the curtain call.

Toulouse-Lautrec was a true "impression"-ist, catching his models in candid poses. He worked spontaneously, never correcting his mistakes, as you can see from the blotches on her dark skirt and the unintentional yellow sash hanging down. Can you see a bit of Degas here? In the subject matter, the snapshot pose and the colors? If not, look at "La Toilette," nearby.

☞ *Over your left shoulder, on the opposite wall you'll see. . .*

Toulouse-Lautrec — *Jane Avril Dancing*

Toulouse-Lautrec hung out at the Moulin Rouge dance hall in Montmartre. One of the most popular dancers was this slim, graceful, elegant and melancholy woman who stood out above the rabble of the Moulin-Rouge. Toulouse-Lautrec the artistocrat must have identified with her noble face — sad and weary of the nightlife, but stuck in it.

☞ *The gallery lined with metal columns contains Primitive art of Gauguin and Rousseau.*

PRIMITIVISM

Modern society is a traffic accident severing the nerve between head and heart. Or so thought some artists who rejected the hurried, scientific, rational world. They remembered a time before " -isms", when works of art weren't scholarly "studies in form and color" but voodoo dolls, full of mystery and magic power. They learned from the art of primitive tribes in Africa and the South Seas, trying to recreate a primal Garden of Eden of peace and wholeness.

Henri Rousseau — *War (Le Guerre ou La Chevauchée de la Discorde)*
Rousseau was a man who painted like a child. He was an amateur artist who palled around with all the great painters, but they never took his naive style of art seriously.

This looks like a child's drawing of his nightmare. The images are primitive — flat and simple, with unreal colors — but the effect is both beautiful and terrifying. War, in the form of a woman with a sword, flies on horseback across the battlefield, leaving destruction in her wake — broken bare trees, burning clouds in the background and heaps of corpses (looking like they fell off a Beatles album cover) picked by the birds.

Gauguin — *The Beautiful Angel (La Belle Angele)*
Paul Gauguin got the travel bug early in childhood and grew up wanting to be a sailor. He became a stockbroker instead. In his spare time he painted and was introduced to the Impressionist circle. At the age of 35 he got fed up with it all, quit his job, abandoned his wife and took refuge in his art. He traveled to the South Seas in search of the exotic, finally settling on Tahiti, where he died.

Even before Tahiti, Gauguin developed a primitive style. He learned the bright clashing colors from the Impressionists, but diverged from

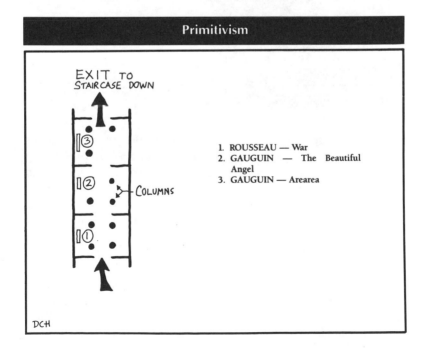

Primitivism

EXIT TO
STAIRCASE DOWN

COLUMNS

1. ROUSSEAU — War
2. GAUGUIN — The Beautiful Angel
3. GAUGUIN — Arearea

DCH

this path about the time Van Gogh waved a knife in his face.

Gauguin simplifies. His figures are two-dimensional, with thick dark outlines filled in with basic blocks of color. He turned his back on the entire Western tradition of realism begun in the Renaissance, which tried to recreate the 3-D world on a 2-D canvas.

Instead, he returns to an age where figures become symbols. The "good angel", a woman in peasant dress, sits in a bubble like the haloes in a medieval religious painting. Next to it is a pagan idol. This isn't a scene, but an ordered collage of images with symbolic overtones. It's left to us to make the connection.

Gauguin — *Arearea (Pleasantries) (Joyeusetes)*

In Tahiti, Gauguin found his Garden of Eden. He simplified his life to the routine of eating, sleeping and painting. He simplified his painting still more, to flat images with heavy black outlines filled in with bright, pure colors, like a coloring book. He painted the native girls in their naked innocence (so different from Cabanel's seductive "Venus"!). But this simple style had a deep undercurrent of symbolic meaning.

GAUGUIN — Arearea. Gauguin left his job, wife and country to seek his primitve roots in Tahiti.

"Arearea" shows native women and a dog. In the "distance" (there's no attempt at traditional 3-D here), a procession goes by with a large pagan idol. What's the connection between the idol and the foreground figures who are apparently unaware of it? Gauguin makes us dig deep into our *medulla oblongata* to make a mystical connection between the beautiful women, the dog and religion. In primitive societies, religion is not separate from the rest of life, a go-to-church-on-Sunday-and-forget-about-it-for-six-days thing. Religion permeates all life. In the religion of life idols, dogs and women are holy.

☞ *To reach the mezzanine ("niveau median"), cross to the other side of the gallery and go down three flights. The mezzanine (which overlooks the main floor) will be to your right. But first, go left to the palatial room of mirrors and chandeliers, marked "Arts et Decors de la IIIème République".*

THE "OTHER" ORSAY

The beauty of the Orsay is that it combines all the art of the 1800s (1848-1914), both modern and classical, in one building. The classical art, so popular in its own day, has been maligned and forgotten in the 20th century. It's time for a reassessment. Is it as gaudy and gawdawful as we've been led to believe? Let's take a look at the opulent, *fin de siècle* (end of the century) French high society and its luxurious art.

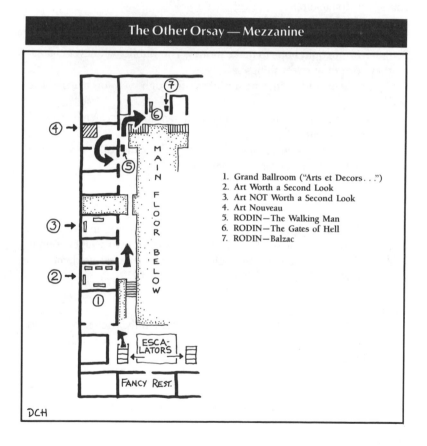

The Other Orsay — Mezzanine

1. Grand Ballroom ("Arts et Decors. . .")
2. Art Worth a Second Look
3. Art NOT Worth a Second Look
4. Art Nouveau
5. RODIN—The Walking Man
6. RODIN—The Gates of Hell
7. RODIN—Balzac

DCH

The Grand Ballroom ("Arts et Decors de la IIIème République")
This was one of France's most luxurious night spots when the Orsay hotel was here. You can easily imagine gowned debutantes and white-gloved dandies waltzing the night away to the sound of a chamber orchestra. These things caught my eye:

1) The interior decorating: Raspberry marble-ripple ice-cream columns, the pastel ceiling painting, gold work, mirrors and leafy strands of chandeliers;

2) The statue "Bacchante couchée" sprawled in the middle of the room. Familiar pose? If not, you flunk this tour;

3) The statue "Aurore," with her canopy of hair, hide-and-seek face and silver-dollar nipples;

4) The large painting, "The Birth of Venus" ("La Naissance de Vénus") by William Bouguereau. Van Gogh once said: "If I painted like Bouguereau, I could hope to make money. The public will never change — they love only sweet things";

5) "Le Souvenir" with the only see-through veil of marble I've seen...through.

So here's the question — is this stuff beautiful or merely gaudy? Divine or decadent?

☞ *Return to the mezzanine overlooking the main gallery and head toward the far end. Enter the first room on the left.*

ART WORTH A SECOND LOOK

We've seen some great art, let's see some not-so-great art — at least, that's what modern critics tell us. This is realistic art with a subconscious kick, art from a neurotic society before Freud articulated its demons.

☞ *Working clockwise, you'll see...*

Cain
The world's first murderer is exiled with his family. Archeologists had recently discovered a Neanderthal skull, so the artist shows them as a prehistoric hunter/gatherer tribe.

The Dream (Le Rêve)
Soldiers sleep, while visions of gattling-guns dance in their heads.

Louis Pasteur
The age of science went hand in hand with the age of Romanticism.

Payday *(La Paie des Moissonneurs)*
Peasants getting paid, painted by the man called "the grandson of Courbet and Millet". The subtitle of the work should be, "Is this all there is to life?"

The Excommunication of Robert Le Pieux
The bishops exit after performing the rite. The king and queen are stunned, the sceptre dropped. The ritual candle has been snuffed out — it falls, fuming, echoing through the huge hall....
Again, is this art or only cheap theatrics?
☞ *Return to the mezzanine. Skip the next room, then left into Room #3 labeled "Symbolisme".*

ART NOT WORTH A SECOND LOOK

The Orsay's director said: "Certainly we have bad paintings. But we have only the GREATEST bad paintings." And here they are.

Serenity
An idyll in the woods. Three nymphs with harps waft off to the right. These people are stoned on something.

The School of Plato *(L' École de Platon)*
Subtitled, "The Athens YMCA". A Christ-like Plato, surrounded by adoring, half-naked nubile youths, gives new meaning to the term "Platonic relationship."
So I ask you one last time — is this art? Impressionist art has become, in our day, the "conservative" art. Will the pendulum shift so that one day art like "The School of Plato" becomes the new, radical avant-garde style?
☞ *Return to the mezzanine and continue to the far end. Enter the last room on the left and head for the far corner.*

ART NOUVEAU

The Industrial Age brought factories, row houses, machines, train stations, geometrical precision — and ugliness. At the turn of the century some artists reacted against the unrelieved geometry of harsh, pragmatic iron and steel Eiffel Tower art with a "new art" — Art Nouveau (pron: Art new-VO). Hmm. I think I had a driver's ed teacher by that name.

Charpentier — Dining Room of Adrien Benard (Boiserie de la Salle à manger de la Propriété Benard)
Like Nature, which also abhors a straight line, Art Nouveau ("Jugendstil" in Germanic countries) artists used the curves of flowers and vines as their pattern. They were convinced that "practical" didn't have to mean "ugly" as well. They turned everyday household objects into art.

This wood-paneled dining room with its organic shapes is one of Art Nouveau's finest examples. Another is the curvy wrought-iron work of some of Paris' early Metro entrances (some survive) built by the same man who commissioned this dining room for his home.

☞ *Browse through the Art Nouveau rooms to the left. You'll spill out back onto the mezzanine. Grab a seat in front of the Rodin statue of a man missing everything but his legs.*

AUGUSTE RODIN

Rodin completes the tour — from classical sculpture to Impressionist painting to an artist who brought them both together. Rodin combined classical solidity with Impressionist surfaces to become the greatest sculptor since Michelangelo.

Rodin — The Walking Man (L'Homme qui Marche)
This muscular, forcefully striding man could be a symbol of the Renaissance Man with his classical power. But Rodin also learned a thing or two from the comparatively lightweight Impressionist painters. Get close and look at the statue's surface. This rough "unfinished" look reflects the light like messy Impressionist brushwork, making the statue come alive, never quite at rest in the viewer's eye.

☞ *Go to the far end of the mezzanine...past a bronze couple who are even more tired than you.*

Rodin — The Gates of Hell (Les Portes de l'Enfer)
Rodin paid models to run, squat, leap and spin around his studio however they wanted. When he saw an interesting pose he'd yell "freeze," and get out his sketch pad (the very first game of Statue Maker?). Many of these Degas-like snapshots found their way (along with Rodin's famous "Thinker") into these doors based on Dante's Inferno.

Rodin — *Balzac*

The great French novelist is given a heroic, monumental ugliness. This is hardly camera-eye realism — Balzac wasn't that grotesque — but it captures a personality that strikes us even if we don't know the man. Wrapped in a long cloak, he thrusts his head out at a defiant angle, showing the strong individualism and egoism of the 19th-century Romantic movement. Balzac is proud and snooty — but his body forms a question mark, and underneath the twisted features we can see a touch of personal pain and self-doubt.

RODIN — Balzac. Rodin combines classical solidity with the rough finish of an Impressionist painting.

From this perch, look over the main floor at all the classical statues between you and the big clock, and realize how far we've come — not in years, but in style changes. Many of the statues below — beautiful, smooth, balanced, and idealized — were done at the same time as Rodin's powerful, haunting works. Rodin is a good place to end the tour — with a stable base of 19th-century stone, he launched art into the 20th century.

Pompidou Modern Art Museum, Paris

More people visit the Pompidou than any other sight in France. Really. Not just because it's (possibly) Europe's best museum of twentieth-century art but because it's an artistic kick in the pants. After the super-serious Louvre and Orsay, go to the Pompidou to have some fun. You won't find classical beauty here, no dreamy Madonnas-and-Children — just a stimulating, offbeat (and, if you like, instructive) walk through nearly every art style of our wild and crazy century.

The Musée National d'Art Moderne in the Centre National d'Art et Culture Georges Pompidou

Hours: Mon., Wed., Thurs., Fri. 12:00-22:00; Sat., Sun. 10:00-22:00; closed Tuesday.

Cost (for permanent collection): 28 F; under 18, free; 18-24 and over 60, 18 F. Sundays free until 14:00.

One-day pass (50 F) gets you into all the building's exhibits.

Tour length: An hour.

Getting there: Metro: Rambuteau. The wild, color-coded exterior makes it about as hard to locate as the Eiffel Tower.

Information: Tel. 4277-1233 or 362-WILD.

Misc.: Cafeteria and restaurant with great views on the fifth floor. Great café neighborhood.

Parisians call the Pompidou "Centre Beaubourg" (pron: boh-BOOR).

Starring: Matisse, Picasso, Chagall, Dali, Warhol.

The Exterior

☞ *View this colorful building from the main square in front.*
That slight tremor you may feel comes from Italy, where Michelangelo has been spinning in his grave at a constant 78 rpms, ever since 1977 when the Pompidou Center first revolted Paris. The Pompidou is a far and mournful cry from Renaissance beauty. But it's an appropriate modern temple for the controversial art it houses.

The building is exoskeletal, with its functional parts — the pipes, heating ducts, and intestinelike escalator — on the outside. This frees up more interior space for displaying art. It's the epitome of modern architecture where "form follows function"; that is, how it looks is secondary to how well it works.

Before judging the Pompidou too harshly, compare it with another famous exoskeletal building here in Paris. It also has its structural elements sticking out the sides in order to make the interior more spacious and full of light. Renaissance artists called this building barbaric and strained, an unstable tangle of angle and lines. We call it Notre-Dame.

☞ *Enjoy the street performers in the square, run through the sprinklers at the colorful Homage to Stravinsky fountain in the square off to the right, and count the seconds down to the next millennium. Then enter and lose your bearings.*

Orientation

The permanent collection (*collection permanente*), which is what we'll see, is on the fourth floor reached by the escalator. But there's plenty more art scattered all over the building, some free, some requiring a separate ticket. Ask at the information booth or just wander. These temporary exhibits are your chance to see the art that will hang over your great-grandchildren's sofas.

The "permanent" collection... isn't. Because the collection changes so often, this chapter will be less of a room-by-room, turn-right-at-the-Madonna tour and more of a general overview of modern art.

☞ *Buy your ticket, then ride up the escalator (or run up the down-scalator to get in the proper mood). When you see the view, your opinion of the Pompidou's exterior should improve a good 15%.*

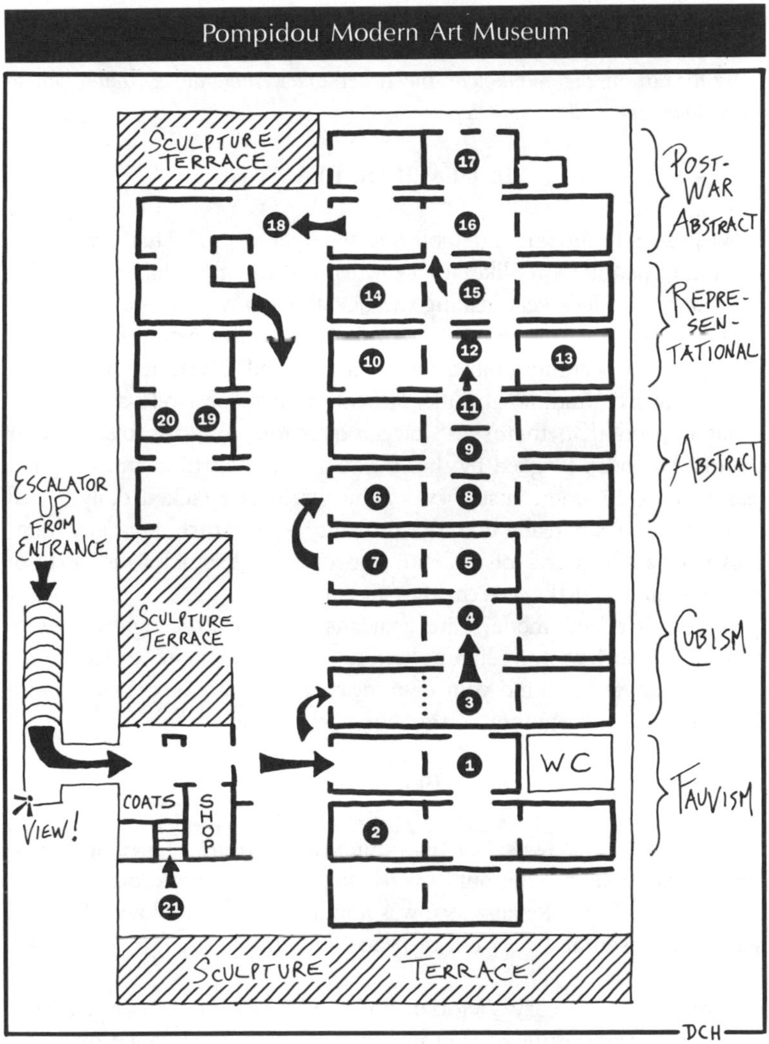

Pompidou Modern Art Museum

FAUVISM
1. Matisse
2. Fauvism

CUBISM
3. Braque and Picasso
4. Later Picasso
5. Leger

ABSTRACT
6. Kandinsky
7. Mondrian
8. Brancusi
9. Klee

REPRESENTATIONAL
10. Expressionism
11. Dada
12. Chagall
13. Rouault
14. Surrealism—Dali

POST-WAR ABSTRACT
15. Miró, Calder, Arp
16. "Patterns and Textures"—Dubuffet
17. Giacometti
18. Abstract—Pollock
19. Design
20. Pop Art
21. Contemporary Collection (3rd floor)

You're looking for the "Musee National d'Art Moderne. Collection Permanente," on the fourth floor.
We'll start in the room near the ticket-taker, then move from room to room down the hall to your left.

THE DEATH OF REALITY

Why doesn't modern art look like the real world? That's the thing that many people don't like about it. It's also exactly what modern art is all about, so let's keep asking the question as we go.

The most obvious response is, if you want reality, get a camera. And if you want a beautiful object, buy it at the mall. Machines have taken over the artist's traditional duties, freeing him to be irrelevant.

But beyond that, there's the bigger question: What *is* reality? Our century has been plagued by that question like no other, and for good reason. Our commonsense view of the world is attacked daily on all fronts. Modern art really *does* reflect reality — the turbulent, anything-goes reality of our end-of-millennium world. It chronicles the death of an old reality and the search for a new one.

If you don't "get" modern art, it means you're on the right track. It's meant to disorient and disrupt our normal outlook, in order to see things in a new way. Find your own meaning. You are a co-creator with the artist and a co-author of this chapter.

1900 A.D.

A new century dawns. War is a thing of the past. Science and technology would soon wipe out poverty and disease. The knowledge that began to bud in the Renaissance was about to reach full flower. Rational Man was poised at a new era of peace and prosperity. . .

Right.

Even before this cozy Victorian dream was shattered by World War, the ground was starting to shift underneath. Darwin stripped off man's robe of culture and found a naked ape beneath. Nietszche murdered God. Freud washed ashore on the beach of a vast new continent, inside each of us. Einstein made every truth merely "relative". Even the fundamental building blocks of the universe, atoms, were behaving erratically.

Technology arrived, but instead of bringing the promised paradise, it brought noise, pollution and ugliness. Worst of all, fast-paced modern life was turning people into robots, leading lives that were empty, programmed and sterile.

Progress was killing them, rationality was approaching a dead-end, and artists were looking for an alternative. They weren't just exploring new art techniques. They were looking for a whole new approach to life.

☞ *Enter the rooms nearest the ticket-taker.*

FAUVISM — Wild Beasts
(Matisse, Derain, Vlaminck, early Braque)

Matisse

Bam. Right off the bat, we know we're not in Kansas anymore. Matisse's colorful, "wallpaper" works are a far cry from the realistic paintings at the Louvre. Most do have a recognizable subject, but the figures are simplified (almost childlike) and distorted, and the colors are unnatural. Also, Matisse obviously didn't try very hard to create the illusion of distance and 3-D that was so important to the Renaissance Italians.

MATISSE — Sadness of the King. Matisse's bright colors and flat style make this more like wallpaper than a 3-D scene. It's best to look "at" this canvas rather than "through" it.

Traditionally, the canvas was like a window that you looked "through" to see a slice of the real world stretching off into the distance. If you try to look "through" a Matisse canvas, you won't get very far. Instead, try looking "at" it, like it was wallpaper. Voila! What was a crudely drawn scene now becomes a sophisticated and decorative pattern of colors and shapes.

☞ *Find the room to the right with works by Matisse's fellow Fauves.*

More Fauves

Matisse was one of the Fauves, or "wild beasts," who tried to inject a bit of the jungle into bored French society. Their style was intentionally crude, with bright, clashing colors. The mask-like faces came from African art and voodoo dolls.

The Fauves were to art what Louis Armstrong was to music and Josephine Baker's topless "Savage Dance" to dance — an attempt to reconnect rational man with his primitive roots.

The Fauves are still painting the real world, but the subject matter is starting to get lost in the blur of paints (think also of Monet's gauzy water lilies and cathedrals). Soon, artists would drop the subject altogether, finding beauty in the colors and shapes themselves — Abstract Art.

And like Cézanne, the Fauves "built" objects using dabs of paint. In early works by Georges Braque ("Le Viaduc a l'Estaque"), he builds his houses with geometrical slabs, early "Cube"-ism.

The Artist as Shaman

Science toppled Man from his place at the pinnacle of the universe. Technology stripped the world bare of mystery, leaving a gray landscape of smoking factories and machines, with man as just another puny cog.

Something was missing. Artists tried to rekindle a sense of wonder in life. They saw art as a way to express some of the — how do I say it? — the holiness? mystery? magic? — that had been lost. With traditional Christianity losing ground, art became a new religion.

They found inspiration in the native peoples of Africa, the South Seas, and Asia, those with "primitive" technologies. Their simple art reflected a whole different outlook, a voodoo world inhabited by spirits and demons.

The modern artist became like their shamans — a wild holy man, living different from "normal" people, who enters a trance connecting him to the hidden world, then "channels" it to us through his art.

The result? Modern art that looked primitive: simple figures, mask-like faces with geometric features, and "flat", two-dimensional scenes.

Artists adopting a more primitive attitude makes some sense, but why return to crude techniques that don't portray the real world? Let's return to that Reality Thing.

3-D — A Western Obsession?

Which is closer — a bear cub at your feet or the mama bear a hundred yards away who's charging at you? If you're painting that scene and want it to reflect your actual experience, you'd make mama huge, terrifying and very close.

Three-dimensional space is just one way to orient ourselves in the world. Renaissance artists seized on 3-D to emphasize a distinct Western trait. We tend to focus our attention strongly on one object (placed prominently in the foreground, center), while we neglect its surroundings (the background).

In art from other cultures, however, the "main" figure is often enmeshed in the web of its surroundings. We see it in context, as part of the big picture, not isolated. Primitive art is less visual, but more visceral and emotional, coming from lower down the brain stem. When the full moon stirs your blood at night, it's so "close" you could hit it with a rock.

☞ *Return to the main hall, then start down toward the far (south end). Take your first right into the Cubist rooms, with several brown Braques.*

CUBISM — Reality Shattered
(Picasso, Braque, Leger, Gris, Picabia)

I throw a rock at a statue made of glass, shatter it, pick up the pieces and glue them onto a canvas. I'm a Cubist.

Braque and Picasso

Braque sees the world through a kaleidoscope of brown and gray. The subjects are somewhat recognizable (with the help of the titles), but they're broken into geometric shards — let's call them "cubes", though there are many different shapes — then pieced back together.

The shards often overlap. More distant objects end up as close to the viewer as near ones. A single shard might contain both an object and the background behind it, both painted the same color. The foreground and background are woven together, destroying the illusion of 3-D and creating interesting new patterns.

Cubism gives us several different sides of the subject at once. For example, to paint a woman's head, Picasso might show us a front view and a side profile together. The result is a face with both eyes on the same side of the nose.

Okay, it's all very interesting, but what's the point?

They were simply taking a new approach to an age-old question, how to paint a three-dimensional world on a two-dimensional canvas. The Cubist "solution" is a kind of Mercator map projection, where the

BRAQUE — Woman with a Guitar.
The Cubists shattered the 3-D world then placed the shards onto a 2-D canvas.
Braque did what all the king's horses and all the king's men couldn't.

round world is pressed flat. (Think of trying to slice up an orange peel so it will lay flat.)

But there's more to Cubism. Traditional art always presented an orderly world, where the most important object sits right up front center, and the less important things are in the distance.

But in fact, life is rarely so orderly. Our attention darts from one thing to the next — from the woman's eyes to her profile to the wall behind her to the guitar in her lap to a memory from childhood and back. It's up to the brain to piece together the flickering snapshots it receives. Cubism simply paints this jumble of sense-data in its raw random form.

Picasso and Braque were shattering the whole Renaissance tradition of realism in art at the same time that science was overturning the three-dimensional space that went with it. Einstein told us there was actually a fourth dimension — time. We experience this dimension when we, say, take 15 seconds to walk around a 3-D object. Picasso saves us the trouble by showing several views at once, translating that fourth dimension into something we can see on a canvas.

☞   *Enter the adjoining room, full of Picassos.*

Pablo Picasso (1881-1973)

Okay, so the Cubists were smarter than Einstein. But why couldn't they draw a picture to save their lives?

Picasso was one modern artist who really could draw and draw well (see his partly finished "Harlequin [Arlequin, 1923]"). But he wasn't content to crank out paintings that look great with a sofa underneath. He constantly explored and adapted his style to new trends, becoming the most famous painter of our century. In these rooms you can stroll through his life and the many styles that influenced artists that followed.

Born in Spain, Picasso moved to Paris as a young man. At first, he felt out of place and lonely, and he painted his fellow loners — thin beggars and haunted outcasts. The dark colors and melancholy mood make this his "Blue" period.

Then he met Georges Braque, and these two modern-day shamans locked themselves into a Paris studio together. They worked on each other's paintings — it's hard to tell whose is whose without the titles — and shared meals, ideas and girlfriends.

Soon Picasso began to build his figures using slabs of overlapping color rather than basic brown cubes. Eventually (1917-1925), he used curved shapes to build the subject, rather than the straight-line, rectangular shapes of early Cubism.

Picasso married and had children. Works from this period (the 1920s) are more realistic, with full-bodied (and big-nosed) women and children, where he tries to capture the solidity, serenity and volume of classical statues.

As his relationships with women deteriorated, he vented his sexual demons by twisting the female body into grotesque balloon-animal shapes (1925-1931).

All through his life, Picasso was always exploring new materials. He made collages, tried his hand at "statues" out of wood, wire, or whatever, and pioneered the use of ready-made objects to build a form (like his famous bull's head made of a bicycle seat with handlebars for horns). These "multimedia" works, so revolutionary at the time, have become stock-in-trade today.

☞ *Enter the next room.*

Leger

Fernand Leger's style has been called "Tubism" — breaking the world down into cylinder shapes rather than cubes. (He supposedly got his inspiration during World War I from the gleaming barrel of a cannon.) Leger captures the feel of the encroaching Age of Machines, with all the world looking like an internal combustion engine.

☞ *Exit Leger into the main hallway and take a breather. The sculpture garden outside is fun. I like the mythical nuclear family — minotaur, mermaid and child.*

Abstract versus Representational

Cubism is a combination of the two main trends in 20th century art. On the one hand, it's "representational", that is, it represents or depicts the real world — a chair, a woman with a guitar, and so on. On the other, it's "abstract", playing with patterns of lines, shapes and colors.

Another way to put it: with representational art you look "through" the canvas like a window. With abstract you look "at" it.

We'll see examples of each of these, though most modern art — like Cubism — is a combination of the two.

ABSTRACT ART — Painting the Hidden Reality
(Kandinsky, Mondrian, Brancusi, Klee)

Abstract art tries to express an idea or feeling through colors and shapes alone. Madison Avenue ad-men are fully aware of the power that a certain color or shape has to make us feel something — red gets us excited, blue calms us, jagged lines suggest turmoil, and so on. Abstract artists use this knowledge of the psychological effects of color and line to try to show on a canvas some of the nonvisual and hidden elements of the world.

What is the "hidden" world? Well, the world of emotions. The world of sounds, smells, taste and touch, things that, while not exactly hidden, are at least nonvisual. Certain abstract concepts like "justice", "beauty" and "2 + 2 = 4" can't be seen, but you could argue that they're real. And finally, there's the world that's been lost in our secular age — the world of holiness, magic, of spirits and demons and angels. All these things may be just as real — and certainly as powerful — as the tables, chairs, nudes and landscapes of realistic painting. But, being unseen, the best way to show them is using abstract designs.

☞   *Enter the next room.*

Kandinsky

The bright colors, bent lines and lack of symmetry tell us that Kandinsky's world was passionate, emotional and intense.

Life assaults our senses in a jumble of sights, sounds and smells. In order to cope, we learn how to simplify and classify it all. Traditionally, the artist helped us find some order out of life's chaos. But nowadays, most of us already live in a programmed, regimented, climate-controlled environment where everything's sorted out for us. So, Kandinsky gives us a slice of the chaotic before it's been tamed and predigested. I don't think he could have done that as well by using recognizable figures.

Notice the titles — "Improvisation", "Composition". Kandinsky was inspired by music, another "abstract" medium that can have a deep emotional impact without portraying any literal reality. Like a jazz musician improvising a new pattern of notes from a set scale, Kandinsky plays with new patterns of related colors, looking for just the right combination that makes us yell, "Go man, go!" (And some paintings, like some songs, "work" for one viewer while to others it's just noise.) Using line and color, Kandinsky translates the unseen reality into a new medium . . . like lightning crackling over the radio.

Mondrian

Reality in the raw may be chaotic, but humans long for order. We find symmetry attractive (maybe because our own bodies are roughly symmetrical) and geometric shapes restful, even worthy of meditation.

Mondrian's T-square style boils painting down to its basic building blocks — black lines, white canvas and the three primary colors. He then arranges them into orderly patterns.

When you come right down to it, that's all painting ever has been, even with Leonardo or Raphael. The only difference is that Renaissance artists made orderly patterns using recognizable people, places and things. If you've ever seen a schematic drawing of, say, the Mona Lisa, you'll know that it's less about a woman than about the triangles and rectangles that she's composed of.

(Are Mondrian's shapes based on anything in the real world? Well, he started out painting realistic landscapes of the orderly fields in his native Holland. Hmm.)

Mondrian appeals to our most basic instinct for order, the instinct that has driven art from earliest times, from the Egyptian pyramids to Stonehenge circles to flanking Greek columns to Roman arches to Renaissance symmetry to the American Indian medicine "wheel".

Brancusi

Imagine how a cave man might feel stumbling across one of Brancusi's curved, shiny statues gleaming in an open field. Think of the sense of wonder, that such a smooth, orderly, confident, geometric form could have emerged out of a rough rock, a tree stump or crude metal. Even for us, the very simplicity strikes us on a primitive level, deep in our collective unconscious, taking us back to a time when sculpture was the ritual circumcision of stones.

Brancusi shows the power of reducing things to their essence. A bird, for example, is shown by the one feature that sets it apart from other animals — a wing, represented by a curved line. This process of "abstracting" general traits from specific objects is what abstract art is about.

The simplicity reminds us that there's more to life than meets the eye. Brancusi doesn't pretend that he's showing us the whole bird. We think instead of what we don't see — the infinite wealth of details that no artist could ever capture. And beyond that, there's the mystery of the "hidden" world — emotions, memories, spirits and demons — that affects us even more than the things we see. What Brancusi leaves out, we fill in.

Klee

Paul Klee's small and playful canvases are deceptively simple.

Klee thought certain shapes were so basic they could be read like universal symbols; think of our modern international traffic symbols. For example, a wavy line would always suggest the idea of motion, and a stick-figure would always mean a human. By the way, Klee's fellow

Swiss, the psychologist Carl Jung, also spoke of universal symbols found in dreams and stories, all part of our "collective unconscious".

But which shapes are truly universal? Klee found a clue in the art of children, and we can see a lot of their playfulness, fantasy and simple figures in his work. Children express themselves more honestly, without censoring their creativity or cluttering it up with learned symbols. If the artist can get in the same uninhibited frame of mind, he too can "channel" the creative impulse. For Klee, the same forces of nature that cause the wave to draw a line of foam on the beach, can cause the artist to draw a line of paint on the canvas. The result is a universal shape. In other words, the true artist doesn't paint Nature, he becomes Nature.

☞ *In the next few rooms, you'll find examples of Dada, Expressionism and the work of Chagall and Rouault.*

REPRESENTATIONAL ART
(Expressionism, Dada, Chagall, Rouault, Dali)

Not every modern artist turned his back on the real world. But camera-eye realism was obsolete. Artists purposely distorted their subjects for effect, to let us see it with fresh eyes.

In a sense, every painting has two "subjects": (1) the subject itself (a chair, a nude woman, a landscape), and (2) the mood or message it conveys. Modern artists are free to distort subject #1 to enhance or clarify #2.

A painting lets us look at the world through the artist's eyes. Sometimes it looks distorted to us, like looking through someone else's glasses. The French writer Proust once said, "Only through art can we get outside ourselves and know another's view of the universe."

World War I — The Death of Values

A soldier shivers in a trench, ankle deep in mud, waiting to be ordered "over the top", to run through barbed-wire, over fallen comrades, and into a hail of machine-gun fire, only to capture a few hundred yards of meaningless territory that would be lost the next day. This soldier was not thinking about art.

World War I left 9 million dead. (France often lost more men in a single day than America lost in all of Vietnam.) The war also killed the optimism and faith in Man that had guided Europe since the Renaissance. Now, rationality just meant scheming, technology meant more machines of death, and morality meant giving your life in an empty cause.

Expressionism — Grosz, Kirchner, Beckmann, Kokoschka

Cynicism and decadence settled over postwar Europe. Artists expressed their disgust by showing a distorted reality that emphasized the ugly. Using the lurid colors and simplified figures of the Fauves, they slapped paint on in thick brushstrokes. This was a new kind of Primitivism — a barbaric, hard-edged, dog-eat-dog world that had lost its bearings. The people have a haunted look in their eyes, the fixed stare of corpses and of those who must bury them.

Dada

When they could grieve no longer, they turned from crying to its giddy twin, laughter. The war killed Renaissance civilization, and all old values became a joke, including artistic ones. The Dada movement, choosing a purposely childish name, made art that was appropriately absurd: a moustache on the Mona Lisa, a shovel hung on the wall with a serious title, or Duchamp's modern version of a Renaissance "Fountain" — a urinal.

It was a dig at all the pompous prewar artistic theories based on the noble intellect of Rational Man. While the experts ranted on, Dadaists sat in the back of the class and made cultural fart noises.

Hey, I love this stuff. My mind says it's sophomoric, but my heart belongs to Dada.

Chagall

Marc Chagall views the world with the wide-eyed wonder of a country boy. Lovers are weightless with bliss. Animals smile and wink at us. Musicians, poets, peasants and dreamers ignore gravity, tumbling in slow-motion circles high above the rooftops. The colors are deep, dark and earthy — a pool of mystery that suggests that if we could plunge in we'd find still more treasures.

Chagall's very personal style fuses many influences. He was raised in a small Russian village, which may explain his "naive" outlook and fiddler-on-the-roof motifs. He paints recognizable things, but they're more like universal symbols (remember Klee?) than specific, real-life objects. Since his upbringing was Orthodox Jewish, Chagall learned early the power of "graven images".

Stylistically, he "builds" his figures like a Cubist, and scatters them in a jumble of images that often overlap. In his early Paris days, he was so poor he had to paint over used canvases — could that explain some of the "double-exposure" effect? And finally, the way he puts powerful images side by side without explaining their connection is something that would later be called Surrealism.

Chagall wasn't just using these techniques for their own sake but to make visible the "hidden", magical aspects of life. This made him a natural for religious works, and his murals and stained glass, with both Jewish and Christian motifs, decorate buildings around the world.

(If you want more Chagall, visit Paris's Garnier Opera House [Metro: Opera] to see his colorful and completely incongruous ceiling painting that somehow works.)

Rouault

Georges Rouault's father made stained-glass windows. Enough said?

The paintings have the same thick, glowing colors, heavy black out lines, simple subjects and (mostly) religious themes. The style is Expressionist, but the mood is medieval, solemn and melancholy. Rouault captures the tragic spirit of those people — clowns, prostitutes and Sons of God — who have been made outcasts by a secular society.

Surrealism — Dali, Magritte, Ernst, de Chirico, Tanguy

Surrealism is a version of connect-the-dots with no numbers. The artist scatters seemingly unrelated images on the canvas, leaving it to us to trace the connection between them. When it does come together, the synergy of unrelated things can be pretty startling. But even if the "juxtaposed" images don't ultimately connect, the artist has achieved one thing: he's made you think, rerouting your thoughts through new neural paths as you try vainly to relate unrelated things. Like with Dada and so much other modern art, if you don't "get" it, you got it.

Dali

Salvador Dali could draw exceptionally well. He painted "unreal" scenes with photographic realism, making us believe they could really happen. Seeing familiar objects in an unfamiliar setting — like a grand piano adorned with disembodied heads of Lenin — creates an air of mystery, the feeling that anything can happen. That feeling is both liberating and unsettling. Dali's images usually pack an emotional punch, things like crucifixes, political and religious figures, and naked bodies.

Many a Surrealist canvas is a "landscape" of the artist's inner world, painted in a stream-of-consciousness frame of mind where nothing is censored. Dreams are a big inspiration. Freud said that the bizarre images of dreams were not just silly fantasies but actually reveal our deepest urges, uncensored by the waking mind.

In dreams, sometimes one object can be two things at once. "I dreamt that you walked in with a cat. . . no, wait, maybe you were the cat. . . no. . ."

DALI — Partial Hallucination: Six Images of Lenin on a Piano. Realistic images side by side in an unreal setting make us think in a new way. What's the connection between Lenin's head and the keyboard?

Surrealists take opposites like these and combine them, like in a dream. Shoes become feet, Greek statues wear sunglasses, and black ants act as musical notes.

Abstract, with a Twist of Surreal — Miró, Calder, Arp

Abstract artists revealed their subconscious using color and shapes alone, kind of like Rorschach inkblots in reverse.

The thin-line scrawl of Joan Miró's work is like the noodling of a three-year-old. You'll recognize crudely drawn birds, stars, animals and strange cell-like creatures with whiskers ("Biological Cubism"). Miró, like Klee, was trying to express the most basic of human emotions, using the most basic of techniques.

Alexander Calder's mobiles hang like Mirós in the sky, waiting for a gust of wind to bring them to life.)

And talk about a primal image! Jean Arp uses amoeba-like shapes to make vaguely recognizable things: "Female Dancer", "Peasant's Head", "Head, Moustache and Bottle", and so on.

POST-WORLD WAR II

Patterns and Textures

As we leave representational art, we have to refocus our eyes once again, looking "at" the canvases, not "through" them. And with that, I hereby retire those prepositions.

We'll enjoy the lines and colors, but let's add a new element — texture. Many works have very thick paint in which you can see the brushstroke clearly. Some have substances besides paint applied to the canvas, like Dubuffet's brown, earthy rectangles of real dirt and organic wastes. Increasingly, art becomes more multimedia (remember Picasso's collages), and we need to pay attention to the materials themselves. Think of the canvas as a tray, serving up a delightful array of different substances with interesting colors, patterns, shapes and textures.

Giacometti

Giacometti's most distinctive statues have the emaciated, haunted and faceless look of concentration camp survivors. Their simplicity is "Primitive", but these aren't stately, sturdy Easter Island heads. Man is weak in the face of technology and the winds of history.

Abstract Expressionism — Pollock, Newman, Rothko, Rauschenberg

America emerged from World War II as the globe's superpower. With Europe in ruins, New York replaced Paris as the art capital. The trend was toward bigger canvases, abstract designs and experimentation with new materials and techniques.

We can get a handle on "Abstract Expressionism" from what we've already seen. It's a way to express strong emotions using color and form alone.

Jackson Pollock

"Jack the Dripper" attacks convention with a can of paint, dripping and splashing a dense web onto the canvas. Picture Pollock in his studio, leaping about, flinging paint in a moment of enlightenment. Of course, the artist loses some control this way — over the paint flying in mid-air and over himself in an ecstatic trance. Painting becomes a whole-body activity, a "dance" between the artist and the elements.

The act of creating is what's important, not the final product. The canvas is only a record of that moment of ecstasy.

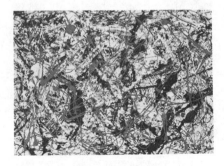

POLLOCK — Peinture. A mess. "Jack the Dripper" attacks convention with a can of paint. His canvases are not a "window" to see through but a "tray" of interesting patterns and textures.

Big, Empty Canvases

All those big, empty canvases with just a few lines or colors — what reality are they trying to show?

Modern man finds himself an insignificant speck in a vast and indifferent universe. Each of us must confront that universe and decide how we're going to make our mark on it. The Existentialist artist confronts the huge, blank canvas in the same way.

Like wow. Another influence on artists was the simplicity of Japanese landscape painting. A Zen master studies and meditates for years to achieve the state of mind in which he can draw one pure line. These canvases, again, are only a record of that state of enlightenment. (What is the sound of one brush painting?)

On more familiar ground, postwar painters were following in the footsteps of artists like Mondrian, Klee and Kandinsky (whose work they must have considered busy). The geometrical forms here reflect the same search for order, but these artists painted to the 5/4 symmetry of "Take Five".

Pop Art

Pop Art is created from the "pop"-ular objects of our everyday throwaway society — a soup can, a car fender, mannequins, tacky plastic statues, movie icons, advertising posters. Take something out of Sears and hang it in a museum, and you have to think about it in a whole different way.

Is this art? Are these mass-produced objects beautiful? Or crap? If not art, why do we work so hard to acquire them? Pop art, like Dada, makes us question our society's values.

Andy Warhol concentrated on another mass-produced phenomenon — celebrities. He took publicity photos of famous people and repeated them. The repetition, like the constant bombardment we get from repeated images on TV, cheapens even the most beautiful things.

Design

If you can't handle modern art, sit on it. Chairs, tables, lamps and vases (the applied arts) are as much a part of the art world as the fine ones. (Some say the first art object was the pot.) This is one area where artists can embrace new technology and mass production.

☞ *Your ticket is also good for the contemporary collection on the third floor. You reach it by way of an escalator (not the one you came up on), located back past the ticket-taker and to the right.*

THE CONTEMPORARY COLLECTION

The modern world is history. Picasso and his ilk are now gathering dust and boring art students everywhere. Let's enter the postmodern world as seen through the eyes of current artists.

You'll see very few traditional canvases. Artists have traded paintbrushes for blowtorches, exploring new materials and new media. (Miró said he was out to "murder" painting.) Mixed-media work is the norm, combining painting, sculpture, photography, welding, film/

slides/video, lighting and sound systems.

One of the "new" materials is using ready-made objects ("found art"), especially the mass-produced, throwaway things we saw in Pop Art and Dada. Artists raid the dumpster, recycling junk into the building-blocks for a larger "assemblage".

Modern artists critique (or deconstruct) society by examining things that are so familiar that we take them for granted. They'll take an object loaded with meaning (a crucifix, for example), remove it from its familiar circumstances (in a church) and put it in a new one (in a jar of urine, to cite one notorious art project). If we now see that object in a different way, it's a reminder that we have beliefs so fundamental that we may never have questioned them.

Installations

An entire room is given to an artist to prepare as he chooses. It's like an art funhouse, where we walk in without quite knowing what to expect. (In the back of my mind, I'm always thinking, Is this safe?) The artist has our complete attention, and we enter without any preconceptions, maybe even with something like the sense of wonder that "Primitives" are supposed to have. The artist engages all our senses, controlling the lights, sounds and sometimes even smells, using the latest technology.

As we explore the room, we are now active participants rather than just passive observers.

Interaction

Some exhibits require your participation, whether it's pushing a button to get the contraption going or just walking around the room or touching something. In some cases, the viewer does art, not just stares at it. If art is really meant to change us, it has to get us involved.

Many artists that in another day and age would have been painting canvases are turning to the performing arts — music, dance, theater and "performance art", which is the mixed-media of live performance. These too have become more interactive, dropping the illusion of a performance and encouraging audience participation. When you finish with the Pompidou, go back outside for some of the live street performers and to see how tame the Homage to Stravinsky fountain now looks.

Versailles, Near Paris

If you've ever wondered why your American passport has French writing in it, you'll find the answer at Versailles. The powerful court of Louis XIV at Versailles set the standard of culture for all of Europe right up to modern times. Versailles was every king's dream palace, and today, if you're planning to visit just one palace in all of Europe, make it Versailles.

Château de Versailles (pron: vehr-SIGH)

Hours: Tues.-Sun. 9:00-18:30; closed Mon. and holidays.

Cost: 31 F; under 18 — free; 18-25 and over 60 — 16 F.
Tours "A" and "B" are an extra 30 F.
Grounds free.

Tour length: Six hours round-trip from Paris (2 in transit, 2 palace, 2 grounds).

Getting there: Take the RER train (40 minutes) to "Versailles R.G." (end of the line). Leaves from RER/Metro stop "Invalides", "Gare d' Austerlitz" or "St. Michel" (20 F r/t). Then walk 10 minutes to the palace.

Information: Information booths at entrances to tour A and B (the two guided tours organized by Versailles).
Best guidebook — *Versailles: The Châteaux, the Gardens, and Trianon.*
English tours to private apartments leave throughout the day.
Tel. 30-84-7400 or 30-84-7618.

Misc.: WC, phones, and cafeteria on opposite side of building from Tour C entrance.

Fountains play at 3:30 each summer Sunday.

Restaurants down the street to right of equestrian statue.

Most crowded on Tuesdays and Sundays daily around 10:00 and 13:00. Less crowded at 9:00 and after 15:00.

Guided tour A gets you into the palace without the long line.

Remember, the crowds gave Marie-Antoinette a pain in the neck too, so relax and let them eat cake.

Starring: Louis XIV and the Old Regime.

Orientation

☞ *Read this on the train ride out there.*

Come the Revolution, when they line us up and make us stick out our hands, will you have enough calluses to keep them from shooting you? A grim thought, I know, but Versailles raises questions like that. It's the symbol of the wealthy Old Regime, where society was divided into the rulers and the ruled, the rich and the poor. To some, it's the pinnacle of civilization, to others the sign of a civilization in decay. Either way, it remains one of Europe's most impressive sights.

Versailles was the residence of the King and seat of France's government for a hundred years. Louis XIV (reigned 1643-1715) moved out of the Louvre in Paris, the previous royal residence, and slowly built up an elaborate palace in the forests and swamps of Versailles, 12 miles west. The reasons for the move were partly personal — Louis loved the outdoors and disliked the sniping environs of stuffy Paris — and partly politics.

Louis was creating the first modern, centralized state. At Versailles he consolidated Paris' scattered ministries, so he could personally control policy. More importantly, he invited to Versailles all of France's nobles, where he could control them. Living a life of almost enforced idleness, the aristocracy couldn't interfere with the way Louis ran things. With 18 million people united under one king (England had only 5.5 million), a booming economy and a powerful military, France became Europe's #1 power.

Versailles was the cultural heartbeat of Europe. Every king wanted a palace like Versailles. Everyone learned French. French taste in clothes, hairstyles, table manners, theater, music, art and kissing spread across the Continent. That cultural dominance has continued, to some extent, right up to the present.

Louis XIV

At the center of all this was Europe's greatest king. He was a true

Renaissance man a century after the Renaissance — athletic, good looking, a musician, dancer, horseman, statesman, art lover, lover. For all his grandeur, he was one of history's most polite and approachable kings, a good listener, who could put even commoners at ease in his presence.

Louis called himself the Sun King, because, like the sun, he gave life and warmth to all that he touched. He was also thought of as Apollo, the Greek god of the sun. Versailles became the personal temple of this god on earth, decorated with statues and symbols of Apollo and the sun.

Louis was a hands-on king, who personally ran affairs of state. All decisions were made by him. Nobles, who in other countries were the center of power, became virtual slaves dependent on Louis' generosity. For 70 years he was the perfect embodiment of the absolute monarch. He summed it up best himself with his famous rhyme — "L'etat, c'est moi!" ("I am the state").

Only Two More "Louis" To Remember

Three kings lived in Versailles during its century of glory. Louis XIV built it and established French dominance. Louis XV, his great- grandson (remember, Louis XIV reigned for 72 years), carried on the tradition and policies but without the Sun King's flair. France's power abroad was weakening and there were rumblings of rebellion from within.

France's monarchy was crumbling, and the time was ripe for a strong leader to re-establish the old feudal order. They didn't get one. They got Louis XVI instead, a shy, meek bookworm, the kind of guy who lost sleep over Revolutionary graffiti...because it was misspelled. Louis XVI married a sweet girl from the Austrian royal family, Marie-Antoinette, and together they retreated into the idyllic gardens of Versailles while Revolutionary fires smoldered.

They finally got their rude awakening in October 1789, when a mob of angry Parisians stormed the palace, trashed it and kidnapped the Royal Family, taking them back to Paris. Four years later they lost their heads under the guillotine, and the Old Regime was dead. No longer the center of Europe, Versailles became a museum.

☞ *Leave the Versailles R.G. train station to the right, walk about a hundred yards, then take your first left, making the grand approach, over Europe's biggest cobblestones, up to the palace. Enter the iron-work gates and stop at the equestrian statue in the middle of the large court. (Or get in line for either Tour A or this self-guided Tour C. Or just step into the shade, but orient yourself from the statue.)*

We'll see the palace, where the kings and queens lived and entertained, and the extensive grounds. The only way to see the "King's Apartments" — the actual bedroom and private rooms — is with the guided tour

(Tour A). The advantages of this tour are: 1) these rooms are more lavishly furnished than the ones we'll see; 2) you visit the Opera House, the single most stunning place in the whole complex; and 3) most importantly, it gets you into the palace (where you can then take this self-guided tour), without standing in line quite so long.

The disadvantages: 1) it costs more; 2) it takes an hour and a half, sometimes with a boring guide; and 3) you see pretty much the same things we'll see. All in all, I recommend it, if you have the time — do it first to get into the palace quicker. For true Versailles-philes, there are two more guided tours of other parts of the palace.

The central palace, the part we'll tour, forms a U around the courtyard in front of you. The right half, known as the King's Wing, is separated from the left half (Queen's Wing) by the Hall of Mirrors ahead of you. Then two long wings shoot out to the right and left (north and south) of this U. In our self-guided tour, we'll walk through the U-shaped part on the middle floor.

The entrance (Tour C) is on the right side of the courtyard — where the line is. The entrance to the guided tours (Tours A and B) is on the left side in an alleyway. The gardens are behind the palace.

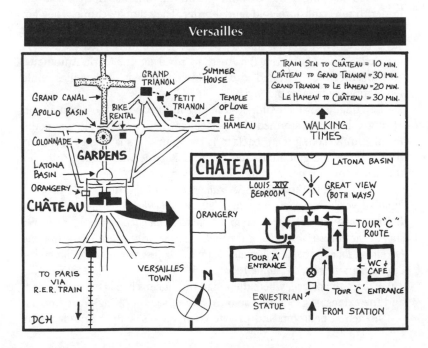

Versailles

TRAIN STN TO CHÂTEAU = 10 MIN.
CHÂTEAU TO GRAND TRIANON = 30 MIN.
GRAND TRIANON TO LE HAMEAU = 20 MIN.
LE HAMEAU TO CHÂTEAU = 30 MIN.

WALKING TIMES

THE ORIGINAL CHÂTEAU

The part of the palace directly in front of you, at the far end of the courtyard, is the original château. Louis XIV's dad used to come out to the forests of Versailles to escape the worries of kingship. Here he built this small hunting lodge. His son spent the happiest times of his boyhood at the lodge, hunting and riding. Louis' bedroom overlooked what is now the courtyard — it's the three arched windows beneath the clock.

When he became king, Louis spent more and more time here, away from the hubbub of Paris. He expanded the lodge, planted gardens and began to entertain guests. The reputation spread about this "Enchanted Island", a kind of Disney World for dukes and duchesses. As visitors flocked here, more buildings were needed to accommodate them.

Louis' architects made plans to demolish this original hunting château, but Louis apparently couldn't bear to destroy all the happy memories. Instead, they kept the château and expanded around it, attaching wings to create the present U-shape. When still more nobles arrived, the long north and south wings were built. The total cost of the project amounted to half of France's entire GNP for one year.

Think how busy this courtyard must have been 300 years ago. There were as many as 5000 nobles here at any one time, each with his own entourage. They'd buzz from games to parties to amorous rendezvous in sedan-chair taxis. Servants ran about doing errands. Horse-drawn carriages arrived at this spot with their finely-dressed passengers, having ridden up the broad boulevard that ran direct from Paris. On either side of the boulevard you can still see the horse stables. Incredible as it seems, both the grounds and most of the palaces were public territory where even the lowliest peasant could come to gawk. Of course this meant that there were, then as now, hordes of tourists.

THE PALACE

☞ *Enter and buy your ticket for the self-guided Tour C. Glance in at the Royal Chapel, then show your ticket and go up the winding staircase for a better view of it from the upper level. If you've taken Tour A, you'll spill out near the view of the upper level of the Royal Chapel.*

Royal Chapel
In the vast pagan "temple" that is Versailles, built to glorify one man,

Louis XIV — the Sun King and Apollo on earth — this Royal Chapel is a paltry tip of the hat to that other god, the Christian one. It's virtually the first, last and only hint of Christianity you'll see in the entire complex. Versailles celebrates Man, not God, by raising Louis to almost godlike status, the personification of all good human qualities. In a way, Versailles is the last great flowering of Renaissance humanism and revival of the classical world.

The chapel is where Louis attended Mass every morning. It was also where all important religious ceremonies took place. Young Louis XVI married Marie-Antoinette in this chapel. The two-story layout meant that the King and Queen didn't have to mingle with the common ordinary nobles below.

☞ *Pass into the next room and take a seat.*

Hercules Drawing Room

Pleasure ruled at Versailles, and here is where the main suppers, balls and official receptions were held. On the wall opposite the fireplace is an appropriate painting, showing Christ in the middle of a Venetian party. The work by Veronese, a gift from the Republic of Venice, was one of Louis' favorites, so they decorated the room around it. The ceiling painting of the "Apotheosis of Hercules" (which gives the room its name) was done in colors meant to harmonize with Veronese's party scene.

☞ *The following rooms are listed in order. The names of the rooms generally come from the decoration. For example, the "Apollo Room" has a painting of the Greek god on the ceiling. From here on, it's a one-way tour — you can't get lost. Follow the crowds exiting the Hercules Room to the right of the Veronese.*

THE KING'S WING

Cornucopia Room

If the party in the Hercules Room got too intense, you could step in here for some refreshments. Silver trays were loaded up with liqueurs, coffee, juice, chocolates, and on really special occasions, three-bean salad.

Louis himself might be here. He was a gracious host who enjoyed letting his hair down at night. If he took a liking to you, he might sneak you through that door — there — into his own private study and show off his collection of medals or his jewels or...the "Mona Lisa" which hung on his wall.

Venus Room

There was one thing you never talked about in Louis' presence —

poverty. Not because he didn't understand it, but because he'd had a taste of it and hated it. Don't let the statue of a confident Louis as a Roman emperor fool you, he started out as a poor little rich kid with a chip on his shoulder. His father had died before he was old enough to rule, and during the regency period, the French Parliament treated little Louis and his mother like trash. They were virtual prisoners, humiliated in their home, the Louvre, surviving on bland meals, hand-me-down leotards and pointed shoes. Maybe Versailles was his way of saying, "Living well is the best revenge."

As if this room weren't grand enough, check out the painting illusion on the left wall that extends it into a mythical courtyard.

Diana Room

This was the billiards room. Games were an important part of Louis' political strategy, known as "the domestication of the nobility". By distracting the nobles with the pleasures of courtly life, he was free to run the government his way. Billiards, dancing and concerts were popular, but the biggest was gambling, usually a card game similar to "21". Louis lent money to the losers, making them even more indebted to him. The good life was an addiction, and Louis held the key to the medicine cabinet.

The ceiling is a painting of Diana (with the bow), the Greek goddess of hunting and Apollo's counterpart. Notice the famous bust by Lorenzo Bernini (in the center) of handsome Louis at age 27.

Mars Room

Decorated with military flair, this was the room for Louis' bodyguards. There's Mars, the Greek god of war, in a chariot on the ceiling. Notice the fat walls that hid thin servants who were to be at their master's constant call — but out of sight when not needed. Also, check out the view of the sculpted gardens out the window.

Mercury Room

Louis' life was a work of art, and Versailles was the display case. Everything he did was a public event designed to show his subjects how it should be done. In this room, the royal family demonstrated the fine art of playing games. Even when Louis went to bed at night, the nearby bedroom was filled with nobles taking part in a solemn ceremony, almost like a mass. They'd fight over who got to hold the candle while Louis slipped into his royal jammies. Bedtime, wake-up and meals were all ritualistic public events.

Apollo Room
This was the grand throne room where Louis held court from a ten-foot silver-canopied throne on a raised platform set against the wall in the center of the room. Everything in here reminds us that Louis was not just any ruler, but the Sun King who lights the whole world with his presence. The ceiling shows Apollo in his chariot, dragging the sun across the heavens every day. Notice the beautifully gilded frame (on the ceiling) with its Goldfinger maidens.

In the corners are the four corners of the world, all, of course, warmed by the Sun. (Counter-clockwise from above the exit door are: 1) Europe, with a sword; 2) Asia, with a lion; 3) Africa, with an elephant; and 4) good old America, an Indian maiden with a crocodile.)

A slightly more human look at Louis is the famous portrait by Rigaud over the fireplace. Here he's shown in his dancing garb, displaying the legs that made him one of the all-time dancing fools of "kingery". Louis had more than 300 wigs like this one, changing them many times a day. This was a fashion "first" which he adopted when his hairline started to recede, but it caught on all over Europe, spreading even to the American colonies in the time of George Washington.

Louis may have been treated like a god, but he was not an overly arrogant man. By posing like a god, he showed the greatness of man. His subjects adored him, because he was a symbol of everything a man could be, the fullest expression of the Renaissance man.

The War Room
Versailles was good propaganda. It showed the rest of the world how rich and powerful Louis was. One look at this eye-saturating view of the gardens sent visitors reeling.

But France's success also made other countries jealous and nervous. Germany, Holland and Spain ganged up on Louis (you can see them with their flags in the semicircles on the ceiling). Two guesses who won. Of course, these mere mortals were no match for the Sun King. The stucco relief on the wall shows Louis on horseback triumphing over his fallen enemies.

But Louis' greatest triumph may be the next room, the one that everybody wrote home about.

THE HALL OF MIRRORS

No one had ever seen anything like this hall when it was opened. Mirrors were still a great luxury at the time, and the number and size of these monsters was astounding. The hall is almost 250 feet long.

There are 17 arched mirrors matched by 17 windows with that breathtaking view of the gardens. Lining the hall are 24 gilded candelabra, eight busts of Roman emperors and eight classical-style statues (seven ancients). The ceiling decoration chronicles Louis' accomplishments political and military, topped off by Louis himself in the central panel (with cupids playing cards at his divine feet) doing what he did best — triumphing.

The Hall of Mirrors. This is where France's beautiful people partied. Pass the Fromage-Whiz.

This was where the grandest festivities were held for the most important ambassadors and guests. Imagine this place filled with guests dressed in silks and powdered wigs, lit by the flames of thousands of candles. The mirrors are a...reflection of an age when beautiful people loved to look at themselves. It was no longer a sin to be proud of good looks or fine clothes or to enjoy the good things in life, laughing, dancing, eating, drinking, flirting and enjoying the view.

In more recent times, this is where the Treaty of Versailles was signed ending World War I (and, some say, starting WWII).

☞ *Enter the small Peace Room and grab a bench.*

The Peace Room

In this sequel to the War Room peace is granted to Germany, Holland and Spain, as cupids play with the discarded cannons, armor and swords. On Sundays, the Queen held chamber music concerts here for family and friends.

Again, check out the nice view of the gardens, overlooking the rectangular area (beyond the railing) of the former Orangerie.

THE QUEEN'S WING

The Peace Room marks the beginning of the Queen's half of the palace.

In Louis' time, the division between the King's and Queen's wings wasn't as distinct as it would later become. True, Louis was not the most faithful husband. There was no attempt to hide the fact that the Sun King warmed more than one bed, for he was above the rules of mere mortals. Adultery became acceptable — even fashionable — in court circles.

Some of Louis' mistresses became more famous and powerful than his rather quiet Queen, but he was faithful to the show of marriage and had genuine affection for his wife. Their private apartments were connected, and Louis made a point of sleeping with the Queen as often as possible, regardless of whose tiara he tickled earlier in the evening.

The Queen's Bedchamber

This room has been recently refurnished to look like it did in October, 1789 when the last Queen left the palace for the last time.

The Queen slept here. Two queens died here. The canopied bed is where 19 princes of blood were born. The chandelier is where two of them were conceived. Just kidding. The rather secret looking doors on either side of the bed were for Louis' late night rendezvous — they lead straight to his rooms.

Drawing Room of the Nobles

The Queen's circle of friends met here. Discussions ranged from politics to gossip, food to literature, fashion to philosophy. The Versailles kings considered themselves enlightened monarchs who promoted the arts and new ideas. Folks like Voltaire, a political radical, and the playwright Moliere participated in the Versailles court. Ironically, these discussions planted the seeds of liberal thought that would grow into the Revolution.

Queen's Antechamber

This is where the royal family dined publicly, while servants and nobles fluttered around them, laughing at the King's jokes like royal Ed McMahons. A typical dinner consisted of four different soups, two whole birds stuffed with truffles, mutton, ham slices, fruit, pastry, compotes and preserves.

At one end is a portrait of Marie-Antoinette with three of her nine children. On the ceiling is a scene showing pilgrims bowing before the woman with the world's shortest legs.

Queen's Guard Room

On October 6, 1789, a mob of Revolutionaries stormed the palace to take the King and Queen back to Paris. They were fed up with the life of luxury led by the ruling class in the countryside while they were starving in the grimy streets of Paris.

The King and Queen locked themselves in. Some of the Revolutionaries got access to this upper floor. They burst into this room where Marie-Antoinette had taken refuge, killed three of her bodyguards and dragged her off. (An obscure legend has it that, as they carried her away, she sang, "Louis, Louis, oh...we gotta go now.") The enraged peasants then proceeded to ransack the place, taking revenge for the years of poverty and oppression they'd suffered.

My question — did the King and Queen deserve it? Were the Revolutionaries destroying civilization or clearing the decks for a new and better one? Is Versailles progress or decadence?

Coronation Room

No sooner did they throw out a king than they got an emperor. The Revolution established democracy, but it was shaky in a country that wasn't used to it. In the midst of the confusion, the upstart general Napoleon Bonaparte took control and soon held dictatorial powers. This room captures the glory of the Napoleon years when he conquered most of Europe. In the huge canvas on the left-hand wall, we see him crowning himself emperor of a new, revived "Roman" Empire. (See the Louvre chapter for a full description of David's "The Coronation of Napoleon.")

Catch the portrait of a dashing, young, charismatic Napoleon by the window on the right. This was done in 1796, when he was just a general in command of the Revolution's army in Italy. Compare this with the portrait next to it from ten years later — looking less like a Revolutionary and more like a Louis. In David's "Distribution of Eagles" (opposite the "Coronation") the victorious general passes out emblems of victory to his loyal troops. In "The Battle of Aboukir" (opposite the window) Napoleon looks rather bored as he slashes through a tangle of dark-skinned warriors. His horse, though, has a look of "What are we doing?! Let's get out of here!!"

Let's.

☞ *There are two exits to the gardens. You can pass through a couple of rooms to the exit staircase on your left. The long Battle Gallery ahead of you is 130 yards of scenes from famous French battles arranged chronologically clockwise around the gallery. The exit staircase puts you outside on the left (south) side of the palace.*

Or, for a longer but more pleasant (and less crowded) exit route, backtrack to the Queen's Guard Room and take the stairs down. You'll see the XVIIIth-century Rooms, the Dauphin's (crown prince's) apartments and lots of royal portraits on your way out. These rooms are open 9:45-12:00 and 2:00-4:30.

THE GARDENS — CONTROLLING NATURE

Louis was a divine-right ruler. One way he proved it was by controlling nature like a god. These lavish grounds, so elaborately planned out, pruned and decorated, showed everyone that Louis was in total command.

☞ *Exiting the palace into the gardens, veer to the left toward the concrete railing about 75 yards away. You'll pass through flowers, cookie-cutter patterns of shrubs and green cones. Stand at the railing overlooking the courtyard below and the Louis-made lake in the distance.*

The Orangerie

The warmth from the Sun King was so great that he could even grow orange trees in chilly France. Louis had a thousand of these and other exotic plants to amaze his visitors. In wintertime, they were kept warm in the long greenhouses (beneath your feet) that surround the courtyard. On sunny days, they were wheeled out in their silver planters and scattered around the grounds.

☞ *From the stone railing, turn about face and walk back toward the palace, veering left toward the two large pools of water. Sit on the top stair, and look away from the palace.*

View Down the Royal Drive

This, to me, is the most impressive spot in all of Versailles. In one direction, the palace. Stretching out in the other, the endless grounds. Versailles was laid out along an eight-mile axis that included the grounds, the palace and the town of Versailles itself — one of the first instances of urban planning since Roman times and a model for future capitals like Washington D.C. and Brasilia.

Looking down the Royal Drive (also known as "The Green Carpet"), you see the round Apollo fountain way in the distance. Just beyond that is the Grand Canal. The groves on either side of the Royal Drive were planted with trees from all over, laid out in an elaborate grid and dotted with statues and fountains. Of the original 1500 fountains, 300 remain.

Looking back at the palace you can see the Hall of Mirrors — it's the middle story, with the arched windows.

☞ *Stroll down the steps to get a good look at the frogs and lizards that fill the round Latona Basin.*

The Latona Basin

The theme of Versailles is Apollo, the god of the sun, associated with

Louis. This round fountain tells the story of the birth of Apollo and his sister Diana. On top of the fountain are Apollo and Diana as little kids with their mother Latona (they're facing toward the Apollo fountain). Latona, an unwed mother, was insulted by the local peasants. She called on the king of the gods, Zeus (the children's father), to avenge the insult. Zeus swooped down and turned all the peasants into the frogs and lizards that ring the fountain.

☞ *As you walk down past the basin toward the Royal Drive, you'll pass by "ancient" statues done by 17th-century French sculptors. The Colonnade is hidden in the woods on the left-hand side of the Royal Drive about three-fourths of the way to the Apollo Basin.*

The Colonnade

It looks like the circular remains of an ancient building, but was actually built as is. It's a 100-foot circle of 64 marble columns supporting arches. Beneath the arches are small bird-bath fountains. Versailles had no prestigious classical buildings, so they built their own — pre-fab Roman ruins.

The Apollo Basin

The fountains of Versailles were its most famous attraction, a marvel of both art and engineering. This one was the centerpiece, showing the Sun God — in other words, Louis — in his sunny chariot, starting his journey across the sky. The horses are half-submerged, giving the impression, when the fountains play, of the sun rising out of the mists of dawn. Most of the fountains were only turned on when the King walked by, but this one played constantly for the benefit of those watching from the palace.

All the fountains are gravity-powered. (Personally, I was amazed when I heard that, so I'll elaborate.) The principle is the same as when you block a hose with your finger to make it squirt. Underground streams flowed from basins up at the palace, then were blocked into smaller pipes at the fountains, forcing columns of water high up into the air.

Looking back at the palace from here, realize that the distance you just walked is only a fraction of this vast complex of buildings, gardens and waterways. Be glad you don't have to mow the lawn.

The Grand Canal

Why visit Venice when you can just build your own? In an era before slide projectors, this was the next-best thing to an actual trip. Couples in gondolas would pole along the waters accompanied by barges with serenading orchestras. The Canal is actually cross-shaped, this being the

long arm, a mile from end to end. It's over four miles to walk around
the whole Canal. Of course, this, too, is a man-made body of water with
no function other than pleasing the whim of one man.

THE TRIANON AREA — RETREAT FROM REALITY

Versailles began as an escape from the pressures of kingship. In a
short time, the palace was as busy as Paris ever was. Louis needed an
escape from his escape, and built a smaller palace out in the boondocks.
Later, his successors retreated still further into the garden, building a
fantasy world of simple pleasures. Meanwhile, the real world was crumbling around them.

☞ *Consider renting a bike here or taking a tram, but only if you're real
tired. The walk is half the fun. It's about a 30-minute walk from here to "Le
Hameau" (the end of the tour), plus another 30 minutes to walk back to the
palace.*

*The Grand Trianon (pron: tree-anon) is 10 minutes northwest of the
Apollo Basin — orient yourself from the palace, which is due east.*

The Grand Trianon

This was the King's private residence away from the main palace.
Louis usually spent of couple nights a week here, but the later Louis's
spent more and more time away from the political center.

The facade of this one-story building is a charming combination of
pink, yellow and white, a real contrast to the imposing baroque facade
of the main palace. Ahead you can see the gardens through the columns.
The king's apartments were to the left of the columns.

The flower gardens were changed daily for the king's pleasure — so
he'd have new color combinations to look at, but also to create "nasal
cocktails", interesting new concoctions of scents.

You can walk around the palace (to the right) if you'd like, for a view
of the gardens and rear facade.

☞ *Facing the front do an about-face. The Summer House is not down
the driveway, but about 200 yards away along the smaller pathway at about
10 o'clock.*

The Summer House of the French Garden

This small white building with four rooms fanning out from the center
was one more step away from the modern world. Here, the Queen spent
summer evenings with family and a few friends listening to music or

playing parlor games. All avenues of the *douceur de vivre* — the sweetness of living — were explored. To the left are the buildings of the Menagerie where cows, goats, chickens and ducks were bred.

☞ *Continue frolicking along the path until you run into...*

The Petit Trianon

Louis XV developed an interest in botany. He wanted to spend more time near the French Gardens, but the Summer House just wasn't big enough. He built the Petit Trianon (the "small" Trianon), a masterpiece of neo-classical architecture. This grey, cubical building has four distinct façades, each a perfect and harmonious combination of Greek-style columns, windows and railings. Walk around it.

Petit Trianon. To escape the pressures of palace life the King and Queen retreated into the safety of their garden and this Neo-classical "cottage."

Louis XVI and his wife Marie-Antoinette made this their home-base. Marie-Antoinette was a sweet girl from Vienna who never quite fit in with the fast, sophisticated crowd at Versailles. Here at the Petit Trianon she could get away and recreate the simple home life she remembered from her childhood. On the lawn outside she installed a merry-go-round.

☞ *Five minutes more will bring you past...*

The Temple of Love

A circle of 12 marble Corinthian columns supporting a dome, decorating a path where lovers would stroll. Underneath, there's a statue of Cupid making a bow (to shoot arrows of love) out of the club of Hercules. It's a delightful monument to a society that could afford that ultimate luxury, romantic love. When the Revolution came, I bet they wished they'd kept the club.

☞ *And finally you'll reach...*

Le Hameau — The Hamlet

Marie-Antoinette longed for the simple life of a peasant. Not the hard labor of real peasants — who sweated and starved around her — but the fairytale world of simple country pleasures. She built this complex of 12 buildings as her own private village.

This was an actual working farm with a dairy, a water-wheel mill and domestic animals. The harvest was served at Marie's table. Marie didn't do much work herself, but she "supervised", dressed in a plain white muslin dress and a straw hat.

The Queen's House is the main building, actually two buildings connected by a wooden gallery. Like any typical peasant farmhouse it had a billiard room, library, elegant dining hall and two living rooms.

Nearby was the small theater. Here Marie and her friends acted out plays far from the rude intrusions of the real world.

☞ *The main palace is a 30-minute walk to the southeast. Along the way, stop at the Neptune Basin near the palace, an impressive mini-lake with fountains.*

Rijksmuseum, Amsterdam

Amsterdam's three great art museums cluster around the city's "Museum Square" (*Museumplein*). In one long afternoon you can follow the course of Dutch art from the Golden Age to the New Age. First, the splendor of Holland's glory days — Rembrandt, Vermeer, Hals and Steen — is captured by the Rijksmuseum collection. Next it's into the 19th century with the best collection anywhere of Holland's great Impressionist, Vincent Van Gogh. The wild and crazy finale is just down the street at the brash and lively Stedelijk Modern Art Museum.

Rijksmuseum (pron: rhymes with yikes)

Hours: Tues.-Sat. 10:00-17:00; Sun. and holidays 13:00-17:00; closed Mon.

Cost: 6.50 Fl; 6-18 years old and over 65, 3.50 Fl. Tickets good all day.

Tour length: 90 minutes

Getting there: Take tram (#16, 24, or 25 to Heineken Brewery or #1 or 25 to Leidseplein) and walk five minutes.

Information: Very helpful information booth upstairs.

A good introductory slide show puts you in a mellow mood for this pleasant art. Free, every 20 minutes, film theater off main lobby.

Tel. 020/673-2121 (English spoken).

Misc.: WCs in basement and near Nightwatch, stamps and phones downstairs.

Pleasant Vondelpark is 5 minutes away.

Starring: Rembrandt, Vermeer, Frans Hals, Jan Steen.

Orientation

☞ *Check your bag (required and free), buy your ticket (required and not free) and head upstairs to the main lobby containing a bookstore desk and information booth. Look down the long gallery to Rembrandt's large canvas of an armed guard called "The Night Watch". Orient from here, facing the "Night Watch".*

Dutch art is meant to be enjoyed, not studied. It's straightforward, meat-and-potatoes art for the common man. The Dutch love the beauty of everyday things painted realistically and with exquisite detail. So set your cerebral cortex on "Low", and let this art pass straight from the eyes to the heart with minimal detours.

We'll concentrate on only four painters — Rembrandt, Frans Hals, Vermeer and Jan Steen. All of them lived during Holland's "Golden Age" of the 1600s when foreign trade made her one of Europe's richest lands. But first, a couple of quick stops to get a feel for Dutch art before this great economic boom.

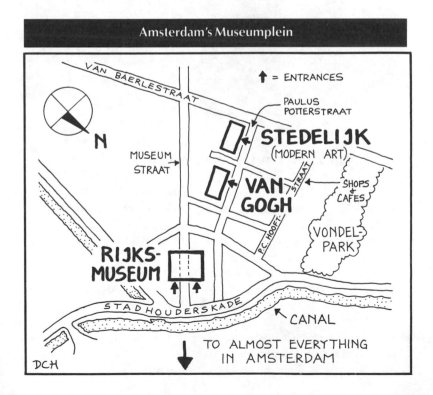

Our entire tour is on this floor to the left of the "Night Watch." To the right is the "Film Theater" (follow signs) with the introductory slide show.

☞ *Start in Room 201, through the door at the left end of the lobby.*

DUTCH ART BEFORE THE GOLDEN AGE (pre-1600)

Eighteen Scenes from the Life of Christ (Achttien Taferelen uit het Leven van Christus) — 15th century
In the days when 90% of Europe was illiterate, art was a way of teaching religious ideas. In these first few rooms, you'll see plenty of Bible scenes. This painting can be "read", "page" by "page", going left to right. In the upper left is the Annunciation, where an angel tells Mary she'll give birth to Christ. "Page 2" is the birth, "page 3" is Jesus being circumcised, then the visit of the Three Wise Men, and so on through Jesus' arrest, execution and resurrection. I like the next-to-last scene of Jesus ascending into heaven. All that's left are his holy toes dangling down from the celestial world.

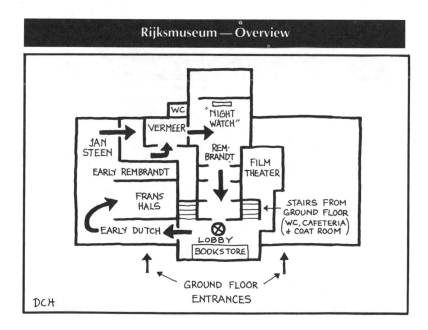

Rijksmuseum — Överview

The Tree of Jesse (De Boom van Jesse)

Here we see Jesus' family tree — literally. At the top is Mary with the baby Jesus. His ancestors are below — David (with the harp), Solomon (with the Scepter), and others stacked like an early version of Hollywood Squares. Again, this is an instructional aid for illiterate masses. But notice the care the artist has taken with the little details, especially the beautiful faces, clothes and scepters. The painting is packed with pretty things to please the eye.

☞ *Walk through the next few rooms of mostly religious scenes, stopping at the three-panel work of colorful people having a party in the countryside.*

The Feast of the Golden Calf (De Aanbidding van het Gouden kalf)

The Dutch love to fill a picture with people having a good time. Here, folks in colorful robes are exchanging good food, wine and conversation in an outdoor setting. In the background, some people are dancing. It's a pleasant scene to look at.

But wait. What's that in the background they're dancing around? It's a golden idol. And who are the two tiny, faint figures in the dark distance at the foot of a smoking mountain? It's Moses (with tablets of stone) and Aaron. Only then do we realize that this colorful work is actually a religious scene from the Bible. The artist used the holy scene as an excuse for painting an unholy joyous feast.

☞ *Now, find a large, appetizing painting.*

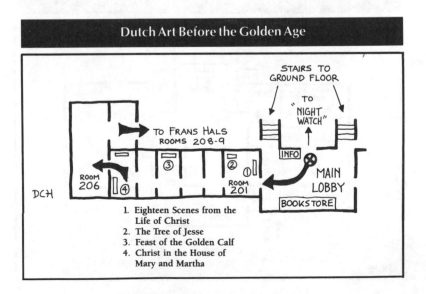

Dutch Art Before the Golden Age

1. Eighteen Scenes from the Life of Christ
2. The Tree of Jesse
3. Feast of the Golden Calf
4. Christ in the House of Mary and Martha

Christ in the House of Mary and Martha (Christus in het Huis van Martha und Maria)

Here we see the Dutch painters' favorite subjects. While Italians painted saints, angels and Madonnas, the Dutch painted...food. For the middle class merchant, food was a religion, and he worshipped thrice daily. Notice the delicious realism — the skin of the cantaloupes and the skin of the plucked birds, the artichokes and other vegetables. And the detail! You can practically count the hares' hairs.

I guess it's no surprise by now that this, too, is a religious scene. In the faint background behind the artichokes someone is preaching. The title is "Christ in the House of Mary and Martha". Compare the sketchy, sloppy work on Christ with the painstaking detail of the food...Dutch priorities. (The dike-digging Dutch love to say, "God made the earth, but the Dutch made Holland.")

In this room and throughout the museum you'll see examples of Holland's three favorite types of paintings — still lifes (of food and everyday objects), landscapes, and portraits (often of groups).

☞ *Enter the large Room 208-209.*

THE GOLDEN AGE (1600s)

Who bought this art? Look around the room and you'll see — ordinary middle class people, merchants and traders. Sure, they're dressed in their Sunday best with those funny stiff ruffled lace collars (which, by the way, were purely for decoration, with no practical function   not even as detachable fans), but underneath it all, you can see that these are hard-working, businesslike, friendly, simple people.

Dutch fishermen sold their surplus catch in distant areas of Europe, returning with goods from these far lands. In time, fishermen became traders, and by 1600, Holland's merchant fleets ruled the waves with colonies as faraway as India, Indonesia and America (New York was originally "New Amsterdam"). The Dutch slave trade — selling Africans to Americans — generated plenty of profit for luxuries, like the art you're looking at.

Look around the room again. Is there even one crucifixion? One saint? One Madonna? I don't think so. This is people art, not church art. In most countries, the Catholic Church and rich kings supported the arts. But Holland was independent, democratic and Protestant, with no taste for saints and Madonnas. There was no Pope, no rich church and no king to pay for Dutch paintings. Instead, Dutch burghers bought portraits of themselves and pretty, unpreachy, unpretentious works for their homes. Even poor people bought smaller canvases by "no-name" artists designed to fit the budgets and lifestyles of this less-than-rich-and-famous crowd.

Frans Hals — *Wedding Portrait of Isaac Abraham (Huwelijksportret van Isaac Abrahamsz)*

Frans Hals (c. 1580-1666) was the premier Golden Age portrait painter. Merchants hired him like we'd hire a wedding photographer today. With a few quick strokes (time was money for businessmen who couldn't sit for hours for a portrait), he captured not only the features but the personality.

In this wedding portrait of a chubby, pleasant merchant and his bride, Hals tells us the story of the Golden Age. This overseas trader was away from home for years at a time on business. So Hals makes a special effort to point out his employer's commitment to marriage: Isaac has his hand over his heart as a pledge of fidelity; the woman's wedding ring is prominently displayed, dead center between them (on her first right-hand finger, Protestant style); the vine clinging to a tree is a symbol of man's support and woman's dependence; and in the distance at right, in the classical love garden, are other happy couples strolling arm in arm along with peacocks, a symbol of fertility.

Claesz — *Still Lifes*

The paintings to the left and right are still lifes by two brothers, Willem and Pieter Claesz. The Dutch people love their homes, cultivating

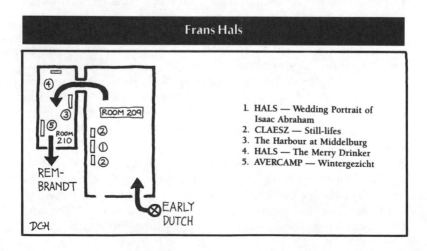

Frans Hals

1. HALS — Wedding Portrait of Isaac Abraham
2. CLAESZ — Still-lifes
3. The Harbour at Middelburg
4. HALS — The Merry Drinker
5. AVERCAMP — Wintergezicht

them like gardens till they're immaculate, decorative and well-ordered. This same sense of pride is reflected in Dutch still-lifes like these, where everyday objects are arranged in the most pleasant way possible. Every detail of the pewterware, the fish, the lemons, the rolls, the glowing goblets is as perfect as a Dutch interior. Get close, and just linger over the little things. You'd swear you can see yourself reflected in the pewter vessel.

On your way out of the large room, glance at the big bright canvas of Prometheus being chained to a rock. It sticks out like an American tourist in Bermuda shorts, doesn't it? This is probably the only Greek myth painting in the entire building, though whole museums in Italy are nothing but classical subjects and nudes.

☞ *Enter Room 210 and moor yourself at the "Harbour at Middelburg" to your left.*

Frans Hals — *The Merry Drinker*
In the "Harbour at Middelburg" (not by Hals, but be patient), we again see Dutch attention to detail — the dog swimming along next to his master on horseback, the shells on the shore, the men in the ship's rigging. The closer you get, the better it looks.

HALS—The Merry Drinker. A "snapshot" catching a fleeting moment. With a few messy brushstrokes Hals creates impressionistic details 200 years ahead of his time.

Now turn 90 degrees (or 450 degrees for an extra thrill) and look across the room at Frans Hals' "The Merry Drinker". Again, notice the details — the happy red face of the man offering us a glass of wine, the lacy collar, the decorative belt buckle, and so on.

Now move in closer. All these "meticulous" details are accomplished with a few quick, thick and messy brush strokes. The beard is only a tangle of brown worms, the belt buckle a smudge of yellow. Even the expressive face is done with a few well-chosen patches of color. Unlike the "Harbour" scene, this canvas is meant to be viewed from a distance, where the colors and brushstrokes blend together.

Hals was a painter with an Instamatic, a "snapshot" portrait painter. Rather than posing his subject, making him stand for hours with "cheese" on his lips, Hals tried to catch him at a candid moment. He often painted common people, fishermen and barflies like this one. He had to work quickly to capture a fleeting gesture like the merry drinker's, so he used this quick, messy brushwork.

This simple technique was a revolution in art. A century later, the Impressionists used the same techniques. In the Van Gogh Museum, you'll see how Van Gogh painted, say, a brown beard, by using thick dabs of green, yellow and red that blend at a distance to make brown. Pretty nifty.

Avercamp — *Winter Scene (Wintergezicht)*

A song or a play is revealed to the audience at the writer's pace. But in a painting, the viewer sets the tempo. He alone chooses where his eyes will go to and how long they'll linger.

AVERCAMP — "Wintergezicht." Crowded with fun, funny details. A typical Dutch painter, Avercamp captures village life on canvas.

Exercise your right to loiter at this winter scene by Hendrick Avercamp. Avercamp, who was deaf and dumb and unfamiliar with the structure of music or theater, would never want to force your attention in any direction. (But I will. Can you find the couple making out in the hay tower? Also, there's a "bad moon on the rise" in the broken-down outhouse at left.) Just look around this painting of Dutch people skating on a frozen river and appreciate its silent beauty and this intimate look at old Holland.

☞ *In Room 211, you'll find several Rembrandts.*

REMBRANDT — EARLY WORKS

Rembrandt van Rijn (1606-1669) is the greatest Dutch painter. Whereas most painters specialized in one field — portraits, landscapes, still-lifes — in order to make a living, Rembrandt excelled in them all. But his technical ability is overshadowed by his complex personality.

Rembrandt — *The Musical Party*

I brake for garage sales. Someday, buried in a stack of old Life Magazines and Herb Alpert records, I'll find a dirty, torn painting. I'll buy it for 75 cents, take it home, have it cleaned and appraised and find out it's worth millions.

That's how Rembrandt's "Musical Party" got here. It was lost for centuries, hidden unknown in some attic, discovered by accident and sold at auction for a small fortune. (The Rijksmuseum acquired a fine collection of Herb Alpert records along with it.) Painted when Rembrandt was 19, it's actually a portrait of his family in funny costumes — his father (in turban), mother, grandmother and himself standing in back.

By the way, of the 500 so-called Rembrandts in existence, 100 have been officially declared fakes by a panel of four Dutch experts. So be careful the next time you plunk down $4 million for a "Rembrandt".

Rembrandt — *Self-Portrait, Age 22 (Zelfportret)*

Rembrandt was a precocious kid. He moved to Amsterdam and entered the highly competitive art world. Amsterdam was a booming town, and, like today, a hip and cosmopolitan city.

Here we see the young country boy fresh in town with an eager and curious attitude, open to whatever life has to offer. But even this early, the boy is something of a mystery. The face is half hidden by hair and shadows, giving him an introspective air.

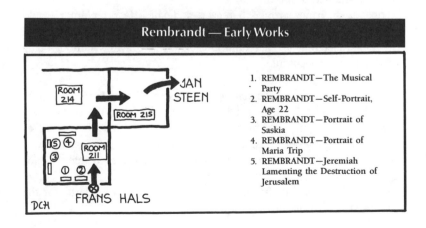

Rembrandt — Early Works

1. REMBRANDT—The Musical Party
2. REMBRANDT—Self-Portrait, Age 22
3. REMBRANDT—Portrait of Saskia
4. REMBRANDT—Portrait of Maria Trip
5. REMBRANDT—Jeremiah Lamenting the Destruction of Jerusalem

Rembrandt — *Portrait of Saskia (Portret van Saskia)*
It didn't take long for the big city to recognize Rembrandt's great talent. Everyone wanted their portrait done by the young master. He became wealthy and famous. He fell in love with and married the rich, beautiful and cultured Saskia.

In this wedding portrait you can understand Rembrandt's popularity. The details of the dress are immaculate, the face literally glows, the features are idealized without seeming phony. You can also see Rembrandt's immense love for Saskia. Just in his early thirties, Rembrandt was the most successful painter in Holland. He had it all.

REMBRANDT—Portrait of Saskia (detail).
Young Rembrandt had money, talent, fame
and a deep love for this woman.

Rembrandt — *Portrait of Maria Trip (Portret van Maria Trip)*
A commissioned portrait by Rembrandt had something extra. The surface details are immaculate — the clothing, jewelry and fine lace work, the subtle face and hands. But Rembrandt gives us not just a person but a personality. This debutante daughter of a wealthy citizen is shy and reserved, maybe a bit awkward in her new dress and adult role, but still self-assured.

Look at the rings around her eyes, a detail a lesser painter would have airbrushed out. Rembrandt takes this feature unique to her and uses it as a setting for her luminous, jewel-like eyes. Without being prettified, she's beautiful.

Rembrandt — *Jeremiah Lamenting the Destruction of Jerusalem*
Rembrandt wasn't interested in cranking out portraits of fat merchants in frilled bibs, no matter what they paid him. He wanted to experiment, trying new techniques and more probing subjects. Many of his paintings weren't commissioned and were never even intended for sale.

His subjects could be brooding and melancholy, a bit "dark" for the public's taste. So was his technique.

You can recognize a Rembrandt canvas by the play of light and dark. Most of his paintings are a deep brown tone, with only a few bright spots glowing from the darkness. This allows Rembrandt to "highlight", literally, the details he thinks are most important.

What's important here isn't the destruction of the city (in the background darkness at left). That's for Spielberg and the big screen. Instead, Rembrandt tells us the whole story in the face of the prophet who predicted the disaster. He's deep in thought, confused and remorseful, trying to understand why this evil had to happen. Rembrandt turns his floodlight of truth on this face.

Light has a primal appeal to humans. (Dig deep into your DNA and remember the time in human prehistory when fire, a sacred thing, was not tamed. Light! In the middle of the night! A miracle! Separating us from our fellow animals.) Rembrandt strikes us at that instinctive level.

☞ *In the next rooms you'll see landscapes, seascapes and church-scapes. Continue to the frolicking man-scapes of Jan Steen in Room 216.*

JAN STEEN (1626-1679)

Not everyone could afford a Rembrandt, like Mr. Trip, but even the poorest people wanted smaller (and cheaper) works for their own homes (the way some people today put paintings of big-eyed children in their bathrooms). Jan Steen, the Norman Rockwell of his day, painted humorous scenes from the lives of the lower classes.

☞ *The next room contains several crowded and frolicking Steens.*

Jan Steen — The Feast of St. Nicholas

It's Christmas Eve, and the kids have been given their gifts. A little girl got a doll. The mother says, "Let me see it," but the girl turns away shyly. In the foreground are the traditional holiday cakes and nuts.

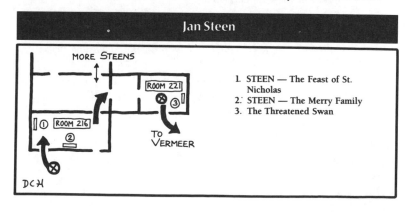

STEEN — Feast of St. Nicholas.
The Norman Rockwell of Holland's
Golden Age, Steen specialized in slices of
life like this Christmas scene.

Everyone is happy except...the boy who's crying. His Christmas present is only a rod in his shoe — like coal in your stocking, the gift for bad boys. The other kids gloat and laugh at him. But wait, it turns out the family is just playing a trick. In the background, the grandmother is beckoning to him saying, "Look, I have your real present in here."

Steen has frozen the moment, sliced a piece off and laid it on a canvas. He's told a story with a past, present and future. These are real people in a real scene that everyone could relate to.

Jan Steen — *The Merry Family*

Steen snuck a moral into this picture of a family eating and drinking as if there's no tomorrow. The broken eggshells and scattered cookware are symbols of waste and extravagance. The proverb tacked to the fireplace reminds us that children will follow the footsteps of their parents. The father in this jolly scene is very drunk — ready to topple over — while in the foreground his mischievous daughter is feeding her brother wine straight from the flask. Mom and Grandma are doing their best to set a good example with a family sing-along, but the child learning to smoke would rather follow dad's lead.

The fun art of Steen in this room reminds us that museums aren't mausoleums.

☞ *If you're keen on Steen, you'll find more in this room and in nearby Room 219.*

Otherwise, cruise through the next few rooms of land- and seascapes to the large Room 221, with a picture of a swan at the far end.

Shhh...Dutch Art

You can be sitting at home late one night and it's perfectly quiet. Not a sound, very peaceful. And then...the refrigerator motor turns off...and it's REALLY quiet.

Dutch art is really quiet art. It silences our busy world to a place where every sound, every motion is noticed. You can hear sheep tearing off grass 50 yards away. Dutch art is still art. It stills our fast-lane world to where we notice the motion of birds. We notice how the cold night air makes the stars sharp. We notice that the undersides of leaves and of cats are always a lighter shade than the tops. Dutch art stills the world — we can hear our own heartbeat and reflect upon that most noble muscle that, without thinking, gives us life.

To see how subtle Dutch art is, realize that the most exciting, dramatic, emotional and extravagant Dutch painting in this whole museum is probably..."The Threatened Swan", on the wall in front of you. Quite a contrast to the rape scenes and visions of heaven of Italian baroque from the same time period.

VERMEER (1632-1675)

Jan Vermeer is the master of quiet and stillness. He creates a still clear pool that is a world in itself. The Rijksmuseum has the best collection of Vermeers in the world — all four of them. (There are only 30 in all.) But each is a small jewel worth lingering over.

☞ *The Vermeer room (221a) is small and often crowded, so you may want to sit here by the Swan and read ahead first.*

Vermeer — *The Kitchen Maid*

Vermeer brings out the beauty in everyday things. The subject is ordinary — a woman pouring milk from a pitcher — but you could look for hours at the tiny details and rich color tones. These are everyday objects, but we see them as though for the very first time, glowing in a diffused light: the bread, the hanging basket, even the nails in the wall. "The Kitchen Maid" practically vibrates with radiant yellow, blue and white. Vermeer squares off a little world in itself (framed by the table in the foreground, the wall in back, the window to the left and the foot stool at right), then fills this space with objects for our perusal.

Vermeer — *The Little Street*

Vermeer lived his whole life in the quiet picturesque town of Delft. This is the view from his front door.

Here, the details actually aren't very detailed — the "cobblestone" street doesn't have a single individual stone in it. What Vermeer wants to show us is the beautiful interplay of colored rectangles on the buildings. Our eye moves from shutter to gable to window, back and forth...and then from foreground to background, as we notice the woman deep in the alleyway.

VERMEER — The Little Street.
Vermeer creates a quiet little world where
we can see the beauty in everyday things.
This was the view from his house in Delft.

Vermeer — *Young Woman Reading a Letter*

Vermeer's placid scenes also have an air of mystery. The girl in blue is reading a letter. Vermeer makes us wonder who it's from, the story behind it. A lover? A father away at sea? She reads it intently, with parted lips and a bowed head. It must be important.

Again, Vermeer has framed off a slice of everyday life. But within this small world are hints of a wider, wilder world outside the frame. The light coming from the left is obviously from a large window, giving us a hint of the world outside. The map hangs prominently, reminding us of travel to exotic lands, most likely where the sender of the letter is.

There's a similar theme in Vermeer's "The Letter" (on the far left), where the ship symbolizes a faraway land. The mysterious letter brought by the servant intrudes like a pebble dropped into the still pool of Vermeer's quiet world.

☞ *Room 223 tells the history of Rembrandt's "Night Watch".*

Night Watch history room

Pause here, and let your retina muscles unclench. We'll go from Vermeer's tiny canvases to the dramatic sweep of Rembrandt. The displays talk about the painting, hanging, cleaning and chopping up of this controversial work. On the right is a small-scale copy showing the original dimensions before the left-hand part was lopped off and lost. The display is interesting, but I've worked most of it into the tour.

☞ *Don't miss the equally wonderful WC before continuing through the glass door into the large "Night Watch" room. The best viewing spot — for the "Night Watch", that is — is to the right of center. This is the angle Rembrandt had in mind when he designed it for its original location.*

REMBRANDT — LATER WORKS

In our last episode, we left Rembrandt at the height of fame, wealth and happiness. He may have had it all, but not for long. We'll see how disappointments in his personal life added a new wisdom to his work.

Rembrandt — *The Night Watch*

This is Rembrandt's most famous painting, though it's not his best. (Sorry, I let an opinion slip out. From now on, just the facts ma'am, just the facts.) Painted in 1642 when he was 36, it was one of his most important commissions — a group portrait of a company of Amsterdam's civic guards to hang in their meeting hall.

REMBRANDT — The Night Watch. Rembrandt makes this much more than a group portrait. It's an action scene, capturing the can-do spirit of the Golden Age.

This is an action shot. The guardsmen (who were really only an honorary militia of rich bigwigs) are moving out on some imaginary assignment, spilling into the street from a large doorway in the back. Flags are flying, the drummer beats a march cadence, the soldiers grab lances and load their muskets. In the center, the commander steps forward energetically with a hand gesture that seems to say, "What are we waiting for? Let's move out!"

Why is the "Night Watch" so famous? Compare it with the less famous group portrait on your left — "Schuttersmaaltijd", by Bartholomeus van der Helst. Every face is visible. Everyone is well lit, flat and flashbulb perfect. These people paid good money to have their mug preserved for posterity, and they wanted it right up front. This colorful, dignified and relaxed work is certainly the work of a master. . . but, ehh, not quite a masterpiece.

By contrast, Rembrandt rousted the Civic Guards off their fat duffs. He took posers and turned them into warriors. He turned a simple portrait into great art.

BARTHOLOMEUS VAN DER HELST — Schuttersmaaltijd.

By adding movement and depth to an otherwise static scene, Rembrandt caught the spirit of Holland in the 1600s. Their war of independence from the Hapsburgs was heading to victory, and their economy was booming. The guardsmen on the move epitomize the proud, independent, upwardly-mobile Dutch.

"The Night Watch", contrary to common myth, was a smashing success in its day. However, there are elements in it that show why Rembrandt soon fell out of favor as a portrait painter. Look at the guy on the right pointing towards the center. Behind the arm is an obscure, half-hidden face. If that was your face and you were proud of it, and you'd paid a good week's wages to have it preserved for posterity, would you be happy? Rembrandt seemed to spend more time painting the dwarf, the dog and the mysterious glowing girl with a chicken (the very appropriate mascot of this "militia" of shopkeepers) than he did the faces of his employers.

Okay, some "Night Watch" scuttlebutt: first off, "The Night Watch" is a misnomer. It's a daytime scene, but over the years, as the preserving varnish darkened and layers of dirt built up, the sun set on this painting, and it got its popular title. At one point, the painting was cropped to fit a smaller room, and the missing piece was lost for good. During World War II it was rolled up and hidden for five years. More recently, a madman attacked the painting, slicing the captain's legs (see the shiny streaks where it was repaired). The madman committed suicide at the police station that night.

Rembrandt's life darkened long before his "Night Watch" did. This work marks the peak of Rembrandt's popularity...and the beginning of his fall from grace. The commissions dried up. The money ran out. His wife Saskia died. His mother died. One by one, his sons died. He had to auction off his paintings and furniture to pay debts. He moved out of his fine house to humble lodgings. He became bitter, disappointed and disillusioned.

He painted masterpieces. Free from the dictates of employers whose taste was in their mouths, he painted what he wanted, how he wanted it. Rembrandt goes beyond mere craftsmanship to probe into and draw life from the deepest wells of the human soul.

☞ *In the long gallery, near "The Night Watch", you'll find. . .*

Rembrandt — St. Peter's Denial

Jesus has been arrested as a criminal. His disciple Peter follows him undercover to the prison to check on the proceedings. A young girl recognizes Peter and asks him, "Don't you know Jesus?" Peter, afraid of being arrested by the Romans, denies it.

Here we see Peter as he answers the girl's question. He must decide where his loyalties lie. With the Roman soldier who glares at him suspiciously from the left, not buying Peter's story at all? Or with his doomed master in the dark background on the right looking knowingly over his shoulder, understanding Peter's complicated situation? Peter must choose. The confusion and self-doubt are written all over his face.

The strong contrasts of light and dark heighten the drama of this psychologically tense scene. The soldier is a blotch of brown. Jesus is a shadowy figure, a lingering doubt in Peter's conscience. The center of the picture is the light shining translucent through the girl's fingers, glowing like a lamp as she casts the light of truth on Peter. Peter's broken-hearted betrayal and sense of guilt could only have been portrayed by an older, wiser — and perhaps himself guilt-ridden — Rembrandt.

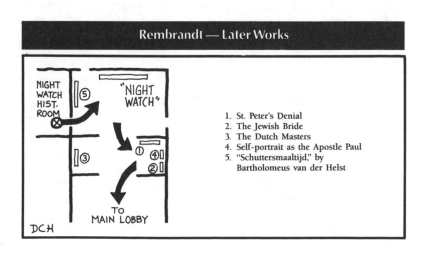

Rembrandt — Later Works

NIGHT WATCH HIST. ROOM ⊗

⑤ "NIGHT WATCH"

③

① ④
②

TO MAIN LOBBY

DCH

1. St. Peter's Denial
2. The Jewish Bride
3. The Dutch Masters
4. Self-portrait as the Apostle Paul
5. "Schuttersmaaltijd," by Bartholomeus van der Helst

Rembrandt — *The Jewish Bride*

Another melancholy, though touching, painting is the uncommissioned portrait known as "The Jewish Bride". This is a truly human look at the relationship between two people in love. The man gently draws the woman toward him. She's comfortable enough with him to sink into thought, but she still reaches back unconsciously to return the gentle touch. The touching hands form the center of this somewhat sad but "yes"-saying work. Van Gogh said, "Rembrandt alone has that tenderness — the heart-broken tenderness."

Rembrandt — *De Staalmeesters*

While commissions were rare, Rembrandt could still paint a portrait better than anyone. Here (in the painting made famous by Dutch Masters cigars) he catches the Draper's Guild in a natural but dignified pose. They've gathered around a table to examine the company's books. They

REMBRANDT — The Dutch Masters (De Staalmeesters). Even in his later years Rembrandt could paint better portraits than anyone. He shows us not just their faces but their personalities as well.

look up spontaneously, as though we've just snapped our fingers to catch their attention. It's as natural as a snapshot, though radiographs show Rembrandt made many changes in posing them perfectly. Even in this simple portrait we feel we can read the guild members' personalities in their faces.

Rembrandt — *Self-Portrait as the Apostle Paul*

Perhaps Rembrandt's greatest legacy is his many self-portraits. They show us the evolution of a great painter's style, as well as the progress of a genius' life. For Rembrandt, the two were intertwined.

Compare this later self-portrait with the youthful, curious Rembrandt of age 22 that we saw earlier. This man has seen it all — success, love, money, fatherhood, loss, poverty, death. He took these experiences and wove them into his art. Rembrandt died poor and misunderstood, but he remained very much his own man to the end.

REMBRANDT — Self-Portrait as the
Apostle Paul. He saw it all — fame,
fortune, love, fatherhood, rejection,
poverty, death. He painted what he
believed in, channeling his life
experiences into his art.

Van Gogh Museum, Amsterdam

The Van Gogh Museum is a cultural high, even to those "not into art". It's a short, well-organized and very user-friendly look at the art of one great and fascinating man. The mix of Vincent's creative genius and his tumultuous life causes many visitors to enjoy this museum even more than the heavyweight Rijksmuseum.

National Museum Vincent Van Gogh
(pron: we say "van-GO,"
though the Dutch say "van-GOCK.")

Hours: Mon.-Sat. 10:00-17:00; Sun. and holidays 13:00-17:00; last entrance 16:30.

Cost: 10 Fl. Those 6-17, over 65 or with one ear, 5 Fl. Family ticket 13.50 Fl.

Tour length: One hour.

Getting there: Follow the tourists 400 yards behind the Rijksmuseum.

Information: No information desk, but bookstore people, while busy, are friendly and speak English.

Good "Vincent" guidebook, big poster tubes, fine reading room and library on entry level.

Tel. 020/570-5200 (English spoken).

Misc.: Fine terrace cafeteria, soup, salads, sandwiches.

WCs are downstairs.

Starring: Take, it Vincent.

Orientation

The core of the museum is on the second floor, one flight up. Here on the ground floor (entry level) are the bookstore, cafeteria, study room and a section for temporary exhibits.

The second floor — the main collection, which we'll see — is arranged chronologically, taking us through the changes in Van Gogh's life and styles.

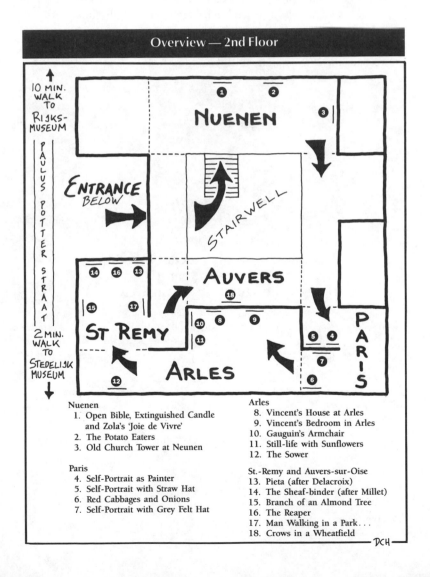

Overview — 2nd Floor

Nuenen
1. Open Bible, Extinguished Candle and Zola's 'Joie de Vivre'
2. The Potato Eaters
3. Old Church Tower at Neunen

Paris
4. Self-Portrait as Painter
5. Self-Portrait with Straw Hat
6. Red Cabbages and Onions
7. Self-Portrait with Grey Felt Hat

Arles
8. Vincent's House at Arles
9. Vincent's Bedroom in Arles
10. Gauguin's Armchair
11. Still-life with Sunflowers
12. The Sower

St.-Remy and Auvers-sur-Oise
13. Pieta (after Delacroix)
14. The Sheaf-binder (after Millet)
15. Branch of an Almond Tree
16. The Reaper
17. Man Walking in a Park . . .
18. Crows in a Wheatfield

The top two floors contain more Van Goghs, including his drawings, works by his friends and colleagues like Gauguin and Toulouse-Lautrec, and temporary exhibits by more recent artists.

VINCENT VAN GOGH

"I am a man of passions..."
You can see Van Gogh's canvases as a series of suicide notes...or as the record of a life full of beauty   too full of beauty. He attacked life with a passion, experiencing life's highs and lows more intensely than the average person. The beauty of the world overwhelmed him, and its ugliness struck him as only another strange form of beauty. He tried to absorb all of life, good and bad, and channel it onto a canvas. The frustration of this overwhelming task drove him to madness.

Van Gogh's life and art were one. His style changed with his circumstances and changing mood. As with Rembrandt, a little knowledge of his life makes the art come alive. For each painting, I'll give just a little background material, and let the painting itself say the rest. Since the museum divides his life and art into distinct periods, let's do the same.

EARLY YEARS (1853-1883) — Wandering

He was the son of a minister from a small Dutch town. At 16 he went to work as a clerk for an art dealership where he worked for several years. But he was restless. His two interests, art and religion, distracted him from his dreary work, and he was finally fired

The next ten years are a collage of dead ends, as he travels through Northern Europe pursuing one path after another. He'd launch into each project with incredible energy, then get disillusioned and move on to something else: teacher at a boarding school, assistant preacher, bookstore apprentice, preacher again, theology student, English student, literature student, art student. He bounces around England, France, Belgium and Holland. He falls in love, but is rejected for someone more respectable. He quarrels with his family and is exiled. He lives with a prostitute and her daughter, offending the few friends he has. Finally, in his late twenties, worn out, flat broke and in poor health, he returns to his family in Nuenen and makes peace. He starts to paint.

☞ *Climb the stairs to the second floor, entering Van Gogh's Nuenen period. You're immediately face to page with a dark, looming Bible.*

NUENEN (Dec. 1883-Nov. 1885) — Poverty and Religion

Open Bible, Extinguished Candle and Zola's Joie de Vivre
  "I have a terrible need of — shall I say the word? — religion. Then I go out and paint the stars."
  A Bible and a book titled *Lust for Life* — these two things dominated his life. In his art, he tried to fuse his religious upbringing with his love of the world's beauty. He lusted after life with a religious fervor. The burned-out candle tells us of the recent death of his father.

The Potato Eaters
  "Those that prefer to see the peasants in their Sunday-best may do as they like. I personally am convinced I get better results by painting them in their roughness...if a peasant picture smells of bacon, smoke, potato steam — all right, that's healthy."
  Van Gogh had dabbled as an artist during his wandering years, sketching things around him and taking a few art classes, but it wasn't until he was 30 that he threw himself into it completely. He painted the dark, dreary countryside of Nuenen in south Netherlands.

The Potato Eaters — Vincent worked with the poorest of the poor. He understood their dark, dreary world and painted it with dignity.

  More importantly, he painted the poor working peasants. He had worked as a lay minister among the poorest of the poor, peasants and miners, launching into it with fanatical zeal. He joined them at work in the mines, taught their children, and even gave away his own few possessions to help them. He was finally dismissed by the church authorities for "excessive zeal", but he came away understanding the poor's harsh existence and the dignity with which they bore it.

The Old Church Tower at Nuenen, 'Cimitière de Paysans'
  The paintings from this time are dark and brown, reflecting the overcast Dutch countryside, the dreariness of these working people's lives. . .and

the loneliness of his own life as he roamed Northern Europe in search of a calling. These are mostly rural scenes, peasants, country buildings. You can see the church and vicarage of his minister father on the opposite wall.

The Old Church Tower at Nuenen — Vincent's father had recently died and was buried near this haunting church tower.

The style is crude — Van Gogh couldn't draw very well (nor would he ever be a great technician). The paint is laid on thick, a technique he'd keep later on. The overall mood of these paintings is of great melancholy, like this bleak cemetery. Notice the crows circling overhead, a reminder of death. His father had died two months earlier.

After his father dies, Van Gogh — in poor health and depressed — moves briefly to Antwerp. He then decides to visit his brother Theo, an art dealer living in the art capital of the world. It was Theo's support — financial and emotional — that would allow Vincent to spend the rest of his short life painting. He moves from rural, religious, poor Holland to...Paris!

☞ *After browsing through the other works from this period, cross to the opposite side of the stairwell.*

PARIS (March 1886-Feb. 1888) — Impressionism

Self-Portrait as Painter

"I am now living with my brother Vincent who is studying the art of painting with indefatigable zeal." — Theo to a friend.

Whoa! Whip out the sunglasses! The colors! In Paris, Vincent is exposed to a thousand different new things. A whole new world of art — and life — is opened up to him. Here he proudly displays his new palette full of bright new colors.

In the cafes and bars of Paris' bohemian Montmartre district, Van Gogh meets the revolutionary Impressionists. He rooms with Theo and becomes friends with other struggling young painters like Gauguin and Toulouse-Lautrec. His health improves, he becomes more sociable, has

Self-Portrait as Painter—In Paris Vincent
gets caught up in the bright colors and
rough brushwork of the Impressionists.

an affair with an older woman, and is generally happy.

He signs up to study under a well-known classical teacher, but quits after only a few classes. He can't afford to hire models, so he roams the streets with sketch pad in hand and learns from his Impressionist friends.

The Impressionists emphasized getting out of the stuffy studio and setting up the canvas outside on the street or in the countryside to paint from nature. There they caught the play of sunlight off the trees, buildings and water.

At first Van Gogh copied from the Impressionist masters. In nearby paintings, you'll see garden scenes like Monet's, cafe snapshots like Degas', still lifes like Cézanne's, "block prints" like the Japanese masters'...and self-portraits like nobody else's.

Self-Portrait with Grey Felt Hat—Caught
in the vortex of bohemian life in Paris.

Self-Portrait with Straw Hat

"You wouldn't recognize Vincent, he has changed so much...The doctor says that he is now perfectly fit again. He is making tremendous strides with his work...He is also far livelier than he used to be and is popular with people."
— Theo to their mother.

The shimmering effect of Impressionist paintings comes from the technique of placing dabs of different colors side by side on the canvas. At a distance, the two colors blend in the eye of the viewer to become a third color. For example, here Van Gogh uses separate strokes of orange, brown and red to create his brown beard — a brown that shivers with excitement.

Red Cabbages and Onions

Despite his new sociability, Van Gogh never quite fits in with his Impressionist friends. He quickly develops his own style — thicker paint, broad, swirling brushstrokes and brighter clashing colors that make even inanimate objects seem to be vibrating with life from within. Here's a flaming onion made of strokes of orange, green, blue, red, and so on. They're supposed to blend to make yellow, but you'd have to back up to Belgium before these colors resolve.

Red Cabbages and Onions — A flaming yellow onion is composed of dabs of red, green and blue that blend and vibrate in your eye at a distance.

Self-Portrait with Grey Felt Hat

"He has painted one or two portraits which have turned out well, but he insists on working for nothing. It is a pity that he shows no desire to earn some money because he could easily do so here. But you can't change people." — Theo to their mother.

In Paris Van Gogh had developed into a good painter, but he was anxious to strike out on his own. Also, the social life of the big city was getting to him. In this painting, his face screams out from a swirling background of molecular activity. Van Gogh wanted peace and quiet where he could throw himself into his work completely. He heads for the sunny south of France.

☞ *Join Vincent in Arles.*

ARLES (Feb. 1888-May 1889) — Sunlight, Beauty and Madness

Vincent's House at Arles — The Yellow House

"It is my intention...to go temporarily to the South, where there is even more color, even more sun."

Winter was just turning to spring when he arrived in Arles near the French Riviera. After the dingy big city, the colors of springtime are overwhelming to Van Gogh. Check out the series of blossoming trees throbbing with new life and drenched in sunlight.

He rents this house with the green shutters. Look at that blue sky! He paints in a frenzy, working feverishly to try and take it all in. He is happy and productive.

Vincent's Bedroom in Arles

"I am a man of passions, capable of and subject to doing more or less foolish things — which I happen to regret, more or less, afterwards."

Vincent's Bedroom at Arles — Living alone in this room in southern France, Vincent enjoys great creativity — but also great loneliness. His friend Gauguin arrives, and they fight. Vincent is overcome with rage, guilt and madness.

Gauguin's Armchair

"Empty chairs — there are many of them, there will be even more, and sooner or later, there will be nothing but empty chairs."

Gauguin arrives. At first they get along great, painting and carousing. But then things start to go bad. They clash over art, life and personalities. Van Gogh, enraged during an argument, pulls out a knife and waves it in Gauguin's face. Gauguin takes the hint and quickly leaves town. Vincent is horrified at himself. In a fit of remorse and madness, he mutilates his own ear.

Still-Life with Sunflowers

"The worse I get along with people the more I learn to have faith in Nature and concentrate on her."

The people of Arles realize they have a madman on their hands, and the local vicar talks him into admitting himself to a mental hospital. Vincent writes to Theo: "Temporarily I wish to remain shut up, as much for my own peace of mind as for other people's."

Even a simple work like these Sunflowers (one of a half-dozen Vincent painted) vibrates with life. Different people see different things in the Sunflowers. Is it a happy mood or a melancholy one? Take your own emotional temperature.

Sunflowers — In his lifetime, Vincent sold only one painting. Today, a "Sunflowers" goes for $40,000,000.

The Sower

A dark, silhouetted figure sows seeds in the burning sun. It's late in the day. The heat from the sun, the source of all life, radiates out in thick swirls of paint. The sower must be a hopeful man, because the field looks slanted and barren. Someday, he thinks, the seeds he's planting will grow into something great, like the tree that slashes diagonally across the scene — tough and craggy but with small optimistic blossoms.

Vincent had worked sowing the Christian gospel (Mark 4:1-9) in a harsh climate. Now in Arles, ignited by the sun, he flung his artistic seeds to the wind, hoping.

But being alone in a strange country has its other side, too. Vincent swings from flurries of ecstatic activity to bouts of great loneliness. Like anyone traveling alone he experiences those high highs and low low lows. This narrow room that's almost folding in on him must have seemed like a prison cell at times. (Psychologists point out that most everything in this painting comes in pairs — two chairs, two paintings, a double bed squeezed down to a single — indicating his desire for a mate. Hmm, maybe.)

He invites his friend Gauguin to join him, envisioning a sort of artists' colony in Arles. He spends months preparing a room upstairs for Gauguin's arrival.

SAINT-REMY (May 1889-1890) — The Mental Hospital

Pietà (after Delacroix)

We see a change from bright, happy landscapes to a more introspective subject. The colors are more surreal, the brushwork even more furious.

It's evening after a thunderstorm. Jesus has been crucified, and the corpse lies at the mouth of a tomb. Mary, whipped by the cold wind, holds her empty arms out in despair and confusion. She is the tender mother who receives us all in death as though saying, "My child, you've been away so long — rest in my arms."

Pietà (after Delacroix) — In the mental hospital, Vincent begins to paint more meditative, swirling and surreal canvases.

Van Gogh continues painting in the asylum. At first the peace and quiet do him good, and his health improves. He copies works by other artists (like this one) and occasionally is allowed outside to paint the gardens and landscapes. Meanwhile the paintings he has sent to Theo begin to attract attention in Paris for the first time. A lady in Brussels buys one of his canvases — the only painting he ever sold during his lifetime. Nowadays, a "Sunflowers" sells for $40 million — that's $5,000 a day for 70 years....

The Sheaf-binder (after Millet)

"I want to paint men and women with that something of the eternal which the halo used to symbolize..."

Van Gogh discovers the equivalence of matter and energy a decade before Einstein. The world he sees is charged from within by spiritual fires.

The fits of madness return. During these spells he loses all sense of his own actions. It means he can't paint, the one thing he feels driven to do. He writes to Theo: "My surroundings here begin to weigh on me more than I can say — I need air. I feel overwhelmed by boredom and grief."

Branch of an Almond Tree
They make plans to move him north to Auvers, a small town near Paris where he can stay at a hotel under a doctor-friend's supervision. On the way there, he visits Theo. Theo's wife had just had a baby which they named Vincent. Van Gogh shows up with this painting under his arm as a birthday gift. Theo's wife later recalls: "I had expected a sick man, but here was a sturdy, broad-shouldered man with a healthy color, a smile on his face and a very resolute appearance."

The Reaper
"*I have been working hard and fast in the last few days. This is how I try to express how desperately fast things pass in modern life.*"
The harvest is here. The time is short. There's much work to be done. A lone reaper works uphill, scything through a swirling wheatfield, cutting slender paths of calm.
Did Vincent suspect that his own days were few?

AUVERS (May 1890-July 1890) — Flying Away

"*[The bird] looks through the bars at the overcast sky where a thunderstorm is gathering, and inwardly he rebels against his fate: 'I am caged, I am caged, and you tell me I have everything I need! Oh! I beg you, give me liberty, that I may be a bird like other birds.' A certain idle man resembles this idle bird...*"
In his new surroundings he continues painting, interrupted by spells of boredom...and of madness. His letters to Theo are generally optimistic, but he worries that he'll succumb completely to insanity and never paint again.

Man Walking in a Park with Falling Leaves
"*...a traveler going to a destination that does not exist...*"
The stark brown trees are blown by the wind. A solitary figure (who?) winds along a narrow, snaky path as the wind blows leaves on him. The colors are surreal — blue, green and red tree trunks with heavy black outlines. A road runs away from us, heading nowhere.

Crows in a Wheatfield
"*This new attack...came on me in the fields, on a windy day, when I was busy painting.*"
On July 27, Vincent leaves his hotel, walks out to a nearby field and puts a bullet through his chest.
This is the last painting Vincent finished. We can try to search the

wreckage of his life for the black box explaining what happened, but there's not much there. His life was sad and tragic, sure, but the record he left is one not of sadness but of beauty. Perhaps too much beauty, experienced too intensely.

Crows in a Wheatfield — A road comes from nowhere, leads to nowhere. The black crows fly ominously overhead. A few weeks later, Vincent shoots himself.

The wind-blown wheat field is a nest of restless energy. Scenes like this must have overwhelmed Van Gogh with their incredible beauty — too much, too fast, with no release. The sky is dark blue, almost nighttime, barely lit by two suns boiling through the deep ocean of blue. The road starts nowhere, leads nowhere and disappears into nothingness in the burning wheat field. Above all this swirling beauty fly the crows, the dark ghosts that had hovered over his life since the cemetery in Nuenen.

Stedelijk Museum, Amsterdam

The Stedelijk has what's new and bizarre in the art world, so the exhibits are always changing, and a set tour is impossible. That's why this museum is so much fun! Just stumble through — looking at, gawking at, and laughing at what passes for art. Much of it is intentionally thumbing its nose at "serious" art, so don't be afraid to laugh. This is your chance to see art before critics and historians have classified, packaged, and judged it — draw your own conclusions.

Stedelijk (pron: STED-uh-lik)

Hours: Daily 11:00-17
Cost: 7 Fl. 7-16 and over 65 — 3.50 Fl.
Tour length: 45 minutes.
Getting there: Next to Van Gogh
Information: Helpful information booth, left of entry.
  Free floor plan with current exhibits.
  Tours for 45 Fl. (includes entry) by appointment, max 15 people.
  Tel. 020/573-2911
Misc.: Good cafeteria and book/poster/card shop.
  Most crowded on Monday when the Rijksmuseum is closed.
Starring: Picasso, Matisse, Chagall, and the folks at "the Beanery".

THE MAIN COLLECTION

A few suggestions. First, pick up a free floor plan at the information desk. You'll need it to confirm how wrong the *Mona Winks* map is — nothing stays put in the unsteady Stedelijk.

If the "permanent" collection is temporarily on display, start there. The chapter on the Pompidou Museum in Paris should be helpful. A walk through the Picassos, Chagalls, Matisses and Mondrians gives a good background. But remember, these once-wild works are now neutered classics as we careen toward another millennium. Anyway, this isn't a museum for chasing famous names — wander ahead of fame.

The Beanery

My favorite is "The Beanery" by Edward Kienholz, an American. We're most comfortable with art that comes in convenient, easily digestible, freeze-dried packets — canvases and statues. But many contemporary artists work in "mixed media", combining painting, sculpture, handicrafts, household appliances, sound, smell and the kitchen sink. One popular trend is toward "installations" where the artist turns an entire room into a full 3-D experience.

"The Beanery" is one of the forerunners of these installations. Kienholz recreates a 1960s cafe down to the smallest detail and peoples it with folks whose faces could stop a clock — or vice versa. Walk in. Poke around discreetly. You may catch yourself saying "excuse me" to a dummy.

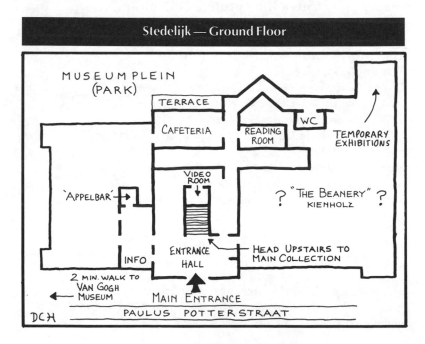

The newspaper at the entrance lets you know what moment in time Kienholz has frozen. Lest you think this is all too heavy, read the rather rude selections on the jukebox.

The Video Room

If everyone in the world, right now, simultaneously picked up their electric can-openers and threw them through their television screens, the world would instantly improve a cool 8%. I'm sure of it. If you don't believe me, check out the exhibition of current video art in the appropriately-named "videotrap". This small amphitheater with two TVs and a barely decent sound system shows delightfully bizarre collages of image and sound. See if you can make the picture and soundtrack synch in your own mind and long for reruns of *Mister Ed.*

Alte Pinakothek, Munich

Munich is Europe's navel, the center of the Continent, where North and South clink cultural steins. The Alte Pinakothek (old art gallery) reflects this meeting of cold, sober North and sunny, happy-go-lucky South. It's a rowdy beerhall of a museum, with art from all over. There's German art, sure, but also one of the world's best collections of Italian Renaissance, Dutch, Flemish, and baroque.

Alte Pinakothek (pron: ALL-tuh peen-ah-ko-tek)

Hours: Tues.-Sun. 9:15-16:30; Tues. and Thurs. also 19:00-21:00; closed Mon.
Cost: 4 DM; students 1 DM; free on Sun.
Tour length: One hour.
Getting there: U-Bahn to "Konigsplatz" or tram 18. 20-minute walk from station.
Misc.: Pleasant, simple cafeteria on ground floor.

Orientation

☞ *Enter and have a seat in the lobby.*
All the paintings we'll see are on the upper floor. Here on the ground floor are the bookstore, information desk, WCs, coffee shop (to the left of the lobby) and more paintings. The upper floor, containing the paintings we'll concentrate on, is laid out like a barbell. We'll start at one fat end

and work our way through the "handle" to the other end.

The Pinakothek has paintings from the North (Germany, Holland, Belgium) and the South (mainly Italy, though even Bavaria has a kind of southern feel). In general, the Northern countries became capitalistic, democratic and Protestant, while Southern countries (including Bavaria) remained more feudal, aristocratic and Catholic. Since art reflects the society that produced it, we'll see two distinct styles.

NORTHERN RENAISSANCE (1450-1550)

The Renaissance began in Italy (as we'll see), but the ideas seeped north. One of the most radical Renaissance attitudes was "humanism" — a confidence in the power of people to control their own destinies. This idea helped fuel the fires of the religious protesters ("Protestants"), who were breaking away from the Catholic church that had dominated Europe through the Middle Ages. In art, this humanism brought a new way for artists to paint people — not as weak sinners before an angry God, but as strong, confident co-creators with God.

☞ *Head upstairs. The stairs branch off in two directions — go left. At the top, through the door, you'll find the Bosch painting on your right.*

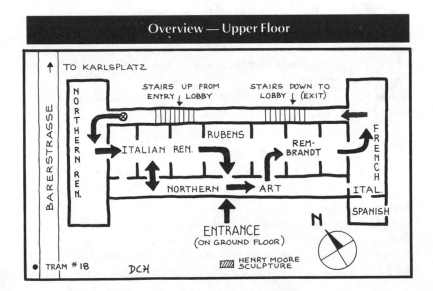

Overview — Upper Floor

Bosch — *Fragment from the Last Judgment (Fragment eines Jungsten Gerichts)*

Look at these puny little guys, tortured by demons. In the Middle Ages, man was seen as a plaything of supernatural forces, a victim of Satan's temptations and God's wrath. In this Last Judgment scene, naked sinners are condemned to Hell to be tormented by half-reptile/half-insect devils. Notice the woman (center right) being carried off by a rooster-like demon. And talk about the Torments of Hell! Catch the odious grey demon (top center) with a mouse's head, pink wings...and a big meal under his belt. Enough to make you beg for fire and brimstone.

   ☞ *Turn left into Room II.*

Cranach — *Crucifixion (Klage unter dem Kreuz)*

Christ's twisted form — distorted, gruesome and unnatural — makes us feel the agony He went through. This is not a majestic Son of God triumphing over Satan but an all-too-human, mortal and weak Jesus suffering for our sins. . .and reminding us none too subtly that ultimately it was sinful man who sent Him to the Cross.

Now contrast Christ's skinny, twisted and ugly body with the massive, majestic forms in Grunewald's painting.

Grünewald — *Saints Erasmus and Maurice (Die Hll. Erasmus und Mauritius)*

These stately figures, painted about the same time as Cranach's crucified Christ, show the influence of the Italian Renaissance. Erasmus in his beautiful jeweled bishop's robes and Maurice in armor are fully three-dimensional, as big and solid as Roman statues. Even more impor-

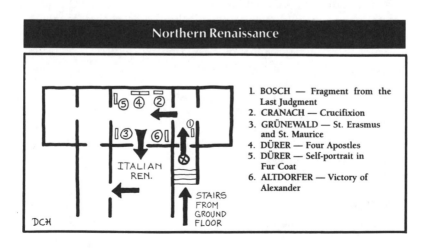

Northern Renaissance

1. BOSCH — Fragment from the Last Judgment
2. CRANACH — Crucifixion
3. GRÜNEWALD — St. Erasmus and St. Maurice
4. DÜRER — Four Apostles
5. DÜRER — Self-portrait in Fur Coat
6. ALTDORFER — Victory of Alexander

ITALIAN REN.

STAIRS FROM GROUND FLOOR

DCH

tant than the sheer mass is their stately bearing, proud and confident, not cowering before supernatural forces.

☞   *Find the two tall paintings that make up one work...*

Dürer — Four Apostles (Johannes und Petrus and Paulus und Marcus)

These four robed apostles (early followers of Jesus) are even more monumental than Grünewald's. Their faces, though, aren't those of idealized Roman statues but of real men with very real human weaknesses. John (at left) seems to be brooding about his receding hairline, while Peter wishes he had a hairline to brood about. In the right-hand panel, bushy-headed Paul looks like a common laborer who just stepped off the rugby field, while Mark eyes the world with fear and suspicion.

The saints we saw by Grünewald were powerful and well-dressed Catholic saints, but these apostles by Dürer are symbols of a brand new and radical religion — Protestantism. Just a few years before, the German monk Martin Luther had defied the Church, been excommunicated by the pope, and started his own church. In the same way that Luther rejected Catholic wealth, worship of saints and authoritarian Church structure, Dürer, in this painting, strips these saints of rich costumes, haloes (contrast with Grünewald's saints) and trappings of authority. These are real, intense, ugly but honest men — the kind to build a new faith on.

Dürer was a child of the Renaissance, open to new ideas, and when Luther's Reformation came along, he joined right in. He painted this work for free, making it a kind of profession of his new faith, complete with an inscription at the bottom warning German rulers to follow the Bible, rather than the orders of Catholic Church leaders. That was quite a statement to make in a time when religious belief was literally a life-and-death matter. The figure of Mark, looking out suspiciously at the far right, is a fitting symbol of these dangerous times — a Bible in one hand and a sword in the other.

Dürer — Self-portrait in Fur Coat (Selbstbildnis im Pelzrock)

...Jesus Christ? Almost. No, this is Albrecht Dürer himself, in the most famous of several famous self-portraits. Solemnly gazing out at us, with his right hand poised almost as though giving us a blessing, this is the ultimate image of Renaissance humanism — the artist as Savior of the World!

It's no accident that Dürer posed himself this way. He'd studied in Italy, where artists were treated like kings, not lowly blue-collar workers. But posing yourself like Jesus Christ?! Isn't that a bit much? Not really.

DÜRER — Self-Portrait in a Fur Coat. In 1500 it was a bold statement to paint yourself at all — much less looking as proud as this. Dürer's message: it's time to start respecting all people, especially artists.

Dürer, a religious man, wouldn't have seen this as a blasphemy against God but as an assertion of Man. He saw humans (especially artists) as instruments of God's continued creation, working under divine inspiration to make beautiful and useful things — co-creators with God.

Dürer's style combines Renaissance solidity with typical Northern attention to detail. Get close and enjoy the incredible intricacy of the plaited hair, the skin texture, and especially the fur collar. To the left of the head is Dürer's famous monogram — "A.D." in the form of a pyramid. With Albrecht Dürer, Renaissance humanism peaked in the north.

Altdorfer — *The Victory of Alexander (Schlacht bei Issus)*

The humanism of the Renaissance met the reality of war...and lost. In 1529 the Moslem Turks were at the gates of Vienna. Meanwhile, throughout Europe, Catholics and Protestants were hacking away at each other with a ferocity that can only happen when each side is convinced that the enemy is Satan himself. By the time the dust settled a century later, Europe was devastated. One out of every three Germans had been killed. The battle Altdorfer portrays here between Greeks and Persians actually took place a thousand years before, but it served as an allegory for the confusion and destruction of what has been called the first "world war".

The battle's outcome is uncertain — as the battles were in Europe when Altdorfer painted it. The masses of soldiers are swept along in the currents and tides of a war completely beyond their control, their confused motion reflected in the swirling sky. We see the battle from a great height, giving us a god-like perspective. The armies melt into a huge landscape, leaving the impression that the battle is being continued into infinity. This is not really a battle scene — it's the picture of a whole world covered with war.

(In the most recent World War, Munich was flattened by Allied saturation bombing. The Pinakothek still bears visible scars on its exterior.

It's rather unsettling to realize that a fraction of a modern bomb could dissolve the entire Pinakothek in a fraction of a second.)

☞ *Enter Room IV, the large Italian Renaissance gallery.*

ITALIAN RENAISSANCE (1450-1550)

The Renaissance — the "rebirth" of interest in the art and learning of ancient Greece and Rome — blossomed in Italy around 1500, spreading from there to the rest of Europe. In art, the Renaissance style meant capturing the realism, three-dimensionality and balance found in classical statues. Italian Renaissance painters learned to paint these three-dimensional figures on a two-dimensional canvas. Their works show a humanistic outlook, even when painting religious subjects — they saw God in the beauty of His greatest creation, the human form.

☞ *We'll return to this room of Renaissance greats in a second, but let's first glance at some of the equally great predecessors of the High Renaissance. Enter the smaller Rooms 1 and 2 by the windows. On the left-hand wall. . .*

Giotto — Christ on the Cross (Christus am Kreuz)
Compare this stately crucifixion with the grotesque crucifixion we saw by Cranach. This Christ is serene and triumphant, not twisted in agony. The mood is enhanced by the symmetry of the painting — Christ is framed on either side by the dripping blood, the angels, the two groups of standing figures and the kneeling figures that balance each other out.

Giotto (pron: ZHOTT-oh) was the first great Renaissance pioneer, though he painted this some two centuries before the High Renaissance.

☞ *Over your left shoulder, you'll find...*

Fra Angelico — Burial of Christ (Grablegung Christi)
This is even more serene despite the tragic subject of Christ's burial. Again, it's the Renaissance balance and symmetry that create the mood. Christ in the center, his luminous body framed by the black mouth of the tomb, is also framed on either side by two mourners. They in turn kneel and bend, echoed by the sloping rock behind them. Even the colors of their robes balance out — each wears matching blues, pinks and gold.

☞ *Return to the main gallery, Room IV.*

Leonardo da Vinci — *Madonna with the Carnation (Maria mit dem Kinde)*

This Virgin Mary with her baby Jesus has no halo, a revolutionary thing at the time. She doesn't need one. We know she's holy and pure simply because she's so beautiful. Tenderness and maternal love radiate from her. This is pure humanism — expressing the divine through the human form.

Leonardo da Vinci, the epitome of the well-rounded Renaissance man, makes Mary a solid mountain of motherly love, a stable pyramid balanced on either side with Renaissance-arch windows. He brings these divine characters down to a very human level. Baby Jesus reaches out to play innocently with a red carnation, unaware that it's a symbol of the blood of the Passion and his eventual death.

☞ *Have a seat on the bench and admire. . .*

Raphael — *The Holy Family (Die Hl. Familie aus dem Hause Cagnigiani),*
The Madonna of the Curtain (Die Madonna della Tenda),
The Madonna Tempi

Like his idol Leonardo, Raphael could combine Renaissance rules of symmetry with the human touch. Compare these three Raphaels with some of the other paintings of Madonnas around the room, for example,

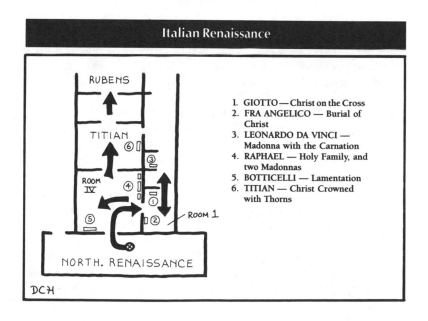

Italian Renaissance

RUBENS

TITIAN

ROOM IV

ROOM 1

NORTH. RENAISSANCE

DCH

1. GIOTTO — Christ on the Cross
2. FRA ANGELICO — Burial of Christ
3. LEONARDO DA VINCI — Madonna with the Carnation
4. RAPHAEL — Holy Family, and two Madonnas
5. BOTTICELLI — Lamentation
6. TITIAN — Christ Crowned with Thorns

the one on the far wall to the right, with Mary flanked on either side by a saint. Dullsville.

RAPHAEL — The Holy Family.
Divine beauty shines through in normal people.

Raphael took Leonardo's pyramid form and ran with it. His "Holy Family" is perfectly balanced without being static and unnatural. Father Joseph is at the peak of the pyramid with his staff forming a strong central axis. Mary and Jesus are to the right of this, balanced by Elizabeth and baby John the Baptist on the left. Within this large pyramid of security are two smaller ones formed by the two mothers with their children.

Raphael's other two Madonnas are also pyramid-shaped compositions, but it's never too obvious or heavy-handed — just enough to give us the subliminal (and sublime) sense of the divine order.

Raphael represents the high point of Renaissance style and humanistic lifestyle. Within a few decades after his death, Europe would be plunged into the religious wars that would soon drain away so much creativity. The warning signs were already apparent in Raphael's lifetime.

☞ *Kitty-corner to the Raphaels you'll see...*

Botticelli — *Lamentation over Christ (Die Beweinung Christi)*

Florence was the cradle of Renaissance free-thinking, the hometown of Leonardo, Michelangelo, Giotto, Fra Angelico and Botticelli. Then, into town rode a charismatic monk named Savonarola preaching medieval fire and brimstone. He took control of the government and ordered that "pagan" books, clothes and paintings be burned. Botticelli, known for his happy-go-lucky lifestyle and worldly paintings, was deeply affected by this religious revival. He burned some of his earlier works and became an ascetic. Later works like this one have a repentant mood.

It looks like Botticelli started to build these figures into a solid Renaissance pyramid à la Raphael...only to have the center collapse and the walls cave in. Mary tries to hold her dead son's body up, but she too has fainted from the enormous weight. The tomb grins darkly behind them, the colors are deathly and surreal, and there's an atmosphere of irretrievable loss. The Renaissance was dying.

☞ *Enter the next large gallery, Room V. On the right-hand wall...*

Titian (Tiziano Vecello) — *Christ Crowned with Thorns (Die Dornenkronung)*

Even Titian, the great Venetian painter of nudes and mythological subjects, was affected by the clamp down on Renaissance ideas. This work — done when he was, get this, 99 years old — is anti-Renaissance in both mood and style. There's no symmetry, no pyramid form and no central figure with balancing figures on the sides. The brushwork is messy and "Impressionistic", the colors dark. The only Renaissance feature is the arch in the background, and it looks cavernous and menacing. Christ with his powerful, statuesque body, sits like a captured Renaissance man, silently taking the abuse of uncivilized fanatics.

RUBENS AND BAROQUE (1600s)

The religious wars split Europe in two — Protestants in the Northern countries, Catholics in the South. (Germany itself was split, with Bavaria remaining Catholic.) The art style of the Catholic countries is known as baroque, characterized by large canvases, bright colors, lots of flesh, rippling motion, wild emotions and grand themes. Baroque art served as propaganda for the sophisticated nobility and Catholic bishops — to impress the masses and keep them loyal to Church and State.

Titian and his fellow Venetians were the jumping-off point for baroque painters. Glance around the room at the large and colorful proto-baroque canvases.

☞ *Now enter the next gallery (VI) noticing the even bigger canvases, lusher colors, more skin, rippling movement...and pudgy winged babies, the sure sign of baroque. Don't be too impressed yet. Continue into the following larger gallery, VII, containing the work of Rubens. Now, be impressed. In the far corner are three autobiographical works.*

Rubens — *Rubens and Isabella Brant*

Peter Paul Rubens of Catholic Flanders (Belgium) is almost universally recognized as the greatest painter ever. Period. Whether he was also the greatest ARTIST is quite another matter, and many people find his work gaudy and superficial. But his command of the brush, of portraying the human figure on canvas from every conceivable angle, is unsurpassed.

Rubens was equally famous in his own day, and here we see him in his prime with his first wife, both of them the very picture of health, wealth and success. They lean towards each other ever so slightly, unconsciously, as people in love will do. The center of this unusually (for Rubens) restrained composition is their two hands, clasped tenderly together in mutual and unpossessive affection.

Rubens — *Hélène Fourment*

When his first wife died, Rubens found a replacement, the youngest of seven sisters famous for their beauty. Hélène was only (gulp) 16 when she married the 53-years-young Rubens ("But Your Honor, she said she was 19, looked 18, and heck, she's almost 17..."), but by all accounts they lived happily ever after. This wedding picture, showing Hélène dressed and seated like a queen, was part of Rubens' own private collection.

Rubens — *Pastoral Scene (Schaferszene)*

Recognize a couple of familiar faces? In this scene of a passionate shepherd with his mate, we see Rubens as the lusty old goat seducing the young, beautiful and only somewhat reluctant Hélène.

Hélène was the model for many of Rubens' women — you can recognize her in the large "Das Apokalyptische Weiss" on the wall to the left. Her blonde hair, blue eyes and small mouth were certainly attractive,

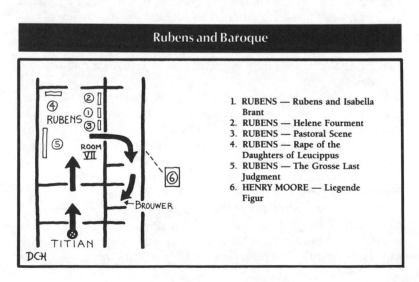

Rubens and Baroque

1. RUBENS — Rubens and Isabella Brant
2. RUBENS — Helene Fourment
3. RUBENS — Pastoral Scene
4. RUBENS — Rape of the Daughters of Leucippus
5. RUBENS — The Grosse Last Judgment
6. HENRY MOORE — Liegende Figur

but Rubens especially loved to paint her full, robust and healthy body. "She never blushed when I took up my brush," Rubens explained. In his own way, Rubens carried on the humanistic tradition of the Renaissance, glorying in the pure, honest beauty of the naked human form.

Rubens — *Rape of the Daughters of Leucippus (Der Raub der Töchter des Leukippos)*

This has many of Rubens' most typical elements — fleshy, emotional, rippling motion, bright colors and a classical subject (Romulus and Remus, the legendary founders of Rome, are taking brides by force from the neighboring Sabines). You'll see many of these features in other paintings around the room.

RUBENS — Rape of the Daughters of Leucippus. The emotional style of Baroque exaggerated sex and violence — or in this case, both.

Looking closer at this swirling mess-terpiece we can see Rubens' standard "X" composition. A diagonal line of motion running from lower left to upper right along the women's flailing arms is crossed by a diagonal from upper left to lower right, running down Romulus' cape and continued in the woman's flowing blond hair. In other words, the intricate counterbalancing of opposite motions — like the weaving counterpoint in a baroque fugue — is based on a solid, balanced, Renaissance structure.

☞ *To view the monstrous "Last Judgment", back up as far away from it as possible, into the spill-over room by the windows. Have a seat by the window.*

Rubens — *The Big Last Judgment (Das Grosse Jungste Gericht)*

At the Last Judgment, Christ will raise the righteous up to Heaven and damn the sinners to Hell. Rubens portrays this as a great cycle of souls, a Christian mandala, with the good people swirling up at left (the right hand of Christ) and the wicked circling down to everlasting torment at right. The only breather for the eyes in this tangle of nudes — by the way, the monastery that commissioned the work rejected it as obscene

— is the donut-hole landscape in the center.

Compare this Big (or, the more appropriate German word, *Grosse*) Last Judgment with this "Small Last Judgment" here in the spill-over room. There's such a jumble of figures that it begins to look like an abstract design. In fact, many modern artists work in exactly this fashion — they accentuate the overall compositional outlines (like this circles of colorful figures) and deemphasize the specific realistic details.

With that in mind, glance over your left shoulder, out the window, to the statue on the lawn about 50 meters away. This abstract work by Henry Moore is a 20th-century version of a full-figured, reclining Rubens nude.

NORTHERN PROTESTANT ART (1600s)

Rubens made a fortune painting for kings, princes and the Catholic Church. But most Northern countries were Protestant and middle class. Protestant churches didn't buy much art — Protestants looked down on the pomp, ceremony and "graven images" in Catholic worship. Instead, Northern art was bought by middle-class merchants and traders, and the subjects reflect it. Saints and Greek gods were out; portraits, landscapes, still-lifes and scenes from everyday life were in. We'll see examples of each of these subjects.

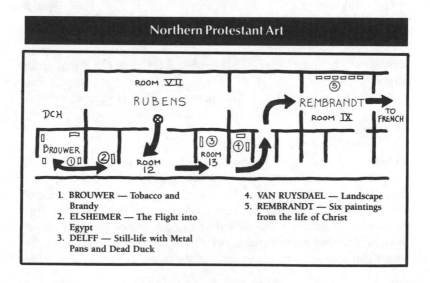

1. BROUWER — Tobacco and Brandy
2. ELSHEIMER — The Flight into Egypt
3. DELFF — Still-life with Metal Pans and Dead Duck
4. VAN RUYSDAEL — Landscape
5. REMBRANDT — Six paintings from the life of Christ

☞ *Facing the "Last Judgment" (as I suppose we all are), turn left and walk, keeping the windows on your left. Pass through the first room, then stop in the second, Room 10.*

Brouwer — *Tobacco (Der Geschmack) and Brandy (Der Gerlich)*

This is a complete about-face from grandiose Rubens to small canvases, natural colors and scenes of everyday life. Adriaen Brouwer also lived a completely different kind of life from his more famous contemporary.

At age 16, Brouwer ran away from home to Holland where he studied art and quickly gained a reputation. He lived a bohemian life, constantly in debt, hanging out in the cheap inns which became his favorite painting subject. He became addicted to tobacco ("Der Geschmack") and brandy ("Der Gerlich"), both of which were practically narcotics in those days, due to the method of preparation. (The paintings confirm this — do these guys look Geschmacked, or what?) He died, burned out from his excesses, at age 32.

Brouwer's style was as radical as his lifestyle. He was one of the first artists to paint the "other side" of life, a kind of 17th-century Kerouac, chronicling life in society's underbelly. He wasn't afraid of ugliness, and he never prettified or glorified the world the way, say, Rubens did. Ironically, Rubens was one of his greatest fans, buying 17 of his works. Take some time here — it's the best collection anywhere of this long-neglected artist.

☞ *Backtrack — keeping the windows on your right — Room 11.*

Elsheimer — *The Flight into Egypt (Flucht Nach Agypten)*

Three refugees — Mary, Joseph and baby Jesus — flee for their lives, adrift in a wide, dark, dangerous world. The true subject isn't the people but the few glimmers of light that they navigate by — the campfire of the shepherds at left (friends or enemies?), Joseph's flickering torch, the Milky Way slanting above, and most of all, the moon with its reflection trapped in water. In this immense night whose dawn is far from inevitable, we sense the fragility of human beings, tiny sparks in a dark world.

The funny measuring devices about two feet off the floor

Seismographs? EKG machines? What are these things?

Try this. Bend over (when the guard's looking away) and blow into the box, as warm and wet and sexy a breath as you can muster (try thinking of Helene Fourment, or Rubens, or both), and watch the needle twitch on the lower drum. See if you can get it above 62, my personal record.

Of course, the lower drum measures relative humidity and the upper one temperature in degrees Celsius, to keep the art in proper atmospheric conditions.

☞ *Pass back through the "Rubens spill-over room" — keeping the windows on your right — and into the next small Room 13. On the left-hand wall hangs . . .*

Delff — *Still-life with Metal Pans and Dead Duck (Stilleben mit Metallgefassen)*
Still-lifes are paintings of everyday objects. By portraying them in perfect detail, artists make us see these common objects as though for the first time. We see the sheen of the pans and the texture of the duck's body, things that we're usually too busy to notice (like the direction the water always swirls when you flush a toilet — is it clockwise or counterclockwise?). By raising the mundane to the level of Art, the artist shows us the beauty residing in all things.

☞ *Continue, keeping the windows on your right, to Room 14.*

Van Ruysdael — *Landscape (Flusslandschaft mit Fahre)*
Rubens would have found this scene boring. But again, the artist gives us the commonplace in all its natural splendor.

☞ *Return to the main gallery, Room IX, containing the brown-toned works of Rembrandt.*

Rembrandt — *Six Paintings From the Life of Christ*
Not every Northern artist was content to paint pots, pans and trees. Rembrandt, the greatest Dutch painter, explored some of the same big themes as his contemporary, Rubens. He matched Rubens for emotion and drama, but always in an understated and human way. He was a Protestant painting for Protestants.

These are six down-to-earth looks at supernatural events. The "Adoration" could just as easily have taken place in a 17th-century Dutch barn as in ancient Bethlehem. Rembrandt often used poor, plain-looking people as his models, even for Mary and Jesus. A true humanist, he saw the divine spark in common folk.

Rembrandt's most typical dramatic trick is strong contrasts of dark and light. The "Adoration" canvas is a moody brown except for one bright patch of light. Where's the light coming from? Certainly not from the dim lantern at left. No, it can't be coming from anywhere else but the baby Jesus himself — literally the "light of the world" shining into the drab existence of everyday people.

In the "Deposition" ("Kreuzabahme") the light again bounces off Christ onto his mother Mary like the sun lighting the moon, showing how his death also hurts her. The drama in these works is underplayed, with subdued emotions. Almost unnoticed is that "The Raising of the Cross" (Kreuzaufrichtung) has a dramatic "X" composition — *à la* Rubens.

☞ *After browsing through the Rembrandts, continue into the next gallery, containing big, colorful canvases in the baroque tradition. Passing from there into the last room (XII), you'll end up face to face with Madame de Pompadour.*

ROCOCO (1700s)

Boucher — *Madame de Pompadour (Marquise de Pompadour 1756)*
In the 1700s, baroque art developed into a lighter, frillier style known as rococo. It appealed to wealthy aristocrats with highly refined tastes — like Madame de Pompadour — who had nothing better to do with their time than dress up and redecorate their palaces. With her dress of pastel colors and surrounded by frilly objects, this mistress of France's Louis XV is rococo incarnate.

☞ *At this point, you may want to explore the colorful art of Italy and Spain in Rooms XIIb and XIII to the right. Otherwise, curtsy and exit to the left of the "Madame".*

Boucher — *Reclining Girl (Ruhendes Mädchen)*
If he'd lived to the age of 150, Rubens would have married this girl. She's both innocent and erotic, the kind of girl to read the Sunday

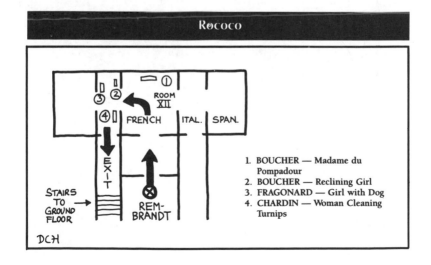

Rococo

1. BOUCHER — Madame du Pompadour
2. BOUCHER — Reclining Girl
3. FRAGONARD — Girl with Dog
4. CHARDIN — Woman Cleaning Turnips

STAIRS TO GROUND FLOOR

ROOM XII

FRENCH   ITAL.   SPAN.

EXIT

REM-BRANDT

DCH

comics in bed with. The pink sheets accentuate her pink skin and fresh, wide-eyed baby face. On the other hand, the rumpled bedding and her suggestive, expectant position make us wonder if maybe we're just seeing a break in the action. Did her lover just slip out for a second to buy her a Slurpee?

BOUCHER — Reclining girl.
French aristocrats loved these frilly titillating rococo scenes.

Fragonard — *Girl with Dog (Mädchen mit Hund)*

In another lecherous "boudoir picture", the artist invites us to ogle a pretty young nymph, looking between her legs at her furry pooch.

Chardin — *Woman Cleaning Turnips (Die Rubenplitzerin)*

God forbid that we end on that note, so contrast the decadent luxury of the rococo world with this woman cleaning turnips. This is French art with a twist of Northern sobriety. While lords and ladies cavort in their boudoirs, this honest working woman pauses from her labors to ask, "Is this all there is to life?"

No, ma'am, it isn't. There's also beer, and that's where I'm headed.

Kunsthistorisches Museum, Vienna

If you like kicking back and enjoying the good things in life, you'd have made a great Hapsburg — and you'll love their museum. The Kunsthistor-whatever-it-is museum houses the beautiful, sensual and light-hearted art collected over the centuries by Austria's beautiful, sensual and light-hearted rulers.

The Kunsthistorisches Museum
(pron: let's just say "Koonst")

Hours: Tues.-Sun. 10:00-18:00; closed Mon. Parts of the painting collection are open Tues. and Fri. 19:00-21:00.

Cost: 45 AS; students 20 AS; first Sun. free.

Tour length: Ninety minutes (for painting gallery only).

Getting there: On Vienna's main ring road across from the Hofburg palace. Subway U-2 to Mariahilfer Strasse or trams 1, 2, D or J.

Information: Information desk on upper floor is friendly and English-speaking. English tours daily at 11:00; Sat. and Sun. at 11:00 and 15:00. Tel. 934541.

Misc.: Expensive coffee shop (salad and Tagesuppe are best deals). Nearby there are several cheap places on Mariahilfer Street, where struggling artists munch Big Macs. Your ticket is good for two fine museums across the Ringstrasse in the Hofburg. 1) The Neue Burg, the lavish newest wing of the Imperial Palace, is filled with Greek armor and historic musical instruments; 2) The Hapsburg royal treasury, in another wing of the Hofburg.

Also excellent and nearby are the Academy of Fine Arts (Bosch, Botticelli, Rubens) and the Albertina Collection of Graphic Arts (with sketches by nearly all the masters).

Starring: Bruegel, Raphael, Titian, Dürer, Rubens.

Orientation

Enter and let yourself be impressed by the marble Entrance Hall with its three-story cupola and broad staircases. The two side stairways to the left and right lead to historical collections which you can visit later. Also, to the right is the cafeteria.

Now, head up the main stairway in front of you toward the statue of "Theseus Clubbing the Centaur" and, to its right, a bust of Kaiser ("Caesar") Franz Joseph I, who was patron to many great artists including his barber. At the top of the stairs you'll find a bookstore and information desk. Have a seat under the cupola.

The Picture Gallery, the heart of what we'll see, is all on this one floor — 1) Italian Art in the right half of the building (as you face in the direction of "Theseus Clubbing the Centaur"), and 2) Northern Art to the left.

Picture Gallery — Overview

Look up into the cupola at the Austrian emperors (in round frames) whose taste in art made this museum necessary. The collection reflects the grandeur and opulence of the Hapsburg family who ruled Austria and its possessions for five centuries, until World War I. At their peak of power in the 1500s, the Hapsburgs ruled Austria, Hungary, North Italy, the Netherlands, Spain, and possessions in America.

They were not merely kings, but "emperors"; not merely emperors but "Roman" emperors; not merely Roman emperors but "HOLY" Roman Emperors. Holy Roman Emperors, Batman!! Claiming to be descended from the great King Charlemagne who united much of Europe in 800 A.D., they were the self-appointed guardians of "civilized" Europe dating back to ancient Rome. The Kunst collection contains many of the most beautiful things that European civilization has created.

☞ *Let's start with the Italian wing, since it gives a good introduction to the opulent Hapsburg style. From the information desk, cross to the opposite side of the stairwell, turning right into the first gallery, marked "Saal I." The Raphaels are on the right-hand wall.*

ITALIAN RENAISSANCE (1450-1550)

You immediately get a sense of the richness of this collection — you've walked right into the High Renaissance. Most museums lead you up to

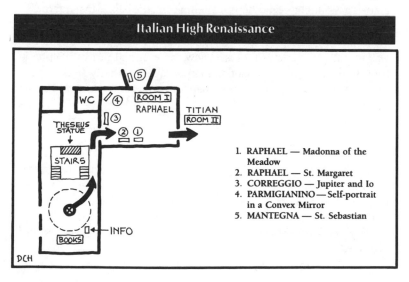

Italian High Renaissance

1. RAPHAEL — Madonna of the Meadow
2. RAPHAEL — St. Margaret
3. CORREGGIO — Jupiter and Io
4. PARMIGIANINO — Self-portrait in a Convex Mirror
5. MANTEGNA — St. Sebastian

this splendor through tortuous rooms of crude medieval crucifixions and altarpieces. But the Hapsburgs had no patience for primitive art.

Raphael — *Madonna of the Meadow (Die Madonna im Grunen)*

May as well start with a bang. Raphael (pron: roff-eye-EL) epitomized the High Renaissance, combining symmetry, grace, beauty and emotion. In true Renaissance fashion, this picture of mother Mary with her child Jesus and the baby John the Baptist (holding the cross) is perfectly balanced — the three figures form a solid pyramid with Mary's face at the peak, her boot as one base and John as the other.

RAPHAEL — Madonna of the Meadow. Renaissance artists showed the orderliness of nature. Notice the symmetry and stability of this human pyramid.

All Renaissance art was balanced, as you can see by glancing around the room (especially to the left) at Madonnas by other artists. But Raphael's balance is more subtle. Baby Jesus and John the Baptist aren't standing stiffly on opposite sides of Mary, but toddling playfully within the triangular outline of her blue and red robe and sloping shoulders. Mary is a mountain of motherly love enfolding the babies in tenderness.

The lovely landscape, serene atmosphere and Mary's adorable face make this a masterpiece of sheer grace, but it also packs an emotional wallop with an ironic fist — we know the eventual deaths of cute little baby Jesus and John the Baptist. Mary's sweet motherly smile is tinged with sadness, as though she too knew the gruesome fate awaiting these two pudgy tykes.

☞ *Just to the right you'll see...*

Raphael — *St. Margaret (Die Heilige Margarete)*

Raphael, a child wonder, had painted the ultra-graceful "Madonna of the Meadow" when he was only 22. In later years, he became impressed by the power and heroic size of Michelangelo's sculptural work, turning to more robust scenes like this female saint who slew a dragon.

Margaret (she's the one with her mouth closed) has a face as beautiful as the Madonna of the Meadow. But her body! She's big as a statue, with forearms that Popeye would die for. Raphael gives us a saint that could kill a dragon with one hand and heft eight steins of beer with the other.

☞ *From Raphael, turn around and notice the next Hapsburg gift to art — plush benches! Art, like sex or a good meal, is best savored slowly. You're not being lazy if you sit down while enjoying a painting. More museums should be so courteous.*

☞ *On the wall to the right of the Raphael wall, find...*

Correggio — *Jupiter and Io*

Jupiter (or Zeus), the king of the Greek gods, has turned himself into a stormy cloud in order to get a date with a beautiful nymph named Io. ("Io, Io, it's off to earth I go.") Isn't that Jupiter's face and hands within the cloud?

This work is typical of the Hapsburg taste in Italian art — fleshy, bright colors, a voluptuous nude, Greek theme, emotional, pretty. Although Correggio was a contemporary of Raphael, he went far beyond Renaissance "balance" — Io may be perched vertically in the center of the canvas right now, but she won't be for long.

☞ *Find the round painting to the right.*

Parmigianino — *Self-Portrait in a Convex Mirror*

This is an obvious attempt to stun the viewer by the sheer difficulty of painting yourself distorted in a fun house mirror. It works. Parmigianino's (pron: like the cheese) exaggerated style — Mannerism — was a favorite of the Hapsburgs. "Io" is also somewhat Mannerist in that it exaggerates reality, creating a world more beautiful than the real world. We'll see plenty of technically polished works of exaggerated beauty in this museum.

☞ *Pop your head through the doorway to the right of Parmigianino. The first painting on your left is...*

Mantegna — *St. Sebastian (Der Hl. Sebastian)*

We've talked about the Renaissance without really saying what it was — the time around 1500 when there was a rebirth of interest in the art, literature, government and science of ancient Greece and Rome. In art, that meant learning the realism and three-dimensionality of ancient statues.

St. Sebastian, an early Christian martyr who was shot through with arrows, stands exactly like a classical Greek statue, leaning on one foot. The anatomy of this human statue is explored meticulously. Mantegna then places the three-dimensional figure into a three- dimensional setting, using floor tiles and roads that recede into the distance to emphasize the depth.

In this Renaissance work full of classical images, there's scarcely a hint of the medieval world...unless it's the knight on horseback in the cloud above.

☞ *Return to the large Raphael gallery, heading left into the next large gallery fully of Titians. On the right hand wall near the far end...*

VENETIAN RENAISSANCE (1500-1600)

Titian — *Danae*

Jupiter is running amok again with a female, this time descending to earth as a shower of gold coins. (And again, his face is barely discernible in the cloud at top.) This is not a restrained classical statue here, but an elegant, colorful and sensuous display of human flesh.

TITIAN — Danae. Luxurious and fleshy Venetian art reflected the values of that merchant city.

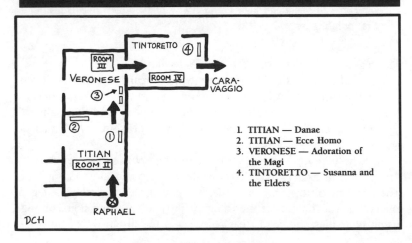

Venetian Renaissance

1. TITIAN — Danae
2. TITIAN — Ecce Homo
3. VERONESE — Adoration of the Magi
4. TINTORETTO — Susanna and the Elders

Yet Titian the Venetian (that rhymes) was also of the Renaissance, believing in a balanced composition. But his balance was that of color, not figures — hot reds and flesh tones on the left, cool blues and greens on the right. Jupiter as the shower of gold spills down connecting the two halves.

☞   *Over your left shoulder, you'll find...*

Titian — *Ecce Homo*

Let your eyes wander over this large canvas for a few seconds. It's a crowd of people, ancient Romans and Jews, all dressed colorfully. But suddenly, there's a commotion, people are whispering to each other and beginning to point. You follow their outstretched hands, up the stairs to a battered figure entering way up in the corner. "Ecce Homo!" ("Behold the man!"), says Pilate and presents Jesus to the crowd. Titian has made a statement. For us, as for the unsympathetic crowd, Christ is not the center of the scene, but almost an afterthought.

☞   *Pass into the next gallery. On the right-hand wall near the center...*

Veronese — *Adoration of the Magi (Die Anbetung der könige)*

Venice was Europe's richest city, the funnel where luxury goods from the exotic East flowed into Northern Europe. Paolo Veronese shows us how East met West in a splendid way. These-Three-Kings-From-Orient-are dressed not in Biblical costume, but in the type of rich silks that Venetian traders imported in Renaissance times. Mary receives them on a Renaissance staircase. Veronese loved silks (and painted them lovingly) and exotic paraphernalia (like the nosy camel sticking his head in the picture).

If Veronese gave us nothing else, he gave us green. (The Kunst has to water these paintings daily, I believe.) Check out "Lukrezia" to the right of the Magi. This Roman heroine is a vision in blond emerging from a sea of green.

☞   *Exit the Veronese gallery, turning right into the next large gallery. At the far end...*

Tintoretto — *Susanna and the Elders (Susanna im Bade)*

First, look around the room at all the highly realistic portraits. Tintoretto mastered the realism of the Renaissance masters, but he was restless to boldly go where no Renaissance man had gone before.

This is a commonly-painted story from the Bible (though it's not in King James' collection of books), common for obvious reasons — it gave the Venetians a chance to show some skin under religious pretenses. In the story, righteous Susanna is spied on by some dirty old men who then wrongly accuse her to hide their own peeping tomfoolery.

We're drawn into the story by Susanna's beauty — and by Tintoretto's craftiness. The wall of flowers extends almost straight back, making the painting an extension of where we stand — we feel like we could step right into the scene. Now notice the one old guy at the far end of the wall leering at Susanna. Who is at this end? There's another old man and then there's...us! The painting's frame is like a window that we're standing here looking through. Tintoretto has made us peeping toms too — as involved in the scene as the characters.

☞ *Enter the next gallery...*

REALISM — CARAVAGGIO AND VELÁZQUEZ (1600-1650)

Caravaggio — *David with the Head of Goliath (David mit dem Haupt des Goliath)*

Artists are always looking for new ways to shock us. And to some extent that's what art is — giving us a new way of looking at things. And the new is almost always scary, the perennial future shock.

Caravaggio (pron: carra-VAH-jee-o) focuses on the one thing that shocks people most — reality. Rather than painting outlandish scenes with unreal colors or distorted figures, he simply painted the real world brutally honest, without glorification.

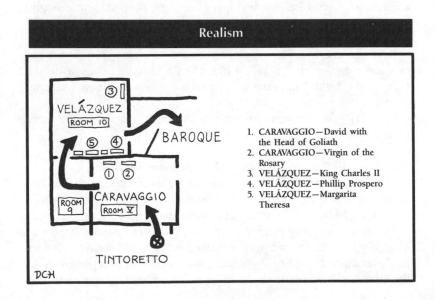

Realism

1. CARAVAGGIO—David with the Head of Goliath
2. CARAVAGGIO—Virgin of the Rosary
3. VELÁZQUEZ—King Charles II
4. VELÁZQUEZ—Phillip Prospero
5. VELÁZQUEZ—Margarita Theresa

CARAVAGGIO — David with the Head of Goliath. By painting himself as Goliath, the shockingly realistic Caravaggio proved he was a head of his time.

Here he turns a third-degree-interrogation light on an old Bible story. David (and, in a sense, Caravaggio himself) is shoving the hideous dripping head of the slain giant right in our noses. Out of deep darkness shine only the few details that Caravaggio shows us, or rather, that he forces us to look at. The painting, bled of color, is practically a black and white photo, slightly over-exposed, like one taken by a police photographer chronicling a crime. The grotesque head of Goliath is none other than Caravaggio himself, a spit-in-your-face self-portrait.

But the most shocking thing to the people of Caravaggio's day wasn't the gory Goliath, but David. This is not a heroic David, or a glorified idealized David like Michelangelo's famous statue. This is no Renaissance man but a grubby street urchin that Caravaggio hired as a model. Caravaggio scandalized the authorities by using common people — servants, beggars and drunkards — as models for his Biblical figures.

☞ *Just to the right...*

Caravaggio — *The Virgin of the Rosary (Die Rosenkranz Madonna)*
Think back on the idealized supernatural beauty of Raphael's "Madonna of the Meadow" and compare it with Caravaggio's plain-faced "Virgin of the Rosary". This "Holy Mother of God" here looks like she could be a maid at a hotel — which she probably was when Caravaggio hired her as his model. In fact, none of these people are glorified.

Caravaggio's hyper-realism was a healthy slap in the face of the art world. It came at a time when lesser painters were copying the grace of Raphael and the sensuousness of the Venetians to churn out sickly-sweet and overly-delicate imitations. And notice the crowning touch of reality in this down-to-earth heavenly vision — the dirt on the feet of the kneeling saints.

☞ *Exit the Caravaggio room to the left (as you face the "Virgin"). Jog to the right, entering the Velázquez room. In the far corner...*

Velázquez — *Portrait of Charles II (König Karl II von Spanien)*
While we're on the subject of gritty realism, check this guy out. Uuuug-ly! Big Durante nose, lips you could balance an egg on and a three-foot jaw. Yet Velázquez — who obviously could keep a firm hand on the brush even while dying of laughter inside — painted him in all his non-glory.

Caravaggio's realism influenced the great painters of Spain's Renaissance of the 1600s, especially the great court painter Diego Velázquez (pron: vel-LOSS-kes). When the Hapsburgs ruled both Austria and Spain, one way these courtly cousins kept in contact was by exchanging portraits of themselves and their children. They hired court painters like we would use an Instamatic to take a family snapshot.

Velázquez was the greatest of "photo-journalist" painters, capturing the likeness of his subjects perfectly, without passing judgment, flattering or glorifying them.

Velázquez — *Portrait of Phillip Prospero (Der Infant Philipp Prosper)*
Little Prince Phillip is only five years old here, but with his elaborate costume and wise, solemn expression, he looks like a tiny priest come to give us a blessing. It's easy to see why Velázquez was such a favorite of the Spanish court. Notice the family puppy in the chair, a happy contrast to the super-sober little Phillip.

☞   *To the right of Phillip are three portraits of...*

Velázquez — *Portraits of Margarita Theresa (Die Infantin Margarita Theresa)*
We get to watch Phillip's sister grow up in these three different portraits at different ages. Margarita was destined from birth to marry the young Austrian prince, and she eventually became Holy Roman Empress. Pictures like these, sent from Spain every few years, were for her pen-pal-and-future-husband to get to know her.

BAROQUE — PUDGY WINGED BABIES (1600s)

Velázquez' just-the-facts-ma'am realism was completely different from most artists of his time. This was the baroque period when motion, emotion, fantasy and surreal colors ruled. Not content with reality, baroque artists painted scenes of exaggerated prettiness, exaggerated violence — or both. If you want to get a quick handle on what "baroque" is, here's a hot tip — pudgy winged babies. If there's a pudgy winged baby in a painting, it's baroque.

☞ *Exit the Velázquez room and pass through four small rooms — how many "p.w.b."s can you spot? Then take your first right into the large Italian Baroque gallery.*

Carracci — *Venus and Adonis*

This vision of exaggerated prettiness has pretty people, lush Venetian-style colors and a Titian-type reclining nude. Oh yes, and a pudgy winged baby.

Manfredi — *Cain Killing Abel (Kain esschlagt Abel)*

In its own way, this is more violent than, say, Caravaggio's more realistic, "David with the Head of Goliath". The artist quickens our heartbeat by showing the moment before the club hits, not after. We anticipate the pain and gore, which is more horrible than actually seeing it.

Giordano — *The Archangel Michael (Der Erzengel Michael)*

Giordano puts violence and prettiness together, as the handsome archangel Michael (with his p.w.b. entourage) subdues shrieking, rebel-

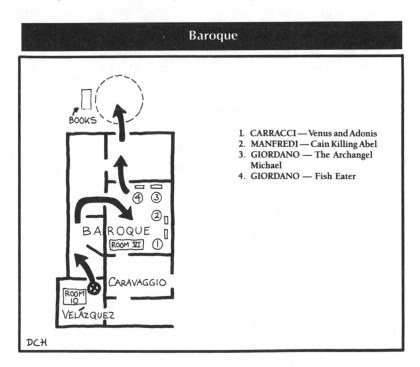

Baroque

1. CARRACCI — Venus and Adonis
2. MANFREDI — Cain Killing Abel
3. GIORDANO — The Archangel Michael
4. GIORDANO — Fish Eater

DCH

lious devils in the battle for heaven. (My favorite face is the dude at lower right; favorite feet, lower left.)

Giordano — *The Fish Eater (Fischesser)*

Giordano must have had a streak of Velazquez in him. This is an honest and ridiculous snapshot of a guy stuffing his face with fish. He pauses and looks at us like, "What's so funny?"

☞   *No doubt this picture has made you hungry. Pass through the last gallery, noticing the portraits of people who actually hung the Fish Eater on the walls of their homes, then head downstairs to the cafe and treat yourself to some good Vienna coffee and pastry...or some fish. Anyway, take a break. Meet you back at the book stand.*

NORTHERN ART

Northern art is so simple, direct and down to earth that you wonder why the luxury-loving Hapsburgs ever bothered with it. But to us it's a strong jolt of good coffee after the saccharine excesses of Italian baroque. Remember that the Low Countries were once part of the Hapsburg

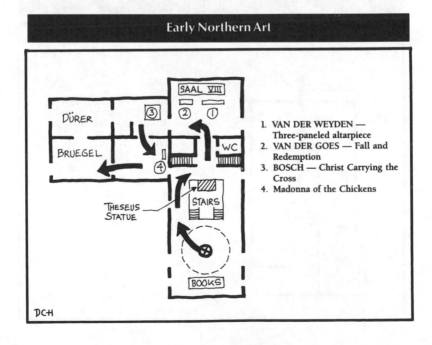

Early Northern Art

SAAL VIII

DÜRER

BRUEGEL

WC

THESEUS STATUE

STAIRS

BOOKS

DCH

1. VAN DER WEYDEN — Three-paneled altarpiece
2. VAN DER GOES — Fall and Redemption
3. BOSCH — Christ Carrying the Cross
4. Madonna of the Chickens

empire. Art-hungry aristocrats bought up Northern paintings almost literally by the gross and sent them home to Vienna. Northern artists always had a great eye for detail. The Northern Renaissance, brought on by the economic boom of Dutch and Flemish trading, wasn't so much a "rebirth" of classical styles as it was a perfecting of the medieval attention to detail. The joy of Northern art is in lingering over canvases that are chock-full of fun, funny, finely-crafted details.

☞ *The first Northern room is "Saal VIII" located at the exact opposite side of the staircase from the bookstore. Inside, find the large triptych (three-paneled painting).*

EARLY NORTHERN ART — Medieval Piety (Before 1500)

Most medieval art was religious. The Church paid artists to decorate churches and paint Bible scenes. The purpose wasn't to paint something beautiful, but something that taught a moral or stoked goodness. The works in this room are a far cry from the ultra-pretty art we saw from the Italian rooms.

Roger Van Der Weyden — *Three-paneled altarpiece (Kreuzinungs Altar)*

The solemn air of the crucifixion scene in the central panel is typical of simple Northern piety — again, a far cry from the emotionalism of Italian baroque (even if there are a few winged angels). Notice the exceptional attention to detail in the robes and the expressive faces.

☞ *Nearby, in a glass case, is the much smaller diptych (two-paneled) altarpiece...*

Hugh Van Der Goes — *Fall and Redemption (Sudenfall und Erlofung)*

Remember Mantegna's "St. Sebastian", the pincushion saint that looked like a Greek statue? Contrast that with the scrawny Adam and Eve in this altarpiece. These naked people ("nudes" is hardly the word) are not heroic Greek gods but fragile human beings. Notice their conveniently covered crotches, a clever touch of medieval modesty. What's amazing is that this "medieval" work was done at roughly the same time as Mantegna's Renaissance masterpiece.

But what these scenes lack in Renaissance three-dimensionality and symmetry they make up for in natural detail. Get close and step into the Garden of Eden, full of tiny little pleasures. The flowers, the shell at the lower right, the blue bird, Eve's shimmering knee-length hair, the intricate muscles of her arm as she reaches for the apple, the serpent with webbed feet, a tail, scaly body and woman's head — this is a true paradise of minute detail. Northern artists meant to have their paintings lingered over, so linger longer.

☞   *Exit Saal VIII to the left. In the small room, find the small painting...*

Bosch — *Christ Carrying the Cross (Kreutzragning)*

Hieronymous Bosch (rhymes with Gosh!) crowded his works with details — human details. How many people are there in this tiny little picture? And each one is a little vignette. Some of Bosch's works are ten times this size, but the figures aren't any bigger — there's just ten times as many of them!

Supposedly, this is Christ carrying the cross, and Jesus is the center of the composition, but he's hardly the center of attention. You could frame off any six-inch section at random, and it would stand on its own, a separate painting you could linger over for hours. Like the criminal in the foreground right confessing to a monk. Is that the executioner standing over him? And is he comforting him? Is that a big tear in his eye, or did Hieronymous "bosch" it?

Bosch's bizarre details and medieval symbolism are often a mystery to us today. The one that really gets me is the shield in front of Christ — what is that, a crucified frog?!

☞   *Exit the small Bosch room into a large gallery. Italians painted Madonnas, saints and angels, the Northern artists painted... food. On the left-hand wall is a painting whose title I forget but whose subtitle must be "Madonna of the Chickens".*

Stroll counter-clockwise around the room, watching scenes of everyday peasant life and more food. This is "meat-and-potatoes" art, literally. Finally, exit into the next large gallery and have a seat.

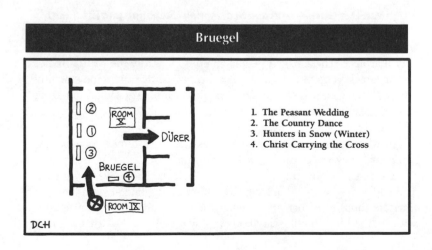

Bruegel

1. The Peasant Wedding
2. The Country Dance
3. Hunters in Snow (Winter)
4. Christ Carrying the Cross

BRUEGEL — Norman Rockwell of the 16th Century

The undisputed master of the slice-of-life village scene was Pieter Bruegel the Elder. This room contains the largest collection of Bruegels in captivity. His works were little known in his day and were quickly forgotten, but the centuries have proved him among the great painters of all time. If we're going to do any major lingering on this tour, let's do it here.

Bruegel (pron: BROY-gull, c. 1525-1569) was a city slicker who liked to dress up like a peasant to observe country folk at play (a trans-fest-ite?) in their native habitat. He poked fun at them not because they were hicks, but because they exemplified weaknesses found in all people.

☞ *Near the center of the main wall, you'll find...*

Bruegel — *The Peasant Wedding (Bauernhochfest)*

His most famous work is not really about a wedding at all but about — what else? — food. There's a whole lotta shovelin' and guzzlin' going on, as the barnful of wedding guests scramble to get their fill of free eats.

The tray of fresh pudding has just been brought in. One guy is grabbing and passing the bowls along, taking our attention with them. We look down the table at people absorbed in eating. In the foreground a child in a drooping red cap licks the bowl with his fingers. The bagpipers have stopped playing to look at the new food brought in. In the midst of this feeding frenzy, look who's been completely forgotten — the demure bride sitting in front of the green cloth.

Besides being a humorous look at village life, Bruegel is making a comment on human greed and gluttony without being heavy-handed. He subtly turns a painting of men into a statement of mankind.

One thing. Is it just me or does the guy carrying the front end of the food tray have one more foot than the standard model? Is he stepping forward with his right or his left — or both?

☞ *Just to the right...*

Bruegel — *The Country Dance (Bauerntanz)*

Speaking of two left feet, these peasants are happily and clumsily clogging to the tune of a bagpiper who wails away while his pit crew keeps him lubed with wine. The main dancer is going at it, while his wife struggles to keep up. Two children are dancing together. Another guy is dragging his reluctant partner out the door to join him. Notice the kissing couple at left. As with Bosch, we are meant to explore the canvas for hidden human treasures.

While Italian art was bought by popes, kings and bishops, Northern art like Bruegel's was bought by middle class merchants, as simple decoration for their homes. They liked pictures of what they liked — food, humorous scenes and pretty landscapes. Above all, nothing heavy or too preachy. There are fewer religious paintings, because most of the North became Protestant in the 1500s, turning away from Catholic-style devotion to saints and the Virgin.

☞ *Look a few paintings to the left...*

Bruegel — *The Hunters in Snow (Die Jäger im Schnee)*
This snowy landscape scene is just what it looks like — a calendar picture, part of a series of six (the other seasons are to the left). It's a slice of winter life. Three dog-tired hunters with their tired dogs return home with only a single fox to show for their efforts. Notice the fun details like the people at the warming fire and the sign over the door dangling from one hinge.

BRUEGEL — The Hunters in Snow. Bruegel's slice-of-life art gives us a pleasant peek at 16th-century Netherlands.

What looks like a simple snapshot of a random scene is actually a careful composition. The left half contains all the dreary work of winter, while the right half is the exhilaration of play. Contrast the haggard hunters with the frolicking skaters playing hockey and curling. And notice how the grove of bare trees suddenly opens up to the spacious landscape on the right — the true subject of this painting — with a glorious distant scene of mountains. The soaring bird is in direct contrast to the weary hunters. It gives a feeling of great freedom, of emerging from the woods after a long journey, of flying forever through infinite space.

Bruegel — *Christ Carrying the Cross (Die Kreutzragung Christi)*
This isn't so much a religious painting as a political one. Like Bosch's similar work, Christ is buried in a festival of figures, and we soon see that this isn't ancient Jerusalem, but 16th century Flanders — see the windmill? And Christ's tormenters in red uniforms aren't Roman soldiers but... Hapsburgs! Bruegel, a fervent nationalist, was bitterly opposed to

the Austrians who ruled his land.

Bruegel's will ordered his wife to destroy this painting in case it should fall into the wrong hands and cause the Hapsburgs to take revenge on his family. Sure enough, it did end up in Hapsburg hands — they loved it! — and paid a small fortune for it! Leave it to an Austrian aristocrat to put beauty over politics.

☞ *Take a seat on the bench.*

A Bruegel's-eye View

Be a Bruegel for a second. Sit on the bench and watch people watching Bruegel. One of the most entertaining things about the Bruegel room is the *Kunst* security system. You may have noticed the electric eyes that buzz when people get too close. It's especially obvious here with Bruegel, as people lean in to look or point at details. It's funny to find people who don't realize they are tripping the buzzer.

Every painting in this room is worth a look — find your own favorite Bruegel and linger. Check out the "Tower of Babel" built by King Nimrod who wanted to shake hands with God. Notice their cranes powered by human treadmills. And spend some time watching "Peasant Children at Play" and their parents at play during *Fasching*, the Austrian Mardi Gras. Get close. They're all full of fun details worth at least two buzzes each. Linger.

I mean it. Linger, I'm in no hurry.

☞ *Exit into the smaller room in the direction of the windows.*

DÜRER AND THE DEUTSCH (1500-1550)

Albrecht Dürer (pron: DEWR-er) was the premier German Renaissance painter. And "Renaissance" really applies here, not only because he studied in Italy at the height of the Renaissance, but also because he was an all-around Renaissance man — the "Leonardo da Vinci of the North" — an architect, engineer, author...and painter.

☞ *The large painting on your left...*

Dürer — *Altarpiece of the Trinity (Die Anbetung der hl. Dreifaltigkeit)*

Dürer combines Northern detail (he was the son of a goldsmith and a renowned engraver) with Italian Renaissance symmetry. At first glance, this altarpiece overwhelms us with a mess of figures — what would you say, a hundred of them? — *à la* Bosch or Bruegel. But on closer inspection, what looks to be a pig-pile of saints turns out to be a neat, geometrical Renaissance composition —*à la* Raphael.

DÜRER — Trinity Altarpiece. Unlike many
of his German contemporaries, Durer
painted religious visions in the grand
Italian Renaissance style.

Dürer has made this painting a series of triangles — appropriate for
a painting about the Trinity. The crucified Christ in the center is in the
shape of a triangle; the clouds that frame him are also triangular; God
the Father is a triangle, as are the crowded crowds of people to the left
and right of the central figures, and so on.

Dürer learned from the Italians how to paint like an artist, but he
also learned how to act like one, to carry himself like an aristocrat and
not a common laborer as most Northern artists were considered to be.
He practically invented the self-portrait as an art form, and here he

Durer and the Deutsch

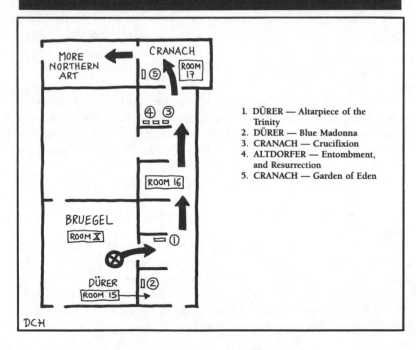

1. DÜRER — Altarpiece of the
   Trinity
2. DÜRER — Blue Madonna
3. CRANACH — Crucifixion
4. ALTDORFER — Entombment,
   and Resurrection
5. CRANACH — Garden of Eden

includes a small likeness of himself — he's the one earthling in this heavenly vision (bottom right). The plaque announces that he, Albrecht Dürer, painted it in 1511.

☞ *Just around the corner to the right are more Dürers, including his otherworldly "Blue Madonna" ("Maria Mit dem Kind") — well worth a peek. From Dürer, keep the windows on your right and pass through three rooms. In the fourth...*

Cranach — Crucifixion (Die kreuznigung)

Contrast Dürer's powerful, serene, Renaissance-style Christ with this crucified Christ — twisted, bleeding, scarred...and vomiting blood! His robe is whipped furiously by the wind as the storm clouds roll in. Obviously, Cranach isn't interested in showing us the geometric perfection of a Renaissance man on a cross. He's communicating with very human details the agony of a tortured man.

☞ *Next to the Crucifixion are two works...*

Altdorfer — Entombment (Die Grablegung Christi) and Resurrection (Die Anferstehung Christi)

These are by another contemporary of Dürer (and Titian and Raphael). They show Christ's tomb at two different times. Jesus was buried on Good Friday, then came back to life on Easter Sunday. In both scenes, Altdorfer misses no chance to strike at our religious emotions.

The Resurrection especially looks like a gaudy poster for a bad horror film — "EASTER SUNDAY III." "He's back from the dead... and He's ticked!" The surreal colors of the morning sky (are the clouds on fire?), the burning halo around Christ's head, and the wind-whipped cloak are all emotional elements that would never find their way into, say, a Raphael Madonna. Yet this was the means for expressing medieval-tinged spirituality, the painter's equivalent of Gothic gargoyles.

In the next room are more medieval-looking works by Cranach. His "Garden of Eden" ("Das Paradies"), with several scenes in one, is especially interesting — notice God's disembodied head spying on Adam and Eve from the clouds.

MORE NORTHERN ART

The Kunst has so many great works by "lesser" Northern artists that we'll have to pass many by. But in your stroll through the next few rooms, here are some pleasant stops along the way.

☞   *Exit the Cranach room, keeping the windows on your right. Follow the map.*

Holbein — *Jane Seymour*

Jane Seymour was one of the VI wives of Henry VIII. Here she is, the former lady in waiting — bland, modest and trying very hard though unsuccessfully to look like a queen. To the right are portraits by Holbein of other members of Henry's court.

Arcimboldo — *Summer (Das Feuer)*

Also known as "Fruit Face". This charming fantasy is one of a series portraying the four seasons as people.

ARCIMBOLDO — Summer.

The Funny-looking machines on the walls

You must have noticed the funny boxes placed around the museum that look like seismographs or EKG charts. They're monitors of relative humidity to make sure the paintings are well-preserved. Blow hot breath on one, and watch the needle twitch.

Brueghel — *The Big Flower Bunch (Der Grosse Blumentraub)*

Still lifes — paintings of everyday objects like fruit, pans or flowers — were a Northern specialty. This vase of flowers was done by Jan Brueghel, the son of the famous Bruegel we just saw. Papa Bruegel had two sons who followed in his footsteps, adding luster and an "h" to his name.

Jan Brueghel was famous for his flowers. Other artists called him to come in and paint flowers for their paintings. This is not a painting from nature, by the way. These are flowers that bloom in all different seasons thrown into one pot. And you'll notice that each flower is arranged perfectly, shown at its best angle and chosen to give a colorful symmetry to the whole piece.

Leaving the simplicity of Northern art — small canvases, small themes, attention to detail — we're about to re-enter the big-canvased broad-stroked world of baroque. But first, let's clear our palate with a look at where we've been.

☞ *Keeping the windows on your right, continue to the very last room along this side of the building. As soon as you enter, turn left to the first two paintings.*

Teniers — *Prince Leopold William in his Gallery in Brussels (Erzerzog Leopold Wilhelm in Serner Galerie in Brussel)*

This Hapsburg governor of the Netherlands was one of history's great collectors of art. Here he is with some of his purchases. Recognize any? There's Raphael's "St. Margaret" and Veronese's "Adoration." Others? Lots of Venetian stuff but very few Northern artists are represented — they're stored in the back room, no doubt.

☞ *Now return to the previous room. Find the portrait on the wall opposite the windows.*

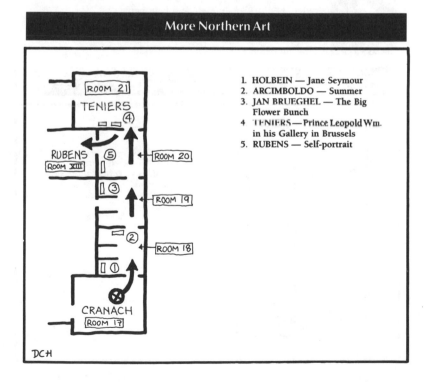

More Northern Art

ROOM 21

TENIERS ④

RUBENS ⑤
ROOM XIII

③

②

①

CRANACH
ROOM 17

ROOM 20

ROOM 19

ROOM 18

1. HOLBEIN — Jane Seymour
2. ARCIMBOLDO — Summer
3. JAN BRUEGHEL — The Big Flower Bunch
4. TENIERS — Prince Leopold Wm. in his Gallery in Brussels
5. RUBENS — Self-portrait

DCH

RUBENS AND REMBRANDT (1600-1670)

Rubens — *Self-portrait (Selbstbildnis)*
Stand here and share in the success of Peter Paul Rubens from Catholic-dominated Flanders (Belgium). He paints himself in his artistic prime — famous, wealthy, well-traveled, intelligent, the friend of kings and princes, an artist, diplomat, man about town, charming, witty and, as the painting shows more than anything else, confident.

Rubens was the greatest baroque painter, even though he was a Northern artist. His patrons were wealthy kings and the wealthy Catholic Church whose tastes ran towards the bright colors, ample flesh and dramatic themes we saw in Italian art.

☞ *On the wall to the right...*

RUBENS — Portrait of Hélène Fourment. Rubens' favorite subject was his young wife. Fleshy enough for two people, she was the perfect model for Mr. Baroque.

Rubens

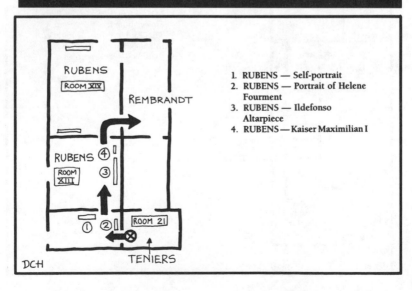

1. RUBENS — Self-portrait
2. RUBENS — Portrait of Helene Fourment
3. RUBENS — Ildefonso Altarpiece
4. RUBENS — Kaiser Maximilian I

Rubens — *Portrait of Hélène Fourment*

At the age of 53, Rubens had everything... except a wife. He married this cute hometown girl of 16, Hélène Fourment, who was to make the last years of his life among the happiest and most productive. Rubens called this painting "The Little Fur" for obvious reasons. That was also his pet name for Hélène for reasons not so obvious, though I could take a guess. This painting was part of Rubens' own private collection. Hélène's full form body was surely an inspiration to Rubens — he painted all the women of his last works with Hélène's sweet face and dimpled proportions.

☞ *Enter the large gallery of large canvases.*

RUBENS

You get a sense of the variety of Rubens by just looking around the room — portraits, religious works, violence, tenderness, pagan myths. He runs the gamut (what is a gamut anyway?) from religious tenderness to Bacchic sensuality. This is the grandeur, motion, emotion and bright colors that appealed to Europe's Catholic rulers.

But, can we be sure it's baroque? Ah yes, there it is in the large "Ildefonso Altarpiece" on the right — pudgy winged babies. It's baroque all right.

Since this has been a lingering kind of tour, just stroll around the Rubens gallery and the one next door. There you'll see two enormous canvases (enormouser than the rest). How could Rubens paint all these in one lifetime? He didn't. He had so many orders that he kept a workshop of assistants busy painting backgrounds and minor figures. He oversaw the work, stepping in at the end to brush on the final touches. Next to the two big canvases done mostly by assistants are Rubens' original "sketches" from which they worked.

☞ *Wherever you may have roamed, end up at the portrait to the left of the "Ildefonso Altarpiece."*

Rubens — *Kaiser Maximilian I*

This is the father of the Hapsburg Empire. He was no doubt a great man, but Rubens has done everything in his painterly power to make him greater. The huge, gleaming armor (which almost dwarfs mild-mannered Max), the rippling clouds in the background, the bright reds and blues, the powerful hand on the sword — all these were Baroque techniques to proclaim the power and authority of rulers like the Hapsburgs.

Just a few miles away from Rubens' workshop in Antwerp lived another great artist who also excelled in many different styles — but the two men were worlds apart.

☞ *From Maximilian, go left into the second Rubens gallery, then take an immediate right into the small room near the windows. On your left you'll see...*

Rembrandt — *Portrait of a Husband (Mannliches Bildnis)*

Compare this Rembrandt portrait with the Rubens we just saw. Rembrandt's subject is no emperor, just an ordinary guy sitting in an ordinary chair with a plain grey background and dressed in ordinary clothes (though they were probably his Sunday best). And Rembrandt has caught him at an ordinary moment — not posing. The man's cheerful personality shines through his red cheeks and he seems to be saying to us, "Hey, let me buy you a drink."

The Protestant middle-class world of Holland called for a different kind of art from the Catholic royalty who bought Rubens' canvases by the yard. The merchants and burghers wanted no-frills portraits, pleasant landscapes and humorous slices of life. Nothing fancy, nothing heavy.

☞ *Continue into the next small room to the left with several Rembrandt portraits.*

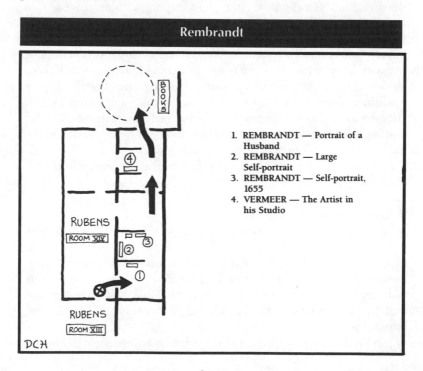

Rembrandt

1. REMBRANDT — Portrait of a Husband
2. REMBRANDT — Large Self-portrait
3. REMBRANDT — Self-portrait, 1655
4. VERMEER — The Artist in his Studio

DCH

Rembrandt — *The Large Self-Portrait (Das Grosse Selbstbildnis)*
Rembrandt always seemed to paint just what he wanted, whether or not it was popular or lucrative to do so. Here we see the hands-on-hips, defiant, open-stance determination of a man who will do what he wants, and if they don't like it — tough.

And he did paint what he wanted. In this room are portraits of family members that surely weren't done for money, like the picture of his son Titus reading a book ("Der Lesende Jungling"). In typical Rembrandt style, most of the canvas is a deep dark brown with only a few light spots glowing from the darkness. (Remember Caravaggio? Rembrandt did). To the right is a portrait of his mother ("Die Mutter des Kunstlers"). These weren't big money-makers, but they merited Rembrandt's full attention.

Rembrandt — *Self-portrait 1655 (Selfbildnis 1655)*
Rembrandt's mother died, his wife died, Titus died, and the commissions for paintings dried up as his style veered from the common path. Rembrandt had to auction off paintings to pay debts and died a poor man.

His numerous self-portraits painted from youth till old age show us a man always changing. From wide-eyed youth, to successful portraitist, to this disillusioned but still defiant old man.

☞ *Let's crown the tour with one last jewel that typifies Northern art so well. From Rembrandt continue down the hall (windows on right) to the next-to-last room.*

Vermeer — *The Artist in his Studio (Allegorie der Malerei)*
The Dutch painter Jan Vermeer quiets the world down to where we can hear our own heartbeat, to where we appreciate the beauty in common things. He creates his own small doll-house world with such detailed clarity, that it's as though we were seeing these everyday items for the first time.

The artist in the painting — probably Vermeer himself — is painting a model dressed in blue; he's just starting with her flowery hat. The studio is its own little world, squared off by the chair in the foreground and the wall in back. Then Vermeer has filled this space with the detailed gems he wants us to focus on — the chandelier, the map, the painter's costume. The curtain drawn aside makes us feel like we're peeking in on this intimate scene.

And throughout it all, the diffused lighting sets a quiet tone, accentuated by cool blue colors, that gives us the peace to meditate on these everyday objects.

Vermeer's paintings all have a quiet element of mystery. What is the map for? The mask on the table? The painting is also called, mysteriously, "An Allegory of Painting". Since the model holds the trumpet and book, traditional symbols of fame, perhaps we are seeing the artist as someone, his back to the public, earnestly and painstakingly trying to capture fleeting fame with a small sheet of canvas.

☞   *This is the end of the tour. However, we've seen only the "Kunst" (art) half of the Kunst-"Historisches" (history) Museum. Gluttons for punishment should head downstairs.*

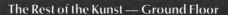

The Rest of the Kunst — Ground Floor

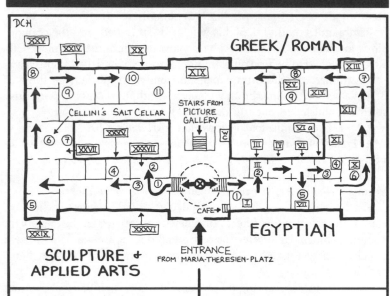

Sculpture and Applied Arts	Egyptian
1. Carved ivory horns	1. Sarcophagus for phat pharaoh
2. Navigational and time-keeping devices	2. Mummified cow's head
3. Backgammon board	3. Mummified crocodiles
4. Model ships done in ivory	4. Cult of the Dead chamber
5. Glass vases and pots	5. Blue hippopotamus
6. Salt Cellar by Cellini	
7. Statuettes by Giovanni Bologna	Greek and Roman
8. Pokals (drinking horns)	6. Athena Parthenos fragment
9. Pokal made of rhinoceros horn	7. Greek and Roman helmets
10. Leopold I statue	8. Onyx cameos
11. Gold breakfast service of Maria Theresa	9. Busts of Roman emperors

THE REST OF THE KUNST

The Picture Gallery on the upper floor should take up most of your time and energy. But the collections on the ground floor are among the best in Europe, and are interesting if only to show the eclectic, garage-sale, scavenger-hunting tastes of the eccentric Hapsburgs.

If you like ancient rubble and medieval curios, take some time to browse through the ground floor. On the map I've highlighted some...highlights. Enjoy.

Cellini — *Salt Cellar (Die Saltera)*

The ground floor has only one sight that's a "must-see" in every guidebook...but this one — Cellini's golden Salt Cellar. Cellini, a famous sculptor whose bronze statue of Perseus stands in the main square in Florence, made this golden receptacle for King Francis I of France (around 1540). It shows Neptune with his trident and Venus reclining on the backs of sea creatures. It's a strange composition, but also strangely balanced, like two people leaning over the sides of a rubber raft — which you'd probably rather be doing after walking all the way to see this silly thing.

CELLINI — Salt Cellar. This exquisitely ridiculous "salt shaker" is typical of the gifts that would gather dust on Hapsburg coffee tables.

Venice — St. Mark's and the Doge's Palace

Venice was once Europe's richest city. As middleman in the trade between Asia and Europe, it reaped wealth from both sides. In 1450, Venice had 150,000 citizens (far more than Paris), and a gross "national" product 50% greater than the entire country of France. The rich Venetians learned to love the good life — silks and jewels from the East, crafts from northern Europe, good food and wine, exotic spices, fine architecture, music, gaiety and laughter. Venice was a vibrant city full of impressed visitors, palaces, canals, glitter, splash and flash. After five centuries, Venice is still very much the same. In this tour, we'll spend a couple of hours in the political and religious heart of this Old World superpower.

Basilica di San Marco

Hours: 9:00-17:00; Sun. 14:00-17:00.
Cost: The Church is free. Charges for Treasury and Loggia.
  Strict dress code (no shorts or bare shoulders), silence requested.
Tour length: One hour.
Getting there: Signs all over town point to San Marco. It's on Piazza San Marco, near the Grand Canal. Vaporetto stop: San Marco.
Information: Cheap, good guidebooks in church atrium bookstand and from hawkers on the piazza.
  Worthwhile recorded phone descriptions throughout (dial English, drop in coins).

Tel. 522-2505

The "I Mosaici di San Marco" slide show (hourly, March-August, next door at Ateneo S. Basso) explains the mosaics.

Misc.: Public pay WC just beyond far end of square.

Starring: St. Mark, Byzantium, Sansovino.

Palazzo Ducale, or Doge's Palace (pron: DOJE-es, not doggies)

Hours: 9:00-19:00 daily; last entrance 18:00.

Cost: 8,000 L; students 4,000 L.

Tour length: One hour.

Getting there: Next to the church.

Information: None anywhere, and no one speaks English. Guidebooks on sale in the Piazza.

Misc.: WC in courtyard near exit.

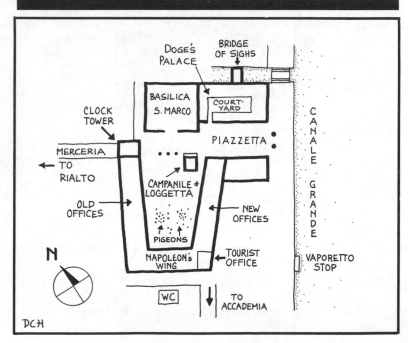

Piazza San Marco

PIAZZA SAN MARCO

☞ *Sit on the steps at the far end (away from the church) in the sun or shade as you wish.*

Bride of the Sea

Imagine this square full of water with gondolas floating where people are now sipping coffee at the cafe tables. That happens every so often at very high tides, a reminder that Venice and the sea are intertwined.

Venetian wealth came from sea trading. As middleman between Europe and the East (the Moslem world of Turkey and the Middle-east), Venice became the wealthiest city in Europe. In St. Mark's Square, the exact center of this East-West axis, we see both the luxury and the mix of Eastern and Western influences.

Basilica San Marco dominates the square with its Greek-Byzantine style domes and glowing mosaics. Mark Twain said it looked like "a warty bug taking a walk". The square itself is almost two football fields long. To the left and right stand the government offices that administered the Venetian Empire's vast network of trading outposts. On the left are the "Old" offices, built in 1530 in solid Renaissance style. The "New" offices on the right, from a century later, are a little heavier and more ornamented, mixing various arches and columns in the Baroque style.

☞ *Behind you are the best public WC in Venice, the post office and American Express office. The Tourist Information office is to your right. With Venice's inconsistent opening hours, it's wise to confirm your sightseeing plans here.*

Walk to the center of the square — to the cool shadow of the bell tower, or Campanile.

The Piazza

Notice how big the square is but also how intimate it feels. Napoleon called it "the most beautiful drawing room in Europe." We have Napoleon himself to thank for the intimate feel. Originally, the far end was open. He closed it off with the wing you were just sitting under.

For architecture buffs, here's three centuries of styles, bam, side by side, *uno due tre*, for easy comparison: 1) Old wing, Renaissance; 2) New wing, Baroque; 3) Napoleon's Wing, Neo-Classical — a return to simpler, more austere classical columns and arches. Napoleon's architects tried to make his wing bridge the styles of the other two. But the height only partly matches the "New" offices and barely matches the "Old". Nice try, guys.

☞   *Meet you at the center flagpole in front of the church. If you're really tired, make your home-base on a bench at the foot of the Campanile, the tall brick bell tower. Watch out for pigeon speckle.*

Basilica San Marco — exterior

Mark was the author of one of the four Bible books telling the story of Jesus' life (Matthew, Mark, Luke and John). Seven centuries after his death his holy body was in Moslem-occupied Alexandria, Egypt. Two visiting merchants of Venice "rescued" the body (euphemism #1 = "stole") from the infidels and spirited it away to Venice, giving the fast-growing city instant religious status as well. They made Mark the patron saint of the city, and you'll see his symbol, the winged lion, all over Venice.

Basilica — Built upon the burgled bones of Saint Mark and decorated with booty from conquered lands, this style could be called "Early Ransack." Onion domes from the East and arches from the West bring tourists from all over.

Above the door on the far left of the church is a mosaic of this event which put Venice on the map. The "Translation" of St. Mark (euphemism #2 = "stole") shows two guys in the center (with the crooked staffs) entering the church and bearing a coffin with the body. Mark looks rather grumpy from the long voyage.

The original church was built (over Mark's dead body!) in the 9th century. The structure we see was begun in the 11th century, with changes made throughout Venice's glory days. In the mosaic, one of the oldest, you can see the church as it looked in the 13th century — even with its famous bronze horses on the balcony. True to its founding, the church is built with columns, stones and decorations translated and rescued from looted buildings throughout the Venetian empire. The style has been called "Early Ransack".

The four bronze horses over the central doorway are the most famous bit of booty. The Venetians stole them from their fellow Christians during the looting of Constantinople (modern Istanbul) and brought them to San Marco. The horses we see overlooking the square are copies, but you can visit the impressive originals housed inside the church museum.

The Clock Tower

Two bronze Moors (African Moslems), "translated" from God knows where, strike the hours atop the clock tower to your left. The dial shows the 24 hours, the signs of the zodiac and the phases of the moon. Above it is the world's first digital clock, which changes every five minutes. There are both Roman numerals and Arabic numerals. (Arabic?! Oh yeah, that's ours.) There's also a lion of St. Mark with alert wings looking down on the crowded square. You can climb the tower for a fine view and be right next to the Moors, as they swing their giant clappers.

Campanile

The original *Campanile* (pron: campa-NEE-lay), or bell tower, was a marvel of 10th-century architecture until the 20th century, when it toppled into the center of the Piazza. It had groaned ominously the night before, sending people in the cafes scurrying. The next morning, crash!

Campanile of St. Mark's — The bell tower collapsed in 1902.

The Campanile fell in 1902 and was rebuilt ten years later. You can ride a lift to the top for the best view of Venice. Notice the photo of the crumpled tower on the wall just before you enter the elevator, giving *deja vu* a profound new meaning.

You don't need a weatherman to know which way the wind blows. Check the golden angel on top of the *Campanile*, who always faces into the breeze.

☞ *Sit at the base of the* Campanile *and face the water. The small square between the church and the water is . . .*

The Piazzetta

This "Little Square" is framed by the Doge's Palace on the left and the Old Library on the right. In former days, it used to be closed off to the general public for a few hours a day, so that government officials and bigwigs could gather in the sun to strike shady deals.

The two large 12th-century columns near the water were rescued (or was it "translated"?) from Constantinople. These columns were used to string up and torture criminals, so the public could learn its lessons vicariously. There's a winged lion on top of one of them, the symbol of Venice's patron saint. The other shows St. Theodore, the former patron saint, who was replaced when they got hold of Mark. I guess stabbing crocodiles in the back isn't classy enough for an upwardly mobile world power.

Venice was the "Bride of the Sea" because she was dependent on sea trading for her livelihood. This "marriage" was celebrated annually by the people. The Doge in full regalia boarded a ritual boat here, at the edge of the Piazzetta, and sailed out into the canal. There, a vow was made, and he dropped a jewelled ring into the water to seal the marriage.

In the distance, across the Grand Canal, is one of the grandest scenes in the city, the Church of San Giorgio Maggiore, designed by the late-Renaissance architect Palladio.

Speaking of architects, I will for the next second-and-a half: Sansovino. The Old Offices, the Old Library and the delicate *Loggetta* you're sitting under (at the base of the *Campanile*) were all designed by him. Take about ten steps toward the Doge's Palace, turn around and you can see all three of these at once. More than any single man, he made Piazza San Marco what it is.

When Venice floods, the puddle appears first around white grates, like the one on the ground between the *Loggetta* and the Doge's Palace.

☞ *Head to the water's edge and turn left. Stop in the middle of the first bridge and look inland.*

The Bridge of Sighs

On your left is the Doge's Palace, where the government doled out justice. On the right were the prisons. (Don't let the palatial facade fool you — see the bars on the windows?) Prisoners sentenced in the Palace crossed to the prisons by way of the covered bridge in front of you. From this bridge they got their final view of sunny, joyous Venice, before entering the black and dank prisons. They sighed.

Venice has been a major tourist center for four centuries. Anyone who ever came here has stood on this very spot, looking at the Bridge of Sighs. Lean on the railing leaned on by everyone from Casanova to Byron to Hemingway.

☞ *Sigh. Then return to the flagpole in front of the Basilica.*

BASILICA SAN MARCO

St. Mark's church is a treasure chest of booty looted during Venice's glory days. That's only appropriate for a church built on the bones of a stolen saint. The first church built over the relics burned down in 976, so what we see dates largely from the 11th century. Succeeding generations plastered it with columns, doors, mosaics and statues plundered by centuries of conquest and aggressive trading.

The facade shows this crazy mix of East and West. The doorways are massive Romanesque (European) arches, but are lined with marble columns from Eastern buildings. The mosaics are mostly Venetian designs executed by Greek craftsmen. There's sculpture from Constantinople, columns from Alexandria and capitals from Sicily. The upper story has some pointed Gothic-style arches, while the whole affair is topped by Greek domes with their Islamic onion-shaped caps. What's amazing isn't so much the variety, as the fact that the whole thing kind of comes together in a bizarre sort of harmony. It remains simply the most unique church in Europe, a church that (borrowing from the writer Goethe) "can only be compared with itself."

☞ *Enter through the central door — a 6th-century bronze-paneled Byzantine job. Turn right in the atrium and drop anchor under the last dome.*

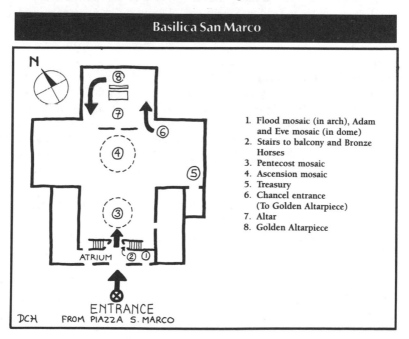

Basilica San Marco

N

1. Flood mosaic (in arch), Adam and Eve mosaic (in dome)
2. Stairs to balcony and Bronze Horses
3. Pentecost mosaic
4. Ascension mosaic
5. Treasury
6. Chancel entrance (To Golden Altarpiece)
7. Altar
8. Golden Altarpiece

ATRIUM

ENTRANCE
FROM PIAZZA S. MARCO

DCH

The Atrium Mosaics

St. Mark's is famous for its mosaics, and the best close-up look at them is actually here in the entrance hall which contains some of the oldest and best. Mosaics are made of small cubes of glass or stone pressed into wet plaster. They were popular in ancient Rome, then carried to the Greek-speaking world when the Roman Empire moved its capital to Constantinople (modern Istanbul). Byzantine churches perfected the gold background effect, achieved with cubes of glass with gold leaf baked right into them.

Medieval mosaics were teaching aids to tell Bible stories to the illiterate masses. Today's literate masses have trouble reading them, so let's look at two simple examples to see how they worked.

In the arch next to the dome you're under is the story of Noah, the Ark and the Great Flood. If you face the *Piazza*, you'll see (on top) Noah building the Ark. Below that are three scenes of him putting all species of animals into the Ark, two by two. Turning around and facing the church interior, you'll see the Flood in full force, drowning the wicked. Noah sends out a dove twice, to see if there's any dry land to dock at. He finds it, leaves the Ark with a gorgeous rainbow overhead and offers a sacrifice of thanks to God. Easy, huh?

Now that our medieval literacy rate has risen, let's try the story that rings the bottom of the dome — Adam and Eve in the Garden of Eden. Stand right under the dome facing the church, crane your neck and read clockwise around the dome:

1) Adam names the animals; 2) God creates Eve from a spare rib and; 3) presents her to Adam; 4) Eve is tempted by the serpent; 5) she picks and gives the forbidden fruit to Adam; 6) They realize that they're naked; and 7) in shame, they try to hide from God; 8) God finds them; and 9) lectures them; 10) He gives them clothes; and 11) pushes them out into the real world where they have to work for a living.

☞ *Enter the church through the central door — just follow the mob up the stairs past the gaily-dressed guard, who makes sure all who enter have covered legs. There are benches along the back wall to both sides of the entry, but wait a second.*

While your eyes adjust to the dark, get a feel for the church. Before reading on, walk up to the center of the church and back. Notice the floor plan of four equal arms radiating from the center. Meet you back here at the bench in five.

The Greek Cross Floor Plan

The central event of Western Christianity is the death of Jesus; the central event for Eastern Christians is His rebirth. That's why most

Western European churches have so many crucifixes, and even the shape of the church itself is often in the form of a crucifix. But look around St. Mark's. Do you see many crucifixes? And the floor plan is not the Latin Cross, symbolizing the crucifixion, but the Greek Cross (+), symbolizing perfection.

Topping the Greek Cross are five domes — one large one in the center and one over each arm, or transept. These are decorated with golden mosaics in the Byzantine style, though many were designed by Italian Renaissance and later artists. The entire upper part is in mosaic, over 4000 square meters' worth (imagine paving a football field with contact lenses). The often-overlooked lower walls are in beautiful marble.

The overall effect is one of "mystical, golden luminosity". It's a subtle effect, one that grows on you, especially as the filtered light changes. There are more beautiful churches, bigger, more overwhelming and even more holy, but none are as stately.

(Hot tip for 21st-century architects: adapt the Greek Cross floor plan to space-age churches. See the chandelier hanging there? It's composed of many six-armed, "three-dimensional" Greek Crosses. Imagine that as an orbiting space-station cathedral . . .)

The Mosaics

From the "Our Lady of Anti-Gravity" chandelier, run your eyes up the support chain to the dome above. This is one of the oldest mosaics in the church, from around 1125. The scene is the Pentecost. The Holy Spirit in the form of a dove sends out tongues of fire — the miracle of speaking in tongues, looking like a red horn on each head — to the 12 Apostles below. (*O sages standing in God's holy fire as in the gold mosaic of a wall, come from the holy fire...and be the singing masters of my soul* — Yeats.) While the mosaics in the Atrium were from the Old Testament, we've now entered the new age of the New Testament.

Mosaic — St. Mark's is covered with intricate Byzantine-style mosaics. Imagine paving a football field with contact lenses.

☞ *Walk up the aisle again to the central dome. Take a seat against a*
pillar. The corner seat is ideal. The nice thing about marble is that it stays
cool even when you sit on it for awhile. Still cool? Sit here and read on.

Central Dome Mosaic

You've probably noticed that the floor is also mosaics, mostly geometrical designs and animals. You've also noticed it rolls like the sea. Venice
is sinking — and shifting — creating these cresting waves of stone.

Gape upwards. (It's fairly safe — there aren't as many pigeons in
here.) The mosaic in the central dome is, again, not the death of Jesus,
but the "Ascension" into heaven after resurrection. This isn't the dead,
crucified mortal Jesus shown in most churches, but a powerful God,
the Creator of All, seated on a crescent moon in the center of starry
heaven, solemnly giving us His blessing. Below Him is Mary (with shiny
golden Greek crosses on each shoulder and looking ready to play patty-
cake) flanked by two winged angels (with Greek crosses on their shoulders too) and the 12 Apostles.

These mosaics are made of tiny bits of glass that look like a whole
picture when seen at a distance, right? Traditional science has told us
that the bench you're sitting on is a "mosaic" of tiny atoms. But now
they see the atom itself as a mosaic of even smaller particles — electrons,
bosons, quarks...is there any end in sight?

Modern physicists (and Zen Buddhists) say no. They look at the whole
system, not its individual parts. To them, traditional science is on a wild
goose chase — like trying to understand this "Ascension" mosaic by
looking at each individual chip separately under a microscope.

Sailing to Byzantium

Two things you should see in the church are the Treasury (Tesoro)
and the Golden Altarpiece (Pala d'Oro). This is your best chance, outside of Istanbul or Ravenna, to experience the glory of the Byzantine
civilization. The Treasury entrance is in the right transept. The Altarpiece is in the apse, though the entrance to it is also in the right transept. (Is the greatest culture in Christendom worth the price of a cup of
coffee? You decide.)

For a thousand years, from 300-1300 A.D., Constantinople was the
greatest city in Europe, perhaps in the world. In 330 A.D., the Emperor
Constantine moved the Roman Empire's capital to the newly-built city
of Constantinople, taking with him Rome's best and brightest. While
the city of Rome decayed and fell, the Eastern half of the Empire lived
on, speaking the Greek language and adopting a more Oriental outlook.

Venetian traders tapped the wealth of this culture during the Crusades, the series of military expeditions to rescue the holy city of Jerusalem from the Moslems. In the Fourth Crusade, in 1204, when Constantinople was threatened by the Turks, they appealed to their fellow Christians in the West for help. The Pope launched a Crusade, the armies marched, they fought the Turks, drove the savage infidel beasts away, entered the city...and proceeded to loot it themselves. (This was perhaps the lowest point in Christian history until the advent of TV evangelism.) Among the treasures shipped back to Venice were the bronze horses and many of the artifacts in the Treasury.

☞ *Enter the Treasury (Tesoro) at the far corner of the right transept.*

Treasury

You'll see Byzantine chalices, silver reliquaries, monstrous monstrances (for displaying the Communion wafer), the marble "Chair of St. Mark" and icons done in gold, silver, enamel, agate, studded with precious gems, etc. This is marvelous handiwork, but all the more marvelous because many were done in 500 A.D., when Western Europe was still rooting in the mud.

☞ *Exiting the Treasury, cross the right transept to the Golden Altarpiece entrance — Pala d'Oro. On the way, notice the door under the rose window at the end of the transept. This was the Doge's private entrance direct from the connecting Doge's Palace. Follow the crowds behind the altar. Read as you shuffle on.*

Golden Altarpiece ("Pala d'Oro")

The first thing you see, after showing your combo ticket, is the high altar itself. Beneath this lies the body of Mark, the Gospel writer (see the tomb through the grate under the altar — it says "Marxus"). Legend has it that before he died he visited Venice, where an angel promised him he could rest his weary bones when he died. Shhh.

Above the altar is a marble canopy. The four supporting columns are wonderful and mysterious — scholars don't even know whether they're from 5th century Byzantium or 13th century Venice! I spent as much time looking at the funny New Testament scenes carved in them as at the Golden Altarpiece with its crowds and glaring lights. (On the right-hand pillar closest to the Altarpiece, fourth row from the bottom — is that a genie escaping from a bottle while someone tries to stuff him back in?)

The Golden Altarpiece is a dazzling gold monstrosity made of 80 Byzantine enamels with religious scenes on them set in gold. Amid the gold are rubies, emeralds, sapphires, pearls, amethysts and topaz. Byzan-

tine craftsmen made this for the Doges over the course of several centuries, 976-1345. It's a bit much to take in all at once, but one figure
you might recognize is in the center of the lower half — Jesus as Creator
of All, similar to the mosaic in the main dome — with Matthew, Mark,
Luke and John around him. Once you've looked at some of the individual
scenes, back up as far as this small room will let you and just let yourself
be dazzled by the "whole picture" — this "mosaic" of Byzantine greatness.

The Bronze Horses and View of the Piazza

☞ *The staircase up to the bronze horses is in the Atrium near the main
entrance. The sign says "Loggia dei Cavalli, Museo."*

Your ticket gives you...

1) A small museum with fragments of mosaics that you can examine
up close;

2) An upstairs gallery with an impressive topside view of the church
interior with its mosaic wallpaper;

3) The Loggia, the balcony overlooking the Piazza. Nice view, fun
people-watching;

The Bronze Horses — What
strange beauty in these
horses drove greedy men to
steal them from Greece to
Rome to Turkey to Venice to
France and back again?

4) The Bronze Horses. You can walk among the copies on the loggia
with their "1978" date on the hoof. Then go inside to a room with the
real things. Very impressive. Stepping lively in pairs with smiles on their
faces. Energy and exuberance. Originally gilded bronze, you can still
see some streaks of gold.

These horses have done some traveling in their day. Made in the time
of Alexander the Great, they were taken by Nero to Rome. Constantine
took them to his new capital in Constantinople. The Venetians then stole
them from their fellow Christians, during the looting of noble Constantinople, and brought them to San Marco.

What goes around comes around, and Napoleon came around and
took the horses, when he conquered Venice in 1797. They stood atop a
triumphal arch in the Louvre courtyard until Napoleon's empire was
"blown-aparte" and they were returned to their "rightful" home.

(What-goes-around-comes-around Dept., P.S.: The horses were again removed from their spot when attacked by their most dangerous enemy yet — 20th-century man. The threat of oxidation from pollution has sent them running for cover inside the church.)

Can you see why they were coveted by so many people, causing so much turmoil? That's not a rhetorical question requiring an obligatory "yes" answer. I mean it — what is it about these brazen beasts that caused greedy people to steal them from Greece to Rome to Turkey to Venice to France and back "home" to this spot?

THE DOGE'S PALACE

☞ *Grab a spot on the bench back at Sansovino's* Loggetta *at the base of the* Campanile.

Venice is a city of beautiful facades — palaces, churches, carnival masks — that can cover darker interiors of intrigue and decay. The Doge's Palace, with its frilly pink exterior, hides the fact that "the Most Serene Republic" in its heyday was far from serene.

The Doge's Palace housed the fascinating government of this rich and powerful Empire. It was the seat of government and home for the Venetian ruler known as the "Doge", or Duke (pron: Doje). For four centuries, this was the most powerful half-acre in Europe. The Doges wanted it to reflect the wealth of the Republic, impressing visitors and serving as a reminder that the Venetians were number one in Europe.

The Exterior

"The Wedding Cake", "The Tablecloth", or "The Pink House" is also sometimes known as the Doge's Palace. The style is called Venetian Gothic, and the arches and windows come to a point like Gothic arches, but the upper half has an Eastern, Islamic flavor with its abstract patterns.

Doge's Palace — The multi-national corporation known as the Venetian Empire was ruled from this palace — the home of its C.E.O., the "Doge" or Duke.

It does look like a tablecloth and the lower columns look like table legs. They originally had pedestals, but these were covered over as the columns sank. If you compare this delicate, top-heavy structure with the massive fortress palaces of Florence, you realize the wisdom of building a city in the middle of the sea — you have no natural enemies.

The palace was originally built in the 800s, but most of what we see came after 1300 as it was expanded to meet the needs of the Empire. Each Doge wanted to leave his mark on history with a new wing. But so much of the city's money was spent on the building that finally a law was passed ordering an enormous fine on anyone who even mentioned any new building. That worked okay for awhile, but Doges had pocketbooks to match their egos. One brave and wealthy Doge proposed a new wing, paid his fine...and started building again.

☞   *The entrance gate is on the Piazzetta, next to the Basilica.*

The Entrance Gate

This is where VIPs and ambassadors entered. Originally the whole gate was painted in bright red, blue and gold.

Pause to look into the nervous eyes of the four cuddly porphyry-stone Tetrarchs. This is an ancient statue ("rescued" from elsewhere and crudely plugged into this wall) of four co-leaders of the Roman Empire. Rome is falling, the Barbarians are closing in and each little guy clutches his neighbor — and his sword. Think of what they've seen on this square. Climb up and pose a photo with them.

☞   *Enter the gate and walk about halfway down the covered entry hall to where the statues above the grand stairway ahead are centered under the arch.*

Imagine yourself as a foreign dignitary on business to meet the Doge. Ahead of you is the grand staircase with two nearly nude statues of, I think, Moses and Paul Newman. The Doge and his aides would be waiting for you at the top. No matter who you were, you'd have to hoof it up — the powerful Doge would descend the stairs for no man.

You'll notice that the entry hall ceiling alternates between Gothic pointed-arch vaulting and round Roman arches. Much of the palace was built on the cusp between medieval and Renaissance.

☞   *The ticket booth is ahead on your left. Then go up the tourists' staircase, and look out over the courtyard (and the backside of Paul Newman) from the top of the VIP staircase.*

From here on, it's hard to get lost (though I've managed). It's a one-way system, so just follow the arrows.

The Courtyard

You have a Doge-eye view of the courtyard. Ambassadors would walk up this staircase to bow to you. The Doge was something like an "elected king" — which makes sense only in the "dictatorial republic" that was Venice. Technically he was just a noble selected by other nobles to carry out their laws and decisions. Gradually, though, the Doges extended their powers to where they ruled more like divine-right kings, striking the fear of death in all who opposed them.

Ahead of you on the right, notice that the palace is attached right to St. Mark's Cathedral. You can see the ugly brick of both structures — the stern inner structure without its painted-lady veneer of marble. On this tour, we'll see the sometimes harsh inner structure of this outwardly serene Republic.

☞ *Head down the loggia to the entrance. Climb the staircase to the first landing.*

The Golden Staircase

The palace was propaganda, designed to impress visitors. This gilded-ceiling staircase was something for them to write home about.

The first floor is where the Doges actually lived. It's usually roped off for temporary exhibitions, but pop your head in. Despite his great power, the Doge had to obey one ironclad rule — he and his family had to leave their own home and live in the Doge's Palace. Poor guy.

☞ *Ascend to the second floor, the small room at the top of the stairs, and grab a bench under the window.*

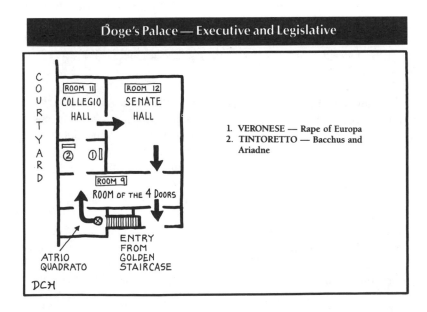

The "Atrio Quadrato"

Look at the ceiling painting, "Justice Presenting the Sword and Scales to Doge Girolano" by Tintoretto. It's a masterpiece by one of the greatest late-Renaissance masters. So what? I'll say it again — so what? May as well adopt the "so what" attitude now, because you'll get it sooner or later. There's so much great art here by great painters — mostly Tintoretto and Veronese — that you can't possibly appreciate it all. Best to treat it not as museum art but as nice wallpaper. Don't analyze, enjoy.

☞   *Enter the next room.*

Room of the Four Doors

This was the central clearinghouse for all the goings-on in the palace. Visitors trying to see the Doge or any other government official had to pass through here to present their papers and explain themselves. The three other doors then led them to their destination — the executive, legislative or judicial branch of government.

The room was designed by Palladio, the architect who did the impressive San Giorgio Maggiore Church you see almost floating across the Grand Canal from St. Mark's Square. On the intricate stucco ceiling, notice the feet of the women dangling down below the edge (above the windows), a typical Baroque technique of creating the illusion of 3-D.

On the wall is a painting by (ho-hum) Titian, showing a Doge kneeling with great piety before a woman embodying Faith holding the Cross of Jesus. Notice old Venice in the misty distance under the cross. This is one of many paintings you'll see of Doges in uncharacteristically humble poses — paid for, of course, by the Doges themselves. Blessed are the earthly, for they shall inherit the meek.

☞   *Enter the small room with the big fireplace and have a seat.*

The Ante-Collegio

It took a big title or bribe to get in to see the Doge. But first you were told to wait here, combing your hair, adjusting your robe, popping a Certs and preparing the gifts you'd brought. While you cooled your heels and warmed your hands at the elaborate fireplace, you might look at some of the paintings — among the finest in the palace, worthy of any museum in the world.

"The Rape of Europa" by Veronese (opposite the window) is a celebration of the luxury and sensuality of Venice at its peak. The Venetian Renaissance looked back to pagan Greece and Rome for subjects to paint, a big change from the saints and crucifixions of the Middle Ages. Here Zeus, the king of the Greek gods, appears in the form of a bull to carry off a beautiful earthling. This is certainly no medieval condemnation of sex and violence, but a celebration in cheery pastel colors of the earthy, optimistic spirit of the Renaissance.

VERONESE — Rape of Europa. One of the world's great masterpieces is just another ho-hum painting — wallpaper in this lavish palace.

Tintoretto's "Bacchus and Ariadne" (next to the window) is another colorful display of Venice's sensual tastes. The god of wine offers a ring to the mortal Ariadne who's being crowned with stars. The ring is the center of a spinning wheel of flesh with the three arms like spokes.

But wait, the Doge is ready for us. Let's go in.

☞   *Enter the next room.*

The Collegio — (Executive Branch)

The Doge would sit on the platform at the far end surrounded by his counselors to receive ambassadors, who laid their gifts at his feet and pleaded their country's case. The gifts were often essentially tribute from lands conquered by Venetian generals. All official ceremonies, such as ratifying treaties, were held here.

At other times it was the private meeting place of the Doge and his cabinet to discuss secrets of state, proposals to give the legislature, or negotiations with the Pope. The wooden benches around the sides where they sat are original. The clock on the wall is a 24-hour clock with Roman numerals and a sword for hands. Wait a minute, there's something wrong here...the order of the Roman numerals. Who says you can't turn back the hands of time?

The ceiling is 24-carat gold with paintings by Veronese. These are not frescoes (painting on wet plaster), like in the Sistine Chapel, but actual canvases painted here on earth and then placed on the ceiling. Venice's humidity would have melted frescoes like so much mascara within years. Check out the painting of the woman with the spider web (on the ceiling, opposite the big window). This was the Venetian symbol of "Discussion". You can imagine the many intricate webs of truth and lies woven in this room by the Doge's sinister nest of advisers.

☞   *Enter the large Senate Room.*

286   *St. Mark's and the Doge's Palace*

The Senate Room — (Legislative Branch)

This was the center of the Venetian government — technically. Venice was technically a republic ruled by the elected Senate that met here, though its power was gradually overshadowed by the Doge and, later, the Council of Ten. Two hundred senators, from the ranks of the nobility, chaired by the Doge, debated and passed laws and made declarations of war in this large, impressive room.

Tintoretto's "The Triumph of Venice" on the ceiling (center) shows the city in all its glory. Venice, as a woman, is up in heaven with the Greek gods, while lesser nations swirl up to give her gifts and tribute. Do you kind of get the feeling the Venetian aristocracy was proud of its city?

On the wall are two large clocks with the signs of the zodiac and phases of the moon. The Senators shared one of them with the Doge next door. And there's one final oddity in this room, in case you hadn't noticed it yet. In one of the wall paintings (above the entry door), there's actually a Doge. . . not kneeling!

☞ *Pass again through the Room of the Four Doors, then through a couple of small rooms to the large hall with a semicircular platform at the far end.*

Room of the Council of Ten — (Judicial Branch)

Venice's worldwide reputation for swift, harsh and secret justice came from the dreaded Council of Ten. This body consisting of the Doge and other elected officials dealt out justice for traitors, murderers and "morals" violators.

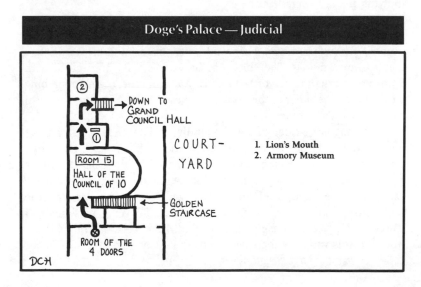

Slowly they developed into a CIA-type (or KGB-type) unit with their own force of policemen, guards, spies, informers and even assassins. They had their own budget and were accountable to no one, soon making them the *de facto* ruling body of the "Republic". No one was safe from the spying eye of the "Terrible Ten". If you were even suspected of disloyalty or troublemaking, you could be swept off the streets, tried, judged and thrown into the dark dungeons in the palace for the rest of your life, without so much as a Miranda warning.

It was in this room that the Council met to decide punishments — who lived, died, was decapitated, tortured or merely thrown in jail. The small door leading off the platform leads through secret passages to the prisons and torture chambers.

The large central oval ceiling painting by Veronese (a copy, actually) shows "Jupiter Descending from Heaven to Strike Down the Vices", redundantly informing the accused that justice in Venice was swift and harsh.

The dreaded Council of Ten was, of course, eventually disbanded. Today, their descendants enforce the dress code for tourists entering St. Mark's.

☞ *Pass through the next room noticing the "Lion's Mouth" to the right of the exit door. These letter boxes, known as "Lions' Mouths" because some had a lion's head, are scattered throughout the palace. Anyone who had a complaint or suspicion about anyone else could accuse him by simply dropping a slip of paper in the mouth. This set the blades of justice turning inside the palace.*

The Armory Museum is up the stairs ahead of you.

Armory Museum

The aesthetics of killing is beyond me, but I must admit I've never seen a better collection of halberds, falchions, mulchers, targes, morions and brigandines in my life. (One of these words is a fake.) There are three small rooms to browse through. If nothing else, this stock of weapons makes you realize how important the military was in keeping the East-West trade lines open.

You'll see artistic shields, a midget's armor, a very very early attempt at a machine gun, old globes and old quivers (but no mulchers). Squint out the window at the far end. It's Palladio's San Giorgio again and Venice's *Lido* (beach) in the distance.

☞ *After the Armory go downstairs, turn left and pass through the long hall with a wood-beam ceiling. Notice the large globes of the world in the second room to the left, a reminder that distant trading was the bread and butter of Venice.*

Now turn right and open your eyes as wide as you can.

Hall of the Grand Council

It took a room this size to contain the grandeur of the Most Serene Republic. This huge room (180 feet long, the second-largest wooden room in Europe after Vienna's Schonbrunn) could accommodate up to 2000 people at once — the nobility who were the backbone of the empire. The Doge, the Senate and the Council of Ten were all subordinate to the Grand Council which elected them from among their ranks.

Once the Doge was elected he was presented to the people of Venice from the balcony on the far end of the room that overlooks the *Piazzetta*. A noble would announce, "Here is your Doge, if it pleases you." That was fine, until one time when the people weren't pleased. From then on they just said, "Here is your Doge."

Ringing the room are portraits in chronological order of 76 Doges. The one at the far end that's blacked out is the notorious Doge Falier, who opposed the will of the Grand Council. He was tried for treason and beheaded. Ironically, the Doge whose memory they tried to blot out is now the best remembered. Fame is great — infamy is better.

TINTORETTO — Paradise. Tintoretto's monsterpiece has more square footage than my apartment. Over 500 (count 'em) figures, including a portrait of his daughter (center) who passed away just before completion.

On the wall over the Doge's throne is Tintoretto's monsterpiece, "Paradise", the largest oil painting in the world. At almost 1700 sq. ft., I could slice it up and wallpaper my entire apartment with it, with enough left over for placemats.

Christ and Mary are at the top of heaven surrounded by 500 saints who ripple out in concentric rings. Tintoretto worked on this in the last years of his long life. On the day it was finished, his daughter died. He got his brush out again and painted her as saint #501. She's dead center with the blue skirt, hands clasped, getting sucked up to heaven. At least, that's what an Italian tour guide told me.

The rest of the room's paintings show great moments in Venice's glory days of military conquest. Veronese's "The Apotheosis of Venice" (on the ceiling at the Tintoretto end) is a typically unsubtle work, showing Venice as a woman being crowned a goddess by an angel. Actually, the Venetians were looking back to better times before the series of military defeats that began her decline. One by one the Turks gobbled up their Eastern trading outposts. In the West the rest of Europe ganged up on Venice to reduce her power. To top it off, by 1500, Portugal had broken Venice's East-West trade monopoly by finding a sea-route to the East around Africa. From 1500 1800 Venice remained a glorious city, but not the great world power she once was.

Out the windows is a fine view of the domes of the Basilica and the palace courtyard below. There's Paul Newman again, and the ugly brick walls and the round- and pointed-arched arcades.

☞ *Read the introduction to the Prisons here in the Grand Council Hall where there are more benches and fewer rats.*

The Prisons

The Palace had its own dungeons. The Doges could sentence, torture and jail political opponents in the privacy of their own home. The most notorious cells were "The Wells" in the basement, so-called because they were deep, wet and cramped.

By the 1500s, the Doges had gone to the Wells once too often, and they were full of political prisoners. New prisons were built across the canal to the east of the palace and connected with a covered bridge — covered so they could still imprison opponents without public knowledge.

☞ *Exit the Grand Hall — next to the monsterpiece — and pass through a series of rooms and once-secret passages, through the covered Bridge of Sighs over the canal to the "New" Prisons.*

Medieval justice was harsh. The cells consisted of cold stone with heavy barred windows, a wooden plank for a bed, a shelf and a bucket. (My question — what did they put on the shelf?)

Circle the cells. Notice the carvings made by prisoners on some of the stone window sills of the cells. My favorites are in the far corner of this rectangular building.

The Bridge of Sighs

Criminals were tried and sentenced in the palace, then marched across the canal here to the dark prisons. On this bridge they got their one last look at Venice. They gazed out at the sky, the water, the beautiful buildings — and sighed.

☞ Cross back over the Bridge of Sighs, pausing to look through the marble-trellised windows at all the tourists and San Giorgio church. If you haven't done so already, sigh.

Accademia,
Venice

The main sight to see in Venice is Venice. I'm a little hesitant to recommend visiting the Accademia if you have only a day in Venice.

Still, the Accademia is the greatest museum anywhere for Venetian Renaissance art, and a good overview of painters whose works you'll see all over town. Venetian art is underrated and, I think, misunderstood. It's nowhere near as famous today as the work of the florescent Florentines — Michelangelo, Leonardo, Botticelli — but it's livelier, more colorful and simply more fun. This tour of Venice's best collection of art will be brief only because there's so much great "art" on the streets and canals of this postcard city.

Gallerie dell' Accademia
(pron: ack-uh-day-mee-uh
while gesticulating spasmodically)

Hours: Tues.-Fri. 9:00-19:30; Mon. & Sat. 9:00-14:00; Sun. 9:00-13:00. Double check these ever-changing hours at the Tourist Info.
Cost: 8000 L.
Tour length: One hour.
Getting there: Walk 15 minutes from San Marco, following signs to "Accademia". Vaporetto #1 to Accademia stop on Grand Canal.
Information: Precious little.
Tel. 522-2247
Misc.: Cheap restaurants and snack stands nearby. The Peggy Guggenheim

Museum of Modern Art is a five-minute walk east along the Grand Canal. Housed in a small palace on the Grand Canal, it's an excellent collection, well displayed and a great introduction to nearly every major movement in modern art (read the Pompidou Gallery chapter for help).

Accademia — Overview

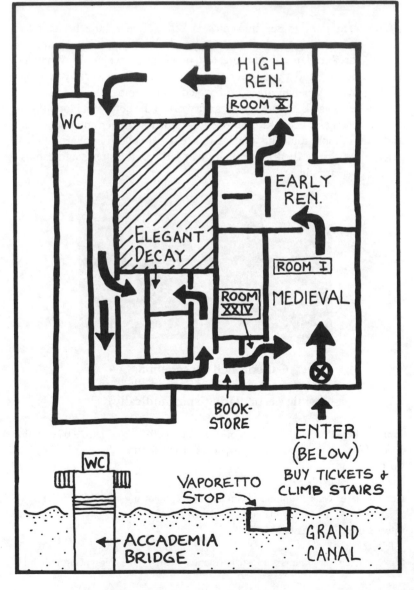

The "Biennale" is a World's Fair of contemporary art that Venice hosts the summer of each even-numbered year. Each country has its own pavilion. (If the Venice map looks like a fish, the Biennale grounds are in the tail.)
Starring: Titian, Veronese, Giorgione, Tintoretto.

VENICE — SWIMMING IN LUXURY

☞ *Buy your ticket, check your bag and head upstairs to a large hall. Immediately past the ticket-taker, turn left and enter the small Room XXIV. Have a seat.*

The Venetian love of luxury shines through in Venetian painting. We'll see grand canvases of colorful, spacious settings, peopled with happy Venetians in luxurious clothes having a great time. Even in solemn religious works, the Venetian love of color and beauty is obvious.

We'll work chronologically from medieval days to the 1700s. But before we start at the medieval beginning, let's sneak a peek at a work by the greatest Venetian Renaissance master, Titian.

Titian — *Presentation of the Virgin (La Presentazione della Vergine al Tempio)*

Look at this masterpiece while I just tick off some of the typical features of Venetian Renaissance art: 1) bright, rich color; 2) big canvases; 3) Renaissance architectural backgrounds; 4) slice of life scenes of Venice (notice the market woman in the foreground selling eggs); and 5) three-dimensional realism. This work is a good example of all of these.

TITIAN — Presentation of the Virgin. Venetian High Renaissance perfection: big canvas, Renaissance architecture, colorful Venetian scene, three-dimensional realism.

The scene is the popular "Biblical" story (though it's not in the Bible) of the child Mary, later to be the mother of Jesus, being presented to the high priest in Jerusalem's temple. But here the religious scene is more an excuse for a grand display of Renaissance architecture and colorful robes — the Venetian love of luxury.

The painting is a parade of colors. Titian (pron: TEESH-un) leads you from color to color. First, the deep blue sky and mountains in the background. Then down to the bright red robe of one of the elders. Then you notice the figures turning and pointing at something. Your eye follows up the stairs to the magnificent jewelled robes of the priests.

But wait! What was that along the way? In a pale blue dress that sets her apart from all the other colored robes, dwarfed by the enormous staircase and columns is the tiny shiny figure of the child Mary, almost floating up to the astonished priest. She is unnaturally small, towered over by the priests and easily overlooked at first glance. When we finally notice her, we realize all the more how delicate she is, a fragile flower amid the hustle, bustle and epic grandeur. Venetians love this painting and call it, appropriately enough, the "Little Mary".

Now that we've gotten a taste of Renaissance Venice at its peak, let's backtrack and see some of Titian's predecessors.

☞ *Return to the large first hall (Room I) stopping at the work closest to the ticket-taker.*

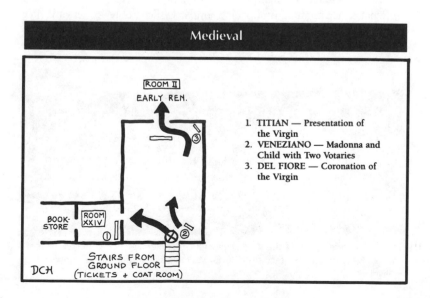

Medieval

ROOM II
EARLY REN.

1. **TITIAN** — Presentation of the Virgin
2. **VENEZIANO** — Madonna and Child with Two Votaries
3. **DEL FIORE** — Coronation of the Virgin

BOOK-STORE   ROOM XXIV

STAIRS FROM GROUND FLOOR
DCH   (TICKETS + COAT ROOM)

MEDIEVAL — PRE-3-D

Medieval painting like you see in this hall was religious. The point was to teach Bible stories and doctrines to the illiterate masses by using symbolism. This art then is less realistic, less colorful and less dramatic than later Renaissance art. Look around the hall and you'll see a lot of gold in the paintings. Medieval Venetians, with their close ties to the East, borrowed techniques like gold-leafing from Byzantine (modern Istanbul) religious icons.

Veneziano — *Madonna and Child with Two Votaries (Madonna in Trono col Bambino e Due Devoti)*
There's a golden Byzantine background of heaven, and the golden haloes let us illiterate masses know that these folks are holy. The child Jesus is a baby in a bubble, an iconographical symbol of His "aura" of holiness.
Notice how two-dimensional and unrealistic this painting is. The size of the figures reflects their religious importance, not their actual size — Mary is huge, being both the mother of Christ as well as "Holy Mother Church". Jesus is next, then the two angels crowning Mary. Finally, in the corner, are two mere mortals kneeling in devotion.
☞ *In the far right corner of the room you'll find...*

Jacobello Del Fiore — *Coronation of the Virgin*
This is a swarming beehive of saints. It's crowded in an attempt to cram as much information as possible into one space. The architectural setting is a clumsy attempt at three-dimensionality. The saints are simply stacked one on top of the other, rather than receding into the distance as they would in real life.
☞ *Enter Room II at the far end of this hall.*

EARLY RENAISSANCE (1450-1500)

Only a few decades later artists rediscovered the natural world and how to capture it on canvas. With this Renaissance, or "rebirth", of the arts and attitudes of ancient Greece and Rome, painters took a giant leap forward. They weeded out the jumble of symbols and fleshed out cardboard characters into real people.

Giovanni Bellini — San Giobbe altarpiece (La Madonna in Trono col Bambino tra i Santi Francesco . . . etc.)
One key to the Renaissance was balance. Here Bellini (pron: bell-EEN-

ee) takes only a few figures, places them in a spacious architectural setting, and balances them half on one side of Mary and half on the other. The overall effect is one of calm and serenity rather than the hubbub of the "Coronation" we just saw.

G. BELLINI — San Giobbe Altarpiece
Titian's teacher gives us a spacious
Renaissance setting with symmetrical
saints — three on the left, three on the
right.

Sure, this is a religious scene — a mythical meeting of Mary and the baby Jesus with saints. But Bellini is more interested in pleasing the eye than teaching Church doctrine. Left to right, you'll find saints Francis (who founded the Franciscan order in the 12th century), John the Baptist, Job, Dominic (founder of another order of monks), Sebastian and Louis.

The painting has three descending arches. The top one is of course the Roman arch above the scene. But below that is a pyramid-shaped arch formed by the figures themselves, with Mary's head at the peak — see it? And nestled beneath that is a smaller arch formed by the three musician angels. Subconsciously, this creates a mood of spaciousness, order and balance.

Bellini was the teacher of two more Venetian greats, Titian and Gior-

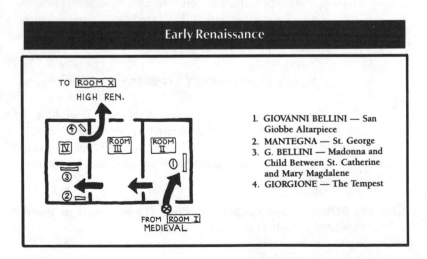

Early Renaissance

TO ROOM X
HIGH REN.

FROM ROOM I
MEDIEVAL

1. GIOVANNI BELLINI — San Giobbe Altarpiece
2. MANTEGNA — St. George
3. G. BELLINI — Madonna and Child Between St. Catherine and Mary Magdalene
4. GIORGIONE — The Tempest

gione. His gift to the Venetian Renaissance was the "haze" he put over his scenes, giving them an idealized, glowing, serene atmosphere. This Vaseline-on-the-lens beauty would be copied by many others.

☞ *Climb the small staircase into Room IV.*

Mantegna — *St. George (San Giorgio)*

This Christian warrior is essentially a Greek nude sculpture with clothes painted on. Notice his stance with the weight resting on one leg (*contrapposto*), the same as a classical sculpture, or Michelangelo's "David", or an Italian guy trying to look cool on the street-corner. Also, Mantegna (pron: mon-TAIN-ya) has placed him in a doorway that's really just an architectural niche designed for a classical statue.

MANTEGNA — St. George. This Greek-statue-with-clothes-on stands proudly in a Renaissance niche. The road snakes into the distance, giving the illusion of even more depth.

The Renaissance began in Florence among sculptors and architects. Even the painters were sculptors, "carving" out figures (like this) with sharp outlines, then filling them in with color. "St. George" is different in that respect from other works in the museum. It has, literally, a harder edge to it compared with the hazy outlines of Bellini.

"St. George" typifies Renaissance balance — a combination of stability and movement, alertness and relaxation, humility and proud confidence. With the broken lance in his hand and the dragon at his feet, George is the strong Renaissance man slaying the medieval dragon of superstition and oppression.

Bellini — *Madonna and Child Between St. Catherine and Mary Magdalene*

In contrast to Mantegna's sharp three-dimensionality, this is just three heads on a flat plane with a black backdrop. Their features are soft, hazy, atmospheric, glowing out of the darkness as though lit by the soft light of a candle. It's not sculptural line that's important here, but color — warm, golden, glowing flesh tones.

Bellini painted dozens of Madonna-and-Childs in his day. This Virgin Mary's okay, I guess (check out his "Madonna of the Small Trees" nearby), but it can't compare with the sheer idealized beauty of Mary Magdalene (on the right). With her hair down like the prostitute she was, yet with a childlike face, thoughtful and repentant, this is the perfect image of the innocent woman who sinned by loving too much.

Giorgione — The Tempest

It's the calm before the storm. The atmosphere is heavy, luminous but ominous. There's a sense of mystery. Who is the woman suckling her baby in the middle of the countryside? And the soldier — is he spying on her or protecting her? Do they know that the serenity of this beautiful landscape is about to be shattered by an approaching storm?

GIORGIONE — The Tempest. Giorgione captures the beautiful, heavy, mysterious calm before the storm — a serene scene about to be shattered by lightning.

The mystery is heightened by contrasting elements. The soldier in armor on the left contrasts with the naked lady with her baby at right. The austere ruined columns contrast with the lusciousness of Nature. And, most importantly, the stillness of the foreground scene is in direct opposition to the threatening storm in the background.

Giorgione (pron: jor-JONE-y) was as mysterious as his few paintings, yet he left a lasting impression. A student of Bellini, he learned to use haziness to create a mood. He also learned to paint with color rather than line. This is a balanced Renaissance work, but balanced with color alone. Patches of green/blue on the sides balance each other perfectly, split down the middle by the grey and yellow of the storm.

This work captures the melancholy mood of beauty. Nothing beautiful lasts. Flowers fade, Mary Magdalenes grow old, and, in "The Tempest," the fleeting stillness of a rare moment of peace is about to be shattered by the slash of lightning — the true center of the composition.

☞ *Exit and turn left, passing through the long Room VI and up the steps to the large Room X.*

VENETIAN HIGH RENAISSANCE — TITIAN, VERONESE, TINTORETTO (1500-1600)

Veronese — *Feast at the House of Levi*

Parrrrty!! Stand about ten yards from this enormous canvas, to where it just fills your field of vision...and hey, you're invited. Venice loves the good life, and the party's in full swing. You're in a huge room with a great view of Venice. Everyone's dressed to kill in brightly colored silks and jewels. The servants bring food and drink while the band rocks out.

VERONESE — Feast of the House of Levi. This was originally titled "The Last Supper," until Veronese was hauled before the Inquisition for painting Christ and His holy apostles in a Venetian orgy. Veronese didn't change a thing . . . except the title.

This captures the Venetian attitude ("More love, less attitude"), as well as the style of Venetian Renaissance painting. Remember? 1) bright colors, 2) big canvases; 3) Renaissance architectural settings; 4) scenes of Venice life; and 5) three-dimensional realism. Painters had mastered realism and now gloried in it.

"The Feast at the House of Levi" is, believe it or not, a religious work painted for a monastery. The original title was "The Last Supper". See

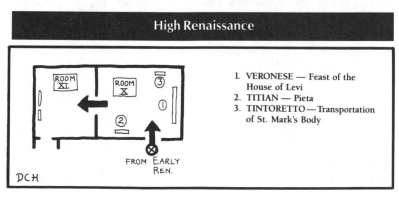

High Renaissance

1. VERONESE — Feast of the House of Levi
2. TITIAN — Pieta
3. TINTORETTO — Transportation of St. Mark's Body

ROOM XI

ROOM X

FROM EARLY REN.

DCH

it? Underneath all the wild goings-on, there's Jesus in the center, flanked by his twelve disciples, celebrating a final meal before being crucified.

This festive feast shows the optimistic spirit of pagan Greece and Rome that was reborn in the Renaissance. Life was a good thing, beauty was to be enjoyed and man was a strong, good creature capable of making his own decisions and planning his own life. Yet to Renaissance men and women this didn't exclude religion. To them, the divine was expressed through natural beauty. God was glorified by glorifying man, His greatest creation. Humanism was an expression of devotion.

Uh-uh, said the Church. In their eyes, the new humanism was the same as the old atheism. The brief *glasnost* of the Renaissance froze quickly after the Reformation, when half of Europe left the Catholic Church and became Protestant. The Church pulled in the wagons and stamped out any hint of free pagan thought that might encourage more deserters.

Veronese (pron: varo-NAY-zee) was hauled before the Inquisition. What did he mean by painting such a bawdy Last Supper? With dwarf jesters? And apostles picking their teeth? And half-dressed ladies? And dogs? And a black man, God forbid? And worst of all, some German soldiers — that is, Protestants (gasp!) — at the far right?!!

Veronese argued that it was just artistic license, so they asked to see his — it had expired. But the solution was simple — rather than change the painting, just fine-tune the title. The "Last Supper" became the "Feast of the House of Levi".

☞ *The Titians are on the wall to the right of Veronese.*

Titian — *Pietà*

The Counter-Reformation even affected the great Titian in his last years. Titian (pron: TEESH-un) was perhaps the most famous painter of his day — even more famous than Michelangelo. He was a great portrait painter and a friend of the dukes, kings and popes he painted. He was cultured, witty, a fine musician and businessman — an all-around Renaissance kind of guy. The story goes that he once dropped his brush while painting a portrait of the Emperor Charles V, the most powerful man in Europe. Charles stooped and picked it up for him, a tribute to Titian's stature and genius.

Titian was 99 years old when he painted this. He had seen the birth, rise and decline of the Renaissance. Remember "Little Mary," the colorful, exuberant Titian painting we saw at the beginning, done at the height of the Renaissance? Now the canvas is darker, the mood more somber. Jesus has just been executed, and His followers have removed His body from the cross. They grieve over it before burying it. Titian painted this to hang over his own tomb.

There are some Renaissance elements, but they create a whole different mood — the optimism is gone. Jesus is in a sculpture niche like Mantegna's confident St. George, but here the massive Roman architecture overpowers the figures, making them look puny and helpless. The lion statues are downright fierce and threatening. Instead of the clear realism of Renaissance paintings, Titian has used rough messy brush strokes, a technique that would be picked up by the Impressionists three centuries later. Instead of simple Renaissance balance, Titian has added a dramatic compositional element — starting with the lion at lower right, a line moves up diagonally along the figures, culminating in the grief-stricken Mary Magdalene who turns away, flinging her arm in despair.

Finally, the kneeling figure of Joseph of Arimathea is a self-portrait of the aging Titian himself, tending to the corpse of the once-powerful, now-dead Renaissance man.

Tintoretto — *Transportation of St. Mark's Body (Trafugamento del corpo di San Marco)*

This is the event that put Venice on the map, painted in the dramatic, emotional style that developed after the Renaissance. Tintoretto would have made a great black-velvet painter. His colors burn with a metallic sheen, and he does everything possible to make his subject popular with the common man. In fact, Tintoretto was a common man himself, self-taught, who took only a few classes from Titian before striking out on his own. He sold paintings in the marketplace in his youth, and he insisted on living in the poor part of town even after he got famous.

TINTORETTO — Transportation of St. Mark's Body. In this sneak preview of Baroque, Tintoretto trades Renaissance balance for heightened emotion. We can almost step right through the canvas into this exciting scene.

Tintoretto has caught the scene at its most dramatic moment. The Moslems in Alexandria are about to burn Mark's body (there's the smoke from the fire in the center), when suddenly a hurricane appears miraculously, sending them running for cover. (See the wisps of baby angel faces in the storm, blowing on the infidels? Look hard on the left side.) Meanwhile, the Venetian merchants whisk the body away.

Tintoretto makes us part of the action. The square tiles in the courtyard run straight away from us, an extension of our reality, as though we could step right into the scene — or the merchants could step into ours.

Tintorettos abound here, in the next room and throughout Venice. Look for these characteristics, some of which became standard features of baroque art that followed the Renaissance: 1) heightened drama, violent scenes, strong emotions; 2) elongated bodies; 3) strong contrasts between dark and light; 4) harsh colors; 5) diagonal compositions.

☞ *Spend some time in this room, the peak of Venice and the climax of the museum. Venice is sinking in works by Titian, Veronese and Tintoretto. After browsing, enter the next large room. At the far end, you'll find a large round framed painting.*

ELEGANT DECAY (1600-1800)

G.B. Tiepolo — *Discovery of the True Cross*

Tiepolo was the last of the great colorful, theatrical Venetian painters. He took the colors of Titian, the grand settings of Veronese and the dramatic angles of Tintoretto, and plastered them on the ceilings of Europe. His best known works are the ceiling decorations in baroque palaces like the Royal Palace of Madrid and the Wurzburg *Residenz*.

Tiepolo was a master of illusion. His works look as though they open up into heaven. Saints and angels cavort overhead as we look up their dresses. His strongly "foreshortened" figures are masterpieces of technical skill, making us feel like the heavenly vision is taking place right above

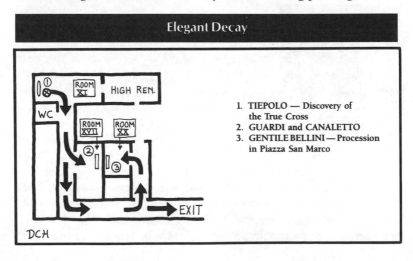

Elegant Decay

HIGH REN.

WC

ROOM XI

ROOM XVII

ROOM XX

EXIT

DCH

1. TIEPOLO — Discovery of the True Cross
2. GUARDI and CANALETTO
3. GENTILE BELLINI — Procession in Piazza San Marco

our heads. Think back on those clumsy attempts at three-dimensionality we saw in the medieval room, and realize how far painting has come.

Nearby is Luca Giordano's "Crucifixion of St. Peter" which also uses a dramatic angle to place us in the thick of the scene — right at the foot of the upside-down cross. The violent subject, rippling muscles and heightened emotion are baroque at its baroque-iest.

☞ *Works of the later Venetians are in rooms branching off the long corridor to your left. Walking down the corridor, the first right leads to the WC. Stop in Room XVII, the first door on the left.*

Guardi and Canaletto ("Antonio Canal")

By the 1700s Venice, retired as a world power, had become Europe's #1 tourist attraction. Wealthy sons and daughters of the nobility traveled here to soak up its art and culture. They wanted souvenirs of their trip, and what better memento than a picture of the city itself?

Guardi and Canaletto painted "postcards" for visitors who lost their heart to the romance of Venice. The city produced less art...but Venice itself was art. Here are some familiar views of a city which has aged gracefully.

Canaletto gives us a camera's-eye perspective on the city, while Guardi sweetens it up. In Guardi's "The Island of S. Giorgio Maggiore" (right in front of you as you enter Room XVII), we see that familiar view across the water from St. Mark's Square. Guardi has caught the play of light at sunset, the green of the water and sky, the pink light off the distant buildings, the Venice that exists in the hearts of lovers — an Impressionist work a century ahead of its time.

☞ *Follow the corridor, turning left at the end. Then take your first left, then left again till there ain't nothing left. Got it? Are you in Room XX?*

Gentile Bellini — Procession in Piazza San Marco (Processione in piazza San Marco)

A fitting end to our tour is a look back at Venice in its heyday. This wide-angle view by Bellini's big brother — more than any human eye could take in at once — reminds us how little Venice has changed over the centuries. There's St. Mark's gleaming gold with mosaics; the three flagpoles out front; the old Campanile on the right; the Doges' Palace. Regardless of its distance from us, every detail is in perfect focus and presented for our inspection. Take some time to linger over it.

Now get outta here, you knuckleheads, and enjoy the real thing.

☞ *Exit by backtracking to the main corridor and turning left past the bookstore. Say Ciao to Titian's "Little Mary" on the way out.*

Florence —
The Renaissance Walk

Florence gave birth to the Renaissance. Europe and its offspring haven't slowed down since. Great and rich as Florence may be, it's easily covered on foot, and while "you could spend a lifetime here", let's pretend we've got five hours — three for a walk through the old town, from "David" to the Duomo to the river, and two for a tour of the Uffizi, the greatest collection of Italian painting anywhere.

The Renaissance sights of downtown Florence (Firenze)

Hours: Accademia (Michelangelo's "David") — Tues.-Sat. 9:00-14:00; Sun. 9:00-13:00; closed Mon. (10,000 L).
The Duomo (cathedral) — daily 10:00-18:00, sometimes closed for lunch (free).
Climb the Dome — Mon.-Sat. 10:00-17:00.
Giotto's Tower — 9:00-19:00 (4,000 L).
Baptistry — 13:00-18:00, Sun. 9:00-13:00 (free).
The famous Baptistry bronze doors are outside, always "open."
Museo del Opera del Duomo ("Piazza del Duomo" #9) — Mon.-Sat. 9:00-19:00; Sun. 10:00-13:00 (4,000 L).

Tour Length: 3 hours.

Getting there: The Accademia is a 15-minute walk from the train station, 10 from the cathedral.

Information: Information office at the train station (try to pick up the Xeroxed update of current museum hours).
Two fine bookshops across from the Accademia.

Accademia tel. 214375.

Misc.: WCs in Accademia (downstairs near ticket booth) inside the Palazzo Vecchio (enter on left side) and in restaurants all along walk.

The Accademia is most crowded on Sun. and Tues. and right at 9:00.

The cheaper cafeterias and ice cream shops are just off Via Dei Calzaiolo.

Starring: Michelangelo, Brunelleschi, Ghiberti, *gelati.*

Orientation

The Duomo, Florence's cathedral with the distinctive red dome, is the center of Florence and the orientation point for this walk. If you ever get lost, home's the dome.

Our slightly-more-than-half-mile walk past Florence's top sights runs from the Accademia (where Michelangelo's "David" is), past the Duomo, down Florence's main pedestrian-only street to the Arno River.

We'll start at the Accademia, though you could easily start at the Duomo and visit the Accademia later.

☞ *Head to the Accademia (two long blocks north of the Duomo). If there's a line, as you shuffle your way along, notice the perspective tricks on the walls of the ticket counter room.*

THE FLORENTINE RENAISSANCE (1400-1550)

In the 13th and 14th centuries, Florence was a powerful center of banking, trading and textile manufacturing. The resulting wealth fertilized the cultural soil. With a boost from Florence's leading family, the art-crazy Medicis, and with the natural aggressive and creative spirit of the Florentines, Florence boomed culturally. It's no wonder the long-awaited Renaissance finally took root here.

The Renaissance — the "rebirth" of Greek and Roman culture that swept across Europe — started around 1400 and lasted about 150 years. In politics, the Renaissance meant democracy. In science, a renewed interest in exploring nature. In art, it was a return to the realism and balance of Greek and Roman sculpture and architecture. The general mood was optimistic and humanistic, with a confidence in the power of the individual.

Medieval Europe had been dominated by the Church. Medieval art was the church's servant. The most noble art form was architecture — churches themselves — and other arts were considered most worthwhile if they embellished the house of God. Painting and sculpture were narrative and symbolic, basically there to tell Bible stories to the devout and illiterate masses.

In the Renaissance, people returned to a pre-Christian world which valued classical Greek thought, logic and reason above superstition and blind faith. In architecture, Roman elements of balance, symmetry, domes and round arches replaced Gothic verticality, spires and pointed arches. In painting and sculpture, Renaissance artists strove for realism. Merging art and science, they used mathematics, the laws of perspective, and direct observation of nature.

This was not an anti-Christian movement, though it was a logical and scientific age. The Church actually supported the Renaissance and commissioned many of its greatest works, with Raphael frescoing Plato and Aristotle on the walls of the Vatican. But for the first time, we also find rich laymen who want art simply for art's sake.

After 1000 years of waiting, the smoldering fires of Europe's classical heritage broke out in flames in Florence.

THE ACCADEMIA — Michelangelo's "David"

Start with the ultimate. When you look into the eyes of Michelangelo's "David", you're looking into the eyes of Renaissance man. Carved by Michelangelo in his mid-20s (from 1501 to 1504), this 14-foot symbol of divine victory over evil represents a new century and a whole new "Renaissance" outlook. This is the age of Columbus and Classicism, Galileo and Gutenberg, Luther and Leonardo. This is Florence — and the Renaissance.

The figure comes from a Bible story. The Israelites, God's chosen people, are surrounded by barbarian warriors led by a brutish giant named Goliath who challenges the Israelites to send out someone to fight him. Everyone is afraid except one young shepherd boy — David. Armed only with a sling which he throws over his shoulder, David picks up some stones in his other hand and heads out to face Goliath.

MICHELANGELO — David. This confident Renaissance Man prepares to slay the ugly giant of medieval superstition, pessimism and oppression. David became the symbol of Florence and the Renaissance.

The statue captures David as he's sizing up his enemy. He stands relaxed but alert, leaning on one leg in a classical pose. In his powerful right hand he fondles the stones he'll fling at the giant. His gaze is steady — searching with intense concentration, but also with extreme confidence. Michelangelo has caught the precise moment when David is saying to himself, "I can take this guy."

Florentines could identify with David. Like David, they considered themselves God-blessed underdogs fighting their city-state rivals. In a deeper sense they were civilized Renaissance men slaying the ugly giant of medieval superstition, pessimism and oppression.

David is a symbol of this Renaissance optimism. He's not a brute. He's a civilized, thinking individual who can grapple with and overcome problems. Man is no longer a plaything of the supernatural, and life is now more than just a preparation for what happens after you die. This is a scientific individual — but this isn't a repudiation of God. Look at his right hand. Many complained that it was too big and over-developed. But this is the hand of God. No boy could slay the giant. But David, powered by God, could...and did.

Originally, the statue was commissioned to go on top of a church, so Michelangelo designed it with head and body out of proportion so that from the distant street level, it would look in proper proportion. The people adopted it as the symbol of their city and wanted it next to the Palazzo Vecchio on the main square (where a copy stands today). Because we don't see David from the angle Michelangelo intended us to, we'll have to live with its funny proportions.

A fine bust of an older Michelangelo (by Volterra) looks on. Also see the model of the cart used to move this giant statue here in 1873. David stands under a wonderful Renaissance dome. Hang around awhile. Freeload on a few English tours.

Prisoners and Pietà

Allow some time to see Michelangelo's "Prisoners" that line the hall leading up to David. These unfinished figures seem to be fighting to free themselves from the stone. Michelangelo believed the sculptor was a tool of God, not creating but simply revealing the powerful and beautiful figures He put in the marble. Michelangelo's job was to chip away the excess, to reveal. The "Prisoners" may have been abandoned before completion, or Michelangelo may have left them unfinished deliberately. Having satisfied himself that he'd accomplished what he set out to do, and seeing no point in polishing them into their shiny, finished state, he went on to a new project. As you study the "Prisoners", notice Michelangelo's love of and understanding of the human body. His greatest days were spent sketching the muscular, tanned and sweating bodies of the workers in the Carrara marble quarries.

Look at the unfinished "Pietà" (the threesome closest to David). Feel the weight of Jesus' dead body. Michelangelo captures that feeling of heaviness by making Christ's body longer than it really was. If he stood up, he'd be seven feet tall!

☞ *Leaving the Accademia, turn left and walk ten minutes to the Duomo. The dome of the Duomo is best viewed just to the right of the facade on the corner of the pedestrian-only street.*

THE DUOMO — Florence's Cathedral

The dome of Florence's cathedral, more than any single thing, is what started the Renaissance. The big but unremarkable church itself (called the "Duomo") is Gothic, built in the Middle Ages by architects who left it unfinished — with a big hole in the roof. In the 1400s, the architect Brunelleschi was called on to finish the job. Rather than capping it with another ho-hum Gothic spire, Brunelleschi decided it was high time for this long awaited "Renaissance" to get off the ground, so he chose a Roman-type dome inspired by the ancient Pantheon in Rome.

He used a dome within a dome. First he built the grand white skeletal ribs which you can see, then filled them in with interlocking bricks.

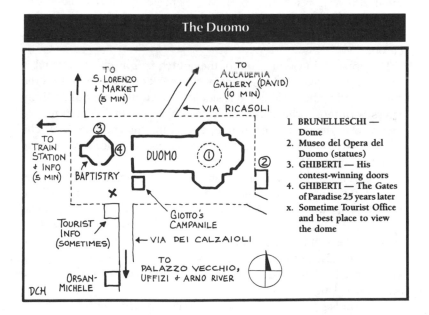

The Duomo

1. BRUNELLESCHI — Dome
2. Museo del Opera del Duomo (statues)
3. GHIBERTI — His contest-winning doors
4. GHIBERTI — The Gates of Paradise 25 years later
x. Sometime Tourist Office and best place to view the dome

The dome grew igloo-style supporting itself as it proceeded from the base upward. His dome, built in only 14 years, was the largest since Rome's Pantheon. Brunelleschi's dome was the wonder of the age, the model for many domes to follow — including Michelangelo's dome of St. Peter's in Rome. People gave it the ultimate compliment saying, "Not even the ancients could have done it." When Michelangelo set out to construct the dome of St. Peter's he said, "I'll make its sister...bigger, but not more beautiful" than the dome of Florence.

BRUNELLESCHI — Duomo dome. Modeled on the ancient Roman Pantheon, this was the greatest feat of engineering since ancient times. Proud Florentines thought of themselves as cultured citizens of a new Rome.

You can climb the dome, but Giotto's Tower (to the right of the facade) is easier and rewards you with a better view. Giotto, like any good Renaissance genius, wore several artistic hats. Considered the father of modern painting, he designed this 274-foot tall bell tower for the Duomo about 200 years before the age of Michelangelo. In his day Giotto was called the ugliest man to ever walk the streets of Florence, but he left the city what, now, many call the most beautiful bell tower in all of Europe.

The ornate Neo-Gothic front of the church is from the 1870s and is generally ridiculed. (Although one of this book's authors thinks it's the most beautiful church facade this side of heaven, the other one naively agrees with those who call it "the cathedral in pajamas".) Thin marble sheets cover the brick construction, decorating the entire exterior. The inside is worth a walk only for its coolness and to notice how bare the terrible flood of 1966 left it.

Either now or later, you may want to visit the wonderful Museo del Duomo (Museum of the cathedral) behind the church. In it you'll see Brunelleschi's wooden model of his dome, a fine collection of Donatello statues and a late Pieta by Michelangelo. You can see part of the Pieta through the window from the museum's courtyard, even when the museum is closed or from the entrance turnstile, without actually going in. The head of Nicodemus (the old guy on top) is a self-portrait of the aging Michelangelo.

☞   *The Baptistry is the small octagonal building in front of the church.*

BAPTISTRY — Ghiberti's Bronze Doors

Florence's Baptistry is dear to the soul of the city. The locals, eager to link themselves to the classical past, believed that this was a Roman building — wishful, but wrong thinking. It is Florence's oldest building (10th century), and most festivals and parades either started or ended here. Go inside for a fine example of pre-Renaissance mosaic art (1300s). The ceiling is a medieval world of religious symbolism — the flat and peaceful reassuring Christ and the tortuous journey to Hell, complete with monsters and poor sinners being gnashed between the teeth of nightmares. This hellish scene looks like something right out of the "Inferno" by Dante...who was dipped into the baptismal waters right here.

Florence had great civic spirit. Different guilds and merchant groups would sponsor contests to embellish their city with great art. The most famous competition was for the commission to redo the Baptistry's north doors (on the right side as you face the Baptistry with the Duomo at your back). All the greats entered, and 25-year-old Ghiberti won easily, beating out heavyweights like Donatello and Brunelleschi (who, having lost the Baptistry gig, was free to build the dome). The entries of Brunelleschi and Ghiberti are in the Bargello — judge them for yourself. In 1425, Ghiberti was given the commission for the east doors (that face the church) — this time there was literally no contest. The bronze panels of these doors (the ones with the crowd of tourists looking on) are the doors Michelangelo said were fit to be the Gates of Paradise. The average tourist finds the nearby pigeons more interesting but give these panels a careful look. They're an example of the Renaissance merging of art and science. Realism was in, and artists used math, illusion and dissection to get it.

GHIBERTI — Story of Jacob and Esau. In this bronze panel from the "Gates of Paradise," Ghiberti uses a series of receding arches to create the illusion of infinite depth.

The "Jacob and Esau" panel (just about eye level on the left) and "King Solomon Receiving the Queen of Sheba" (bottom right) are good examples of how the artist used receding architectural lines and banisters to divide foreground and background — anything to show a 3-D scene on that 2-D surface. Ghiberti spent 27 years (1425-1452) working on these panels. His self-portrait bust is atop the second row of panels in the center of the door frame — the guy on the left with the shiny bald head.

☞ *Facing the Duomo, turn right and cross to the head of the pedestrian-only street which runs from here towards the Arno River.*

VIA DEI CALZAIOLI

The busy and pleasant pedestrian-only Via dei Calzaioli leads from the Duomo to Florence's main square and the Uffizi Gallery. This was "Main Street" for the ancient Roman camp that became Florence. Throughout the city's history, this street has connected the religious center (where we are now) with the political center (where we're heading), a ten-minute walk away. In the last decade traffic jams have been replaced by potted plants, and this is a pleasant place to stroll, people-watch, window shop and catch the drips on your ice cream cone.

Enjoy this stroll past shops of Florentine chic and tempting pizza, *gelati* and pastry shops. For a refreshing break or light meal, these places are touristy but fast, easy and reasonable — the chilled fruit cups are as good as they look. There's a good self-service place at #34 Via Vacchino, just two blocks down Via Tosinghi. (Most of these places have toilets in their basements, so if nature is screaming, don't ask permission, just wander down, and take care of business.)

If you're in the mood for some of the world's best edible art, take a left off Via dei Calzaioli at Via degli Speciali Corso, and drop by an ice cream parlor called "Festival del Gelato" for a cup of their famous *gelato.* If your tongue has never experienced a real orgasm, sit down before you put anything in your mouth.

GELATI — Edible art. Lick a little Italy.

Gelati tips: *Nostra Produzione* and *Produzione Propia* mean they make it on the premises. Also, metal tins rather than the normal white plastic indicate it's most likely homemade. (While one of the authors thinks the rice flavor (*riso*) is the greatest experience this side of the Duomo facade, the other is partial to coffee flavor.)

ORSANMICHELE CHURCH — Florence's Medieval Roots

The Orsanmichele church (at the intersection with Via Dei Tavolini) provides an interesting look at Florentine values. It's a combo- church/granary. Originally this was an open loggia with a huge warehouse upstairs to store grain to feed the city during sieges. The arches of the loggia were artfully filled in, and the building gained a new purpose — a church. Step inside and stand before the altar. Find the pillars with spouts in them (about two feet off the ground) for delivering grain from the storage rooms upstairs. Dream upon the Gothic tabernacle for awhile. (One hundred lire in the coin box buys one minute of light.) Notice its medieval elegance, color and disinterest in depth and realism. This is a wonderfully medieval scene — Florence in 1350. Remember the candle-lit medieval atmosphere that surrounds this altarpiece as you view similar works out of context in the Uffizi gallery.

Back outside, circle the church. Each niche is filled with an important statue. Some are very Gothic — set deeply in the niches, sculpted at a time when statues were justified only because they embellished the house of God. Others, like Donatello's great "St. George", are alert, stepping out, announcing the new age with its new outlook. (The original of this statue is in the Bargello.) Compare Donatello's Renaissance-style

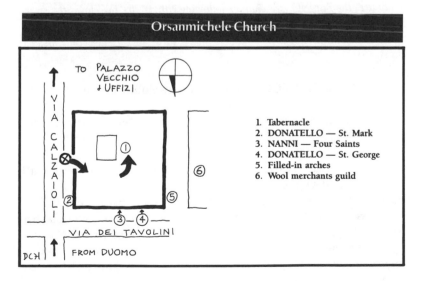

Orsanmichele Church

TO PALAZZO VECCHIO & UFFIZI

VIA CALZAIOLI

VIA DEI TAVOLINI

FROM DUOMO

DCH

1. Tabernacle
2. DONATELLO — St. Mark
3. NANNI — Four Saints
4. DONATELLO — St. George
5. Filled-in arches
6. Wool merchants guild

St. George with the deeply-set and less-sophisticated "Four Saints" statue to its left.

Below some of the niches you'll find the symbols of various guilds and groups that paid for the art, like the carpenters' guild below the "Four Saints". Step around the back to see the old loggia arches filled in. Behind you is the headquarters of the wool merchants guild — just another rich old building rotting in the shadow of the Florentine superstars. Thirsty? How about a cold glass of *aqua con gas* or *te freddo* in the bar opposite the Four Saints?

Renaissance Man steps out. (Left) These medieval-looking saints hide in the church's protective niche. (Right) Donatello's confident "St. George" steps right up to the edge of his niche and looks boldly into the future.

Moving back out to the front of the church, on Via dei Calzaioli, find Donatello's "St. Mark" (in the far right niche as you face the church), a fine example of the new Renaissance style and advances. Notice his classical *contrapposto* (weight on one foot) stance. And his anatomy is fully there — even though he's fully clothed.

☞ *The interesting House of Dante and Florence's best collection of sculpture, the Bargello (see chapter following Uffizi), are just down the street as you leave the main pedestrian street to the left. But let's skip those for now and continue down the mall 50 more yards to the huge and historic square.*

PALAZZO VECCHIO — Florence's Political Center

Via dei Calzaioli empties into the main civic center of Florence, with the Palazzo Vecchio, the Uffizi Gallery and the marble greatness of old Florence littering the cobbles. This square still vibrates with the echoes of Florence's past — executions, riots and great celebrations. Today, it's a tourist's world with pigeons, postcards, horse buggies and tired hubbies. Stand in the center. Before you towers the Medicis' palatial city hall — a fortress designed to contain its riches and survive the many riots that went with local politics. The windows are just beyond the reach of angry stones, the tower was a handy lookout, and justice was doled out sternly on this square. The original "David" once stood where the pigeon-stained replica stands today. During one riot, a bench was thrown out of a palace window and knocked David's arm off.

To the right is the Loggia, once a forum for public debate but later, when the Medici figured good art was more desirable than free speech, it was turned into an outdoor sculpture gallery. Notice the squirming Florentine themes — rapes and severed heads, Sabines and Perseus. Benvenuto Cellini's "Perseus", the Loggia's most noteworthy piece, shows the Greek hero who decapitated the ugly snake-headed Medusa. They say Medusa was so ugly she turned humans who looked at her to stone — though one of this book's authors thinks she's kinda cute.

☞ *Step past the David replica through the front door into the Palazzo Vecchio's courtyard.*

This palace replaced the Bargello as Florence's civic center. You're surrounded by art for art's sake — a statue frivolously marking the courtyard's center, ornate walls and columns. Such luxury was a very big change for man 500 years ago.

☞ *The Palazzo is not worth touring on a quick visit like ours. Return to the square and head right as you leave the palace door, over towards the big fountain by Ammanati that Florentines (including Michelangelo) consider a huge waste of marble — though one of this book's authors...*

Palazzo Vecchio

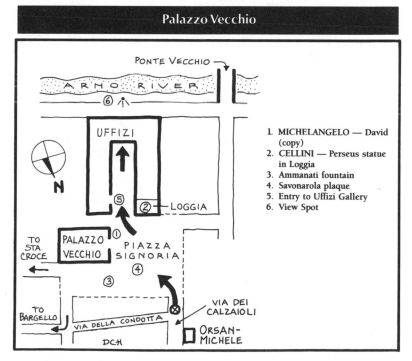

1. MICHELANGELO — David (copy)
2. CELLINI — Perseus statue in Loggia
3. Ammanati fountain
4. Savonarola plaque
5. Entry to Uffizi Gallery
6. View Spot

Find the round bronze plaque in the cobbles ten steps in front of the fountain. The plaque says, "On this spot where Savonarola once had the decadence and vanities of Florence burned, Savonarola himself was burned to death." (Fascinating history. Study the turbulent years of the Medicis and Savonarola, the austere monk who made Florence a theocracy for awhile in the days of Michelangelo.) The burning of Savonarola in the year "MCCCCXCVIII" (1498, I think) really marked the end of the Florentine Renaissance. The Medicis were driven out and so was much of the artistic spirit. Florentine optimism was gone, the artists were somber, and, with papal financing, the Renaissance set up shop in Rome.

SANTA CROCE

If you have a few extra minutes, walk five minutes east to the Santa Croce area — fun shopping (leather and gold), fine church and great *gelati*. The church of S. Croce contains the tombs of Michelangelo, Galileo and Machiavelli, a memorial to Dante, and (to the right of the altar) some great Giotto frescos of the life of St. Francis. There's a leather shop also to the right of the altar (with free and clean WCs). Next door is the fine little Pazzi Chapel by Brunelleschi, possibly the best example of Renaissance architecture in town. Best ice cream is at Vivoli's on via Stinche. You owe it to yourself.

☞ *The glory days of Florence were over — and so, almost, is this walk — but as a postscript, let's wander over to the Uffizi, the two-toned horseshoe-shaped building the fake David is looking at.*

UFFIZI COURTYARD — The Renaissance Hall of Fame

The top floor of this building, known as the "Uffizi" (offices) during the Medici days, is filled with the greatest collection of Florentine painting anywhere and is one of Europe's top four or five galleries (see next chapter).

The Uffizi courtyard is filled with merchants and hustling young artists, overlooked by statues of the great figures of the Renaissance. We tourists focus on the visual art and accomplishments of this culture explosion. Now pay tribute to the nonvisual Renaissance by pausing in front of the statues representing Florence's Hall of Fame.

☞ *Stroll down the left side of the courtyard from the Uffizi entrance to the river, noticing...*

1) Lorenzo the Magnificent (next to the Uffizi entrance). Excelling in many things — though not modesty — he set the tone for the Renaissance. A great art patron and cunning broker of power; 2) Giotto; 3) Donatello; 4) Leonardo da Vinci; 5) Michelangelo; 6) Dante, considered

the father of the Italian language, who was the first Italian to write a popular work ("The Divine Comedy") in non-Latin, using the Florentine dialect which soon became "Italian" throughout the country; 7) Petrarch; 8) The devious-looking Machiavelli is the father of modern cutthroat ways of governing. His book, The Prince, taught "Machiavellian" ends-justifies-the-means thinking, paving the way for the slick and cunning politics of today. And finally, 9) Amerigo Vespucci (in the corner nearest the river), an explorer who gave his name to a fledgling New World.

☞ *Finish our walk at the Arno River. There's a good resting point overlooking the river just across the street from the Uffizi.*

PONTE VECCHIO

Before you is the Ponte Vecchio (Old Bridge). A bridge has spanned this narrowest part of the Arno since Roman times. In the 1500s the Medici kicked out the butchers and tanners and installed the gold and silversmiths you'll see and be tempted by today. (A fine bust of the greatest goldsmith, Cellini, graces the central point of the bridge.) Notice the Medici's protected and elevated passageway that led from the Palazzo Vecchio through the Uffizi, across the Ponte Vecchio and up to the immense Pitti Palace, just beyond the bridge. During WWII, the local German commander was instructed to blow the bridge up. But even some Nazis appreciate history — he blew up the buildings at either end leaving the bridge impassable but intact. *Grazie.*

MORE MICHELANGELO

One more "must-see" sight and I'm history. But if you're a fan of Earth's greatest sculptor, you won't leave Florence until there's a check next to each of these:

* Medici Chapel (The "Night" and "Day" statues, plus others done for the Medici tomb. Located at Church of S. Lorenzo.)

* Bargello Museum (Several "minor" sculptures. See the chapter in *Mona.*)

* Duomo Museum (Another moving Pietà. Located behind the Duomo at #9.)

* Laurentian Library (He designed the entrance staircase. Located at Church of S. Lorenzo.)

* Uffizi Gallery (A rare Michelangelo canvas. See the chapter in *Mona.*)

* Casa Buonarotti (A house Michelangelo once owned, at Via Ghibellina 70.)

* Michelangelo's tomb (Church of Santa Croce.)

Uffizi Gallery, Florence

In the Renaissance, Florentine artists rediscovered the beauty of the natural world. Medieval art had been symbolic, telling Bible stories. Realism didn't matter. But Renaissance people saw the beauty of God in nature and the human body. They used math and science to capture the natural world on canvases, as realistically as possible.

The Uffizi Gallery has the greatest overall collection anywhere of Italian painting. We'll trace the rise of realism and savor the optimistic spirit that marked the Renaissance.

My eyes love things that are fair,
and my soul for salvation cries.
But neither will to Heaven rise
unless the sight of Beauty lifts them there.
—Michaelangelo—sculptor, painter and poet.

Galleria dell' Uffizi (pron: oo-FEETS-ee)

Hours: Tues.-Sat. 9:00-19:00; Sun. and holidays 9:00-13:00; closed Mon.
Last entry one hour before closing.
Hours can be erratic — double-check.
Cost: 10,000 L.
Tour length: Two hours.
Getting there: On the Arno river near the Palazzo Vecchio and Ponte Vecchio, a 20-minute walk from the station.
Information: Only books from street vendors. Nothing inside.
Tel. 218341.

Misc.: Only one WC, near exit.

The Uffizi can be hot and mobbed — 16:00 is a good time.

Snack bar with salads, desserts, fruit cups and a great terrace with a Duomo/
Palazzo Vecchio view. A cappuccino here is one of Europe's great bargains.

Starring: Botticelli, Venus, Raphael, Giotto, Titian, Leonardo, Michelangelo.

Orientation

☞ *Enter the Uffizi from the courtyard, buy your ticket, then take the lift or walk up the four flights of the "Monumental" staircase. Your brain should be fully aerated from the hike up.*

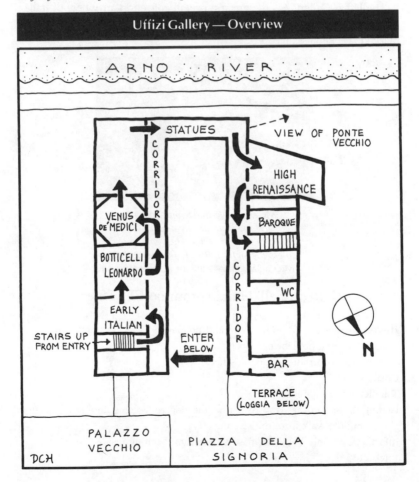

The U-ffizi is U-shaped, running around the courtyard you entered from. The entire collection is on this one floor, displayed chronologically. This left wing contains Florentine painting from medieval to Renaissance times. The right wing (which you can see across the courtyard from here) has Roman and Venetian High Renaissance and the Baroque that followed. Connecting the two is a short corridor with sculpture. We'll concentrate on the Florentine section — naturally, the Uffizi's strong point — then get a taste of the art it inspired.

☞ *Head down the hall and enter the first door on the left. The Madonna and Child by Giotto is straight ahead of you.*

MEDIEVAL — WHEN ART WAS AS FLAT AS THE WORLD (1200-1400)

Giotto — *Madonna and Child (Madonna Col Bambino Gesù, Santi E Angeli)*

For the Florentines, "realism" meant "three-dimensionality". In this room are pre-Renaissance paintings that show the slow process of learning to paint a three-dimensional world on a two-dimensional canvas.

Before concentrating on the Giotto, let's look at some others in the room. First look at the Crucifixion on your right (as you face the Giotto). This was medieval "three-dimensionality" — paint a crude two-dimensional

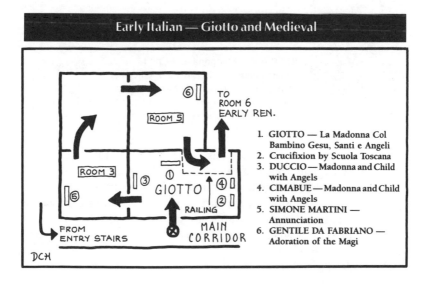

Early Italian — Giotto and Medieval

TO ROOM 6 EARLY REN.

1. GIOTTO — La Madonna Col Bambino Gesu, Santi e Angeli
2. Crucifixion by Scuola Toscana
3. DUCCIO — Madonna and Child with Angels
4. CIMABUE — Madonna and Child with Angels
5. SIMONE MARTINI — Annunciation
6. GENTILE DA FABRIANO — Adoration of the Magi

work...then physically tilt the head forward. Nice try.

The three Madonna-and-Bambinos in this room were all painted within a few decades of each other around the year 1300. The one on the left (as you face Giotto), by Duccio, is the most "medieval" and two-dimensional. There's no background. The angels are just stacked one on top of the other, floating in an unreal space. Mary's throne is crudely drawn — the left side is at a three-quarters angle while the right is practically straight on. Mary herself is a wispy cardboard-cutout figure, seemingly floating a half inch above the throne.

On the opposite wall, Cimabue's is a vast improvement. The large throne creates an illusion of depth. Mary's foot actually sticks out from the throne towards us. Still, the angels are stacked like sardines, serving as a pair of heavenly bookends.

Now let's look at the Giotto. Giotto (pronounced ZHOTT-oh) creates a space and fills it. Like a set designer he builds a three-dimensional "stage" — the canopied throne — then peoples it with real beings. We know the throne has depth because there are angels in front of it and prophets behind. The steps leading up to it give even more depth. But the real triumph here is Mary herself — big and monumental, like a statue. Beneath her robe she has a real live body — her knees and breasts stick out at us. This three-dimensionality was revolutionary in its day, a taste of the Renaissance a century before it began.

GIOTTO — Madonna and Child.
Single-handedly, Giotto nearly started the Renaissance a century before its time. Pioneering the illusion of 3-D he paints sculptural people in realistic settings.

Giotto was one of the first "famous" artists. In the Middle Ages, artists were mostly unglamorous craftsmen like carpenters or real-estate salesmen. They cranked out generic art and could have signed their work with a bar code. Giotto was the first to be recognized as a genius, a unique individual. He died in a plague which devastated Florence. If there had been no plague, would the Renaissance have started 100 years earlier?

☞ *Enter Room 3, to the left of Giotto.*

Simone Martini — *Annunciation (Annunciazione Con I Santi Ansano E Giulitta)*

After Giotto's spasm of Renaissance-style realism, painting returned to two-dimensionality for the rest of the 1300s. But several medieval works eased Florence into the Renaissance.

Martini's "Annunciation" has medieval features you'll see in many of the paintings in the next few rooms: 1) religious subject; 2) gold background; 3) two-dimensional; 4) meticulous details.

SIMONE MARTINI — Annunciation. In medieval paintings, realism was sacrificed to tell Bible stories more clearly. When necessary, the message was actually spelled right out.

This is not a three-dimensional work. But remember, the point of medieval art was not to recreate reality but to teach religion, especially to the illiterate masses. So Martini has boiled things down to the four basic figures needed to get the message across: 1) The angel appears to sternly tell 2) Mary that she'll be the mother of Jesus. In the center is 3) a vase of lilies, a symbol to tell us Mary is pure. Above, is the 4) Holy Spirit as a dove about to descend on her. If the symbols aren't enough to get the message across, Martini has spelled it right out for us: "Hail, favored one, the Lord is with you." Mary doesn't look exactly pleased as punch.

This isn't a beautiful Mary or even a real Mary. She's a generic woman without distinctive features. We know she's pure, not from her face, but because of the symbolic flowers. Before the Renaissance, artists didn't care about the beauty of individual people.

☞ *Pass through the next room, stopping at the far end of Room 5.*

Gentile Da Fabriano — *Adoration of the Magi (Adorazione Dei Magi)*

Look at the incredible detail of the Three Kings' costumes, the fine horses, the cow in the cave. This work is literally crammed with realistic details — but it's still far from realistic. The point was to tell a story. So we see the Magi not only worshipping baby Jesus, but also in the background heading home.

☞ *Exit to your right and hang a U-turn left into Room 6.*

EARLY RENAISSANCE (mid-1400s)

In the 1400s painters worked out the problems of painting realistically. They concentrated on "perspective" (using mathematics to create the illusion of three-dimensionality), and how to paint the human body.

Uccello — *The Battle of San Romano (La Battaglia di S. Romano)*

Paolo Uccello almost literally went crazy trying to conquer the problem of perspective. He was a man obsessed with the three dimensions (thank God he was born before Einstein discovered one more). This canvas is not so much a piece of art as an exercise in perspective. Uccello (pron: oo-CHELL-o) has challenged himself with every possible problem.

UCCELLO — Battle of San Romano. Uccello almost went crazy trying to master three-dimensionality on a canvas. There's some good, some mediocre and some atrocious attempts, like the 40-foot rabbit in the background.

The broken lances at left set up a 3-D "grid" in which to place this crowded scene. The fallen horses and soldiers are experiments in "foreshortening" — shortening the figures (and parts of figures) that are

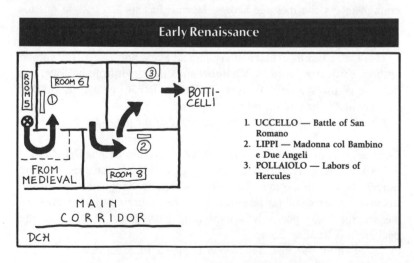

Early Renaissance

1. UCCELLO — Battle of San Romano
2. LIPPI — Madonna col Bambino e Due Angeli
3. POLLAIOLO — Labors of Hercules

farther away from us to create the illusion of distance. Some of the figures are definitely A-plus material, like the fallen grey horse in the center and the white horse at right riding away. But some are more like B-minus work — the kicking red horse has legs that look like hamhocks at this angle, and the fallen soldier at far right would only be four feet tall if he stood up.

And then there's the D-minus "Are-you-on-drugs?" work. The converging hedges in the background create a nice illusion of a distant hillside maybe 75 or 100 yards away. So what are those soldiers doing there the size of the foreground figures? And jumping the hedge, is that a 40-foot rabbit? Uccello got so wrapped up in three-dimensionality he kind of lost...perspective.

☞   *Enter Room 8.*

Fra Filippo Lippi — *Madonna and Child with Two Angels (Madonna Col Bambino E Due Angeli)*

Compare this Mary with the generic female in Martini's "Annunciation". We don't need the tiny halo over her head to tell us she's holy — she radiates sweetness and light from her divine face. Heavenly beauty is expressed by a physically beautiful woman.

Fra ("Brother") Lippi was a monk who lived a less than monkish life. He lived with a nun who bore him two children. He spent his entire life searching for the perfect Virgin. Through his studio passed Florence's prettiest girls, many of whom decorate the walls here in this room.

Lippi painted idealized beauty, but his models were real flesh and blood human beings. You could look through all the thousands of paintings from the Middle Ages and not find anything so human as the mischievous face of one of Lippi's little angel boys.

☞   *Enter Room 9. Pollaiolo is in the glass case.*

Pollaiolo — *Labors of Hercules (Fatiche d'Ercole)*

While Uccello worked on perspective, Pollaiolo studied anatomy. In medieval times, dissection of corpses was a sin and a crime (the two were one then), a desecration of the human body which was the temple of God. But Pollaiolo was willing to sell his soul to the devil for artistic knowledge. He dissected.

These two small panels are experiments in painting anatomy. The poses are the wildest imaginable, excuses to see how the muscles twist and tighten.

There's something funny about this room that I can't put my finger on...I've got it — no Madonnas. Not one. We've seen how early Renaissance artists worked to conquer reality. Now let's see the fruits of their work, the flowering of Florence's Renaissance.

☞ *Enter the large Botticelli room and take a seat.*

FLORENCE — THE RENAISSANCE BLOSSOMS (1450-1500)

Florence in 1450 was in a firenz-y of activity. There was a can-do spirit of optimism in the air. There were prosperous merchants and bankers and a strong middle class. The government was reasonably democratic, and Florentines saw themselves as citizens of a strong republic like ancient Rome. Their civic pride showed in the public monuments and artworks they built. Man was leaving the protection of the Church to stand on his own two feet.

Lorenzo de' Medici, head of the powerful Medici family, epitomized this new humanistic spirit. Strong, decisive, handsome, poetic, athletic, sensitive, charismatic, intelligent, brave-clean-and-reverent Lorenzo was a true Renaissance man deserving the nickname he went by — "The Magnificent". He gathered Florence's best and brightest around him for evening wine and discussions of great ideas. One of this circle was the painter Botticelli (pron: botti-CHELL-y).

Botticelli — *Allegory of Spring (Allegoria della Primavera)*
Here is the Renaissance in its first bloom, its "springtime" of innocence. Madonna is out, Venus is in. Adam and Eve hiding their nakedness are

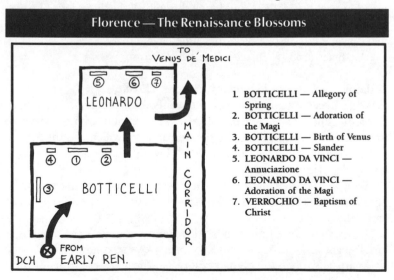

Florence — The Renaissance Blossoms

1. BOTTICELLI — Allegory of Spring
2. BOTTICELLI — Adoration of the Magi
3. BOTTICELLI — Birth of Venus
4. BOTTICELLI — Slander
5. LEONARDO DA VINCI — Annuciazione
6. LEONARDO DA VINCI — Adoration of the Magi
7. VERROCHIO — Baptism of Christ

out, glorious flesh is in. This is a return to the pre-Christian pagan world of classical Greece where things of the flesh are not sinful. But this is certainly no orgy — just fresh-faced innocence and playfulness.

BOTTICELLI — Allegory of Spring. Pagan innocence. Botticelli was part of a youthful band of Florentines who saw beautiful things as an expression of the divine.

It's springtime in a citrus grove. The winds of spring blow in (Mr. Blue at right) causing Flora to sprout flowers from her lips. Meanwhile the figure of Spring walks by spreading flowers from her dress. At the left are Mercury and the Three Graces, dancing a delicate maypole dance. The Graces may be symbolic of the three forms of love — love of beauty, love of people, and sexual love, suggested by the raised intertwined fingers. (They forgot love of peanut-butter-on-toast.) In the center stands Venus, the Greek goddess of love. Above her flies Cupid with a blindfold, blindly and happily shooting his arrows of love without worrying whom they'll hit.

Botticelli has painted a scene of exquisite beauty. The lines of the bodies, especially of the Graces in their see-through nighties, have pleasing curves. The faces are idealized but have real human features. There's a look of thoughtfulness and even melancholy in the faces — as though everyone knows that the innocence of spring must soon pass.

☞ *Look at the next painting to the right.*

Botticelli — *Adoration of the Magi (Adorazione dei Magi)*

Here's the rat pack of confident young Florentines, who reveled in the optimistic pagan spirit. Botticelli painted himself into the scene, looking vain in the yellow robe, at far right. I hardly need to say which one is Lorenzo — he's the Magnificent-looking guy at the far left.

Botticelli — *Birth of Venus (Nascita di Venere)*

This is the purest expression of Renaissance beauty. Venus' naked body is not sensual but innocent. Botticelli thought that physical beauty was a way of appreciating God. Remember Michelangelo's poem: souls will never ascend to Heaven "...unless the sight of Beauty lifts them there."

BOTTICELLI — Birth of Venus. Beauty or porn? It depends on who's behind the pulpit. Two generations earlier, this "Venus on a Half Shell" would have gotten Botticelli in hot water. By the end of his life, it did.

According to myth, Venus was born from the foam of a wave. Still only half-awake, this fragile newborn beauty is kept afloat on a clam shell, while the winds come to blow her to shore, where her maiden waits to cover her. The pose is the same S-curve of classical statues (as we'll soon see). Botticelli's pastel colors, recently restored, make the world itself seem fresh and newly born. The details show Botticelli's love of the natural world — Venus' windblown hair, the translucent skin, the braided hair of her handmaiden, the flowers in the dress, the slight ripple of the wind's chest muscles, and the flowers tumbling in the slowest of slow motions, suspended like musical notes, caught at the peak of their brief but beautiful life.

☞   *It goes without saying, but "Venus on the Half-shell" — as many tourists call this — is one of the masterpieces of Western art. Take some time with it. Then find the small canvas on the wall to the right, near "La Primavera."*

Botticelli — *Slander (La Calumnia)*
    The spring of Florence's Renaissance had to end. Lorenzo died young. The economy faltered. Into town rode the monk Savonarola, preaching medieval hellfire and damnation for those who embraced the "pagan" Renaissance spirit. "Down, down with all gold and decoration," he roared, "Down where the body is food for the worms." He presided over huge bonfires where the people threw in their fine clothes, jewelry, pagan books...and paintings.
    Botticelli listened to Savonarola. He burned some of his own paintings and changed his tune. The last works of his life were darker, more somber and pessimistic of humanity.
    "Slander" spells the end of the Florentine Renaissance. The setting is classic Brunelleschian architecture, but look what's taking place beneath those stately arches. These aren't proud Renaissance men and women but a ragtag, medieval-looking bunch, squatters in an abandoned hall of justice. Here in this chaotic Court of Thieves, the accusations fly, and

everyone is condemned. The naked man pleads for mercy, but the hooded black figure, a symbol of his execution, turns away. Once-proud Venus — straight out of "The Birth of Venus" — looks up to heaven as if to ask, "What has happened to us?" The classical statues in their niches look on in disbelief. One statue can't even bear to look, to see how low man has sunk.

The German poet Heine said, "When they start by burning books, they'll end by burning people." Savonarola, after four short years of power, was burned on his own bonfire in the Piazza della Signoria, but by then the city was in shambles. The brief *glasnost* of the Renaissance was over.

☞ *Enter the next room.*

Leonardo Da Vinci — *Annunciation*

Leonardo was a Florentine who had to move away to achieve fame. A scientist, architect, engineer and musician, Leonardo was a true Renaissance man. He worked at his own pace rather than to please an employer, so he often left works unfinished. The two in this room aren't his best, but even a mediocre Leonardo is enough to put a museum on the map, and they're definitely worth a look.

LEONARDO DA VINCI — Annunciation. Grace, balance and human realism. Leonardo captures a supernatural scene in believable terms. Compare this with Martini's bare-bones medieval Annunciation.

Think back on Martini's "Annunciation" to realize how much more natural, relaxed and realistic Leonardo's is. He's taken a miraculous event — an angel appearing out of the blue — and made it seem almost everyday. He constructs a beautifully landscaped "stage" and puts his characters in it. Gabriel has walked up to Mary and now kneels on one knee like an ambassador, saluting her. Look how relaxed his other hand is draped over his knee. Mary, who has been reading, looks up with a gesture of surprise and curiosity. Leonardo has taken a religious scene and presented it in a very human way.

Leonardo — *Adoration of the Magi*
Leonardo's human insight is even more apparent in this unfinished work. The poor kings are amazed at the Christ child — even afraid of him. They scurry around like chimps around fire, looking, but making sure they don't get too close. Leonardo was pioneering a new era of painting, showing not just the outer features but the inner personality.

(If you just can't get enough of Leonardo, glance at the next painting to the right, "Baptism of Christ" by Verrochio, Leonardo's teacher. Legend has it that Leonardo painted the angel on the far left when he was only 14 years old. When Verrochio saw that some kid had painted an angel better than he ever would, he hung up his brush for good.)

Florence saw the first blossoming of the Renaissance. But when the cultural climate turned chilly, artists flew south to warmer climes. The Renaissance shifted to Rome.

☞ *Exit into the main corridor. Breathe. Sit. Admire the ceiling. Look out the window. See you in five.*

Back already? Now continue down the corridor and turn left into the octagonal Venus de' Medici room. You'll recognize it by the line outside — they only allow 25 people in at a time. Read while you wait.

CLASSICAL SCULPTURE

If the Renaissance was the foundation of the modern world, the foundation of the Renaissance was classical sculpture. Sculptors, painters and poets alike turned for inspiration to these ancient works as the epitome of balance, 3-D, human anatomy and beauty. While the best

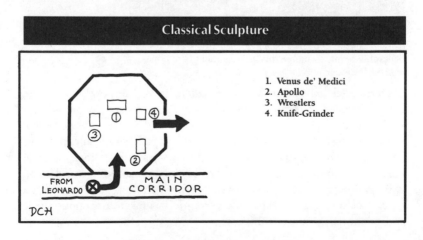

Classical Sculpture

1. Venus de' Medici
2. Apollo
3. Wrestlers
4. Knife-Grinder

FROM LEONARDO ⊗   MAIN CORRIDOR

DCH

collection of Renaissance sculpture is in the nearby Bargello, these classical statues illustrate nicely what a profound effect the art of the ancient world had on Renaissance artists.

The "Venus de' Medici", or Medici Venus ("Venere de' Medici"), ancient Greece.

Is this pose familiar? Botticelli's "Birth of Venus" has the same position of the arms, the same S-curved body and the same lifting of the right leg. A copy of this statue stood in Lorenzo the Magnificent's garden where Botticelli used to hang out. This one is a Roman copy of the lost original by the great Greek sculptor Praxiteles.

PRAXITELES — Venus de' Medici.
The ideal of classical beauty and Botticelli's model for the "Birth of Venus." Nineteenth-century tourists used to swoon in ecstasy at her loveliness. (Or was it just that the Uffizi was as hot and crowded back then as it is today?)

Perhaps more than any other work of art, this statue has been the epitome of both ideal beauty and sexuality. In the 18th and 19th centuries, beauty and sexuality were one and the same. Sex was considered a dirty thing, so the sex drive of cultured aristocrats was channeled into a love of pure beauty. Wealthy sons and daughters of Europe's aristocrats made the pilgrimage to the Uffizi to complete their classical education...where they literally swooned in ecstasy before the cold beauty of this Goddess of Love.

Louis XIV had a bronze copy made. Napoleon stole her away to Paris for himself. And in Philadelphia, USA in the 1800s, a copy had to be kept under lock and key to prevent the innocent from catching the Venere-al disease. It may be difficult for us to appreciate such passionate love of art, but if any generation knows the power of sex to sell something — be it art or underarm deodorant — it's ours.

The Other Statues

The Medici Venus is a balanced, harmonious, serene statue from Greece's "Golden Age", when balance was admired in every aspect of life. Its male counterpart is behind you to the right. "Apollino" (a.k.a. "Venus with a Penis") is also by the master of smooth, cool lines, Praxiteles.

The other works are later Greek (Hellenistic), when quiet balance was replaced by violent motion and emotion. "The Wrestlers", to the left of Venus, is a study in anatomy and twisted limbs — like Pollaiolo's paintings a thousand years later.

The drama of "The Knife Grinder", to the right of Venus, stems from the off-stage action — he's sharpening the knife to flay a man alive.

☞ *Exit the Tribune room passing through five rooms of masterpieces which you may want to return to. In the second room, check out the two portraits (on the left) of Martin Luther by his friend Lukas Cranach, then move on Exit to a great view of the Arno. Stroll through the sculpture wing.*

The Sculpture Wing

A hundred years ago, no one even looked at Botticelli — they came to the Uffizi to see the sculpture collection. Why isn't the sculpture as famous now? Stop at the "Boy Pulling a Spine from his Foot" on your left. This is a famous statue, right? And it must be old because the label says "UN ORIGINALE" in big block letters. But now read the fine print — the tiny little "da" in front. It's not an original at all, but a copy "from" ("da") an original...which is in Rome.

☞ *There are benches at the other end of the Sculpture Wing with a great view.*

View of the Arno

Florence's best view of the Arno and the Ponte Vecchio. You can also see the red-tiled roof of the Vasari Corridor, the "secret" passage connecting the Palazzo Vecchio, the Uffizi, the Ponte Vecchio and the Pitti Palace on the other side of the river (not visible from here) — a half mile in all. This was the private walkway, wallpapered in great art, for the Medici family's commute from home to work.

As you appreciate the view, remember that it's this sort of pleasure that Renaissance painters wanted you to get from their paintings. For them, a canvas was a window you looked through to see the wide world. By contrast, a medieval painting surface wasn't a transparent window, but a page on which to write a story using pictures as words. In the 20th century, some artists have rejected the canvas-as-window approach also.

We're headed down the home stretch now. If your feet are killing you, and it feels like torture, remind yourself it's a pleasant torture and smile...like the statue next to you.

☞ *In the far corridor, turn left into the first room (#25) and grab a blast of cold from the air-conditioner vent below the chairs to the left.*

HIGH RENAISSANCE — MICHELANGELO, RAPHAEL, TITIAN
(1500-1550)

Michelangelo — *Holy Family (Sacra Famiglia)*
This is the only completed easel painting by the greatest sculptor in history. Florentine painters were sculptors with brushes, and this shows it. Instead of a painting it's more like three clusters of statues with some clothes painted on. The main subject is the holy family — Mary, Joseph and baby Jesus — and in the background are two groups of nudes looking like classical statues. The background represents the old pagan world, while Jesus in the foreground is the new age of Christianity. The figure of young John the Baptist, at right, is the link between the two.

Michelangelo was a Florentine — in fact he was like an adopted son of the Medicis who recognized his talent — but much of his greatest work was done in Rome as part of the Popes' facelift of the city. We can see here some of the techniques he used on the Sistine Chapel ceiling that revolutionized painting — monumental figures, dramatic angles (we're looking up Mary's nose), accentuated rippling muscles and bright

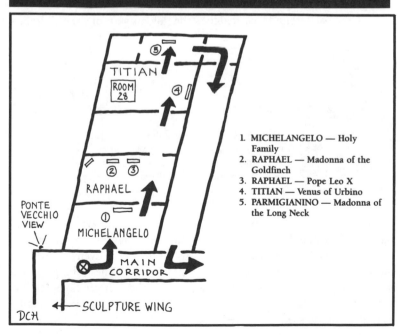

High Renaissance — Michelangelo, Raphael, Titian

1. MICHELANGELO — Holy Family
2. RAPHAEL — Madonna of the Goldfinch
3. RAPHAEL — Pope Leo X
4. TITIAN — Venus of Urbino
5. PARMIGIANINO — Madonna of the Long Neck

clashing colors (all the more apparent, since both this work and the Sistine have been recently cleaned). These added an element of dramatic tension lacking in the graceful work of Leonardo and Botticelli.

☞   *Enter Room 26.*

MICHELANGELO — Holy Family.
Michelangelo insisted he was a sculptor, not a painter — and this painting shows it.

Raphael (Raffaello Sanzo) — *Madonna of the Goldfinch (La Madonna del Cardellino)*

Raphael (pron: roff-eye-ELL) perfected his craft in Florence, following the graceful style of Leonardo. Like Leonardo, he adds the human touch to a religious subject. In typical Leonardo fashion, this group of Mary, John the Baptist and Jesus is arranged in the shape of a pyramid with Mary's head at the peak. It's a tender scene, painted with warm colors and a hazy background that matches the golden skin of the children.

RAPHAEL — Madonna of the Goldfinch.
Perfect Renaissance balance. Mary forms a pyramid with the two children on either side. The features are idealized and graceful *à la* Da Vinci.

The two halves of the painting balance perfectly. Draw a line down the middle, through Mary's nose and down through her knee. On the left is John the Baptist balanced by Jesus on the right. Even the trees in the background balance each other, left and right. These things aren't immediately noticeable, but they help create the subconscious feeling of balance and order that reinforce the atmosphere of maternal security in this domestic scene — pure Renaissance.

Raphael — *Leo X and the Cardinals (Leone X con i Cardinali)*

Raphael was called to Rome at the same time as Michelangelo, working next door while Michelangelo did the Sistine Ceiling. Raphael peeked in from time to time, learning from Michelangelo's monumental, dramatic figures. His later work is grittier and more realistic than the idealized, graceful and "Leonardesque" Madonna. Pope Leo is big, like a Michelangelo statue. And Raphael captures some of the seamier side of Vatican life in the cardinals' eyes — shrewd, suspicious and somewhat cynical. With Raphael, the photographic realism pursued by painters ever since Giotto, was finally achieved.

If pressed to name a date for the end of the Renaissance, many scholars would say 1520 — the year Raphael died. Raphael (see his self- portrait to the left of the Madonna) is considered both the culmination and conclusion of the Renaissance. The realism, balance and humanism we associate with the Renaissance are all found in Raphael's work. He combined the grace of Leonardo with the power of Michelangelo. With his death, the Renaissance shifted again — to Venice.

☞ *Pass through the next room containing Pontormo's "Last Supper at McDonald's," then continue into Room 28.*

Titian (Tiziano) — *Venus of Urbino (La Venere di Urbino)*

Compare this Venus with Botticelli's newly-hatched Venus, and you get a good idea of the difference between the Florentine and Venetian Renaissance. Botticelli's was pure, innocent and otherworldly. Titian's should have a staple in her belly-button. This isn't a Venus, it's a centerfold — with no purpose but to please the eye and other organs. While Botticelli's allegorical Venus is a message, this is a massage.

TITIAN — Venus of Urbino. Botticelli's Venus was an allegory — this is a centerfold. The Venetian Renaissance was sensual and colorful.

Titian (pron: TEESH-un) and his fellow Venetians took the pagan spirit pioneered in Florence and carried it to its logical hedonistic con- clusion. Using bright rich colors they captured the luxurious life of happy-go-lucky Venice.

Remember how balanced Raphael's "Madonna of the Goldfinch" was?

Every figure on one side had a balancing figure on the other. Titian balances his painting a different way — with color. The canvas is split down the middle by the curtain. The left half is dark, the right half warmer. The two halves are connected by a diagonal slash of luminous gold — the nude woman.

By the way, visitors from centuries past also panted in front of this Venus. The poet Byron called it "THE Venus". With her sensual skin, hey-sailor look and suggestively placed hand, she must have left them blithering idiots.

☞   *Enter the n-n-n-next room.*

Parmigianino — Madonna of the Long Neck (Madonna dal Collo Lungo)

Raphael, Michelangelo, Leonardo and Titian mastered reality. They could place any scene onto a canvas with photographic accuracy. How could future artists top that?

"Mannerists" like Parmigianino tried to by going beyond realism, exaggerating it for effect. Using brighter colors and elongated figures (two techniques explored by Michelangelo), they created scenes more elegant and more exciting than real life.

By stretching the neck of his Madonna, Parmigianino (pron: like the cheese) gives her an unnatural swan-like beauty. She has the same pose and position of hands as Botticelli's Venus and the Venus de' Medici. Her body forms an arcing S-curve — down her neck as far as her elbow, then back the other way along Jesus' body to her knee, then down to her foot. The baby Jesus seems to be blissfully gliding down this slippery-slide of sheer beauty.

☞   *Pass through several rooms, returning to the main corridor where, by the window, you'll see the famous "Venus de' Mallard" statue.*

THE REST OF THE UFFIZI

As art moved into the baroque period, artists took Renaissance realism and exaggerated it still more — more beautiful, more emotional or more dramatic. There's lots of great stuff in this wing, and I'd especially recommend Tintoretto's "Leda" (Room 35), the enormous canvases of Rubens (Room 41) and the shocking ultra-realism of Caravaggio's "Bacchus" and "Abraham Sacrificing Isaac" (Room 44).

☞   *But first — or last, if you've had plenty of art for the day — head to the end of the corridor to the last room for a true aesthetic experience.*

The Little Cappuchin Monk (*Cappuccino*) — by an anonymous Italian.
This drinkable art form, born in Italy, is now enjoyed all over the world. It's called "The Little Cappuchin Monk", because its frothy milk foam gives the coffee a light-and-dark-brown look, like the two-toned cowls of the Cappuchin order. Drink it on the terrace in the shadow of the towering Palazzo Vecchio and argue Marx and Hegel — was the Renaissance an economic phenomenon or a spiritual one? Or don't. Saluté.

Bargello, Florence

The Renaissance began with sculpture. All the great Florentine painters were "sculptors with brushes." You can see the birth of this revolution of 3-D in the Bargello, which boasts the best collection of Florentine sculpture. It's a small, uncrowded museum, and a pleasant break from the intensity of the rest of Florence.

Museo Nazionale in the Bargello (pron: bar-jello)

Hours: Tues.-Sat. 9:00-14:00; Sun. 9:00-13:00; closed Mon.
Cost: 6000 L.
Tour length: Forty-five minutes.
Getting there: Five-minute walk NE of Uffizi. Facing the Palazzo Vecchio, head to the far left corner of the square, turning right onto Via della Condotta. At the next intersection, look kitty-corner to the left for a rustic brick building with a spire that looks like a baby Palazzo Vecchio. When lost ask, "Doe-vay bar-jello?"
Information: None.
 Tel. 210801.
Misc.: Best WC in Florence.
Starring: Michelangelo, Donatello, Brunelleschi, Ghiberti, and four different Davids.

Orientation

☞ *Buy your ticket and take a seat in the courtyard.*

The Bargello, built in 1255, was Florence's City Hall. The heavy fortifications tell us that politics in medieval Florence had its occupational hazards. After the administration shifted to the Palazzo Vecchio, this soon became a police station ("bargello") and prison.

The Bargello is a three-story rectangular building which surrounds this central courtyard. (The cool, quiet courtyard is practically worth the price of admission — just to escape Florence's traffic-filled streets.) The best statues are found in two rooms — the one on the ground floor at the foot of the stairs, and the room one flight above it. We'll proceed logically in a chrono- kind of way.

But first, meander around this courtyard and get a feel for sculpture in general and rocks in particular. Sculpture is a much more robust art form than painting. Think of the engineering problems alone of moving these stones from a quarry to an artist's studio. Then the sheer physical strength of chiseling away for hours on end. A sculptor must be powerful yet delicate, controlling the chisel to chip out the smallest details. Think of Michelangelo's approach to sculpting — he wasn't creating a figure but only liberating it from the rock that surrounded it.

Finally, a viewing note. Every sculpture has an invisible "frame" around it — the stone block it was cut from. Visualizing this frame helps you find the statue's center of balance.

Donatello Room

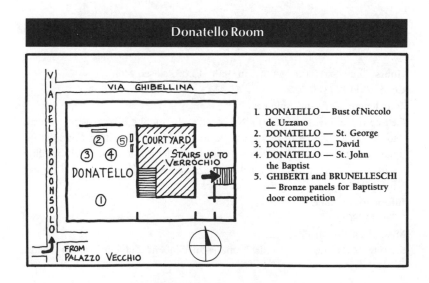

1. DONATELLO — Bust of Niccolo de Uzzano
2. DONATELLO — St. George
3. DONATELLO — David
4. DONATELLO — St. John the Baptist
5. GHIBERTI and BRUNELLESCHI — Bronze panels for Baptistry door competition

☞ *The large Donatello room is on the next floor up. Pause at Donatello's painted bust of Niccolo de Uzzano.*

DONATELLO (1386-1466)

Donatello was the first great Renaissance genius, a model for Michelangelo and others. He mastered realism, creating the first truly lifelike statues of people since ancient times. Donatello's work is highly personal. Unlike the ancient Greeks, he always sculpted real people, not idealized versions of pretty gods and goddesses. Some of these people are downright ugly. In the true spirit of Renaissance humanism, Donatello was the first to appreciate the beauty of flesh-and-blood human beings — even ugly ones like "Niccolo de Uzzano" here.

Donatello's personality was also a model for later artists. He was moody and irascible, purposely setting himself apart from others in order to concentrate on his sculpting. He developed the role of the "mad genius" that Michelangelo would later perfect.

☞ *At the far end of the room, "St. George" stands in a niche in the wall.*

Donatello — St. George

A century before Michelangelo sculpted his famous "David", this was the unofficial symbol of Florence. George, the Christian slayer of dragons, was just the sort of righteous warrior that proud Renaissance Florentines could get behind in their struggles with nearby cities. He stands on the edge of his niche looking out alertly with the same relaxed intensity that Michelangelo used for his "David". This is the original marble statue — a bronze version stands in its original niche at Orsanmichele church.

☞ *On the floor to your left you'll find...*

Donatello — David

This boyish-approaching-girlish David is quite a contrast with Michelangelo's powerful version at the Accademia. Donatello's smooth-skinned warrior sways gracefully, poking his sword playfully at the severed head of the giant Goliath. He has a *contrapposto* stance similar to Michelangelo's, resting his weight on one leg in the classical style, but it gives him a feminine rather than ultra-masculine look. Gazing into his coy eyes is a very different experience from Michelangelo's tough Renaissance man.

This David paved the way for Michelangelo. It was the first free-standing male nude done in a thousand years. In the Middle Ages, the human body was considered a dirty thing, a symbol of man's weakness, something to be covered up in shame. The Church prohibited exhibitions of nudity like this one and certainly would never decorate a church with it. But in the Renaissance, a new class of rich and powerful merchants appeared who bought art for their own personal enjoyment. This particular statue stood in the courtyard of the Medici's palace...where Michelangelo, practically an adopted son, grew up admiring it.

(This is the first of four different "Davids" in the Bargello: 1) This one 2) Another version by Donatello — look over your left shoulder 3) Verrochio's "David" upstairs (which we'll visit) and 4) Michelangelo's other unfinished version we'll see downstairs. Compare and contrast the artists' styles as you see them. How many ways can you slay a giant?)

☞ *Donatello's "St. John the Baptist" is to the right of David #1.*

Donatello — St. John the Baptist (S. Giovanni Battista)

John the Baptist was the wild-eyed wildcat prophet who lived in the desert, preaching, eating bugs and honey, and baptizing Saviors of the World. Donatello, the mad prophet of the coming Renaissance, must have identified with this original eccentric. Circle John with his sandals and that halo which must be super-glued on.

☞ *On the wall near "John" you'll find some bronze relief panels.*

Ghiberti and Brunelleschi — Baptistry Door Competition Entries (two different relief panels, titled "Il Sacrificio di Abramo")

Don't look at the labels just yet. These two versions of "Abraham Sacrificing Isaac" were finalists in the contest to decide who would do the bronze doors of the Baptistry. (Donatello also entered but lost.) Ghiberti eventually won and later did the doors known as the Gates of Paradise. Brunelleschi lost — fortunately for us — freeing him to design the Duomo's dome.

You be the judge. Here are the two finalists for the Baptistry door competition — Ghiberti's and Brunelleschi's. Which do you like the best?

(Ghiberti's, on the left, won.)

You be the judge. It's obvious who won...Right...?

☞ *Leave the Donatello room, and cross to the opposite side of the courtyard, then climb the red-carpeted stairs to the next floor up. At the top of the stairs, turn left, then left again. Verrochio's "David" stands in the center of the room.*

Verrochio — David
Verrochio is best known as the teacher of Leonardo da Vinci, but he was also the premier sculptor between the time of Donatello and Michelangelo. This saucy, impertinent David is more masculine than Donatello's, but a far cry from Michelangelo's monumental version.

☞ *Nearby, in a glass case, is a small work by Antonio del Pollaiuolo*

Pollaiuolo — Hercules and Antaeus (Ercole e Anteo)
Antaeus was invincible as long as he was in contact with the earth, his mother. So Hercules just picked him up in a Renaissance half-nelson and crushed him to death.

More than any early Renaissance artist, Pollaiuolo studied the human body in motion. These figures are not dignified Renaissance men, but brutish, violent, animal-like beasts. Yet in this tangled pose of flailing arms and legs there still is a Renaissance sense of balance — all the motion spins around the center of gravity where their hips meet.

☞ *Poke around the statues and the armaments collection on this floor, then descend back to the courtyard on the ground floor. We'll see the last room on the ground floor at the foot of the outside stairway.*

LESSER MICHELANGELOS

Michelangelo — Bacchus (Bacco)
Maybe Michelangelo had a sense of humor after all. Compare this tipsy Greek God of Wine with his sturdy, sober David. Bacchus isn't nearly so muscular, so monumental...or so sure on his feet. Hope he's not driving. The pose, the smooth muscles and curving belly and hips look more like Donatello's boyish David.

☞ *Just to the left you'll find...*

Michelangelo — Bruto
Another example of the influence of Donatello is this so-ugly-he's-beautiful bust by Michelangelo. His sheer ugliness gives him the look of a man who has succeeded against all odds, a dignity and heroic quality that would be missing if he were too pretty.

The subject is Brutus, the Roman lover of liberty who murdered his friend and dictator, Julius Caesar ("Et tu...?"). Michelangelo could understand this man's dilemma. He himself had close ties to the

344   *Bargello, Florence*

Medici, his adopted family, who could also be corrupt and tyrannical. So he gives us two sides of a political assassin. The right profile (the front view) is heroic. But the hidden side, with the drooping mouth and squinting eye, makes him more cunning, sneering and ominous.

Michelangelo — David (also known as Apollo)

This is the last of the Davids in the Bargello, a good time to think back on those we've seen: Donatello's girlish, gloating David; Verrochio's boyish, impish version; and now this unfinished one by Michelangelo. He certainly learned from these earlier versions, even copying certain elements, but what's truly amazing is that his famous David in the Accademia is so completely different — so much larger than life in every way — from the earlier attempts.

In the glass cases to your left are small-scale copies of some of Michelangelo's most famous works.

☞   *On the other side of the room...*

Giambologna — Mercury

Catch this statue while you can—he's got flowers to deliver. Despite all the bustle and motion, Mercury has a solid Renaissance core: the line of balance that runs straight up the center, from toes to nose.

Giambologna — Florence Victorious over Pisa (Firenze Vittoriosa su Pisa)

This shows the fierce Florentine chauvinism born in an era when Italy's cities struggled for economic and political dominance...and Florence won.

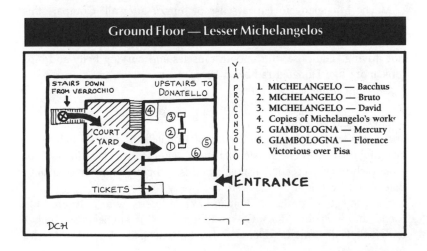

A Walk Through Ancient Rome

Rome has many layers — modern, baroque, Renaissance, Christian — but let's face it, "Rome" is Caesars, gladiators, chariots, centurions, thumbs up or thumbs down, "Et tu, Brute," trumpet fanfares and Roman Meal bread. That's the Rome we'll look at. On our Caesar Shuffle, we'll see the downtown core of ancient Rome, from the Colosseum, through the Forum over the Capitol Hill and to the Pantheon.

Colosseo, Foro Romano, Campidoglio, Pantheon

Hours and Cost (confirm at tourist office):
  Colosseum — Mon., Tues., Thurs., Fri., Sat. 9:00-19:00; Sun. and Wed. 9:00-13:00; off-season 9:00-15:00 most days. (Admission is free; upper level costs 6,000 L.)
  Forum — Mon., Wed., Thurs., Fri., Sat. 9:00-18:00; Tues. and Sun. 9:00-13:00; off-season 9:00-15:00 (10,000 L).
  Mamertine Prison — 9:00-12:30 and 14:30-18:00 (donation, 300 L?).
  Pantheon — Daily 9:00-17:00, Sun. 9:00-13:00 (Free).
  Again, hours are notoriously unreliable in Rome. Call tourist office at 488-3748 or 488-1851.
Tour length: Four hours.
Getting there: Subway to "Colosseo" stop, or taxi.
Information: No information service anywhere; only guidebooks from street vendors.

The excellent small red "Rome: Past and Present" book has overlay reconstructions of many of the monuments on this tour (pay between 10,000 and 12,000 L).

Misc.: Restaurants near Victor Emmanuel Monument, and good self-service cafeteria at Largo Argentina near the Pantheon.

Bring a water bottle and consider a picnic lunch.

Forum has drinking fountains.

WCs behind Colosseum, at Forum entrance, in Capitoline Museum, and in cafes near Pantheon.

ROME — REPUBLIC AND EMPIRE (500 B.C.-500 A.D.)

Ancient Rome spanned a thousand years, 500 B.C.-500 A.D. In that thousand years, Rome expanded from a small tribe of barbarians to become ruler of a vast Mediterranean empire, then dwindled slowly to city-size again. The first 500 years, when Rome's armies made her ruler of the Italian peninsula and beyond, Rome was a republic governed by elected senators. The next 500 years of world conquest and eventual decline, Rome was an empire ruled by a dictator backed by the military.

Julius Caesar bridged the Republic and the Empire. This ambitious general and politician, popular with the people because of his military victories and charisma, suspended the constitution and assumed dictatorial powers (around 50 B.C.). His adopted son Augustus took over, and soon "Caesar" was not just a name but a title. Emperor Augustus ushered

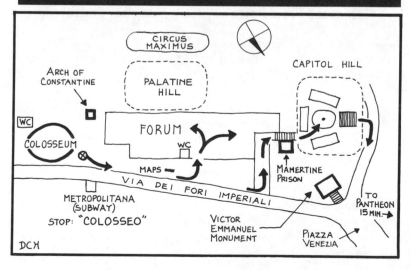

Rome Walk — Overview

in the "Pax Romana" or Roman peace (1-200 A.D.) when Rome reached her peak, controlling an empire stretching even beyond Eurail — from Scotland to Egypt, from Turkey to Morocco.

THE COLOSSEUM

☞ *View the Colosseum from the grassy patch across the street from the "Metropolitana" subway building.*

Built when the empire was at its peak (80 A.D.), this represents Rome at its grandest. The Flavian Amphitheater (its real name) was a stadium for gladiator contests and public spectacles. The design was simple — take two Greek theaters and stick them together. It was built by making a shell of brick, filling it in with concrete, then facing it with travertine stone held in place by iron pegs. The final structure was colossal, a "coloss-eum", the wonder of its age, seating 50,000 people.

Colosseum (Flavian Amphitheater). When killing became a spectator sport, the Romans wanted to share the fun with as many people as possible. By sticking two Greek theaters together, they created a stadium that could accommodate 50,000 roaring fans (100,000 thumbs).

The exterior says a lot about the Romans. They were great engineers, not artists. While the essential structure is Roman, the facade is Greek, decorated with the three types of Greek columns — Doric on bottom, Ionic in the middle and Corinthian on top. Originally, copies of Greek statues stood in the arches of the upper two stories. The Colosseum was meant to be functional, not necessarily beautiful. (If an ancient Roman visited the USA today as a tourist, he'd send home postcards of our greatest works of "art" — freeways.)

☞ *Enter by the west entrance, the one in front of you. Move up to a railing overlooking the arena.*

Interior

You're on arena level. What we see now are the underground passages beneath the playing surface. The oval-shaped arena (86 by 50 yards) was originally covered with boards, then sprinkled with dirt. Like modern stadiums, the spectators ringed the playing area. The brick masses around you supported the first small tier of seats, and you can see two larger slanted supports higher up. Wooden beams stuck out from the top to support an enormous canvas awning in sections, which could be hoisted across by armies of sailors to provide shade for the spectators — the first domed stadium.

"Hail, Caesar! We who are about to die salute you!" The gladiators would enter the arena from this west end, parade around to the sound of trumpets, stop at the emperor's box at the "50-yard-line" on the right (opposite where the cross stands today), raise their weapons, shout this salute...and the fights would begin. The fights pitted men against men, men against beasts and beasts against beasts.

The gladiators were usually slaves, criminals or poor people who got their chance for freedom, wealth and fame in the ring. They learned to fight in training schools, then worked their way up the ranks. The best were rewarded like our modern sports stars with fan clubs, great wealth and product endorsements.

The animals came from all over the world — lions, tigers, bears, oh my, crocodiles, elephants and hippos (not to mention exotic human "animals" from the "barbarian" lands). They were kept in cages beneath the arena floor, then lifted up in elevators where they'd pop out from behind blinds into the arena — the gladiator never knew where, when or by what he'd be attacked. Nets ringed the arena to protect the crowd. The stadium was inaugurated with a 100-day festival in which 2000 men and 9000 animals were killed. Colosseum employees squirted perfumes around the stadium to mask the stench of blood. For a light-hearted change of pace between events, the fans watched dogs bloody themselves fighting porcupines.

And Christians? Did they throw Christians to the lions like in the movies? Christians were definitely thrown to the lions, made to fight gladiators, crucified and burned alive...but probably not here in this particular stadium. Maybe, but probably not.

The Romans were — in their fantasies — a nation of warriors who built an empire on conquest. In reality, they were city-slicker bureaucrats who got vicarious thrills watching brutes battle to the death. The contests were always free, sponsored by politicians to buy votes or to keep Rome's growing mass of unemployed rabble off the streets.

Only a third of the original Colosseum remains. As Rome decayed, the Christians took over and closed it to games. Earthquakes destroyed some of it, but most was carted off as easy pre-cut stones for other buildings during the Middle Ages and Renaissance.

☞ *With these scenes in mind, wander around. For a few thousand lire you can go up to the upper deck for a more colossal view (stairs near the entrance).*

Leaving the Colosseum the way you came in, the Roman Forum is directly in front of you (though you can't enter it from this end), the subway stop is on your right, and the Arch of Constantine is on your left.

Arch of Constantine

If you are a Christian, were raised a Christian or simply belong to a so-called "Christian nation", ponder this arch. It marks one of the great turning points in history — the military coup that made us all Christians. In 312 A.D. an upstart general named Constantine, who claimed he was guided by a religious vision, defeated the Emperor Maxentius in one crucial battle. Constantine became Emperor and promptly legalized Christianity. With this one battle, an obscure Jewish sect with a handful of followers became the state religion of the entire Western world. In the year 300 A.D., you could be killed for being a Christian — by 400 you could be killed for not being one. Church enrollment boomed.

☞ *The entrance to the Roman Forum is 400 yards west along Via dei Fori Imperiali. The entrance building will be on your left. Remember, there are other "Forums" nearby — you're looking for "Foro Romano".*

About 100 yards along the way to the entrance stop at the "Let's Watch Rome Grow" maps which show how Rome grew to the point where the Mediterranean was called "Our Lake".

Buy your ticket (WCs on the left after you enter). Walk down the ramp, then go right about 20 yards. Find a seat on a piece of rubble. I know it's hot, but Roman history is most enjoyable when consumed while sitting on a broken slice of column. Sit with your back to the entrance.

ROMAN FORUM ("FORO ROMANO") — Heart of the Empire

The Forum was the political, religious and commercial center of the city. Rome's most important temples and halls of justice were here. This was the place for religious processions, elections, important speeches and parades by conquering generals. As Rome's empire expanded, these few acres of land became the center of the civilized world.

The hill ahead of you and slightly to the left, with all the trees, (the south border of the Forum) is the Palatine Hill where Rome started in 753 B.C. According to legend, twin brothers named Romulus ("Rome") and Remus were orphaned in infancy and raised by a she-wolf on top of the Palatine. Growing up, they found it hard to get dates. So they and their cohorts attacked the nearby Sabine tribe, fought them here in this valley and stole their women. After they made peace, the marshy valley became the meeting-place, and then the trading center, for the scattered tribes on the surrounding hillsides. Rome was born right here.

The valley is rectangular, running roughly east-west. At the far east end (to the left, out of sight) is the Colosseum. To the right rises the Capitol Hill. Running left to right at your feet is the rocky path known as the Via Sacra, the main street which runs down to the right past the large brick Senate building (*Curia*) to the well-preserved Arch of Septimius Severus.

The original "forum", or main square, was the flat patch about the size of a football field — just ahead of you and stretching out to the right. As Rome's empire grew, new buildings were built in the direction of the Colosseum.

There are three types of structures in the Forum: temples, basilicas and triumphal arches. We'll look at one of each of these. The Forum is now rubble, no denying it. We'll have to raise our imaginations to near-psychedelic levels in order to turn ruins into temples.

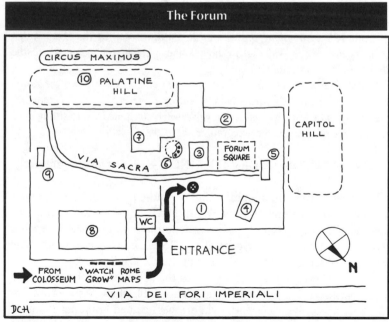

The Forum

x. Sit Here	4. Senate House	8. Basilica Maxentius
1. Basilica Aemelia	5. Arch of Septimius Severus	9. Arch of Titus
2. Basilica Julia	6. Temple of Vesta	10. Ruins of emperors' palaces
3. Temple of Julius Caesar	7. House of the Vestal Virgins	and view of Circus Maximus

The Forum's Main Square

The square where Romans met was bordered on our side by the Via Sacra and the Basilica Aemilia — we're sitting on the ruined columns of Aemilia's front porch. Now nothing but rubble, it was originally an impressive marble hall of justice as tall as the triumphal arch to the right. On the far side of the square was the Basilica Julia, an even bigger hall of justice built by Julius.

The Forum Square (existing rubble in dark). View from the Forum entrance toward Capitol Hill. For 500 years this square, surrounded by temples and government buildings, was the center of the Western world.

At either end of the square were speakers' platforms. The eastern one (our end) was at the Temple of Julius Caesar ("Templo dei Giulio"), the squat brick foundations ahead of you. It was a Greek-style temple ringed with 40-foot columns which are no longer there. From the front steps looking out over the square, emperors, senators and famous orators addressed the people of Rome. After Julius Caesar had been assassinated, this is where Mark Antony stood up to say (in Shakespeare's words), "Friends, Romans, countrymen, lend me your ears. I come to bury Caesar, not to praise him." In true Roman fashion, after they had killed Caesar, they made him a god, giving this temple its present name.

The most important political building was the Senate House (*Curia*), the well-preserved brick building with the triangular roof and one big window located between us and the triumphal arch. Three hundred Senators elected by the citizens of Rome met here to debate and create the laws of the land. Even when emperors became the supreme authority, the Senate was a power to be reckoned with.

This square was the busiest, most crowded — and often the seediest — section of town. Besides the senators, politicians and currency exchangers, there were even sleazier types — souvenir hawkers, fortune- tellers, gamblers, slave marketeers, drunkards, hookers and lawyers.

Walk around the square and mentally replace tourists in T-shirts with tribunes in togas. Imagine the buildings towering and the people buzzing around you, while an orator gives a rabble-rousing speech from the temple steps. Stumble through the stubble of columns in the Basilica Aemilia, and try to recreate the floor plan. Check out the front of the Senate House where senators plotted Caesar's assasination. If things still look like just a pile of rocks, at least tell yourself, "But Julius Caesar once leaned against these rocks."

☞   *Now dive into the interior of the Forum (keeping the entrance behind you). Head for the higher ground toward the Palatine Hill behind the remains of the small circular temple. Find two rectangular brick pools and a row of statues on pedestals.*

Temple of Vesta and House of the Vestal Virgins

This was Rome's most sacred spot. The Temple of Vesta (the small white circular ruins you passed on the way here) was the oldest in the city and housed the Sacred Flame of Rome. As long as this flame burned, Rome would stand. The flame was tended by priestesses known as Vestal Virgins.

House of the Vestal Virgins. This place was the model — both architecturally and sexually — for monasteries and convents throughout the Middle Ages.

The Vestal Virgins lived where you're standing in a two-story building surrounding a central courtyard with these two pools at one end. The rows of statues to the left and right mark the long sides of the building. This place was the model — both architecturally and sexually — for almost all convents and monasteries in the Middle Ages.

The six Vestal Virgins were chosen from noble families before the age of ten, serving a 30-year term. They were honored and revered by the Romans. They had their own box opposite the emperor in the Colosseum, and even consuls had to yield the right of way to them on the street.

As the name implies they were virgins, having taken a vow of chastity. If a virgin served her term faithfully — abstaining for 30 years — she was given a huge dowry, a statue in her honor (like the ones at left) and allowed to marry ("Life begins at 40?"). But if they found any virgin who wasn't, she was strapped to a funeral car, paraded through the streets of the Forum, taken to a crypt, given a loaf of bread and a lamp...and buried alive. Many girls chose the latter fate.

☞　*After some photo fun on an empty pedestal or with a headless statue, return to the Via Sacra and turn right. Head up the slight slope in the direction of the Colosseum.*

Via Sacra

The "Sacred Way" was Rome's Main Street, the oldest in the city and site of the grandest and holiest parades. It ran east-west from the Arch of Titus on the east end to the Arch of Septimius Severus on the west, then jogging left to the Temple of Saturn (the large columns at the foot of Capitol Hill). Religious processions by torchlight passed along here. And when conquering generals returned to Rome, they paraded their booty, exotic animals and prisoners from the conquered lands for all Rome to see. Many of the large basalt stones under your feet were walked on by Caesar Augustus, 2000 years ago.

☞　*As you head up the Via Sacra you'll see three enormous arches off to the left. Follow the lane to the left and find shade near a brick pillar or under an arch.*

Basilica Maxentius

The three arches are only one third of this grand hall of justice. They were matched by a similar set along the Via Sacra side. Between them ran the central hall, spanned by a roof 120 feet high, or about 50 feet higher than the side arches. The stubs of brick arcing out from the three arches were supports for this immense barrel-vaulted ceiling. The hall itself was a football-field long. At the far (west) end stood an enormous statue of the emperor on a throne.

Basilica Maxentius (Interior — existing rubble in dark). A Roman hall of justice, 100 yards long. The three standing arches were only the side aisles of this enormous structure, supporting a central roof that towered much higher.

Here is where justice was dispensed and common people came to plead their cases. Imagine this huge hall lavishly furnished with colorful inlaid marble, fountains and statues, and filled with strolling Romans. This building is larger than the Basilica Aemilia or Basilica Julia but has the same general shape — a rectangular building with a long central hall flanked by two side halls. (This floor plan is easy to see in the Basilica Aemilia — glance to your left as you exit the Forum.)

ROME FALLS

This peak of Roman grandeur is a good place to talk about the Fall of Rome. Again, Rome lasted a thousand years — 500 years growing, 200 years at its peak, and 300 years of gradual decay. The Fall had many causes. Christians blame it on moral decay. Marxists blame it on a shallow economy based on spoils of war. (Ronald Reagan blames it on Marxists.) Whatever the reasons, the far-flung empire could no longer keep its grip on conquered lands, and they pulled back. Barbarian tribes from Germany and Asia attacked the Italian peninsula and even looted Rome itself in 410 A.D., leveling many of the buildings in the Forum. In 476, the last emperor checked out, switched off the lights, and Europe plunged into centuries of ignorance, poverty and weak government — the Dark Ages.

But Rome lived on in the Catholic Church, the state religion of Rome's last generations. Emperors became popes (both called themselves "Pontifex Maximus"), senators became bishops, orators became priests...and basilicas became churches. Christian worship services required a larger meeting hall than Roman temples provided, so they used the spacious Roman basilica (hall of justice) as the model for their churches. Cathedrals from France to Spain to England, from Romanesque to Gothic to Renaissance all have the same basic floor plan as a Roman basilica. And remember that the goal for the greatest church of all, St. Peter's, was to "put the dome of the Pantheon atop the Basilica Maxentius". The glory of Rome never quite died.

☞   *Return to the Via Sacra and turn left, following it as it curves up toward Palatine Hill. Stop at the triumphal arch on the left...and the drinking fountain on the right. There's an impressive view of the Colosseum through the arch.*

Arch of Titus

Conquest and booty fueled Rome's incredible expansion. Conquering generals brought the spoils of war back home to parade them in front of the hometown folks. They built these triumphal arches to march under and to commemorate their victories.

This arch celebrated the Roman victory over the province of Judea (Israel) in 70 A.D. The Romans had a reputation as benevolent conquerors, tolerating the local customs and rulers. All they required was allegiance to the Empire, shown by worshipping the current emperor as a god. No problem for most conquered people, who already had half a dozen gods on their prayer lists. But the Israelites' god was jealous, and refused to let his people worship the emperor. Israel revolted, but after a short, bitter war, the Romans defeated the rebels, took Jerusalem and sacked their temple.

The propaganda value of Roman art is clear on the inside of this arch. On the left side, a relief shows the emperor Titus in a chariot being crowned by the goddess Victory (though they both look like they've been through the wars as modern pollution takes its toll). The right side shows the sacking of the temple — soldiers carrying the Jewish candelabrum, silver trumpets and the table for the holy bread from the temple. The two plaques on poles were to have listed the conquered cities but were unfinished.

The brutal crushing of this rebellion (and one 60 years later) devastated the nation of Israel. With no temple as a center for their faith, they were scattered throughout the world (the Diaspora). There was no Jewish political entity again for 2000 years, until after World War II when modern Israel was created.

PALATINE HILL AND CIRCUS MAXIMUS (OPTIONAL)

The Palatine Hill was the birthplace of Rome and the site of the luxurious palaces of the emperors ("palatine" gives us our word "palace"). The ruined palaces are hardly luxurious today, looking similar to the ruins of the Palace of Caligula at the foot of the hill overlooking the Forum. However, the hike up the hill is worth it, if for no other reason than for the view of the Circus Maximus. It's about a 10-minute hike up.

☞   *The Circus Maximus is on the far side of the Palatine Hill. Follow the colossal cobbles uphill from the Arch of Titus. At the summit, bear either left or right around the modern-looking building to the railings overlooking the Circus.*

Circus Maximus

This was a huge race course. Chariots circled around the cigar- shaped mound in the center. Bleachers (now grassy banks) originally surrounded the track. The track was 400 yards long while the whole stadium measured 650 by 220 yards, seating — get this — 300,000 people. The wooden bleachers once collapsed during a race, killing 13,000.

Races consisted of seven laps (about a mile altogether). In such a small space, collisions and overturned chariots were very common. The charioteers were usually poor low-borns, who used this dangerous sport to get rich and famous. Many retired as millionaires.

Circus Maximus (model) — If the gladiator show at the Colosseum was sold out, you could always get one of the 300,000 seats at the Circus Max. In an early version of today's Demolition Derby, Ben Hur and his fellow charioteers raced recklessly around the oval course. Notice the emperors' palaces on Palatine Hill conveniently located overlooking the finish line.

The public was crazy about it. There were 12 races a day, 240 days a year. Four teams dominated competition — Reds, Whites, Blues and Greens — and every citizen was fanatically devoted to one of them. Obviously, the emperors had the best seats in the house from their palaces on the hill. They occasionally had the circus floor carpeted with designs in colored powders for their pleasure.

The spectacles continued into the Christian era (until 549) despite Church disapproval.

☞ *Exit the Forum by the way you came in (not at the Colosseum end). Head west again (left) alongside Via dei Fori Imperiali for another 200 yards, taking your first left.*

Enjoy the view of the Forum from the railing at the huge Arch of Septimus Severus. Until modern times the history of Rome and its remains were no big deal. The Forum lay buried to the height we're at now. Only a few tips of columns interrupted what for centuries was called "the cow field". One evening two hundred years ago, Edward ("Rise and Decline") Gibbon stood here. He heard the song of Christian monks praying among pagan ruins and pondered the cyclical history of civilization...

Now turn about face and view the Capitol Hill. Ahead of you is a stair-case to the top. To the right of that is a dark building with a black iron fence labeled "MAMERTINUM". Let's drop in.

CAPITOL HILL

Mamertine Prison

Tip the monk (300 L will do), pass through the turnstile and descend into the 2500-year old cistern. There came a time when Rome needed prisons more than extra water, and this former cistern became the Mamertine Prison noted for its famous inmates. Inside, on the wall near the entryway you'll see lists of the most important prisoners and how they died. Secular criminals are listed on the left, Christian ones on the right. *Suppliziato* means quartered, *strangolati* is strangled, *morto di fame* is starvation...Saints Peter and Paul are said to have done time here. The floor of the prison has a hole with a grate over it. Long before pilgrims added the more convenient stairs, this was the standard entry way. Walk down the stairs past a supposed miraculous image of Peter's face, when a guard pushed him into the wall. Downstairs you'll see the column that Peter was chained to, and in this room a miraculous fountain sprang up, so Peter could baptize other prisoners. The upside-down cross commemorates Peter's upside-down crucifixion.

☞ *Escape the prison and climb the long hot stairs up Capitol Hill, past the guy who'll give you a deal on more slides and postcards of Rome than you could ever use, and on up until you find a great fountain. Block the spout with your finger, and a cool jet of refreshing water will fly up. Continue up to the large square on the hilltop.*

On the left-hand corner at the summit is the statue of the symbol of Rome — Romulus and Remus being suckled by the she-wolf. These

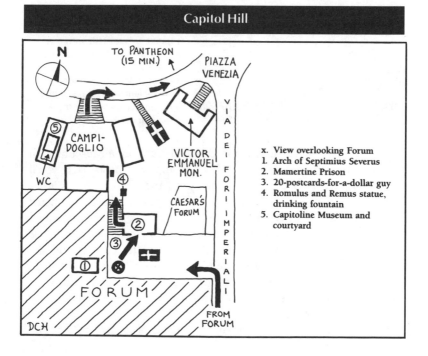

Capitol Hill

N

TO PANTHEON
(15 MIN.)

PIAZZA
VENEZIA

VIA DEI FORI IMPERIALI

CAMPI-
DOGLIO

VICTOR
EMMANUEL
MON.

WC

CAESAR'S
FORUM

FORUM

FROM
FORUM

DCH

x. View overlooking Forum
1. Arch of Septimius Severus
2. Mamertine Prison
3. 20-postcards-for-a-dollar guy
4. Romulus and Remus statue,
    drinking fountain
5. Capitoline Museum and
    courtyard

were the mythological founders of Rome who, according to legend. . .okay, I know it's hot — let's skip the legend. This hilltop has been sacred to Romans ever since 500 B.C., when an Etruscan Temple of Jupiter stood here.

☞ *Enter the square designed by Michelangelo and head for the stairs at the far end. Go down a dozen stairs or so, then turn around and come back up, entering the square the way Michelangelo wanted you to.*

Michelangelo's Renaissance Campidoglio

The Piazza del Campidoglio is the Renaissance square bounded by three palaces designed by Michelangelo. Michelangelo masterfully created a beautiful layout without much to start with. You'll notice that this square isn't. The buildings on the sides converge toward the far building. Yet Michelangelo has given a beautiful harmony to a setting that was not at all symmetrical. Notice, too, how the columns of the buildings ignore the fact that there are two stories, uniting the upper and lower halves and making the square a bit more intimate. The building with the fountain houses the offices and official residence of Rome's mayor. The other two are classical museums.

Campidoglio — Michelangelo capped Capitol Hill with this ingeniously designed Renaissance square. His use of Roman-style columns shows how ancient Rome was reborn a thousand years later in the Renaissance.

The building on the right is the excellent Capitoline Museum with many ancient statues including a gallery of emperors' busts. Here you'll find the original Etruscan "Capitoline Wolf", the famous "Boy With a Thorn in his Foot", and a seductive statue of the demonic Emperor Commodus dressed as Hercules. In its courtyard, you'll be entertained by chunks of a giant statue of Constantine. How creative can you be with your camera? (A rare public WC lurks in the corner. And the museum bookstand is one of Rome's better ones. Check out the huge wall map of ancient Rome.) The entry to this building lists local marriages, and there are always plenty. It's not uncommon to see newlyweds here in cummerbunds of bliss.

☞ *Now descend the stairs for good and pause at the bottom.*

The Modern World

Look to your left a few blocks at the building which incorporates an ancient Roman colonnade into its walls. Then turn right, and look up the long stairway to the early Christian church high above you. There's an obscure Etruscan statue in there that we absolutely must see — meet you at the top. Just kidding! Be thankful you don't need to climb these steps.

Follow the sidewalk to the right along the immense white Victor Emmanuel II monument. As you go, look down at the forgotten parts of ancient Rome that lie quietly under the entire city. Leave the ancient world for a minute and walk to the center of the monument for a look at Italy's guarded Tomb of the Unknown Soldier and the eternal flame. Turn around to see the busy Piazza Venezia. The balcony of the palace on the right is where Mussolini would whip his fans into a fascist fury. The long Via del Corso stretching away from you is Rome's grand boulevard. Much of it is closed to traffic each early evening for the daily *paseo* ritual — "cruising" without cars.

☞ *Now get our your Rome city map and find the Pantheon. It's about a 15-minute walk northwest — about 500 yards as the pigeon flies.*

THE PANTHEON

☞ *Face the Pantheon from the obelisk fountain in front.*

Exterior

It doesn't look like much from here, but this is perhaps the most influential building in art history. Its dome was the model for the Florence cathedral dome which launched the Renaissance and for Michelangelo's dome of St. Peter's which capped it all off. Even Washington D.C.'s Capitol building was inspired by this dome.

The Pantheon was a Roman temple dedicated to all (*Pan*) the gods (*theos*). First built in 27 B.C., it was completely rebuilt around 120 A.D. by the Emperor Hadrian. In a gesture of modesty, admirable in anyone but astounding in a Roman emperor, Hadrian left his own name off it, putting the name of the original builder on the front — "M. Agrippa".

☞ *Pass between the enormous one-piece marble columns and through the enormous original bronze door. Stand awestruck for a moment, then take a seat on the bench to your right.*

Interior

The dome, the largest made until modern times, is set on a circular base. The mathematical perfection of this dome-on-a-base design is a testament to Roman engineering. The dome is as high as it is wide —

142 feet — making it one half of a perfect sphere. (Imagine a basketball set inside a wastebasket so that it just touches bottom.)

Pantheon (Interior) — A dome set on a circular base with perfect proportions — 142 feet high, 142 wide. This dome was the model for many that followed. The interior, looking much like it did 2,000 years ago, gives us a feel for the grandeur of Rome.

The dome is made from concrete that gets lighter and thinner as it reaches the top. The walls at the base are 20 feet thick made from heavy travertine concrete, while near the top they're only five feet thick made of a light volcanic rock. Both Brunelleschi and Michelangelo studied this dome before building their own. Remember — and this is the last time I'll say it, I promise — St. Peter's Cathedral is really only "the dome of the Pantheon on top of the Basilica Maxentius".

The *oculus*, or eye-in-the-sky at the top, the building's only light source, is almost 30 feet across. No, they don't close the window when it rains — the 1800-year-old floor has holes in it and slants towards the edges to let the water drain. The marble floor is largely restored, though the designs are close to the originals.

This is Rome's best preserved ancient building. What you see is what Hadrian, Constantine, Augustine, Charlemagne, Michelangelo, Dean Martin and all other visitors to Rome have seen for the last 2000 years. The barbarians passed it by when they sacked Rome. Early in the Middle Ages, it became a Christian church (from "all the gods" to "all the martyrs"), saving it from architectural cannibalism and ensuring its up-keep through the Dark Ages. The only major destruction came in the 17th century when the pope stole the bronze plating and melted it down to build the huge bronze canopy over the altar at St. Peter's ("What the Barbarians didn't do, the Barberini did"). About the only new things in the interior are the decorative statues and the tombs of famous people, like the artist Raphael (to the left of the main altar, in the glass case), and modern Italy's first king, Victor Emmanuel II (on the right).

The Pantheon is the only continuously used ancient building in Rome. When you leave, you'll notice how the rest of the city has risen on 20 centuries of rubble.

The Pantheon also contains the world's greatest Roman column. There it is spanning the entire 142 feet from heaven to earth — the pillar of light from the *oculus*.

St. Peter's, Rome

St. Peter's is the greatest church in Christendom. Not only is it the largest, but it represents the power and splendor of Rome's 2000-year domination of the Western world. Built on the memory and grave of the first Pope, St. Peter, this is where the grandeur of ancient Rome became the grandeur of Christianity.

Basilica di San Pietro, Vatican

Hours: Daily, 7:00-19:00. Mass daily at 17:00. Lift to the dome 8:00-18:00.
Cost: Free. Strict dress code — no shorts or bare shoulders. Mechanical ascension to the dome 3000 L.
Tour length: One hour, plus another hour if you climb the dome.
Altitude gain: 300 feet.
Getting there: Subway to "Ottaviano", then 15-minute walk south on Via Ottaviano.
   Several city buses go right to St. Peter's Square.
   Taxis are cheap.
   A shuttle bus (twice an hour, 2000 L) connects the church and the Vatican Museum.
Information: Helpful booth just inside front door.
   Tourist office on left side of square is excellent. (Pick up free Vatican and church map and list of current hours. This office conducts several special insider tours of Vatican gardens, etc. Open Mon.-Sat. 8:30-19:00.)

Free, 90-minute English tours leave from information booth usually at 10:15
and 15:00.

Tel. 698-4466.

Misc.: WCs to right of church and on the roof.

Drinking fountains at obelisk and near WCs.

Post office next to tourist office on left of square (Vatican post is more reliable
than Italian).

Best time to visit is early or late.

Starring: Michelangelo, Bernini, Bramante, St. Peter, a heavenly host and, occasionally, the Pope.

OLD ST. PETER'S

☞ *Find a shady spot where you like the view under the columns around*
St. Peter's circular "square". Sit — if the pigeons left you a clean spot.

Nearly 2000 years ago this area was the site of Nero's Circus, a huge
Roman chariot racecourse. The obelisk you see in the middle of the
square was the centerpiece of the course. The Romans had no marching
bands, so for half-time entertainment they killed Christians. This persecuted minority was forced to fight wild animals and gladiators, or they
were simply crucified. Some were tarred up, tied to posts and burned
— human torches to light up the evening races.

One of those killed, around 65 A.D., was Peter, Jesus' right-hand man
who had come to Rome to spread the message of love. Peter was crucified
— but on an upside-down cross at his own request, because he felt
unworthy to die as his master had. His remains were buried in a nearby
cemetery, where they were quietly and secretly revered for two centuries.

When Christianity was finally legalized in 312, the Christian emperor
Constantine built a church on the site of the martyrdom of this first
"pope", or bishop of Rome, from whom all later popes claimed their
authority as head of the Church. "Old St. Peter's" lasted 1200 years
(324-1500 A.D.).

By the time of the Renaissance, Old St. Peter's was falling apart and
was considered unfit to be the center of the Western church. The new
larger church we see today was begun in 1506, and actually built around
the old one. As it was completed 120 years later, after many changes of
plans, Old St. Peter's was dismantled and carried out the doors of the
new one.

☞ *Ideally you should head out to the obelisk to view the square and*
read this. But let me guess — it's 95 degrees, right? Okay, stay in the shade
of these stone sequoias a while longer and read on.

ST. PETER'S SQUARE

St. Peter's Square with its ring of columns is meant to symbolize the arms of the church reaching out to its people. It was designed by the Baroque architect Bernini, who also did much of the work we'll see inside. Numbers first — 284 columns 50 feet high in stern Doric style. Topping them are Bernini's 140 favorite saints, 10 feet tall. The "Square" itself is elliptical, 200 by 150 yards.

The obelisk in the center is 80 feet of solid granite weighing over 300 tons. Think for a second of how much history this monument has seen. Erected originally in Egypt over 2000 years ago, it witnessed the fall of the pharaohs to the Greeks and then to the Romans. It was then moved to Imperial Rome where it stood impassively watching the slaughter of Christians at the racecourse. Today it watches over the church, a reminder that each civilization builds on the previous ones. The puny cross on top only serves to remind us that much of our Christian culture is but a thin veneer over our pagan origins.

☞ *Now venture out across the burning desert to the obelisk, which always provides a narrow sliver of shade.*

Face the church, then turn about face and say "*Grazie, Benito.*" I don't make a habit of going around thanking Fascist dictators, but Benito

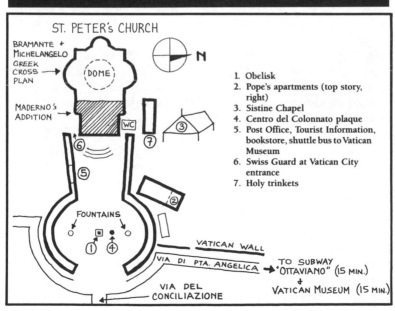

St. Peter's Square

ST. PETER's CHURCH

BRAMANTE + MICHELANGELO GREEK CROSS PLAN →

(DOME)

MADERNO'S ADDITION →

WC

N

1. Obelisk
2. Pope's apartments (top story, right)
3. Sistine Chapel
4. Centro del Colonnato plaque
5. Post Office, Tourist Information, bookstore, shuttle bus to Vatican Museum
6. Swiss Guard at Vatican City entrance
7. Holy trinkets

FOUNTAINS

VATICAN WALL

VIA DI PTA. ANGELICA → TO SUBWAY "OTTAVIANO" (15 MIN.)

VIA DEL CONCILIAZIONE

VATICAN MUSEUM (15 MIN.)

Mussolini did, at least, one good thing in his day. This broad boulevard he built in the 1930s finally let people see the dome of St. Peter's that the facade had hidden for centuries. From here at the obelisk, Michelangelo's magnificent dome can only peek its top over the bulky Baroque front entrance. You have to back up into Mussolini's boulevard to truly appreciate Michelangelo's original vision.

The building at two o'clock to the right (as you face the church), rising up behind Bernini's colonnade, is where the Pope lives. The last window on the right of the top floor is his bedroom. The window to the left of that is his study, the "window on the world", where he appears occasionally to greet the masses. If you come to the square at night as a Poping Tom, you might see the light on — the Pope burns much midnight oil.

From here you can also see the near end of the Sistine Chapel, the triangular-shaped brown stone roof just to the right of St. Peter's facade. The tiny chimney at the peak of the roof (with the long antenna) is where the famous smoke signals announce the election of each new pope. If the smoke is black, a 75% majority hasn't been reached. White smoke means a new pope has been selected.

Walk to the right and stand on the fifth plaque from the obelisk, marked "Centro del Colonnato". From here all of Bernini's columns on the right side line up. The curved Baroque square still pays its respects to Renaissance mathematical symmetry.

☞ *Climb the gradually sloping stairs past crowd barriers and the huge statues of St. Paul with his two-edged sword and St. Peter with his bushy hair and keys.*

Stop by the Vatican City entrance on the left side of the church. Guarding this border crossing into Vatican City — a separate country — are the mercenary guards from Switzerland. Their colorful uniforms are said to have been designed by Michelangelo, though he was not known for his sense of humor.

☞ *Enter the atrium of the church passing under the balcony where the Pope appears on special occasions to bless everyone. You'll pass by the dress-code enforcers and a gaggle of ticked-off guys in shorts.*

THE BASILICA

The Atrium
The atrium is itself bigger than most churches. Facing us are the five famous bronze doors. Each symbolic door leads into the main church. The central door, made from the melted-down bronze of the original door of Old St. Peter's, is only opened on special occasions.

The far right entrance is the Holy Door, opened only during Holy Years. On Christmas Eve, every 25 years, the Pope knocks three times with a silver hammer, and the door is opened. At the end of the year, he bricks it up again with a ceremonial trowel to await another 24 years. On the door, note Jesus' shiny knees, polished by pious pilgrims, who touch them for a blessing.

The other doors are modern, reminding us that, amid all this tradition, the Catholic Church has changed enormously, even during our lifetime. The "Door of Death" on the far left shows the many ways mortals may die. It also has a portrait of a kneeling pope, John XXIII, who presided over the landmark Vatican II council in the early 1960s. This meeting of Church leaders brought the medieval church into the modern age, making old doctrines — like the use of Latin in the mass — "relevant" to the 20th century. The most recent door (1977, second from the left), is called "Good and Evil". Which is which?

☞ *Now for one of Europe's great wow experiences. Enter the church. Walk to the rear of the center door or sit on the base of a square column at the back wall. Look around and gape for awhile. I'll wait.*

St. Peter's Basilica

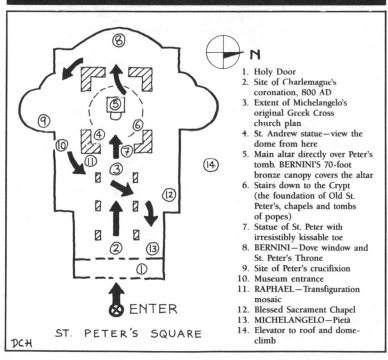

1. Holy Door
2. Site of Charlemagne's coronation, 800 AD
3. Extent of Michelangelo's original Greek Cross church plan
4. St. Andrew statue—view the dome from here
5. Main altar directly over Peter's tomb. BERNINI'S 70-foot bronze canopy covers the altar
6. Stairs down to the Crypt (the foundation of Old St. Peter's, chapels and tombs of popes)
7. Statue of St. Peter with irresistibly kissable toe
8. BERNINI—Dove window and St. Peter's Throne
9. Site of Peter's crucifixion
10. Museum entrance
11. RAPHAEL—Transfiguration mosaic
12. Blessed Sacrament Chapel
13. MICHELANGELO—Pietà
14. Elevator to roof and dome-climb

The Church

Again, let's start with size, then turn to beauty. The golden window at the far end is two football fields away. The dove in the window above the altar has the wingspan of a 747 (okay, maybe not quite, but it is big). The church covers six acres — if planted with wheat it could feed a small city. The babies on the columns along the main hall (the nave), are taller than you are. The lettering in the gold band along the top of the columns is six feet high. The church has a capacity for 95,000 standing worshippers (that's over 2000 tour groups!). It's the largest church in the world.

St. Peter's Nave—While ancient Rome fell, its grandeur survived. Roman basilicas became churches, Senators became Bishops, and the Pontifex Maximus . . . remained the Pontifex Maximus. This church is the largest in Christendom. (It's so big that the lint from its nave alone could fill all the mattresses of Rome's cheap hotels.)

The church is huge and it feels huge, but everything is actually designed to make it seem smaller than it really is. Its baroque architects went to great lengths to give it a surprisingly intimate and homey atmosphere, despite the overwhelming size and decoration. For example, the statue of St. Theresa at the bottom of the first pillar on the right is 15 feet tall. The statue above her, near the top, looks the same size but is actually six feet taller, giving the impression that it's not as far away as it really is. Similarly, the fancy bronze canopy over the altar at the far end is as tall as a seven-story building. That makes the great height of the dome seem smaller.

Looking down the nave, we get a sense of the grandeur of ancient Rome that was carried on through the Middle Ages by the Catholic Church. The floor plan is based on the ancient Roman basilica, or law court building, with a central aisle (nave) flanked by two side aisles. The goal of this unprecedented building project was to "put the dome of the Pantheon on top of the Roman Forum's Basilica Maxentius". If you've seen these two Roman structures you have an idea of this mega-vision. In fact, many of the stones used to build St. Peter's were scavenged from the ruined basilicas of the ancient Roman Forum.

On the floor in front of the central doorway is a round slab of porphyry stone in the purple/red color of ancient Roman officials. This is the spot where, on Christmas night, 800 A.D., the French King Charlemagne was crowned "Holy Roman Emperor", again making Rome the center of a briefly united Europe.

You're surrounded by marble, gold, stucco, mosaics, columns of stone and pillars of light. This is baroque, the decorative style intended to overwhelm and impress the masses with the authority of the Church. St. Peter's was very expensive to build and decorate. The Popes financed it by selling "indulgences", or papal pardons. The rich could literally buy forgiveness from the Church. This kind of corruption inspired an obscure German monk named Martin Luther to rebel and start the Protestant Reformation. The baroque interior by Bernini was part of the Church's Counter-Reformation, showing the glorious golden vision of heaven available to everyone — if they remained a good Catholic.

☞ *Walk straight up the center of the nave toward the altar.*

Michelangelo's Church — The Greek Cross

The plaques on the floor show where other, smaller churches of the world would end if they were placed inside St. Peter's: St. Paul's Cathedral in London ("Londinese"), the Florence Cathedral, and so on.

You'll also walk over circular golden grates. Stop at the second one (at the third pillar from the entrance). Look back at the entrance, and realize that if Michelangelo had his way, this whole long section of the church wouldn't exist. The nave was extended after his death.

Michelangelo was 72 years old when the Pope persuaded him to take over the church project and cap it with a dome. He agreed on three conditions: 1) that he receive no payment; 2) that he have a thousand workers at his disposal in order to finish it in his lifetime; and 3) that he could put the dome over a "Greek Cross" floor plan. Of these three conditions, the Pope was more than happy to meet the first one. But Michelangelo died (18 years later) before the project was completed, and later architects changed his original design.

The Greek Cross plan (+) called for a central dome topping four equal arms. In Renaissance times this symmetrical arrangement symbolized perfection — the orderliness of the created world and the goodness of man (who was created in God's image). But Michelangelo was a Renaissance Man in Counter-Reformation times. The Church, struggling against Protestants and its own corruption, opted for a plan designed to impress the world with its grandeur — the Latin Cross of the Crucifixion — with its extended nave to accommodate the grand religious spectacles of the baroque period.

☞ *Continue toward the altar, entering "Michelangelo's Church". Park yourself in front of the statue of St. Andrew to the left of the altar, the guy*

*holding an X-shaped cross. Gaze up into the dome. Gasp if you must —
never stifle a gasp.*

The Dome

The dome soars higher than a football field on end, 390 feet to the
top of the lantern. It glows with light from its windows, the blue and
gold mosaics creating a cool, solemn atmosphere. In this majestic vision
of heaven, we see Jesus, Mary and a ring of saints, more rings of angels
above them, and way up in the ozone, God the Father.

Listen to the hum of visitors echoing through St. Peter's. Churches
are an early form of biofeedback, where we can become aware of ourselves, our own human sounds, and can reflect on our place in the
cosmos. Half animal, half angel, stretched between heaven and earth,
born to live a short while only to die, a bubble of foam on a great
cresting wave...humanity.

Peter

The base of the dome is ringed with a banner telling us in letters six
feet tall why this church is the most important in Catholicism. According
to Catholics, Peter was selected by Jesus to head the Church. The banner
in Latin quotes from the Bible where Jesus says to him, "You are Peter
(*Tu es Petrus...*) and upon this rock I will build my church" (Matthew
16:18). Peter was the first bishop of Rome, and his authority has supposedly passed in an unbroken chain to each succeeding bishop of Rome
— that is, the 250-odd popes that followed.

Michelangelo's dome —
Towering high above Peter's
bones, the dome's huge
lettering reminds us of Christ's
words: "You are Peter (Tu es
Petrus) and upon this rock I will
build my church."

Under the dome, under the bronze canopy, under the altar, under
the marble floor some twenty feet rest the bones of St. Peter, the "rock"
that this particular church was built upon. Go to the railing and look
down into the small lighted niche eight feet below the altar with a box
containing bishops' shawls — a symbol of how Peter's authority spread
to the other churches.

Are the bones of Jesus' apostle really here? According to a papal pronouncement: definitely maybe. The traditional site of his tomb was sealed up when Old St. Peter's was built on it in 326 A.D. and remained sealed until 1940, when it was opened for archeological study. Bones were found, dated from the first century, of a robust man who died in old age, whose body was wrapped in expensive cloth. Various inscriptions and graffiti in the tomb indicate that 2nd and 3rd century visitors thought this was Peter's tomb. Does that mean it's really Peter? Who am I to disagree with the Pope? Definitely maybe.

If you line up the cross on the altar with the dove in the window, you'll notice that the niche below the cross is a foot and a half off-center left with the rest of the church. Why? Because Michelangelo designed the church around the traditional location of the tomb, not the actual location discovered by modern archeology.

☞ *You can go down to the crypt and the foundations of Old St. Peter's, containing tombs of popes and memorial chapels. The staircase is to your right. It's free, but the visit takes you back outside the church, a 15-minute detour ending up at a water fountain, WC, and a wacky-sometimes-tacky religious souvenir store.*

In the nave (over your right shoulder) is a bronze statue of Peter — one of a handful of pieces of art that was in the earlier church. In one hand he holds the keys, the symbol of the authority given him by Christ, while with the other he blesses us. He's wearing the toga of a Roman senator. It may be that the original statue was of a senator, and the bushy head and keys were added later to make it Peter. Peter's big right toe has been worn smooth by the lips of pilgrims. Stand in line and kiss it, or, if you're worried about hoof-and-mouth disease, touch your hand to your lips, then rub the toe. This is simply an act of reverence with no legend attached, though you can make one up if you like.

The Altar

The main altar beneath the dome is used only when the Pope himself says mass. He often conducts the Sunday morning service when he's in town, a sight worth seeing. I must admit, though, it's a little strange being frisked at the door for weapons at the holiest place in Christendom.

The white marble slab of the altar would be lost in this enormous church, if it weren't for the seven-story bronze canopy by Bernini which "extends" the altar upward and reduces the perceived distance between floor and ceiling. Bernini, who designed the baroque interior, gave a surprising unity to an amazing variety of pillars, windows, statues, chapels and aisles. The canopy is his crowning touch. The corkscrew columns, "the epitome of baroque", are actually copies of ancient columns from Old St. Peter's. The bronze that was used was stolen and melted down from the ancient Pantheon.

On the columns, you see three bees on a shield, the symbol of the Barberini family who commissioned the work and ordered the raid on the Pantheon. As the saying went, "What the Barbarians didn't destroy, the Barberini did."

Starting from the column to the left of the altar, walk clockwise around the canopy. Notice the female faces on the marble bases, about eye-level above the bees. Someone in the Barberini family was pregnant during the making of the canopy, so Bernini put the various stages of childbirth on the bases. Continue clockwise to the last base to see how it came out.

☞ *Walk into the apse — the area with the golden dove window — and take a seat.*

The Apse

Bernini also did the dove window over the smaller front altar, which is used for everyday services. The Holy Spirit, in the form of a six-foot dove, shines light on the faithful, as sunlight pours through the alabaster windows, turning into artificial rays of gold and reflecting off swirling gold clouds, angels and winged babies. This really is the epitome of baroque — a highly decorative, glorious, mixed-media work designed to overwhelm the viewer.

Beneath the dove is the centerpiece of this structure, the so-called "Throne of Peter", an oak chair built in medieval times for a Holy Roman Emperor and, subsequently, encrusted with tradition and encased in bronze by Bernini, as a symbol of papal authority. Statues of four early Church fathers support the chair, a symbol of how bishops should support the Pope in troubled times — times like the Counter-Reformation. Bernini's baroque was great propaganda for the power of the Catholic Church.

This is a good place to remember that this is a church, not a museum. In the apse, mass is said daily at 5:00 pm for pilgrims and Roman citizens alike. (You're welcome to take communion during any mass.) Wooden confessional booths are available for Catholics to tell their sins to a listening ear and receive forgiveness and peace of mind. The faithful renew their faith, and the faithless gain inspiration. Sit here, look at the light streaming through the windows, turn and gaze up into the dome and quietly contemplate your god.

Or...

Contemplate this: the mystery of empty space. The bench you're sitting on and the marble at your feet, solid as they may seem, consist overwhelmingly of open space — 99.9999 percent open space. The atoms that form these "solid" benches are, themselves, mostly open space. If the nucleus of your average atom was as large as the period at the end of this sentence, its electrons would be specks of dust orbiting around it...at the top of Michelangelo's dome. Empty space. Perhaps matter is only an aberration in an empty universe.

☞ *Poke around the south transept, the arm to the left of the bronze canopy, (as you approach from the entrance). Look at the Bernini doorway with the gold skeleton smothered in jasper poured like maple syrup. Bizarre baroque.*

Stop at the altar at the far end with the painting of St. Peter crucified upside down.

Left Transept

You are now standing on the exact spot (according to tradition) where Peter was killed 1900 years ago.

Persecution of Christians was actually a rare thing in ancient Rome, and the Romans were exceptionally tolerant of other religions. All they required of their conquered peoples was allegiance to the Empire by worshipping the Emperor as a god. For most religions this was no problem, but monotheistic Christians were children of a "jealous" God who would not allow worship of any others. They refused to worship the Emperor and valiantly stuck by their faith, even when burned alive, crucified and thrown to the lions. Their bravery, optimism in suffering, and message of love struck a chord among slaves and members of the lower classes. The religion started by a poor carpenter grew, despite occasional "pogroms" by fanatical emperors. In three short centuries, Christianity went from a small Jewish sect in Jerusalem to the official religion of the world's greatest empire.

☞ *If you like old jewels and papal robes, the St. Peter's Museum is just around the corner to your right as you leave the transept. It displays the treasures and splendors of Roman Christianity, a marked contrast to the poverty of early Christians.*

Heading back towards the central nave, look to your left and pause for a bit at the copy of Raphael's huge painting "The Transfiguration", especially if you won't be seeing the original in the Vatican Museum. This "painting" is no painting at all. It's a mosaic, like all but one of the pictures in St. Peter's, since smoke and humidity would damage real paintings. If the light's right, you can see through these mosaics made with thousands of colored chips the size of your little fingernail.

☞ *Cross the nave to the other side of the church, then head towards the entrance along the right (north) aisle. You're welcome to step into the Blessed Sacrament Chapel, an oasis of peace reserved for prayer and medita-*

tion inside metalwork gates.
Continue toward the entrance of the church. On your left behind bullet-proof
glass is...

The Pietà

Michelangelo was 24 years old when he completed this Pietà. A pietà (pron. pee-ay-TAH), literally meaning pity, is any work showing Mary with the dead body of Christ taken from the cross. Here, Mary cradles her crucified son in her lap.

Michelangelo, with his total mastery of realism, captures the sadness of the moment. Christ's lifeless right arm drooping down lets us know how heavy this corpse is. His smooth skin is accented by the rough folds of Mary's robe. Mary tilts her head downward, looking at her dead son with sad tenderness. Her left hand is upturned as if asking, "How could they do this to you?"

MICHELANGELO — Pietà. Done by a 24-year-old Michelangelo, Mary is a solid pyramid of maternal tenderness cradling the unnaturally small body of her dead son.

Michelangelo didn't think of sculpting as creating a figure, but as simply freeing the God-made figure from the prison of marble around it. He'd attack a project like this with an inspired passion. (Sound spacey? Think for a second of some 24-year-old you know. Imagine giving him a chisel and some marble...)

Realistic as this work is, its true power lies in the subtle "unreal" features. Look how small and childlike Christ is compared with the massive Mary. Unnoticed at first, this accentuates the subconscious impression of Mary enfolding Jesus in her maternal love. Again, notice how young Mary is. She's the mother of a 30-year-old man, but here she's portrayed as a teenage girl. This caused a scandal in Michelangelo's day, but now we realize he did it to show how Mary was the eternally youthful "handmaiden" of the Lord, always serving Him even at this moment of supreme sacrifice. She accepts God's will, even if it means giving up her own son to help others.

The statue is a solid pyramid of maternal tenderness. Yet within this, Christ's body tilts diagonally down to the right, and Mary's hem flows with it. Subconsciously we feel the weight of this dead God sliding from her lap to the ground.

And Mary's face...'nuff said.

On Christmas morning, 1972, a madman with a hammer entered St. Peter's and began hacking away at the Pietà. The damage was eventually repaired, but that's why there's the shield of bulletproof glass.

This is Michelangelo's only signed work. The story goes that he overheard some people praising his finished Pietà, but attributing it to a second-rate sculptor from a lesser city. He was so enraged that he grabbed his chisel and chipped "Michelangelo Buonarotti of Florence did this" in the ribbon running down Mary's chest.

On your right is the inside of the Holy Door, mortared up until it will be opened next on Christmas Eve, 1999. If there's a prayer inside you, you might ask that when it's opened for Holy Year 2000, St. Peter's will no longer need security checks or bulletproof glass.

Up to the Dome

A nice way to finish a visit to St. Peter's is to go up to the dome for a view of Rome. Take either the elevator located just to the left of where you entered the church (next to the Baptistry), or the one near the north transept behind Peter with the well-worn foot (often, one or the other is closed). These take you to the roof with a nice view of St. Peter's Square, Rome across the Tiber and the dome itself — almost terrifying in its nearness — looming behind you.

If you're energetic, climb the dome for the best view of Rome anywhere. The staircase actually winds between the outer shell and the inner one. It's a long, sweaty, stuffy ten-minute climb up but worth it. The view from the summit is great, the fresh air even better. Find the big white Victor Emmanuel Monument with the two statues on top and the Pantheon with its large light shallow dome. The large rectangular building to the left of the obelisk is the Vatican Museum stuffed with art. Survey the Vatican grounds with its mini-train system and lush gardens. The climb back down is much faster and easier — in these stairways, people circulate better than air.

(The dome is open 8:00-18:00. Allow one hour for the full trip up and down, a half hour to go only to the roof and gallery.)

Even if you don't hike all the way to the top, from the elevator everyone goes up a few steps to the gallery ringing the interior of the dome. From here you look down inside the church. Notice the dusty top of Bernini's seven-story-tall canopy far below, study the mosaics up close...and those huge letters! It's worth the elevator ride for this view alone, to look down into the church and on the tiny pilgrims buzzing around its empty space.

The Vatican Museum, Rome

Many tourists see the Vatican Museum as an obstacle between them and its grand finale, the Sistine Chapel. True, this huge, confusing and crowded mega-museum can be a jungle, but with this book as your vine, you should swing through with ease, enjoying the highlights, and getting to the Sistine just before you collapse. On the way, we'll enjoy some of the less-appreciated but equally important sections of this warehouse of Western civilization.

Museo Vaticano (pron: moo-SAY-oh vah-tee-KAHN-oh)

Hours: July-Sept. — Mon.-Fri. 8:45-16:30; Sat. 8:45-14:00; closed Sundays except last Sunday of the month.

Oct.-June — Mon.-Sat. 8:45-13:45.

Closed 13 religious holidays including Corpus Christi and St. Peter and Paul day in June, and Assumption Day in early or mid-August.

Some individual rooms close at odd hours, especially after 13:00. A lighted board at the ground level entrance lists closures. The rooms we'll see are generally open.

Modest dress (no short shorts) is appropriate and often required to visit the museum.

Last entrance is one hour before closing, Sistine closes 30 minutes early.

Cost: 10,000 L, free on last Sundays.

Tour length: Until you expire, or 2½ hours, whichever comes first.

Getting there: It's a 15-minute walk from St. Peter's Square. Subway to "Ottaviano" and a 15-minute walk.

Bus #19, 23, 30, 32, 49, 50, 64, 77, 81, 913, 991, and a special shuttle bus to save you the long exhausting walk from the church (2000 L).

Taxis are reasonable (just move your hands and say "moo-SAY-oh vah-tee-KAHN-oh").

Information: Information booth on ground floor at entry (English spoken).

The museum has signs to four color-coded self-guided tours but very little English explanation.

The black "Guide to the Vatican" book is best.

You can (but I wouldn't) rent cassette tours of the entire museum at the entry, or for the Raphael rooms and Sistine just before the Raphael rooms.

Introductory movie is in the theater to the right of the ticket turnstile.

Tel. 698-4628.

Misc.: Cafeteria is clean, not cheap, great view.

There's a great produce market three blocks directly in front of the entrance. Post office, writing room, exchange bank and book shop next to ticket booth. Generally hot and crowded. Sat., Sun. and Mon. are worst, late afternoons are best.

Starring: Michelangelo, Raphael, Laocoön, the Greek masters and their Roman copyists.

Vatican Museum — Upstairs Lobby

THE POPE'S COLLECTION

☞ *Leave Italy by entering the doors. Climb the impressive modern double-spiral staircase — why does everyone seem to be going your way? — or take the lift. At the top are the ticket windows.*

Find a quiet spot to read ahead — try the writing tables in the lobby post office. Or, buy your ticket, pass through the entry, then pull off into the courtyard immediately to your left, or the courtyard near the cafeteria.

With the fall of Rome, the "Catholic" (or "universal") Church became the great preserver of civilization, collecting artifacts from cultures dead and dying. A walk through here is like regressing into your past lives, a dip into the "collective unconscious" of the Western mind.

Renaissance popes collected most of what we'll see. Those lusty priests-as-Roman-emperors loved the ancient world. They built these palaces for themselves and decorated them with classical statues and Renaissance paintings. They combined the Classical and Christian worlds, finding the divine in the creations of man.

We'll concentrate on classical sculpture and Renaissance painting. But along the way (and there's a lot of along-the-way in this place) we'll stop to leaf through a few yellowed pages from the 5000-year-old scrapbook of mankind. The museum's one-way-only policy makes it difficult to get lost, so directions will be kept to a minimum.

This heavyweight museum is shaped like a barbell — two buildings connected by a long hall. The building you're now in contains the ancient world, the one at the far end (near St. Peter's) is the Renaissance (including the Sistine Chapel). The halls there and back are a mix of old and new.

We're headed to see three of the greatest Greek sculptures, but we have to pass through the Egyptian collection first. Move quickly — don't burn out before the Sistine Chapel at the end — but by pausing to look at some of the things along the way, you'll see how each civilization

Vatican Museum — Overview

borrows from and builds on the previous one.

☞   *Follow the crowds, turn left up the stairs, then right into the Egyptian Rooms. Get wrapped up in the mummies, then follow the yellow arrow into the next room.*

EGYPT (3000-1000 B.C.)

Egyptian art was for religion, not decoration. A statue or painting preserved the likeness of someone, giving him a form of eternal life. Most of the art was for tombs, where they put the mummies you see. Notice that the art is only realistic enough to get the job done. You can recognize that it's a man, a bird or whatever, but these are stiff, two-dimensional, schematic figures. They are functional, rather than beautiful.

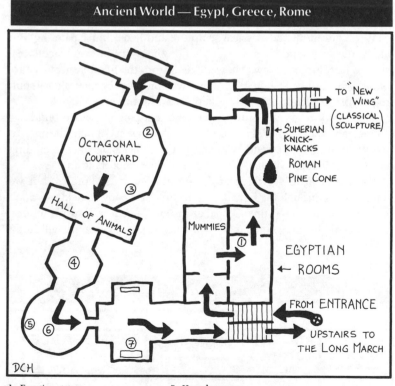

Ancient World — Egypt, Greece, Rome

1. Egyptian statues
2. Apollo Belvedere
3. Laocoön
4. Belvedere Torso

5. Hercules statue
6. Porphyry basin
7. Mrs. Constantine's sarcophagus

Egyptian Statues

Keep these statues in mind as you look at later, more realistic Greek sculpture. Stiff and unnatural, they step out awkwardly with arms straight down at their sides. In Egyptian belief, a stable statue like this could be a place of refuge for the wandering soul of a dead man.

☞ *Continuing on, you'll turn left down a curving corridor. Look outside to the right. This enormous pine cone (or is it an artichoke?) once decorated the top of a huge Roman column.*

Continue through three more rooms, pausing at the glass case on your right in the third room, containing brown clay tablets.

Sumerian knickknacks

Even before Egypt, civilizations flourished in the Middle-east. The Sumerian culture in Mesopotamia (modern Iraq) invented writing around 3000 B.C. You can see the clay tablets with this cuneiform (wedge-shaped) script. Also see the ingenious cylinder seals with which they made impressions in soft clay to seal documents and mark property.

☞ *Pass through the next small room of Assyrian bas reliefs and go left. But first, look to your right down the stairs into the "New Wing".*

New Wing (Braccio Nuovo) of classical statues

A warehouse of Greek and Roman statues. There are 976 statues (I counted them myself) including busts of famous Romans. If you have the energy to walk down the wing — I'll wait for you here — try playing "20th-Century Look-alike". Doesn't the Emperor Vespasian look like L.B.J.?

☞ *Leaving the "New Wing", turn left (catching the view of Rome out the window to your right) into the octagonal courtyard. There are benches in the middle.*

SCULPTURE — GREECE AND ROME (500 B.C.-500 A.D.)

This palace wouldn't be here, this sculpture wouldn't be here, and you'd be spending your vacation in South Dakota at Reptile Gardens if it weren't for a few thousand Greeks in a small town about 450 years before Christ. Athens set the tone for the rest of the West. Democracy, theater, economics, literature and art all got their start there in an extremely short 50-year period. Greek culture was then passed on to Rome, and revived again 1500 years later during the Renaissance. The Renaissance Popes built and decorated these palaces to recreate the glory of the classical world.

Apollo Belevedere

The Greeks loved balance. A well-balanced man was both a thinker and an athlete, a poet and a warrior. In their art they also wanted balance, and the "Apollo Belevedere" is possibly the best example in the world. Apollo, the god of the sun and also music, is hunting. He has spotted his prey and is about to go after it with his (missing) bow and arrows.

Apollo Belvedere — The epitome of classical Greek balance, grace and idealized beauty, this sun god blends motion and stability.

Compare this with the stiff Egyptian statues we saw. Here, the great Greek sculptor Praxiteles has fully conquered realism. The anatomy is perfect, the pose is natural. Instead of standing at attention, face forward with his arms at his sides, Apollo is on the move, stepping forward slightly with his weight resting on one leg.

Though this is an action shot, the overall mood is of balance and serenity. Apollo eyes his target, but hasn't attacked yet. He's moving, but not out of control. He's also a balance between a real person and an ideal god. And the smoothness of his muscles is balanced by the rough folds of his cloak.

During the Renaissance, when this Roman copy of the original Greek work was discovered, it was considered the most perfect work of art in the world. The handsome face, eternal youth and the body that seems to float a half-inch off the pedestal made it an object of wonder and almost worship. Apollo's grace was something superhuman, divine and godlike, even for devout Christians.

Laocoön

Apollo was famous, but the most famous Greek statue in ancient Rome was the "Laocoön" (pron: lay-OKK-o-wahn). The ancient Romans considered it "superior to all other sculpture or painting". It was famous in the Renaissance, too...though no one had seen it, only read about it from ancient accounts. Then, in 1506, it was unexpectedly unearthed in Rome. The discovery caused a sensation. They cleaned it off and paraded it through the streets before an awestruck populace. No one had ever seen anything like it, having been raised on a white bread diet of pretty, serene and balanced Apollos. The "Laocoön" was an eye-opener. One of those who saw it was a young Michelangelo, and it was a revelation to him. The Renaissance was about to take another turn.

Laocoön — Unearthed in Rome in 1506, this sculpture caused a sensation and changed Renaissance artists' ideas about classical beauty. Michelangelo was affected by the powerful, muscular, twisted figures and dramatic movement.

Laocoön was a pagan high priest of Troy, the ancient city attacked by the Greeks. When the Greeks brought the Trojan Horse to the gates as a ploy to get inside the city walls, Laocoon tried to warn his people not to bring it inside. But the gods wanted the Greeks to win so they sent huge snakes to crush him and his two sons to death. We see them at the height of their terror, when they realize that, no matter how hard they struggle, they're doomed.

The Laocoön is Hellenistic, done four centuries after the Golden Age, after the scales of "balance" had been tipped. Where Apollo is a balance between stillness and motion, this is motion run wild. Where Apollo is serene, this is emotional. Where Apollo is idealized grace, this is powerful and gritty realism. The figures (carved from a single block of marble!) are monumental in size, not light and graceful. The poses are as twisted as possible, accentuating every rippling muscle. The line of motion starts from Laocoön's left leg, runs up his body and out his right arm (which some historians think has been badly restored and was originally extended straight out even more dramatically).

The motion and emotion of this statue were unsurpassed in the ancient world and in the Early Renaissance. Two years after seeing it, though, Michelangelo began work on the Sistine Chapel, and the High Renaissance kicked into gear.

☞ *Leave the courtyard. Pass through the Hall of Animals, a jungle of beasts real and not so real, to the "Torso" in the middle of the next large hall.*

Belvedere Torso

For most of us, our entire experience with statues consists of making snowmen. But, standing face to face with this hunk of shaped rock makes us appreciate the sheer physical labor involved in chipping a figure out of solid rock. It takes great strength but, at the same time, great delicacy.

Belvedere torso — Michelangelo loved this old rock and actually thought it was beautiful. Its twisted musculature and brute bulk show up in his later work.

This is all that remains of an ancient statue of Hercules seated on a lion skin. Michelangelo loved this old rock. He'd caress it lovingly and tell people, "I am the pupil of the Torso." To him, it contained all the beauty of classical sculpture. But it's not beautiful. It's ugly. Compared with the pure grace of the Apollo, it's downright hideous.

But Michelangelo, an ugly man himself, was looking for a new kind of beauty — not the beauty of idealized gods, but the innate beauty inside every person, even so-called ugly ones. With its knotty lumps of muscle the Torso has a brute power and a distinct personality despite — or because of — its rough edges. Remember this Torso because we'll see it again later on.

☞   *Enter the next "domed" room.*

Round Room

This room, modeled on the Parthenon interior, gives some idea of how the Romans took Greek ideas and made them bigger. Like the big bronze statue of Hercules with his club found near the Theatre of Pompey. Or the enormous Roman hot-tub/bird-bath/vase made of porphyry.

☞   *Enter the next room.*

Sarcophagi

These two large coffins made of — you guessed it — porphyry marble (purple was a rare, royal, expensive and prestigious color in pre-Crayola days), held the bodies of Roman Emperor Constantine's mother and daughter. They were Christians and, therefore, criminals until Constantine made Christianity legal (313 A.D.).

☞   *See how we've come full circle in this building — the Egyptian Rooms are ahead on your left. We now start the Long March toward the Sistine*

Chapel and Raphael Rooms.
Go up the stairs one flight and prepare to enter the long, long hall lined with statues.

THE LONG MARCH — SCULPTURE, TAPESTRIES, MAPS AND VIEWS

Remember, this building was originally a series of palaces for the popes. They loved beautiful things and, as heirs of Imperial Rome, they felt they deserved such luxury. This quarter-mile walk gives you a sense of the scale that Renaissance popes built on. The palaces and art represent both the peak and the decline of the Catholic Church in Europe. It was extravagant spending like this that inspired Martin Luther to rebel, starting the Protestant Reformation.

Gallery of the Candelabra — Classical Sculpture
This statue gallery is named for the large Roman candlesticks that separate the "rooms". In the second "room", stop at the statue of "Diana the Huntress" on the left. Here, the virgin goddess goes out hunting. Roman hunters would pray to statues like this in order to get divine help in their hunt for food.

Farmers might pray to another version of the same moon goddess — "Artemis", on the opposite wall. This billion-boobed beauty stood for fertility.

☞ *Move into the next "room".*

The Long March — Sculpture, Tapestries, Maps and Views

1. Diana the Huntress
2. Artemis
3. Bacchus
4. 3-D illusion on ceiling
5. Supper at Emmaus tapestry
6. Good view of gardens and dome

Fig Leaves

Why do the statues have fig leaves? Like the one on the left with a baby Bacchus on his shoulder? In fact, all these statues looked much different, originally, than they do now. First off, they were painted, usually in gaudy colors. (Even the "Apollo Belvedere" whose cool grey tones we now admire as "classic Greek austerity" probably had a hot pink cloak or some such.) Also, many of them had glass eyes like the little Bacchus here.

Fig leaf — After the brief *glasnost* of the Renaissance, the Catholic Church clamped down on free thinking and pagan ideals. They plastered fig leaves over all the classical crotches in their collection.

And the fig leaves? Those came from 1550-1800 when the Church decided that certain parts of the human anatomy were obscene. (Why they didn't pick the feet, which are universally ugly, I'll never know). Or perhaps the Church leaders associated these full-frontal statues with the outbreak of Renaissance humanism that reduced their power in Europe. Whatever, they reacted by covering classical crotches with plaster fig leaves, the same leaves Adam and Eve had used when the concept of "privates" was invented.

Note: The leaves could be removed at any time if the museum officials were so motivated. There are suggestion boxes around the museum. Whenever I see a fig leaf I get the urge to picket. We could start an organ-ized campaign....

☞ *Cover your eyes in case they forgot a fig leaf or two and continue to the Tapestries.*

Tapestries

On the left are tapestries designed by Raphael showing the life of Christ. They were made in workshops in Brussels, done in 5 by 5 foot sections sewn together.

Check out the beautiful sculpted reliefs on the ceiling, especially the panel near the end of the first Tapestry room showing a centurion ordering Eskimo Pies from a vendor. Admire the workmanship of this relief, then realize that it's not a relief at all — it's painted on a flat surface!

Illusions like this were proof that painters had mastered realism. In the tapestry "The Supper at Emmaus" at the end of the second Tapestry room, watch how the head of the table follows you as you walk past.

Map Gallery

This gallery gives your best view of the Vatican gardens. Look out the third or fourth window on your right. The Vatican is a separate state formed in 1929. It has its own radio station, as you see from the tower on the hill. What you see here is just about all there is — these gardens, the palaces you're in and St. Peter's. If you lean out and look left you'll see the dome of St. Peter's the way Michelangelo would like you to see it — without the bulky baroque facade.

This gallery's ceiling is a good example of papal splendor. The maps are decorations from the 16th century. You can plan the next leg of your trip with the two maps of Italy at the far end of the hall — "New Italy" and "Old Italy" — both with a smoking Mt. Vesuvius near Napoli/Neapolis/Naples. There's a nice map of Venice on the right as you exit.

☞ *Take a breather in the next small tapestry hall before turning left into the crowded Raphael Rooms.*

RENAISSANCE ART
RAPHAEL ROOMS — PAPAL WALLPAPER

We've seen art from the ancient world; now we'll see its "rebirth" in the Renaissance. We're about to enter the main palaces built by the great Renaissance popes. This is where they lived, worked and worshipped. They wanted these rooms to reflect the grandeur of their position. They hired the best artists — mostly from Florence — to paint the walls and ceilings. The decorations combine classical and Christian values.

We'll see a suite of several rooms painted by Raphael and then the Sistine Chapel by Michelangelo.

☞ *Turn left, and pass through two rooms. The first has a huge non-Raphael painting on the wall. The second celebrates the doctrine of the Immaculate Conception. Next you'll pass along an outside ramp overlooking a courtyard (is that the Pope's car?), ending up in the first of the Raphael Rooms — the Constantine Room.*

Constantine Room

Only one of these scenes from the life of Constantine was personally designed by Raphael (pron: roff-eye-ELL), but the room is fascinating anyway.

The frescoes celebrate the passing of the baton from one culture to the next. Remember, Rome was a pagan empire persecuting a small but fanatic cult from the East, Christianity.

Then, on the night of October 27, 312 A.D. (left wall), as Constantine was preparing his troops for a coup d'etat, he saw something strange. A cross appeared in the sky with the words, "You will conquer in this sign".

Next day (front wall), his troops raged into battle with the Christian symbol marked on their shields. There's Constantine in the center, slashing through the enemy, with God's warrior angels riding shotgun overhead.

The victorious Constantine was supposedly baptized a Christian (right wall). As emperor, he legalized Christianity and worked hand in hand with the pope (window wall). Rome soon became a Christian empire that would dominate Europe. Even after the government fell, Rome's glory lived on through the Dark Ages in the pomp, pageantry and learning of the Catholic Church.

Look at the ceiling painting. A classical statue falls and crumbles before the overpowering radiating force of the Cross. Woh! Christianity triumphs over pagan Rome. (This was painted, I believe, by Raphael's colleague, Salvadoro Dalio.)

☞   *In the next room, there's a small chapel in the far corner. Check out*

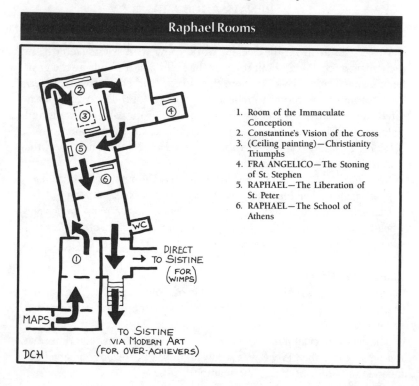

Raphael Rooms

1. Room of the Immaculate Conception
2. Constantine's Vision of the Cross
3. (Ceiling painting)—Christianity Triumphs
4. FRA ANGELICO—The Stoning of St. Stephen
5. RAPHAEL—The Liberation of St. Peter
6. RAPHAEL—The School of Athens

WC

DIRECT TO SISTINE (FOR WIMPS)

MAPS

TO SISTINE VIA MODERN ART (FOR OVER-ACHIEVERS)

DCH

the fresco there on the left wall, upper part.

The Stoning of St. Stephen

Raphael wasn't the only famous painter to work here. The Florentine monk, Fra Angelico, decorated part of this tiny room. In this scene the early Christian martyr is stoned during a heavenly vision (pun intended, if not funny). The apostle Paul, who started out as a harsh critic of Christianity, stands to the side holding the cloaks of the executioners.

☞ *Return to the main room and enjoy one of the rarest of rare artifacts, the bench in the corner.*

RAPHAEL

Raphael was only 25 when Pope Julius II invited him to paint the walls of his private apartments. Julius was so impressed by Raphael's talent that he had the work of earlier masters scraped off and gave Raphael free rein to paint what he wanted.

Raphael lived a charmed life. He painted masterpieces effortlessly. He was handsome and sophisticated, and soon became Julius' favorite. In a different decade, he might have been thrown out of the Church as a great sinner, but his love affairs and devil-may-care personality seemed to epitomize the optimistic pagan spirit of the Renaissance. His works are graceful, but never lightweight or frilly — they're strong, balanced and harmonious in the best Renaissance tradition. When he died young in 1520, the High Renaissance died with him.

☞ *Continue through the next small hallway. In the following room look above the windows in front of you.*

The Liberation of St. Peter

Peter, Jesus' right-hand man, was thrown into prison in Jerusalem for his beliefs. In the middle of the night, an angel appeared and rescued him from the sleeping guards (Acts 12). The chains fell away miraculously (and were later brought to the St. Peter in Chains church in Rome) and the angel led him to safety (right) while the guards took hell from their captain (left). This little "play" is neatly divided into three separate acts that make a balanced composition.

Raphael makes the miraculous event even more dramatic with the use of three kinds of light illuminating the dark cell — half-moonlight, the captain's torch, and the radiant angel. Raphael's mastery of realism, rich colors and sense of drama made him understandably famous.

☞ *Enter the next room.*

The School of Athens

In both style and subject matter, this fresco sums up the spirit of the Renaissance.

The Renaissance was not only the rebirth of classical art, it was a rebirth of learning, of discovery, of the optimistic spirit that man is a rational creature. Raphael pays respect to the great thinkers and scientists of ancient Greece gathered together at one time in a mythical school setting.

RAPHAEL — School of Athens. The ultimate example of the Renaissance in both subject matter and style. Great Greek thinkers are like haloed saints in the holy pursuit of Knowledge.

In the center are Plato and Aristotle, the two greatest. Plato points up, indicating his philosophy that mathematics and pure ideas are the source of truth (right side of the brain thinking?) while Aristotle points down, showing his preference for scientific study of the material world (left side). There's Socrates, midway to the left, ticking off arguments on his fingers. And in the foreground at right, Euclid bends over a slate to demonstrate a geometrical formula.

But this isn't just a celebration of classical learning, but a chance to show that Renaissance thinkers were as good as the ancients. The bearded figure of Plato is none other than Leonardo da Vinci, whom Raphael worshipped. That's Raphael himself among the greats, next to last on the far right, with the black beret, looking out at us. And the "school" building is actually a Renaissance setting taken from early designs for St. Peter's.

The balanced style is also the epitome of Renaissance. Raphael has created a spacious three-dimensional setting of Renaissance architecture and peopled it with figures balanced evenly, left and right. Look at the tops of the columns that support the arches. If you laid a ruler over them and extended the line that recedes into the arch, it would run right to dead center of the picture. Similarly, the floor tiles in the foreground all point to dead center. All the "lines of sight" draw our attention to the center of the picture, Plato and Aristotle, and to the small arch over their heads — a "halo" over these two secular saints in the divine pursuit of knowledge.

Raphael painted this room while Michelangelo was at work down the hall in the Sistine Chapel. Raphael popped in on the sly to see the master at work. He was astonished. Raphael's early work had always been graceful, pretty and delicate (like the "Apollo Belvedere"). When he saw Michelangelo's powerful figures and dramatic scenes, he began to beef up his work to a more heroic level. As he was finishing up "The School of Athens", perhaps his greatest work, he tipped his brush to the master by painting Michelangelo into the scene — the brooding, melancholy figure in front leaning on a block of marble.

☞ *Get ready. It's decision time. From here there are two ways to get to the Sistine Chapel. One is definitely the better way, so pay attention.*

Passing through the next room, you'll soon see two arrows — one pointing left to the Sistine and one pointing right to the Sistine. GO RIGHT. Meet you on a bench at the bottom of the stairs.

Whew! Glad you made it. The advantage of this route (which really isn't much longer) is that you can sit down in peace and quiet to read ahead before entering the hectic Sistine Chapel. Also, you get to stroll through the impressive Modern Religious Art collection on the way to the Sistine, a few minutes' walk away.

Sit, relax and read the introduction to the Sistine Chapel here.

THE SISTINE CHAPEL

The Sistine Chapel contains: 1) Michelangelo's Ceiling; and 2) Michelangelo's huge "Last Judgment", painted 25 years later on the wall over the altar. For now, let's concentrate on the Ceiling.

When Julius II asked him to decorate the popes' personal chapel, Michelangelo said no way. Michelangelo insisted he was a sculptor, not a painter. The Sistine ceiling was a vast undertaking and he didn't want to do a half-vast job. But the Pope pleaded, bribed and threatened until Michelangelo finally consented on the condition he be able to do it all his own way.

Julius had asked for only 12 Apostles along the sides of the ceiling, but Michelangelo had a grander vision. The next four years (1508-1512) were spent lying on his back on scaffolding six stories up covering the entire ceiling with frescoes of scenes from the Old Testament. With frescoes, painting on wet plaster, if you don't get it right the first time, you have to scrape the whole thing off, replaster it and start over. In sheer physical terms, it's an astonishing achievement: 600 square yards with every inch done by his own hand. (Raphael only designed most of his Rooms, letting assistants do the grunt work.) The physical effort, the paint dripping in his eyes, the creative drain and the mental stress from a pushy Pope combined to almost kill him.

But when it was finished and revealed to the public, it simply blew 'em away. Like the "Laocoön" statue discovered six years earlier, it was unlike anything seen before. It both caps the Renaissance and turns it in a new direction. In perfect Renaissance spirit, it mixes Old Testament prophets with classical and classical-looking figures. But the style is more dramatic, shocking and emotional than the balanced Renaissance works before it. This is a very personal work — the Gospel according to Michelangelo — but its themes and subject matter are universal. Almost without exception, art critics concede that the Sistine Ceiling is the single greatest work of art by any one human being.

The Sistine Ceiling — Understanding What You're Standing Under

The Ceiling shows the history of the world before the birth of Jesus. We see God creating the world, creating man and woman, destroying the earth by flood, etc. Along the sides we see the Old Testament prophets and pagan Greek prophetesses that foretold the coming of Christ. Dividing these scenes and figures is a painted architectural framework (a 3-D illusion) decorated with nude figures with symbolic meaning.

The key is to see these three simple divisions underneath the tangle of bodies:

- The central spine of rectangular panels with nine scenes from Genesis.
- The two rows of panels on either side with prophets.
- The triangles in between the prophets showing the ancestors of Christ.

☞ *Signs will direct you through the Modern Art section to the Sistine. Enter the Chapel and grab a seat at the screen (if possible) two-thirds of the way back.*

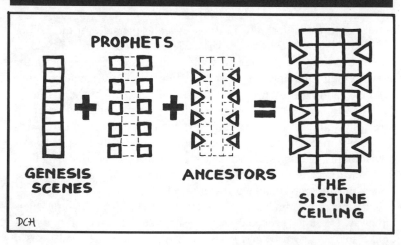

The Sistine Ceiling-Understanding What You're Standing Under

PROPHETS

GENESIS SCENES

ANCESTORS

THE SISTINE CEILING

DCH

Face the altar and get oriented. There's the "Last Judgment" on the big wall behind the altar. Now look up to the ceiling and find:
1) The central spine of Genesis scenes.
2) The prophets along the sides of this spine.
3) The ancestors in the triangles.
Got it? The "Creation of Adam" is near the very center of the ceiling.

The Creation of Adam

God and Man are equal in this Renaissance version of creation. Adam, newly formed in the image of God, lounges dreamily in perfect naked innocence. God, with his entourage, swoops in, in a swirl of activity. Their reaching hands are the center of this work. Adam's is limp and passive, God's is strong and forceful, His finger twitching upward with energy. Here is the very moment of creation, as God passes the spark of life to man, the crowning work of His creation.

This is the spirit of the Renaissance. God is not a terrifying giant reaching down to puny and helpless man from way on high. Here they are on an equal plane, co-creators, divided only by the diagonal patch of sky. God's billowing robe and the patch of green upon which Adam is lying balance each other. They are like two pieces of a jigsaw puzzle, or two long-separated continents, or like the yin and yang symbols finally coming together, uniting, complementing each other, creating

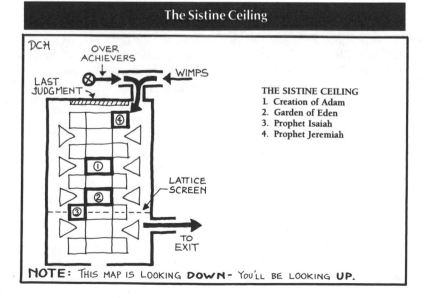

The Sistine Ceiling

THE SISTINE CEILING
1. Creation of Adam
2. Garden of Eden
3. Prophet Isaiah
4. Prophet Jeremiah

NOTE: THIS MAP IS LOOKING **DOWN** - YOU'LL BE LOOKING **UP**.

wholeness. God and man work together as equals in the divine process of creation.

MICHELANGELO — The Creation of Adam. Renaissance man and God are equals as a fatherly God reaches out to give the spark of life to His greatest creation.

☞ *Two panels away towards the rear of the chapel, you'll find...*

The Garden of Eden: Temptation and Expulsion

In one panel we see both scenes from the Garden of Eden, highlighting the contrast. On the left is the leafy garden of paradise where Adam and Eve lie around blissfully. But the devil comes along as a serpent with a woman's torso and winds around the forbidden Tree of Knowledge. The temptation to gain new knowledge is too great for these Renaissance people, so they eat the forbidden fruit.

At right, the angel drives them from Paradise into the barren plains. They're grieving, but they're far from helpless. Adam's body is thick and sturdy, and we know they'll survive in the cruel world. Adam's gesture to the angel is strong, like he's saying, "All right, already! We're going!"

Take some time with these Genesis scenes, the highlight of the ceiling. They run in sequence, starting at the front showing: 1) God dividing light from darkness; 2) Creation of the sun, moon and vegetation; 3) God separating land and water; 4) Creation of Adam; 5) Creation of Eve; 6) Garden of Eden; 7) Noah's Sacrifice; 8) The Flood; 9) The Drunkenness of Noah.

Prophets

By 1510 Michelangelo had finished the first half of the ceiling, the end farthest from the "Last Judgment" wall. When they took the scaffolding down and Michelangelo could finally see what he'd been working on for two years, he wasn't satisfied. As monumental and powerful as his figures are, from the floor they didn't look dramatic enough for Michelangelo. For the other half he pulled out all the stops.

Compare an early prophet with a later one. "Isaiah" (find him on the map) is shown in a pose like a Roman senator. He is a stately, sturdy, balanced, composed Renaissance Man. Now look at "Jeremiah" in the corner by the Last Judgment. This prophet, who witnessed the destruction of Israel, is a dark, brooding figure. He slumps his chin in his hand and ponders the fate of his people. The difference between the dignified Isaiah and the dramatic Jeremiah is like the difference between the "Apollo Belvedere" and the "Laocoön". This sort of emotional power was a new element in Renaissance painting.

The Cleaning Project

The ceiling and the "Last Judgment" have been cleaned — a 12-year project that removed centuries of dirt and soot from candles, oil lamps and the annual Papal Barbecue (just kidding), plus animal glues used to preserve the works. Read the explanation at the base of the cleaning shaft.

The project was controversial. The bright, bright colors that emerged upset those who grew up with the Sistine's darker tones. Critics charge that the cleaners were also removing shading deliberately put on by Michelangelo. The colors are a bit shocking, forcing many art experts to re-evaluate Michelangelo's style.

☞ *The "Last Judgment" is best viewed from the screen where, hopefully, you've found a spot on the bench.*

The Last Judgment

When Michelangelo was asked to paint the altar wall 22 years later, the mood of Europe — and of Michelangelo — was completely different. The Protestant Reformation had forced the Catholic Church to clamp down on free thought, and the Renaissance spirit of optimism was fading. Michelangelo, himself, had begun to question the innate goodness of mankind.

It's Judgment Day, and Christ — the powerful figure in the center, raising his arm to strike down the wicked — has come to find out who's naughty and nice. Beneath him, a band of angels blows its trumpets Dizzy Gillespie-style to wake the dead. The dead at lower left leave their

MICHELANGELO — The Last Judgment (detail). Thirty years after painting the Sistine ceiling, Michelangelo portrayed Christ as a powerful, wrathful and terrifying deity poised to strike down the wicked. Renaissance optimism had ended.

graves and prepare to be judged. The righteous, on Christ's right hand (the left side of the picture), ascend to the glories of Heaven. The wicked on the other side are hurled down to Hell where demons wait to torture them.

One of the wicked (to the right of the trumpeting angels) has an utterly lost expression, like saying "How could I have been so stupid!" Two demons grab him around the ankles to pull him down to the bowels of Hell where he's been condemned to an eternity of constipation.

The Last Judgment

1. Christ with Mary at His side
2. Trumpeting Angels
3. The dead come out of their graves. The righteous ascend.
4. One of the damned
5. Charon in his boat
6. The demon/critic of nudity
7. St. Bartholomew with flayed skin containing Michelangelo's self-portrait

Charon, from the underworld of Greek mythology, waits below to ferry the souls of the damned to their hellish destination.

But it's a terrifying Christ, Himself, who dominates this scene. As He raises His arm to smite the wicked, He sends a ripple of fear through everyone, and they recoil. Even the saints that surround Him — even Mary beneath His arm — shrink back in terror. His expression is completely closed, and He turns his head, refusing to even listen to the whining alibis of the damned. Look at Christ's bicep! If this muscular figure looks familiar to you, it's because you've seen it before — "the Belvedere Torso".

When the Last Judgment was unveiled to the public in 1544, again, it caused a sensation and changed the course of art. The complex composition with more than 300 figures swirling around the figure of Christ was far beyond traditional Renaissance balance. The twisted figures shown from every angle imaginable challenged other painters to try and top this master of creating the illusion of 3-D. And the sheer terror and drama of the scene was a far and mournful cry from the placid optimism of, say, Raphael's "School of Athens". Michelangelo had Baroque-en all the rules of the Renaissance, signaling a new era of art.

Originally, everyone in the "Last Judgment" — Christ, the saints, even Mary — was stark naked. In the Renaissance, the naked human body was seen as an expression of God's glorious creative powers. But in darker times, this didn't sit well with the Catholic Church. To them, such pagan ideas were "germs" threatening the body of the Church. Rather than tolerating these "germs" (and building up a healthy immunity), they chose to sterilize society, eradicating Renaissance ideas.

Even as Michelangelo painted it, he got murmurs of discontent from the Church authorities. He rebelled by painting his chief critic into the scene — in Hell. He's the demon in the bottom right corner with a serpent wrapped around his body.

After Michelangelo's death, there was no defense. The prudish Church authorities enforced the new Vatican penal code, hiring an artist to paint the wisps of decency over their privates. In Mary's case, she got a whole new wardrobe. (P.S. The artist who did it — known to history as "The Tailor" — got in one lick for his beloved Michelangelo. Out of all 300 figures who were covered up, the only one that was left buck naked was. . .the critic in the corner.)

The Last Judgment marks the end of Renaissance optimism. Think back on "The Creation of Adam", with its innocence and exaltation of man. There he was the equal of a fatherly God. Here, man cowers in fear and unworthiness before a terrifying, wrathful deity. Michelangelo himself must have questioned his own innate goodness. Look at St.

MICHELANGELO — The Last Judgment
(detail). A disillusioned and self-doubting
Michelangelo paints his own face in the
flayed, wretched skin in St. Bartholomew's
hand.

Bartholomew, the bald bearded guy at Christ's left foot (our right). In the flayed skin he's holding is a barely recognizable face — the twisted self-portrait of a self-questioning Michelangelo.

☞ *Exiting the Sistine you'll soon find yourself facing the Long March Back to the museum's entrance. You're one floor down from the long corridor you walked to get here.*

THE LONG MARCH BACK

Along this corridor you'll see some of the wealth amassed by the popes, mostly gifts from royalty. There are lavishly decorated hammers and trowels. These are the ceremonial tools the pope uses to open and close St. Peter's Holy Door during Holy Years. Find your hometown on the map of the world from 1529 (in a glass case near an astrological globe) — look in the land called "Terra Incognita". The elaborately decorated Library that branches off to the right contains rare manuscripts. Finally, near the end of the hall you'll see a couple of small benches — thanks a lot, 1-1/4 miles from the ticket-taker.

☞ *Exiting the corridor, turn left. At the courtyard with a great view of the dome, turn left again towards the cafeteria (going right takes you to the exit). The Pinacoteca is to the right of the cafeteria entrance.*

PINACOTECA (PAINTING GALLERY)

How would you like to be Lou Gehrig — always batting behind Babe Ruth? That's the Pinacoteca's lot in life. Who needs more art after being wowed and exhausted by the Sistine & Co.? But after the Vatican's artistic feast, this little U-shaped collection of paintings is a 15-minute after-dinner mint.

See this gallery of paintings as you'd view a time-lapse blossoming of a flower, walking through the evolution of painting from medieval to baroque with just four stops.

☞ *Enter and stroll up to Room IV.*

Melozzo Da Forli — *Musician Angels*

Salvaged from a condemned church, this playful series of frescoes shows the delicate grace and nobility of Italy during the time known fondly as the *quattrocento* (1400s). Notice the detail and the classical purity given these religious figures.

☞ *Walk on to the end room (Room VIII) where they've turned on the dark to let Raphael's* Transfiguration *shine. Take a seat, rest, read and ponder.*

Raphael   *The Transfiguration*

Raphael's "Transfiguration" shows Christ on a mountain top visited in a vision by the prophets Moses and Elijah. Peter, James and John cower in awe under Jesus, "transfigured before them, his face shining as the sun, his raiment white as light." (As described by the Evangelist Matthew — taking notes in the painting's lower left.)

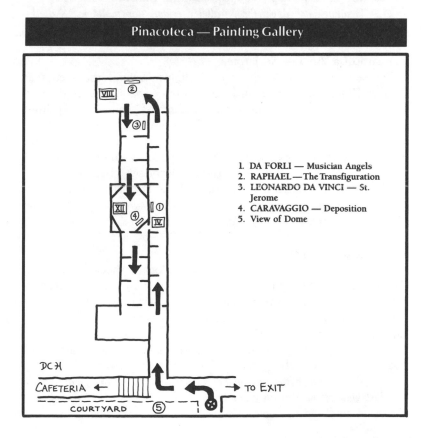

Pinacoteca — Painting Gallery

1. DA FORLI — Musician Angels
2. RAPHAEL — The Transfiguration
3. LEONARDO DA VINCI — St. Jerome
4. CARAVAGGIO — Deposition
5. View of Dome

The nine remaining Apostles try in vain to heal a boy possessed by demons. Jesus is gone, but "Lady Faith" in the center exhorts them to carry on.

RAPHAEL — The Transfiguration (detail). As he was dying, Raphael set his sights on heaven and painted possibly his most beautiful work — the heavenly face of Jesus.

Raphael died young, in 1520, leaving this final work to be finished by his pupils. The last thing Raphael painted was the beatific face of the ecstatic Jesus, perhaps the most beautiful Christ in existence.

☞ *Heading back down the parallel corridor, stop in Room IX at the brown unfinished work by Leonardo.*

Leonardo Da Vinci — *St. Jerome*

This unfinished work gives us a glimpse behind the scenes at Leonardo's technique. Even in the brown undercoating we see the psychological power of Leonardo's genius. The intense penitence and painful ecstasy of the saint comes through loud and clear in the anguished body on the rocks and in Jerome's ecstatic eyes, which see divine forgiveness. Leonardo wrote that a good painter must paint two things: "man and the movements of his spirit." (The patchwork you see is because Jerome's head was cut out and used as a seat of a stool in a shoemaker's shop.)

☞ *Roll on through the sappy sweetness of the Mannerist rooms into the shocking ultra-realistic world of Caravaggio, Room XII.*

Caravaggio — *Deposition*

Caravaggio was the first painter to intentionally shock his viewers. By exaggerating the light/dark contrasts, shining a brutal third-degree-interrogator-type light on his subjects, and using low-life models in sacred scenes, he takes a huge leap away from the Raphael-pretty past and into the "expressive realism" of the modern world.

A tangle of grief looms out of the darkness as Christ's heavy, dead body nearly pulls the whole group with him from the cross into the tomb.

☞ *Walk through the rest of the gallery's canvas history of art, enjoy one last view of the Vatican grounds and Michelangelo's dome, then follow the grand spiral staircase down. Go in peace.*

The Prado, Madrid

The Prado is the greatest painting museum in the world. If you like art and you plan to be in Europe, it makes a trip to Madrid a must. In its glory days, the Spanish Empire was Europe's greatest, filling its coffers with gold from the New World and art from the Old. While there are some 3000 paintings in the collection, we'll be selective, focusing on just the top 1500 or so.

Museo del Prado (pron: PRAH-doh)

Hours: Tues.-Sat. 9:00-19:00; Sun. and holidays 9:00-14:00; closed Mon.

Cost: 400 ptas; students free; tickets include Guernica.

Tour length: Three hours, plus 30 minutes from Guernica.

Getting there: 15-minute walk from Puerta del Sol; bus #9, 10, 19, 27, 34, 45; subway to "Banco de España" or "Atocha" and 10-minute walk; cheap taxis (say "moo-SAY-oh del PRAH-doh").

Information: Good small pamphlets on Flemish, Goya and Velázquez on racks in appropriate rooms.

Museum tel. 420-2836.

Misc.: Good, reasonable cafeteria in basement at south end.

The royal gardens are just south, and the huge, pleasant Retiro park is three blocks east.

Most crowded Tues. and Sun. and all mornings. Least crowded in late afternoons.

Starring: Bosch, Goya, Titian, Velázquez, Dürer, El Greco.

NEW WORLD GOLD — OLD WORLD ART

Heaven and earth have always existed side by side in Spain — religion and war, Grand Inquisitors and cruel conquistadors, spirituality and sensuality, holiness and horniness. The Prado has a surprisingly worldly collection of paintings for a country in which the medieval Inquisition lasted up until modern times. But it's just this mix of worldly beauty and heavenly mysticism that is so typically Spanish.

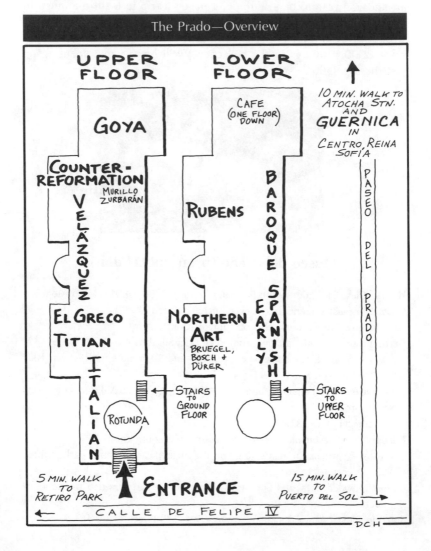

The Prado—Overview

Gold from newly-discovered America bought the sparkling treasures of the Prado. Spain, the most powerful nation in Europe in the 1500s was growing rich on her New World possessions just about the time of the world's greatest cultural heyday, the Renaissance.

The collection's strengths reflect the tastes of Spain's cultured kings from 1500-1800: (1) Italian Renaissance art (especially the lush and sensual Venetian art which was the rage of Europe); (2) Northern art (from the Spanish-controlled Netherlands) with its detailed celebration of the natural world; and (3) their own Spanish court painters. This tour will concentrate on these three areas, with a special look at some individual artists, who are especially well-represented here — Velazquez, Goya, Titian, Rubens, El Greco and Bosch.

☞ *Enter the Prado at the north end, upper floor (the "Puerta de Goya"). Orient yourself from the rotunda.*

From the rotunda, look through the huge doorway marked "Escuela Española", down the long gallery. The Prado runs north-south. Rooms branch off to the left (east) of this long hall. The layout is similar on the floor below.

We'll start with Italian Renaissance art on this floor. Then downstairs to Northern Renaissance art. Then back upstairs for Spanish art.

☞ *Enter Room 4, the door to left marked "Escuela Italiana" (Italian School) and belly up to the Annunciation altarpiece on your right.*

ITALIAN RENAISSANCE (1400-1600)

Modern Western Civilization as we know it (or wish we knew it), began in the prosperous Renaissance cities of Italy during the years 1400-1600. Florence, Rome and Venice led the way out of the Gothic Middle Ages, building on the forgotten knowledge of ancient Rome and Greece. So it's fitting that we start our tour here.

Unlike the heaven-centered medieval artists, Renaissance artists gloried in the natural world and the human body. They painted things as realistically as possible. For the Italians, "realistic" meant "three-dimensional", and they set out to learn how to capture the 3-D world on a 2-D canvas.

Fra Angelico — *The Annunciation (La Anunciación)*
Fra Angelico was a mix of the passing Middle Ages and the coming Renaissance. He was a monk of great piety (his nickname means "Angelic Brother") who combined medieval religious sentiment with new Renaissance techniques. This is more like two separate paintings in one: 1) on the left, the medieval-style story of Adam and Eve in the Garden of Eden; and 2) on the right (under the porch), the Renaissance-style scene of the angel telling Mary she'll give birth to the Messiah.

The Fall (on the left side) expresses a characteristic medieval idea — man is sinfully weak and undeserving of the pleasures of Paradise. Adam and Eve, scrawny and two-dimensional, seem to float in an unrealistic space above the foliage. Eve folds her hands nervously, scrunching down, waiting for her spanking from an angry God. The style is also medieval, with detailed flowers, a labor of love by a caring monk who was also a miniaturist. Another medieval element is the series of story-telling scenes below illustrating events in the life of Mary for the illiterate faithful.

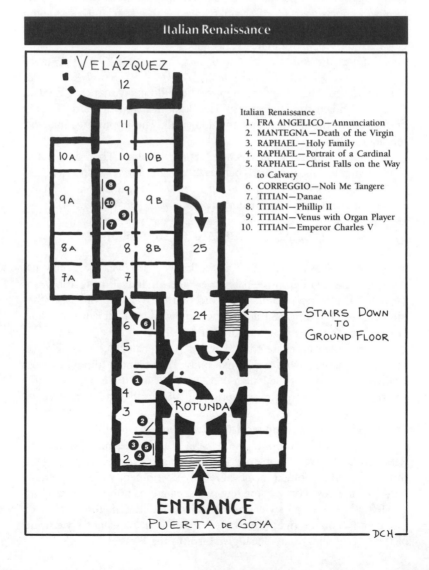

Italian Renaissance

Italian Renaissance
1. FRA ANGELICO—Annunciation
2. MANTEGNA—Death of the Virgin
3. RAPHAEL—Holy Family
4. RAPHAEL—Portrait of a Cardinal
5. RAPHAEL—Christ Falls on the Way to Calvary
6. CORREGGIO—Noli Me Tangere
7. TITIAN—Danae
8. TITIAN—Phillip II
9. TITIAN—Venus with Organ Player
10. TITIAN—Emperor Charles V

FRA ANGELICO — The Annunciation.
Delicate, serene and spiritual. The
"Angelic Brother" combines medieval
piety with Renaissance technique.

The Annunciation scene on the right is early Renaissance. The porch makes a 3-D setting. Then Fra Angelico fills it with two massive, almost sculptural bodies. The message of the scene is upbeat and humanistic, as the Angel tells Mary she'll give birth to a Savior who'll redeem sinful man from the Fall. (Is it good news to Mary? She doesn't look too thrilled.)

Still, the painting is flat by modern standards, and the study in depth perspective is crude. Aren't the receding bars of the porch's ceiling a bit off? And Mary's hands just aren't right — like when you have to wash the dishes with two left-hand rubber gloves. But it's a lot better (and more 3-D) than its medieval neighbors here.

Above all, notice the serene atmosphere of the painting. There are no harsh shadows or strong light sources. Everything is bathed in a pristine, glowing, holy light. The only movement is the shaft of light shooting down from the hands of God, bringing redemption from the Fall, connecting the two halves of the painting and fusing medieval piety with Renaissance humanism.

☞ *Face the windows, then turn left around the partition into the next small alcove (Room 3).*

Mantegna — *Death of the Virgin (El Tránsito de la Virgen)*

The true pioneer of Renaissance 3-D was Andrea Mantegna (pron: mon-TAYN-ya). He creates a spacious setting, then peoples it with sculptural figures.

The dying mother of Christ is surrounded by statue-like apostles with plates on their heads and pots in their hands. The architectural setting is heroic and spacious. Follow the lines in the floor tiles and side columns. See how they converge toward the window, then seem to continue on to the far horizon in the lines of the bridge? This creates a subconscious feeling of almost infinite spaciousness, bringing a serenity to an otherwise tragic death scene. You can imagine Mary's soul leaving her body and floating easily out the window, disappearing into the infinite distance.

☞ *Turning the corner into Room 2, your eye will go immediately to some large Raphael canvases. Let them overwhelm you, then turn about face and refocus your eyes on the tiny "Holy Family with a Lamb". The sheer difference in size and scope of these works gives you a sense of Raphael's vision.*

Raphael — Holy Family with a Lamb (*Sagrada Familia del Cordero*)

It took artists (like Fra Angelico and Mantegna) centuries to master reality. It took Raphael only 20 years — and then he went beyond it. He could reproduce reality perfectly on a canvas, but also give it harmony, geometry and heroism that made it somehow more real than reality. Combining idealized beauty with down-to-earth realism, he was the ultimate Renaissance painter.

Raphael (pron: roff-eye-ELL) was only 21 when he painted this. He learned Leonardo da Vinci's technique of *sfumato*, spreading a kind of hazy glow around the figures (the technique that gives the "Mona Lisa" her vague, mysterious smile). He also used Leonardo's trademark pyramid composition — the three figures form a pyramid with Joseph's head at the peak.

Raphael — Portrait of a Cardinal (*Cardenal Desconocido*)

Compare the idealized beauty of the "Holy Family" with the stark realism of this portrait. This isn't an idealized version of an ideal man, but a living, breathing — in this case almost sneering — man. Raphael captures not just his face, but his personality — the type of man who could become a cardinal at such a young age in the Renaissance Vatican's priest-eat-priest jungle of holy ambition. He's cold, intelligent, detached and somewhat cynical — a gritty portrayal of a gritty man.

Raphael — Christ Falls on the Way to Calvary (*Caída en el Camino del Calvario*)

Raphael puts it all together — the idealized grace of the "Holy Family" and the realism of the "Cardinal". Look at the detail on the muscular legs of the guy in yellow (at left) and the arms of Simon who has come to help Jesus carry his cross. Then contrast that with the idealized beauty of the mourning women. When this painting was bought in 1661, it was the costliest in existence.

Raphael has added drama to the work by splitting the canvas into two contrasting halves. Below the slanting line made by the crossbar is a scene of swirling passion — the sorrow of Christ and the women, the tangle of crowded bodies. Above it is open space and indifference — the bored soldiers and onlookers and the bleak hill in the background where Jesus is headed to be crucified.

☞ *Backtrack to Fra Angelico's "Annunciation", then continue past it to Room 6.*

Correggio — *Noli Me Tangere (Don't Touch Me)*
Raphael could paint idealized beauty, but this is simply the most beautiful painting in captivity. That's it. Period. If it were any sweeter you could get diabetes just looking at it.

It's Easter morning and Jesus has just come back to life. One of his followers, Mary Magdalene, has run into him in the garden near the tomb. She is amazed and excited and reaches toward him. "Don't touch me!" (*"Noli me Tangere"*) says Jesus (though he spoke neither English nor Latin), and points up to Heaven.

The colors accentuate the emotion of the scene. Blazing like a flame against the cool landscape of blue and green, Mary Magdalene   the ex-prostitute in a fiery yellow dress and yellow hair — is hot to touch the cool Christ with his blue cloak and pale, radiant skin. The composition also accentuates the action. The painting's energy runs in a diagonal line up the rippling Mary, through Christ and his upstretched arm to heaven, where he will soon go.

☞ *Enter Room 7 and continue straight ahead to the large Room 9.*

Titian (Tiziano, c. 1490-1576)
Look around. What do you see? Flesh. Naked bodies in various poses; bright, lush, colorful scenes. Many scenes have "pagan" themes, but even the religious works are racier than anything we saw from the Florentine and Roman Renaissance.

Venice in 1500 was the richest city in Europe, the middleman in the lucrative trade between Europe and the Orient. Wealthy, cosmopolitan and free, Venetians loved the fine things of life — rich silks, beautiful people, jewels, banquets, music, wine, and impressive buildings — and Venetian painters enjoyed painting them in bright colors.

The chief Venetian was Titian (they rhyme). Titian ("Tiziano" in Spain) was possibly the most famous painter of his day — more famous than Raphael, than Leonardo and even than Michelangelo. His reputation reached Spain, and he became the favorite portraitist for two kings who bought many of his works.

Titian — *Danae*
In Greek mythology, Zeus, the king of the gods, was always zooming to earth in the form of some creature or other to fool around with some mortal woman or other. Here, he descends as a shower of gold to consort with the willing Danae. You can almost see the human form of Zeus within the cloud. Danae is rapt, opening her legs to receive him, while her servant tries to catch the heavenly spurt with a towel.

This is one of the world's finest and most famous nudes. Danae's rich luminous flesh on the left of the canvas is set off by the dark servant at right and the threatening sky above. The white sheets beneath her make her glow even more.

TITIAN — Danae. This Renaissance Playmate aroused the interest of Spain's ascetic kings.

But this is more than a classic nude — it's a Renaissance Miss August. How could Spain's ultra-conservative Catholic kings have tolerated such a downright pagan and erotic painting?

Titian — *Phillip II (Felipe II)*

The mystery is heightened when we look at the man who bought this and many other nudes, King Phillip II. Phillip deserved his reputation as a repressed prude — pale, suspicious, lonely, a cold fish, the sort of man who would build the severe and tomb-like Escorial Palace. Freud would have had a field day with such a complex man who could be so sternly religious and yet have such sensual tastes. Here, he is looking as pious and ascetic as a man can while wearing that outfit.

Titian — *Venus with the Organ Player (Venus El Amor y La Música)*

A musician turns around to leer at a naked woman while keeping both hands at work on his organ. This was another painting that aroused Phillip's interest. The message must have appealed to him — the conflict between sacred, artistic pursuits as symbolized by music and worldly, sensual pursuits as embodied in the naked lady.

Titian emphasizes these two opposites with color — "cool" colors on the left, hot crimson and flesh on the right. The center of the painting is where these two color schemes meet, so even though the figures lean and the poplar trees in the background are "off-center", the painting is balanced and harmonious in the Renaissance tradition.

A century after Phillip's reign, his beloved nudes were taken down from the Escorial and Royal Palace and hidden away as unfit to be seen. For over a century these great Titians were banned.

Titian — *Emperor Charles V on Horseback (El Emperador Carlos V en la Batalla de Muhlberg)*

Are you glad to be here? If so, then tip your book to that guy on horseback, the father of the Prado's collection.

In the 1500s, Charles was the most powerful man in the world. He was not merely King Charles of Spain, but Holy Roman Emperor of possessions stretching from Spain to Austria, from Holland to Italy, from South America to Burgundy. He was defender of the Catholic Church against infidel Turks, French kings and, in this picture, rebellious Protestants.

Here, Titian shows him in the classic equestrian pose of a Roman conqueror. His power is accentuated by his control over his rearing horse and the lance with its optimistic tilt.

Once Charles met Titian and saw what he could do, he never wanted anyone else to paint him. And the story goes that, while sitting for a portrait one day, this greatest ruler in the world actually stooped over to pick up a brush Titian dropped.

We've seen painting move from Gothic two-dimensionality to Renaissance realism and balance. The next style — baroque — took Renaissance realism to unrealistic heights. But before we get tangled in the steaming jungle of baroque, let's take a refreshing break in the cooler climes of the Northern countries. Their down-to-earth realism is a delightful contrast to the idealized beauty of the Italian school.

☞ *The Northern art is downstairs. Return to the rotunda and take the staircase to the ground floor. Start down the long gallery, then take your first left, into Room 57B. We'll start in Room 58.*

NORTHERN ART

Master of Flemalle (Robert Campin) — *St. John the Baptist*

The Northern "Renaissance" was less a rebirth of classical ideas than an improvement on medieval painting. Remember the detailed flowers in Fra Angelico's "Annunciation"? That sort of attention to detail is the first thing we notice in Northern art. Here, not only are the wood, the glass and the cloth done with loving care, but look at the curved mirror in the middle — the whole scene is reflected backwards in perfect detail!

Roger Van Der Weyden — *Descent From the Cross (El Descendimiento)*

In this powerful and sober "Descent", again, it's the detail that first draws our attention — notice the robe of Joseph of Arimathea holding Christ's feet. And look at the veins in Joseph's forehead!

This is a human look at a traditional scene. Each of the faces is a different study in grief. Joseph's expression seems to be asking, "Why do the good always die young?" Look how Mary has swooned in the same S-curve as Jesus' body — the death of her son has dealt her a near-fatal blow as well. But the overwhelming tone of the scene is one of serenity. These are people of Northern piety who know and accept that Jesus must die.

Along with Titian's nudes, this was one of Phillip II's favorite paintings — quite a contrast! Yet this "Descent" and Titian's "Danae" both have the power to send us into ecstasy. Hmm.

Northern Art (Ground Floor)

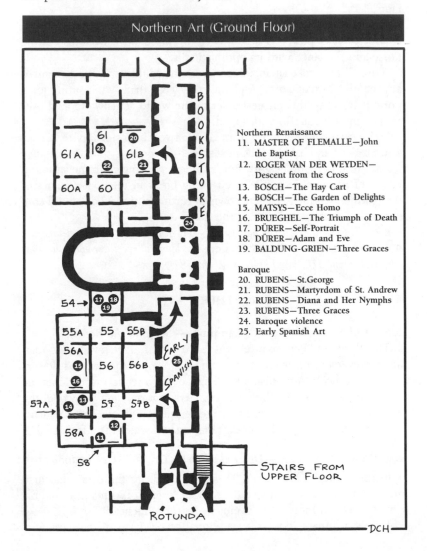

Northern Renaissance
11. MASTER OF FLEMALLE—John the Baptist
12. ROGER VAN DER WEYDEN—Descent from the Cross
13. BOSCH—The Hay Cart
14. BOSCH—The Garden of Delights
15. MATSYS—Ecce Homo
16. BRUEGHEL—The Triumph of Death
17. DÜRER—Self-Portrait
18. DÜRER—Adam and Eve
19. BALDUNG-GRIEN—Three Graces

Baroque
20. RUBENS—St.George
21. RUBENS—Martyrdom of St. Andrew
22. RUBENS—Diana and Her Nymphs
23. RUBENS—Three Graces
24. Baroque violence
25. Early Spanish Art

☞ Exit the real world and enter into the Garden of Delights, Room 57A.

Bosch (c. 1450-1516)

The work of Hieronymous Bosch can be summed up in one word — wow! It's difficult to be any more articulate because his unique vision lends itself to so many different interpretations.

Bosch (rhymes with "Gosh!") was born, lived and died in a small town in Holland — that's about all we know of him, his life being as mysterious as his work. He was much admired by his contemporaries, who understood his symbolism better than we.

Here are some possible interpretations of Bosch's work — he was: 1) crazy; 2) commenting on the decadence of his day; 3) celebrating the variety of life and human behavior; 4) painting with glue in a badly ventilated room. Or perhaps it's a combination of these.

Bosch — The Hay Cart (El Carro de Heno)

Before unraveling the tangle of the cryptic triptych "The Garden of Delights", let's warm up on a "simpler" three-paneled work. Its message is that the pleasures of life are transitory, so we'd better avoid them or we'll wind up in hell.

CENTER PANEL: An old Flemish proverb goes, "Life is a cart of hay from which everyone takes what they can." The whole spectrum of greedy, grabby humanity is here: rich and poor, monks and peasants, scrambling for their share of worldly goods. Even the Pope and the Holy Roman Emperor (with the sword) chase the cart on horseback. In the very center is a man with a knife at another man's throat, getting his share by force. Two lovers on top of the cart are oblivious to the commotion, but are surrounded by symbols of hate (the owl) and lust (the jug). The cart itself is drawn by Satan's demons.

With everyone fighting for his piece of the pie, it's easy to overlook the central figure — Christ above in Heaven, watching unnoticed. Is He blessing them or throwing up His hands?

Bosch describes the world's pleasures in the center panel, then puts them in the eternal perspective. The left panel tells us where this crazy world of temptation came from, while the right panel reminds us where it leads.

LEFT: The story of the Creation and the Garden of Eden can be "read" from top to bottom. At the top, God has sprayed D-Con and rousted Satan's vermin from Heaven, setting them loose on earth. Then God creates Eve from Adam's rib, Eve gets tempted by a (female) serpent, and finally, they're driven from Paradise. It was this first sin which brought evil into the world.

RIGHT: Here's the whole point of Bosch's sermon — worldly pleasures lead to Hell. Animal-like demons symbolizing various vices torture those who succumbed to the temptation of hay-cart planet earth.

Bosch — *The Garden of Delights (El Jardin de las Delicias)*

With this traditional Christian interpretation in mind, let's turn to the overwhelming "Garden". To make it less overwhelming, I'd suggest "framing off" one-foot squares to peruse at your leisure.

In its day, The "Garden" was interpreted as we've interpreted the Hay Cart; that is, the pleasures of the world are transitory, so you'd better watch out or you'll wind up in hell.

BOSCH — Garden of Delights. This three-paneled altarpiece takes you from the Creation to the gnashing torments of Hell via the fleeting "delights" of earthly life.

In the central panel men on horseback ride round and round searching for but never reaching the elusive Fountain of Youth. Lower down and to the left are two lovers in a bubble, illustrating that "pleasure is as fragile as glass" and will soon disappear. Just to their right is a big mussel shell, a symbol of the female sex, swallowing up a man. My favorite is the kneeling figure in front of the orange pavilion in the foreground — talk about "saying it with flowers!"

One of the differences between "The Hay Cart" and "The Garden of Delights" is Columbus. Discoveries of new plants and animals in America gave Bosch a whole new continent of sinful pleasures to paint — some real, some straight out of the Star Wars bar. In the left panel, check out the cactus tree in the Garden of Eden and the bizarre two-legged dog near the giraffe.

Bosch was certainly a Christian, but there's speculation he was a heretical Christian painting forbidden rites of a free-wheeling cult called Adamites. The Adamites were medieval nudists who believed the body was good (as it was when God made Adam) and that sex was healthy. They supposedly held secret orgies. So, in the central panel we see Adamites at play, frolicking two-by-two and two-by-three, etc. in the meadows as innocent as Adam and Eve in the garden. Whether or not

Bosch approved, you must admit that some of the folks in this Garden are having a Delightful time.

This "Adamist" interpretation makes a lot of sense in the left panel. Here the main scene, virtually non-existent in the Bible, is the fundamental story of the Adamites — the marriage (sexual union) of Adam and Eve. God himself is performing the ceremony, wrapping them in the glowing warmth of His aura.

The right panel is Hell, a burning, post-holocaust wasteland of perverse creatures and meaningless rituals where sinners are tortured by half-human demons. In this Hell, "poetic justice" reigns supreme with every sinner getting his just desserts — a glutton is eaten and re-eaten eternally, while a musician is crucified on a musical instrument for neglecting his church duties. Other symbols are less obvious. Two big ears pierced with a knife blade mow down all in the way. A pink bagpipe symbolizes the male and female sex organs (call Freud for details). In the center, Hell is literally frozen over. At lower right a pig dressed as a nun tries to seduce a man. And in the center of this wonderful nightmare is a creature with a broken egg-shell body, tree trunk legs, a witch's cap and...the face of Bosch himself staring out at us.

☞ *This room is crawling with Bosches. Take some time to look around. Don't miss the illustrated table, the nun that looks like a haystack and the guy with the Tin Man's funnel doing brain surgery on Andy Rooney. When you're done, let's meet in Room 56A.*

NORTHERN RENAISSANCE (1500-1600)

The sunny optimism of the Italian Renaissance didn't quite penetrate the cold Northern lands. Italian humanists saw Man as almost like a Greek god — strong, handsome and noble — capable of standing on his own without the help of anyone, including God and the Catholic Church.

On the other hand, when you divorce Man from what's holy, life on earth can seem pretty pointless. Northern artists concentrated on the folly of Man (think of Bosch's puny humans) cast adrift in a chaotic world.

Matsys — *Ecce Homo (Cristo Presentado al Pueblo)*
The mob — a menagerie of goony faces — is railing on the prisoner Christ before his execution. Christ seems quite fed up with it all. The painting is especially effective because of our perspective. We're looking up at Christ on the balcony — we've become part of the hooting mob.

Brueghel — *The Triumph of Death (El Triunfo de la Muerte)*
The brief flowering of the Renaissance couldn't last. The optimism and humanism of the Renaissance met the brutal reality of war. . .and lost. The openness of the Renaissance fueled the Reformation, the bitter break between the Catholic Church and the "Protest"-ants. The resulting wars involved almost every nation of Europe (remember Charles V who led the Catholics). The Northern countries were the hardest hit — in Germany alone, a third of the population died. The battles were especially brutal, with atrocities on both sides — the predictable result when politicians and generals claim God is on their side.

Pieter Brueghel the Elder (pron: BROY-gull) lived in these violent times, witnessing the futility of this first "World War". In violent times the message turns simple and morbid — no one can escape death.

BRUEGHEL—The Triumph of Death. Renaissance optimism was massacred by the brutal religious wars that swept through Europe during the Reformation.

The canvas is one big chaotic, non-symmetrical, confusing battle scene. Death in the form of skeletons (led by the one on horseback with a scythe) attacks a crowd of people, herding them into a tunnel-like building (reminiscent of a Nazi death camp?!). Elsewhere, other skeletons dole out the inevitable fate of all flesh. No one is spared. Not the jester (lower right, crawling under the table), not churchmen, not the Emperor himself (at lower left, whose gold is also plundered), not even the poor man (upper right) kneeling, praying for mercy with a cross in his hands.

We can imagine these scenes being played out in real life on the battlefields of Europe, leaving countries as wasted as the barren countryside in the background. In the end, after a hundred bloody years of war, a truce divided countries into the Catholic or Protestant folds (divisions that survive today), and Europe began to learn the lesson of tolerance — to exist we must coexist.

☞ *Continue to Room 54.*

Dürer — *Self-Portrait (Autoretrato)*
Wow. That was intense.
Before looking into the eyes of 26-year old Albrecht Dürer, look first

at his clothes and hairdo — they tell half the story of this remarkable personal statement. It's the look of a mod/hip/fab/rad young guy, a man of the world. The meticulous detail-work (Dürer was also an engraver) is the equivalent of preening before a mirror. Dürer (pron: DEWR-er), recently returned from Italy, wanted to impress his bumpkin fellow Germans with all he had learned.

But Dürer wasn't simply vain. Renaissance Italy treated its artists like princes, not workmen. Dürer learned not only to paint like a great artist, but to act like one as well.

DÜRER — Self-Portrait. The first true self-portrait ever. Dürer expected the same respect at home in Germany as he'd received in Renaissance Italy. Here he shows himself as a cultured, hip, rather arrogant man of the world.

Now look into his eyes, or rather, look up at his eyes, since Dürer composed the painting so that he is literally looking down on us. We see an intelligent, bold and somewhat arrogant man, confident of his abilities. The strong arms and hands reinforce this confidence.

This is possibly the first true self-portrait. Sure, other artists used themselves as models and put their likeness in scenes (like Bosch in Hell), but it was a whole new thing to paint your own portrait to proudly show your personality to the world. Dürer painted probably ten of them in his life — each showing a different aspect of this complex man. At the time it was arrogance itself for an artist to think he was as important as the gods, saints, kings and princes he usually painted.

Dürer put his mark on every painting and engraving. Note the pyramid-shaped "A.D." (D inside the A) on the window sill — Albrecht Dürer.

Dürer — *Adam and Eve (two separate panels)*

These are the first full-size nudes in Northern European art. It took the boldness of someone like Dürer to bring Italian fleshiness to the more modest Germans.

The title is Adam and Eve, but of course that's just an excuse to paint two nudes in the classical style. Or maybe we should say to "sculpt" two nudes, because they are more like Greek statues on pedestals than paintings. Dürer emphasized this by taking the one scene (Eve is giving Adam the apple — notice how their hair is blown by the same wind) and splitting it into two canvases — each "statue" has its own niche. Compared with Bosch's smooth-limbed, naked little *homunculi*, Dürer's Adam and Eve are three-dimensional and solid, with anatomically correct muscles. They're a bold humanistic proclamation that the body is good, man is good, the things of the world are good.

☞ *Now, look backwards, both literally and figuratively, at the two panels on the opposite wall that face Adam and Eve*

Hans Baldung-Grien — The Three Graces
Painted about the same time as Dürer's works, these, too, have a classical touch — the Graces were goddesses of joy in Greek mythology — but what a different message! While Durer portrayed the Renaissance glory of man, the Three Graces are a gloomy medieval reminder that all flesh is mortal and we're all on the same moving sidewalk to the junk pile.

In the left panel are the Three Graces in youth — beautiful, happy, in a playful green grove with the sun shining, surrounded by angelic babies. But with grim Northern realism, the right panel shows what happens to all flesh (especially that of humanists!). The Three Graces become the three stages of sagging decay — middle age, old age, and death. Death holds an hourglass of that devouring army of ants, Time.

☞ *Return to the main gallery and turn left, heading toward the far (south) end of the museum. Near the bookstore, you'll see a bull raping a woman, a man preparing to hack a baby in two and Hercules riding four white horses up to heaven. Welcome to baroque.*

Rubens's work is in Rooms 61 and 61B just off the main gallery. But first, take a seat in the long gallery (Room 75) and soak in baroque.

RUBENS AND BAROQUE (1600s)

You're surrounded by baroque. Large canvases, bright colors, rippling bodies, plenty of flesh, violent scenes. This room contains more rapes per square foot than any gallery in the world.

Baroque art overwhelms. It plays on our emotions, titillates our senses and carries us away. Baroque was made to order for the Catholic Church and absolute monarchs who used it as propaganda to combat the dual threats of Protestantism and democracy. They impressed the common masses with beautiful palaces and glorious churches, showing their strength and authority.

Peter Paul Rubens of Flanders (Belgium) was the favorite of Catholic rulers. He painted the loves, wars and religion of Catholic kings. His huge canvases were in great demand, and Rubens — like Titian before him — became rich and famous, a cultured, likeable man of the world, who was even entrusted with diplomatic missions by his employers.

☞ *Enter the first Rubens room (61B) through the door midway down the gallery.*

Rubens — *St. George Slaying the Dragon (San Jorge y El Dragón)*

This was a popular subject for Catholic kings involved in the wars of the Counter-Reformation. Like the legendary early Christian warrior who killed a dragon to save a princess, these kings saw themselves as righteous warriors saving the holy Church from the dragon of Protestantism.

In this typically baroque tangle of bodies, we see the exciting moment just as George, who has already speared the dragon, is about to apply the *coup de bludgeon* with his sword. The limp princess has a lamb, the symbol of Christ and His church.

Baroque art often looks confusing, but it's always anchored in Renaissance-style balance. This painting has an X-like composition, the rearing horse slanting one way and George slanting the other. Above where the X intersects are the two stars of the scene, George with his rippling plumed helmet and the horse, with its rippling mane.

Speaking of X-like compositions, check out the "Martyrdom of St. Andrew" on an X-cruciating cross. All around these rooms are Rubens paintings of religious subjects. Glance at the series of smaller paintings with titles championing the Catholic cause — "Triumph of the Church", "Triumph of the True Catholic", etc.

Rubens — *Diana and Her Nymphs Discovered by a Satyr (Ninfas y Satiros)*

A left to right rippling wave of figures creates a thrilling chase scene. Four horny satyrs (half-man, half-beast — though why mythical creatures like this never have their human half at the bottom, I'll never know) have crashed a party of woodland nymphos who flee from left to right. Only the Greek goddess Diana, queen of hunting, stands with her spear to try to stem the tide of flailing limbs.

All the elements of a typical Rubens work are here — action, emotion, sensuality, violence, bright colors, fleshy bodies, and rippling clothes and hair, like Rubens turned his wind machine on high.

Another typical feature is that it wasn't all painted by Rubens. Rubens was in such demand that he couldn't fill all the orders himself. In his home/studio/factory in Antwerp, he put assistants to work with the backgrounds and trivial details of his huge works, then, before shipping a canvas out the doors, Rubens would bring the work to life with a few final strokes.

Rubens — *The Three Graces (Las Tres Gracias)*
Have a seat and gaze at the pure beauty of Rubens' "Three Graces". These ample, sensual bodies — like all his women — with glowing skin, rhythmic limbs, grace and delicacy against a pleasant background, are Rubens at his best. This particular painting was for his own private collection. His young second wife was the model for the Grace at left. She shows up fairly regularly in Rubens' paintings. Remember that in later, more prudish years many of Rubens' nudes, like Titian's, were wrapped in brown paper and locked in the closet.

PETER PAUL RUBUNS — The Three Graces. After flesh fell out of fashion in Spain, these typically robust Rubens women were locked away.

☞ *Break time? The cafeteria is not far away, in the basement at the south end of the museum.*

Most of the Spanish art is upstairs on the upper floor, but let's start here on the ground floor in the long Spanish Primitives gallery (Rooms 48-49) back near the rotunda.

SPANISH ART

The final section we'll look at is Spanish painting, the Prado's *forte*. The three big names — El Greco, Velázquez and Goya — are well represented, but we'll glance at a few others, as well.

Spanish religious devotion and fanaticism are legendary. Look around. In this whole room of medieval Spanish art, is there even one painting that isn't of saints or Bible stories? I found one once. It shows heretics being punished by the Inquisition during an auto da fé — a combination revival meeting and barbecue (coals provided, B. Y. O. sinner). An estimated 2,000 enemies of God were burned alive during the reign of one notorious Grand Inquisitor.

One reason for Spanish fanaticism is that they had to literally fight for their religion. Moslems from North Africa (the Moors) controlled much of the peninsula for five centuries, making Christians a second-class and sometimes persecuted minority. It took centuries of fierce warfare to finally drive the Moors out. Spain couldn't officially call herself a "Christian" nation until the same year Columbus sailed for America. The iron-strong Spanish faith was forged in the fires of those wars.

Later, in the Counter-Reformation, when the Catholic Church shored up its defenses against the threat of the Protestant Reformation, Spain's militant religion was rallied against the Protestant "infidels". Much of the Spanish art we'll see was affected by the struggles between Catholics and Protestants, art designed to inspire the common people to have faith in the Catholic church.

☞ *Head upstairs. From the rotunda, start down the long gallery, then take your first left, into the El Greco Rooms 9B and 10B.*

EL GRECO (c. 1540-1614)

The first great Spanish painter was Greek. El Greco (Spanish for "the Greek") was born in Greece, trained in Venice, then settled in Toledo, Spain. The combination of these three cultures, plus his own unique personality, produced a highly individual style. His paintings are Byzantine icons drenched in Venetian color and fused in the fires of Spanish mysticism.

Phillip II, the ascetic king with sensual tastes who bought so many Titians, didn't like El Greco's bizarre style (perhaps because the figures — thin and haunting — reminded him of himself!?). So El Greco left the Spanish court at El Escorial and moved south to Toledo where he was accepted. He married and spent the rest of his life there. If you like El Greco, make the 90-minute trip there.

El Greco — *Christ Carrying the Cross (Cristo Abrazado a la Cruz)*
Even as the blood runs down his neck and he trudges toward his death, Christ accepts his fate in a trance of religious ecstasy. Notice how the crossbar points upward. Jesus, clasping the cross lovingly to him, sights along it like a navigational instrument to his destination — Heaven.

EL GRECO — Christ Carrying the Cross. Even facing death, El Greco's Christ burns with religious ecstasy. The shining eyes sight along the crucifix like a navigational instrument toward heaven.

However, it's the upturned eyes that are the soul of this painting. (Someone has suggested it be titled "The Eyes of Jesus".) They are close to tears with humility and sparkle with joyful acceptance. (Warning: Do not get too close to this painting. Otherwise you'll see that the holy magic in the eyes is only a simple streak of white paint.)

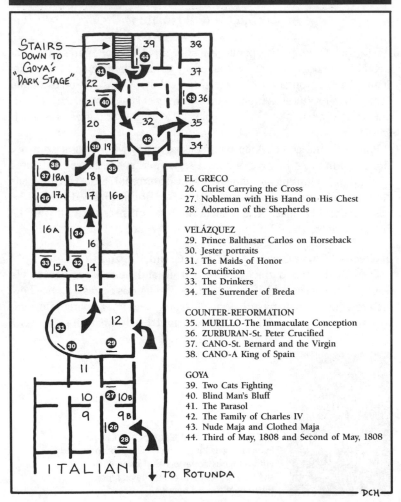

Spanish Art (Upper Floor)

STAIRS DOWN TO "GOYA's DARK STAGE"

EL GRECO
26. Christ Carrying the Cross
27. Nobleman with His Hand on His Chest
28. Adoration of the Shepherds

VELÁZQUEZ
29. Prince Balthasar Carlos on Horseback
30. Jester portraits
31. The Maids of Honor
32. Crucifixion
33. The Drinkers
34. The Surrender of Breda

COUNTER-REFORMATION
35. MURILLO-The Immaculate Conception
36. ZURBURAN-St. Peter Crucified
37. CANO-St. Bernard and the Virgin
38. CANO-A King of Spain

GOYA
39. Two Cats Fighting
40. Blind Man's Bluff
41. The Parasol
42. The Family of Charles IV
43. Nude Maja and Clothed Maja
44. Third of May, 1808 and Second of May, 1808

ITALIAN   ↓ TO ROTUNDA

DCH

El Greco — The Nobleman with His Hand on His Chest (El Caballero de la Mano al Pecho)

For all the mysticism of his paintings, we should remember that El Greco was not a mystic, but a well-traveled, learned, sophisticated, down to earth man. Despite his distorted paintings with their elongated bodies and bright unreal colors (which he may have learned during his training with Titian in Venice), he could paint realistically.

This is an exceptionally realistic and probing portrait. The sitter was an elegant and somewhat arrogant gentleman, who was obviously trying to make an impression. The sword probably indicates the portrait was done to celebrate his becoming a knight. El Greco reveals the man's personality, again, in the expressive eyes and in the hand across the chest. Notice how the middle two fingers touch — El Greco's trademark way of expressing elegance. Look for it in other works.

The signature is on the right in faint Greek letters — "Domenicos Theotocopoulos", El Greco's real name.

El Greco — The Adoration of the Shepherds (La Adoración de los Pastores)

El Greco painted this for his own burial chapel in Toledo, where it hung until the 1950s. It combines all of his trademark techniques into a powerful vision.

The shepherds, with elongated bodies and expressive hands, are stretched upward, flickering like flames toward heaven, lit from within by a spiritual fire. Christ is the light source, shining out of the darkness, giving a sheen to the surrounding colors. These shepherds will never be able to buy suits off the rack.

Notice El Greco's typical two-tiered composition — earth below, Heaven above. Over the Christ Child is a swirling canopy of clouds and angels. Heaven and earth seem to intermingle, and the earthly figures look as though they're about to be sucked up through a funnel into the vault of heaven. There is little depth to the picture — all the figures are virtually the same distance from us — so our eyes have nowhere to go but up and down, up and down, linking heaven and earth, God and man.

☞ Continue down the main gallery, turning left into the large lozenge-shaped Velázquez Room 12 and adjoining Rooms 13-16.

VELÁZQUEZ (1599-1660)

For 35 years, Diego Velázquez (pron: vel-LOSS-kes) was the King of Spain's court painter. Look around the room. While El Greco and other Spanish artists painted crucifixions, saints and madonnas, Velázquez painted what his boss, the king, told him to — mostly portraits.

Unlike the wandering, independent Greco, Velázquez was definitely a career man. Born in Seville, apprenticed early on, he marries the master's daughter, moves to Madrid, impresses the king with his skill and works his way up the ladder at the king's court — valet to the king, director of new buildings, director of festivities, etc. He becomes the king's friend and art teacher and, eventually, is knighted.

What's amazing in this tale of ambition is that, as a painter, Velázquez never compromised. He was the photo-journalist of his time, chronicling court events for posterity.

Velázquez — Prince Balthasar Carlos on Horseback (El Príncipe Baltasar Carlos)

As court painter, this was exactly the kind of portrait Velázquez was called on to produce — the prince, age five, looking like the masterful heir to the throne. But the charm of the painting is the contrast between the pose — the traditional equestrian pose of a powerful Roman Conqueror — with the fact that this "conqueror" is only a cute, tiny tyke in a pink and gold suit. The seriousness on the prince's face adds the crowning touch. We can see why Velázquez was such a court favorite.

While pleasing his king, Velázquez was also starting a revolution in art. Stand back and look at the prince's costume — remarkably detailed, right? Now move up closer — all that "remarkable detail" is nothing but messy splotches of pink and gold paint! In the past, artists painted details meticulously. But Velázquez learned how just a few dabs of colors on a canvas blend in the eye when seen at a distance to give the appearance of great detail. Two centuries later this technique would eventually be taken to its extreme by the Impressionists.

Velázquez — Jester Portraits (Bufones)

In royal courts, dwarfs were given the job of entertaining the nobles. But some also had a more important task — social satire. They alone were given free rein to say anything they wanted about the king, however biting, nasty, or — worst of all — true. Consequently, these dwarfs were often the wittiest and most intelligent people at court, and Velázquez, who must have known them as colleagues, paints them with great dignity.

Velázquez — The Maids of Honor (Las Meninas)

Velázquez has made the perfect blend of formal portrait and candid intimate snapshot. It's a painting about the painting of a portrait. Here's what we're seeing:

One hot summer day in 1656, Velázquez (at left) with brush in hand and looking like Salvador Dali (which is a little like saying that Jesus looked like John Lennon) is painting a formal portrait of King Phillip and his wife. They would be standing where we are, and we only see them reflected in the mirror in the distance.

Their daughter, the Infanta Margarita (the main figure in the center), has come to watch her parents being painted. With her are her two attendants (*meninas*, or girls), one of whom is kneeling, offering her a cool glass of water. Also in the picture is the young court jester (far right) poking impishly at the family dog. A female dwarf looks on, as do others in the background. Also, at that very moment, a member of court is passing by the doorway in the distance on his way upstairs, and he, too, looks in on the progress of the portrait.

VELÁZQUEZ —The Maids of Honor. A behind-the-scenes look at the royal family. There's more history in this casual glimpse of the young princess and her attendants than in a thousand official royal portraits. If you were the ruler of Spain in 1656 this is what you'd see — the princess, her attendants, and Velázquez himself (far left).

Velázquez was smart enough to know that the really interesting portrait wasn't the king and queen, but the action behind the scenes. We're sucked right in by the natural-ness of the scene and because the characters are looking right at us. This is true Spanish history, and Velázquez the journalist (who is shown wearing the red cross of knighthood, painted on after his death — possibly by Phillip IV himself) has told us more about this royal family than in volumes of history books.

The scene is lit by the window at right. Using gradations of light, Velázquez has split the room into four receding planes: 1) the king and queen, standing where we are; 2) the main figures, lit by the window; 3) the darker middle distance figures (including Velázquez); 4) the black wall; and 5) the lit doorway. We are drawn into the painting, living and breathing with its characters, free to walk behind them, around them and among them. This is art come to life.

Velázquez — Crucifixion

King Phillip IV was having an affair. He got caught and, being a good Christian king, was overcome with remorse. He commissioned this work to atone for his adulterous ways. (That's Phillip, pious and kneeling, to the left of the Crucifixion.)

Velázquez's Crucifixion must have matched the repentant mood of his king (and friend). You can often tell the tone of a Crucifixion by the tilt of Christ's head. Here, it's hanging down, accepting His punishment, humble and repentant.

Meditating on this Christ would truly be an act of agonizing penance. We see him straight from the front, no holds barred. Every detail is laid out for us, even down to the knots in the wood of the crossbar. And the dripping blood! We feel how long Jesus has been hanging there by how long it must have taken for that blood to drip ever so slowly down.

Velázquez — *The Drinkers (Los Borrachos)*

Velázquez's objective eye even turns Greek gods into everyday folk. Here the Greek god of wine crowns a drinker for his deeds of debauchery. Bacchus is as finely painted as anything Titian or Rubens ever did, but what a difference in scenes! The real focus isn't the other-worldly Bacchus who seems quite indifferent, but his fellow, human merrymakers.

This isn't a painting, it's a polaroid snapshot in a blue-collar bar. Look how natural the guy is next to Bacchus, grinning at us over the bowl of

VELÁZQUEZ — The Drinkers. In this blue-collar snapshot, Velázquez captures peasants drinking (while beating Bacchus at strip poker).

wine he's offering us — and the guy next to him, clambering to get into the picture and mugging for the camera! Velázquez was the master at making a carefully composed scene look spontaneous.

Velázquez — *The Surrender of Breda (La Rendición de Breda)*

Here's another piece of artistic journalism, the Spanish victory over the Dutch after a long siege of Breda, a strongly fortified city.

The scene has become famous as a model of fair play. The defeated Dutch general is offering the keys to the city to the victorious Spaniards. As he begins to kneel in humility, the Spanish conqueror restrains him — the war is over and there's no need to rub salt in the wounds. The optimistic calm-after-the-battle mood is enhanced by the great open space highlighted by the 25 lances (the painting is often called "The Lances") silhouetted against the sky.

☞ *From the cool objectivity of Velazquez, enter the heat and passion of Spain's religious art of the Counter-Reformation, in Rooms 16B-18.*

COUNTER-REFORMATION ART —
FIGHTING BACK WITH BRUSHES (1600s)

Europe was torn in two by the Protestant Reformation. For 100 years, Catholics and Protestants bashed Bibles in what has been called the first "world war". The Catholic Church also waged a propaganda campaign (the Counter-Reformation) to bolster the faith of the confused and weary masses. Art was part of that campaign. Pretty pictures brought abstract doctrines down to the level of the common man.

Murillo — *The Immaculate Conception (La Immaculada)*
For centuries, the #1 deity in the Christian pantheon was the goddess Mary. This painting is a religious treatise, explaining a Catholic doctrine that many found difficult to comprehend — the Immaculate Conception of Mary. Since all humans are stained by the original sin of Adam (so the doctrine went), didn't that mean Jesus was as well, since His mother was human? Not so, said the Catholics. Mary, by a special act of God, was conceived and born without taint of original sin.

MURILLO — Immaculate Conception. This "immaculately" pure Virgin Mary is a floating Ivory Soap commercial for Catholicism.

The Spanish have always loved the Virgin. She's practically a cult figure. Common people pray directly to her for help in troubled times. Murillo (pron: mur-REE-oh) used this fanatic devotion to Mary to teach the dull, theological concept of Immaculate Conception. He painted a beautiful, floating and Ivory-Soap-pure woman — the most "immaculate" virgin imaginable — radiating youth and wholesome goodness.

Zurbarán — *St. Peter Crucified appearing to Peter Nolasco*
After Murillo's sweet beauty, Zurbarán is like a bitter jolt of *café solo*.
In Spain miracles are real. When legends tell of a saint who was beheaded but didn't die, that isn't an "allegory on eternal life" to the Spanish — they picture a real man walking around with his head under his arm.
So, when Zurbarán paints a mystical vision, he gives it to us in

photographic realism. Bam, there's the Apostle Peter crucified upside down right in front of us. Nolasco looks as shocked as we at the reality of the vision. This is "People's Art" of the Counter-Reformation, religious art for the masses. (Zurbarán has the sort of literal-minded religion that makes people wonder things like — "When the Rapture comes, what if it catches me sitting on the toilet?")

Cano — St. Bernard and the Virgin

Here's another heavenly vision brought right down to earth. St. Bernard is literally enjoying the "milk of paradise", a vision he had of being suckled on the heavenly teat of Mary. When God's word was portrayed in this realistic way, the common folk lapped it up.

Cano — A King of Spain (Un Rey de España)

By 1600, Spain had peaked as Europe's great power. The quick wealth from the Americas began to dry up, the Spanish fleet was defeated by the British, and France emerged as a European power. Spain's influence sank.

I like to think of Cano's "A King of Spain" as a picture of the country at the moment it passed its peak. This unknown king in mythical dress, slumped unhappily on his throne, with a globe of the world in his hands, waves his sword, bored. There's nothing left to conquer. His look is like, "I've got the whole world. Now what?"

☞   *Enter the Early Goya Rooms, 19-23.*

GOYA (1746-1828)

Goya's "Two Cats Fighting" ("Gatos Riñendo") represents the two warring halves of a human soul, the dark and light sides, anger and fear locked in immortal combat, fighting for dominance of a man's life. Hey, if you can't tell from the painting, take a clue from this melodramatic, purple prose — we're entering the Age of Romanticism.

Francisco de Goya, a true individual in both his life and his painting style, is hard to pigeonhole — his personality and talents were so varied. We'll see several different facets of this rough-cut man — cheery apprentice painter, loyal court painter, political rebel, scandal-maker, disillusioned genius. His work runs the gamut, from pretty rococo to political rabble-rousing, to Romantic nightmares.

For convenience, let's divide Goya's life into three stages — Court Painter, Political Rebel and "Dark" Stage.

Goya: Court Painter

Born in a small town, Goya, unlike Velázquez, was a far cry from a precocious painter destined for success. In his youth he dabbled as a matador, kicking around Spain before finally landing a job in the Royal Tapestry. The canvases in these rooms were designs made into tapestries bound for the walls of nobles' palaces.

Browse through these rooms and watch lords and ladies of the 1700s with nothing better to do than play — toasting each other at a picnic, dancing with castanets, flying kites, playing paddleball, listening to a blind guitarist, walking on stilts or playing Blind Man's Bluff.

GOYA — The Parasol ("El Quitasol"). In his early years as court painter Goya's art was light and frilly.

Notice how — how do I say this? — how BAD the drawing is in some of these canvases, especially early ones. However, in the few short years he worked in the "tapestry" department, Goya, the inexperienced apprentice slowly developed into a good, if not great, draftsman. "The Parasol" ("El Quitasol") was one of his first really good paintings, with a simple composition and subtle shadings of light. Goya worked steadily for the court for 25 years, dutifully cranking out portraits before finally becoming First Court Painter at age 53.

☞ *Exiting the "tapestry" rooms, turn right and walk down the hall, entering the octagonal-or-something-agonal Room 32 to the left. Here you'll find portraits of Goya's employers, the Royal Family of Spain.*

Goya — The Family of Charles IV (La Familia de Carlos IV)

They're decked out in all their finest, wearing every medal, jewel and ribbon they could find for this impressive group portrait. Goya has captured all the splendor of the Court in 1800 — but with a brutal twist of reality. For underneath all the royal finery, he captured the inner personality — or lack thereof — of these shallow monarchs.

This isn't so much a royal portrait as it is a stiff family photo of Ma and Pa Kettle in their Sunday best. The look in their eyes seems to say "I can't wait to get this monkey-suit off." (I always picture Goya deliberately taking his own sweet time making them stand and smile for hours on end.)

Goya, the budding political liberal, shows his disgust for the shallow king and his family. King Charles, with his ridiculous hairdo and silly smile is portrayed for what he was — a vacuous, good-natured fool, a henpecked husband controlled by his domineering queen. She, the true center of the composition, is proud and defiant. She was vain about the supposed beauty of her long, swan-like neck, and here she stretches to display every centimeter of it. The other adults, with their bland faces, are bug-eyed with stupidity. Catch the crone looking out at us bird-like, fourth from left.

As a tribute to Velázquez' "Maids of Honor", Goya painted himself painting the scene at far left. But here Goya stands back in the shadows looking with disdain on the group. Only the children escape Goya's critical eye, painted with the sympathy he always showed to those lower on the social ladder.

☞ *Look around the room at other portraits, equally judgmental of the King, Queen and Prince, then cross the hall into Room 36.*

Goya: Political Rebel

Goya — Nude Maja (La Maja Desnuda) and Clothed Maja (La Maja Vestida)

Goya remained at Court because of his talent, not his political beliefs — or his morals. Rumors flew that he was fooling around with the beautiful, intelligent and vivacious Duchess of Alba. Even more scandalous was a painting, supposedly of the Duchess in a less-than-devout-Catholic pose.

A *maja* was a hip working-class girl. Many of Goya's early tapestries show royalty dressed in the garb of these colorful commoners. Here the Duchess has undressed as one.

"The Nude Maja" was a real shocker. Spanish kings enjoyed the sensual nudes of Titian and Rubens, but it was unheard of for a pious Spaniard to actually paint one. Goya incurred the wrath of the Inquisition, the Catholic court system that tried heretics and sinners.

The painting caused such a stir that, supposedly, that's why Goya dashed off another version with her clothes on. The quick brushwork is sloppier, perhaps because Goya was in a hurry, or because he was anxious to invent Impressionism. The two paintings may have been displayed in a double frame — the nude could be covered by sliding the clothed *maja* over it to hide it from Inquisitive minds that wanted to know.

Artistically, the nude is less a portrait than an idealized nude in the tradition (and reclining pose) of Titian's "Venus and the Organ Player." The pale body is highlighted by the cool green sheets à la Titian, as well. Both paintings were locked away in obscurity, along with the Titians and Rubenses until 1901.

☞   *Down the hall, in Room 39, you'll find . . .*

Goya — *Third of May, 1808* and *Second of May, 1808*

Goya became a political radical, a believer in democracy in a world of kings. During his time, the American and French Revolutions put the fear of God in the medieval minds of Europe's aristocracy. In retaliation, they were determined to stamp out any trace of political liberalism.

GOYA — 3rd of May, 1808. French soldiers cut down brave Spaniards with all the compassion of a lawnmower. Napoleon's brutal invasion of Spain contributed to Goya's increasing disillusionment.

Goya admired the French leader Napoleon, who fought for the democratic ideals of the French Revolution against the kings of Europe. But then Napoleon invaded Spain (1808), and Goya saw war firsthand. What he saw was not a heroic war liberating the Spaniards from the feudal yoke, but an oppressive, brutal, senseless war in which common Spaniards were the first to die.

The "Second of May, 1808" and "Third of May, 1808" show two bloody days of the war. On the 2nd, the common citizens of Madrid rebelled against the French invaders. With sticks, stones and kitchen knives they rallied in the Puerta del Sol in protest. The French sent in their fearsome Egyptian mercenary troops to quell the riot. Goya captures the hysterical tangle of bodies as the Egyptians wade through the dense crowd hacking away at the overmatched *Madrilenos* who have nowhere to run.

The next day the French began reprisals. They took suspected rebels to a nearby hill and began mercilessly executing them. The "Third of May, 1808" is supposedly a tribute to those brave Spaniards who rebelled against the French, but it's far from heroic. In fact, it's anti-heroic, showing us the irrationality of war — an assembly line of death, with each victim toppling into a crumpled heap. They plead for mercy and get none. Those awaiting death bury their faces in their hands, unable to look at their falling companions. The central victim in luminous white spreads his arms Christ-like and asks, "Why are you doing this to us?"

Goya goes beyond sympathy for the victims. In this war, even the executioners are pawns in the game, only following orders without understanding why. The colorless firing squad, with guns perfectly level and feet perfectly in step, is a faceless machine of murder, cutting people down with all the compassion of a lawnmower. They bury their faces in their guns as though they, too, are unable to look their victims in the eye. This war is horrible, and what's worse, the horror is pointless.

The violence is painted with equally violent techniques. There's a strong prison-yard floodlight thrown on the main victim, focusing all our attention on his look of puzzled horror. The distorted features, the puddle of blood, the twisting bodies, the thick brushwork — all are features of the Romantic style that emphasized emotion over beauty. It all adds up to a vivid portrayal of the brutality and ultimate senselessness of war. Like the victims, we ask, "How can one human being do this to another?"

Goya was disillusioned by the invasion of his "hero" Napoleon. Added to this he began to go deaf. His wife died. To top it off, he was exiled as a political radical. Goya retreated from court life to his own private, quiet — and dark — world.

☞ *To get to the "Black Paintings", exit back into the hallway, turn right, silently flagellate yourself, then turn right again winding down the stairs. At the foot of the stairs continue straight, then take the first right into Room 67.*

Goya's Dark Stage

In 1819 Goya — deaf, widowed, and exiled — moved into a villa and began decorating it with his own oil paintings. The works were painted right on the walls of rooms in the villa, later transferred to canvas.

You immediately see why these are the "Black", or "Dark" paintings — both in color and mood. They're nightmarish scenes, scary and surreal, the inner visions of an embittered man smeared onto the walls as though finger-painted in blood.

Goya — *The Witches' Sabbath (Aquellare)*

Dark forces convened continually in Goya's dining room. This dark coven of crones swirls in a frenzy of black magic around a dark, Satanic goat in monk's clothes who presides, priest-like, over the obscene rituals. The main witch, seated in front of the goat, is the very image of wild-eyed adoration, lust and fear. (Notice the one noble lady sitting just to the right of center with her hands folded primly in her lap — "I thought this was a Tupperware party....")

Goya — *Battle to the Death (Duelo a Garrotazos)*

Two giants buried up to their knees, face to face, flail at each other with clubs. Neither can move, neither can run, neither dares rest or the other will finish him off. It's a standoff between superpowers caught in a never-ending cycle of war. Can a truce be reached? It looks bleak.

The "Black Paintings" foreshadow 20th-century Surrealism with their dream images, and Expressionism with their thick, smeared style and cynical outlook. Are these really by the same artist who did the frilly "Blind-Man's Bluff" in the "tapestry" room?

Goya — *Saturn Devouring One of His Sons (Saturno Devorando a un Hijo)*

Fearful that his sons would overthrow him as king of the gods, the Roman god Saturn ate them. Saturn was also known as Cronus, or Time,

GOYA — Saturn Devouring One of His Sons. Here, Goya's gory message is that Time devours us all. By the way, the Prado cafeteria is just downstairs.

and this may be an allegory of how Time devours us all. Goya was a dying man in a dying, feudal world. The destructiveness of time is shown in all its horror by a man unafraid of the darker side.

☞ *Rather than end the Prado on this dreary note, walk to the nearby "Guernica" annex to end on a different dreary note.*

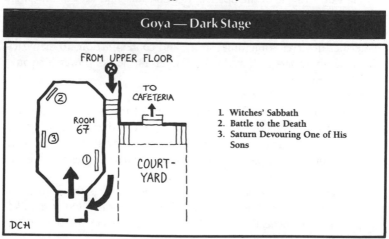

Goya — Dark Stage

FROM UPPER FLOOR

TO CAFETERIA

ROOM 67

COURT-YARD

1. Witches' Sabbath
2. Battle to the Death
3. Saturn Devouring One of His Sons

DCH

GUERNICA

Picasso's monumental canvas "Guernica" is not only a piece of art but a piece of history. It's one of Europe's must-see sights, so leave time for it.

☞ *"Guernica" is in the Centro Arte Reina Sofia, Madrid's slick new modern art museum located three long blocks south of the Prado across the street from the Atocha train station (open 10:00-21:00, closed Tuesday, tel. 467-5062).*

"Guernica" is the product of the right artist in the right place at the right time. Pablo Picasso, a Spaniard, was in Paris in 1937, preparing an exhibition of paintings for its World's Fair. Meanwhile, a bloody civil war was being fought in his own country. The legally elected democratic government was being challenged by traditionalist right-wing forces under Francisco Franco. Franco would eventually win and rule the country with an iron hand for three decades.

Guernica was a small town in northern Spain of no strategic importance, but it became the target of the world's first saturation-bombing raid. Franco gave permission to his Fascist ally, Hitler, to use the town as a guinea pig to try out Germany's new air force. The raid leveled the town, causing destruction that was unheard of at the time — though by 1944 it would be commonplace.

News of the bombing reached Picasso in Paris. He scrapped earlier plans and immediately set to work on the Guernica mural for the Spanish pavilion. It was finished in a matter of weeks. Thousands of people attended the fair, and the Guernica mural had a profound impact on those who saw it. They witnessed the horror of modern technology of war, the vain struggle of the Spanish Republicans, and the cold indifference of the Nazi war machine. It was a prophetic vision of the World War to come.

Guernica deserves some time, study, and contemplation. To many, it's difficult to appreciate at first. Linger longer and let its power hit you.

Pablo Picasso — *Guernica*

Picasso shows Guernica in the aftermath of the bombing. It's as if he'd picked up the shattered shards and "pasted" them onto a canvas. It looks like a jumble of overlapping shades on first sight, but looking closer, we can see each piece of this broken city. The figures are twisted, but recognizable. Let's sort the main ones out.

On the left is a bull. In typical Cubist fashion, we see the head from two angles at once. The body extends to the left, ending with a tail like a wisp of smoke. Beneath the bull is a modern "Pietà" — a grieving mother with her dead child.

The central figure is a horse with a twisted head and a sword piercing its newsprint body. The rider has fallen, dismembered, at the horse's feet. We see his severed head and severed arm with a broken sword.

On the right, a woman runs screaming. Above her, another pokes her head out a window, shining a shaft of light on the horse and the woman below. To the far right another figure cries with grief inside a building.

PICASSO — Guernica. Fascist bombs shattered Europe. Picasso throws the jumbled pieces onto a canvas to show the senselessness of modern war.

This is a gruesome and, despite the modern "abstract" style, remarkably realistic portrayal of the bombing's destruction. But Picasso has suggested a symbolic interpretation that raises the work to the universal level, a commentary on all wars.

Picasso himself said that the central horse, with the spear in its back, symbolizes humanity succumbing to brute force. The bull represents brutality, standing triumphant over the mourning mother and child.

The Guernica raid was a completely senseless and pointless act of brute force without any military purpose. In fact, the entire Spanish Civil War was an exercise in brutality. As one side captured a town, it might systematically round up every man, old and young — including priests — line them up and shoot them in revenge, for atrocities by the other side. The bare bulb at the top of the canvas shines an interrogator's third-degree light on all this ugliness.

To the right of the bull is a crying dove, the symbol of peace in defeat. The rider's broken sword could be the futility of trying to fight brutality with brutality.

This is a scary work. The drab concrete-colored grey tones create a depressing, almost nauseating mood. We are like the terrified woman at right, trying to run from it all. But her leg is too thick, dragging her down, like trying to run from something in a nightmare. The figure thrusting her head out of the window with a lamp in her hand, is humanity itself, coming out of its shell, seeing for the first time the harsh horror of modern war.

A New Enlightenment Through Travel?

Thomas Jefferson said "Travel makes you wiser but less happy." We think he was right. And "less happy" is a good thing. It's the growing pains of a broadening perspective, a tearing off of the hometown blinders. It exposes you to new ways of thinking and to people who have a completely different set of "self-evident" truths. We've shared with you a whole book of our love of travel. Now allow us one page to share some thoughts on how travel has given us new ways of thinking.

On any trip, the biggest culture shock can occur when you return home. America is a land of unprecedented material wealth. Though comprising only 5 percent of the world's people, we control over 30 percent of the global economic pie. We've built a wall of money around our borders, insulating ourselves from world problems. We can't see that our rampant pursuit of wealth, both as individuals and as a society, has global repercussions—long-term damage to the earth, impoverishment of weaker nations, and military aggression to maintain our disproportionate standard of living. Only by traveling can we see ourselves as others see us and see how our life-style affects others.

For us (Rick and Gene), travel has brought a new perspective. Like the astronauts, we've seen a planet with no boundaries. It's a tender green, blue, and white organism that will live or die as a unit. We're just two of five billion equally precious people. And by traveling we've seen humankind as a body that somehow must tell its fat cells to cool it . . . because nearly half of the body is starving and the whole thing is threatened.

Returning home, we've found that you can continue the mind-expanding aspect of travel by pursuing new ideas. Expose yourself to some radical thinking.

A new enlightenment is needed. Just as the French Enlightenment led us into the modern age of science and democracy, a new Enlightenment must teach us the necessity of realistic and sustainable affluence, global understanding, peaceful coexistence, and controlling nature by obeying it.

We hope that your travels give you a fun and relaxing vacation or adventure . . . and also that they'll make you an active patriot of the planet. The future is in our hands.

Rick and Gene

Index
of Artists and Styles

About the Authors

Rick Steves (1955-)

Rick has gained notoriety as a guru of alternative European travel. Since 1980 he has led "Back Door" tours of Europe and written twelve travel guidebooks including the classic *Europe Through The Back Door*, now in its eleventh edition, which started a cult of people who insist on washing their socks in sinks and taking showers "down the hall" even when not traveling. Rick also publishes the "Back Door" travel newsletter, writes a weekly newspaper column, hosts and co-writes a PBS television series, "Travels in Europe with Rick Steves," and gives travel lectures throughout the U.S. As a native of Seattle, Washington, he graduated from the University of Washington with degrees in European History and Business Administration.

Gene Openshaw (1956-)

Gene is both an author and a composer. After graduating from Stanford University, he promptly put his degree to work by writing joke books and performing stand-up comedy. He also has worked as a travel guide, schoolteacher, roofer, movie projectionist, musician and political pamphleteer. As a composer, his works include a few minor classical pieces, music for theatrical productions, an obscure album of songs, "Method in the Madness," and an opera, "Matter."

Rick Steves' BACK DOOR CATALOG

All items field tested, highly recommended, completely guaranteed, discounted below retail and ideal for independent, mobile travelers. Prices include tax (if applicable), handling, and postage.

The Back Door Suitcase / Rucksack $70.00

At 9"x22"x14" this specially designed, sturdy functional bag is maximum carry-on-the-plane size (fits under the seat) and your key to foot-loose and fancy-free travel. Made of rugged water resistant Cordura nylon, it converts easily from a smart-looking suitcase to a handy rucksack. It has hide-away padded shoulder straps, top and side handles and a detachable shoulder strap (for toting as a suitcase). Lockable perimeter zippers allow easy access to the roomy (2,700 cubic inches) central compartment. Two large outside pockets are perfect for frequently used items. Also included is one nylon stuff bag. Over 40,000 Back Door travelers have used these bags around the world. Rick Steves helped design and lives out of this bag for 3 months at a time. Comparable bags cost much more. Available in navy blue, black, or grey.

Moneybelt $8.00

This required, ultra-light, sturdy, under-the-pants, nylon pouch is just big enough to carry the essentials (passport, airline ticket, travelers checks, and so on) comfortably. I'll never travel without one and I hope you won't either. Beige, nylon zipper, one size fits nearly all, with "manual."

Catalog   FREE

For a complete listing of all the books, travel videos, products and services Rick Steves and Europe Through the Back Door offer you, ask us for our 64-page catalog.

Eurailpasses . . .

...cost the same everywhere. We carefully examine each order and include for no extra charge a 90-minute Rick Steves VHS video Train User's Guide, helpful itinerary advice, Eurail train schedule booklet and map, plus a free 22 Days book of your choice! Send us a check for the cost of the pass(es) you want along with your legal name (as it appears on your passport), a proposed itinerary (including dates and places of entry and exit if known), choice of 22 Days book (Europe, Brit, Spain/Port, Scand, France, or Germ/Switz/Aust) and a list of questions. Within 2 weeks of receiving your order we'll send you your pass(es) and any other information pertinent to your trip. Due to this unique service Rick Steves sells more passes than anyone on the West Coast and you'll have an efficient and expertly-organized Eurail trip.

Back Door Tours

We encourage independent travel, but for those who want a tour in the Back Door style, we do offer a 22-day "Best of Europe" tour. For complete details, send for our free 64 page tour booklet/catalog.

All orders will be processed within 2 weeks and include tax (where applicable), shipping and a one year's subscription to our Back Door Travel newsletter. Prices good through 1993. Rush orders add $5. Sorry, no credit cards. Send checks to:

Europe Through The Back Door ● 120 Fourth Ave. N.
Box   2009 ● Edmonds, WA 98020 ● (206) 771-8303

Other Books from John Muir Publications

Adventure Vacations: From Trekking in New Guinea to Swimming in Siberia, Bangs 256 pp. $17.95

Asia Through the Back Door, 3rd ed., Steves and Gottberg 326 pp. $15.95

Belize: A Natural Destination, Mahler, Wotkyns, Schafer 304 pp. $16.95

Bus Touring: Charter Vacations, U.S.A., Warren with Bloch 168 pp. $9.95

California Public Gardens: A Visitor's Guide, Sigg 304 pp. $16.95

Costa Rica: A Natural Destination, 2nd ed., Sheck 288 pp. $16.95

Elderhostels: The Students' Choice, 2nd ed., Hyman 312 pp. $15.95

Environmental Vacations: Volunteer Projects to Save the Planet, 2nd ed., Ocko 248 pp. $16.95

Europe 101: History & Art for the Traveler, 4th ed., Steves and Openshaw 372 pp. $15.95

Europe Through the Back Door, 11th ed., Steves 448 pp. $17.95

Europe Through the Back Door Phrase Book: French, Steves 112 pp. $4.95

Europe Through the Back Door Phrase Book: German, Steves 112 pp. $4.95

Europe Through the Back Door Phrase Book: Italian, Steves 112 pp. $4.95

Floating Vacations: River, Lake, and Ocean Adventures, White 256 pp. $17.95

A Foreign Visitor's Survival Guide to America, Baldwin and Levine 224 pp. $12.95

Great Cities of Eastern Europe, Rapoport 256 pp. $16.95

Guatemala: A Natural Destination, Mahler 288 pp. $16.95

Gypsying After 40: A Guide to Adventure and Self-Discovery, Harris 264 pp. $14.95

The Heart of Jerusalem, Nellhaus 336 pp. $12.95

Indian America: A Traveler's Companion, 2nd ed., Eagle/Walking Turtle 448 pp. $17.95

Interior Furnishings Southwest: The Sourcebook of the Best Production Craftspeople, Deats and Villani 256 pp. $19.95

Mona Winks: Self-Guided Tours of Europe's Top Museums, 2nd ed., Steves and Openshaw 456 pp. $16.95

Opera! The Guide to Western Europe's Great Houses, Zietz 296 pp. $18.95

Paintbrushes and Pistols: How the Taos Artists Sold the West, Taggett and Schwarz 280 pp. $17.95

The People's Guide to Mexico, 9th ed., Franz 608 pp. $18.95

The People's Guide to RV Camping in Mexico, Franz with Rogers 320 pp. $13.95

Ranch Vacations: The Complete Guide to Guest and Resort, Fly-Fishing, and Cross-Country Skiing Ranches, 2nd ed., Kilgore 396 pp. $18.95

The Shopper's Guide to Art and Crafts in the Hawaiian Islands, Schuchter 272 pp. $13.95

The Shopper's Guide to Mexico, Rogers and Rosa 224 pp. $9.95

Ski Tech's Guide to Equipment, Skiwear, and Accessories, ed. Tanler 144 pp. $11.95

Ski Tech's Guide to Maintenance and Repair, ed. Tanler 160 pp. $11.95

A Traveler's Guide to Asian Culture, Chambers 224 pp. $13.95

Traveler's Guide to Healing Centers and Retreats in North America, Rudee and Blease 240 pp. $11.95

Understanding Europeans, Miller 272 pp. $14.95

Undiscovered Islands of the Caribbean, 3nd ed., Willes 264 pp. $14.95

Undiscovered Islands of the Mediterranean, 2nd ed., Moyer and Willes 256 pp. $13.95

Undiscovered Islands of the U.S. and Canadian West Coast, Moyer and Willes 208 pp. $12.95

A Viewer's Guide to Art: A Glossary of Gods, People, and Creatures, Shaw and Warren 144 pp. $10.95

The Visitor's Guide to the Birds of the Eastern National Parks: United States and Canada, Wauer 400 pp. $15.95

2 to 22 Days Series
Each title offers 22 flexible daily itineraries that can be used to get the most out of vacations of any length. Included are not only "must see" attractions but also little-known villages and hidden "jewels" as well as valuable general information.

22 Days Around the World, 1993 ed., Rapoport and Willes 264 pp. $13.95

2 to 22 Days Around the Great Lakes, 1993 ed., Schuchter 192 pp. $10.95

22 Days in Alaska, Lanier 128 pp. $7.95

2 to 22 Days in the American Southwest, 1993 ed., Harris 176 pp. $10.95

2 to 22 Days in Asia, 1993 ed., Rapoport and Willes 176 pp. $10.95

2 to 22 Days in Australia, 1993 ed., Gottberg 192 pp. $10.95

2 to 22 Days in California, 1993 ed., Rapoport 192 pp. $10.95

22 Days in China, Duke and Victor 144 pp. $7.95

2 to 22 Days in Europe, 1993 ed., Steves 288 pp. $13.95

2 to 22 Days in Florida, 1993 ed., Harris 192 pp. $10.95

2 to 22 Days in France, 1993 ed., Steves 192 pp. $10.95

2 to 22 Days in Germany, Austria, & Switzerland, 1993 ed., Steves 224 pp. $10.95

2 to 22 Days in Great Britain, 1993 ed., Steves 192 pp. $10.95

2 to 22 Days in Hawaii, 1993 ed., Schuchter 176 pp. $10.95

22 Days in India, Mathur 136 pp. $7.95

22 Days in Japan, Old 136 pp. $7.95

22 Days in Mexico, 2nd ed., Rogers and Rosa 128 pp. $7.95

2 to 22 Days in New England, 1993 ed., Wright 192 pp. $10.95

2 to 22 Days in New Zealand, 1993 ed., Schuchter 192 pp. $10.95

2 to 22 Days in Norway, Sweden, & Denmark, 1993 ed., Steves 192 pp. $10.95

2 to 22 Days in the Pacific Northwest, 1993 ed., Harris 192 pp. $10.95

2 to 22 Days in the Rockies, 1993 ed., Rapoport 192 pp. $10.95

2 to 22 Days in Spain & Portugal, 1992 ed., Steves 192 pp. $9.95

2 to 22 Days in Texas, 1993 ed., Harris 192 pp. $10.95

2 to 22 Days in Thailand, 1993 ed., Richardson 180 pp. $10.95

22 Days in the West Indies, Morreale and Morreale 136 pp. $7.95

Parenting Series
Being a Father: Family, Work, and Self, *Mothering* Magazine 176 pp. $12.95
Preconception: A Woman's Guide to Preparing for Pregnancy and Parenthood, Aikey-Keller 232 pp. $14.95
Schooling at Home: Parents, Kids, and Learning, *Mothering* Magazine 264 pp. $14.95
Teens: A Fresh Look, *Mothering* Magazine 240 pp. $14.95

"Kidding Around" Travel Guides for Young Readers
Written for kids eight years of age and older.
Kidding Around Atlanta, Pedersen 64 pp. $9.95
Kidding Around Boston, 2nd ed., Byers 64 pp. $9.95
Kidding Around Chicago, 2nd ed., Davis 64 pp. $9.95
Kidding Around the Hawaiian Islands, Lovett 64 pp. $9.95
Kidding Around London, Lovett 64 pp. $9.95
Kidding Around Los Angeles, Cash 64 pp. $9.95
Kidding Around the National Parks of the Southwest, Lovett 108 pp. $12.95
Kidding Around New York City, 2nd ed., Lovett 64 pp. $9.95
Kidding Around Paris, Clay 64 pp. $9.95
Kidding Around Philadelphia, Clay 64 pp. $9.95
Kidding Around San Diego, Luhrs 64 pp. $9.95
Kidding Around San Francisco, Zibart 64 pp. $9.95
Kidding Around Santa Fe, York 64 pp. $9.95
Kidding Around Seattle, Steves 64 pp. $9.95
Kidding Around Spain, Biggs 108 pp. $12.95
Kidding Around Washington, D.C., 2nd ed., Pedersen 64 pp. $9.95

"Extremely Weird" Series for Young Readers
Written for kids eight years of age and older.
Extremely Weird Bats, Lovett 48 pp. $9.95
Extremely Weird Birds, Lovett 48 pp. $9.95
Extremely Weird Endangered Species, Lovett 48 pp. $9.95
Extremely Weird Fishes, Lovett 48 pp. $9.95
Extremely Weird Frogs, Lovett 48 pp. $9.95
Extremely Weird Insects, Lovett 48 pp. $9.95
Extremely Weird Primates, Lovett 48 pp. $9.95
Extremely Weird Reptiles, Lovett 48 pp. $9.95
Extremely Weird Sea Creatures, Lovett 48 pp. $9.95
Extremely Weird Spiders, Lovett 48 pp. $9.95

Masters of Motion Series
For kids eight years and older.
How to Drive an Indy Race Car, Rubel 48 pages $9.95
How to Fly a 747, Paulson 48 pages $9.95
How to Fly the Space Shuttle, Shorto 48 pages $9.95

Quill Hedgehog Adventures Series
Green fiction for kids. Written for kids eight years of age and older.
Quill's Adventures in the Great Beyond. Waddington-Feather 96 pp. $5.95
Quill's Adventures in Wasteland, Waddington-Feather 132 pp. $5.95
Quill's Adventures in Grozzieland, Waddington-Feather 132 pp. $5.95

X-ray Vision Series
For kids eight years and older.
Looking Inside Cartoon Animation, Schultz 48 pages $9.95
Looking Inside Sports Aerodynamics, Schultz 48 pages $9.95
Looking Inside Sunken Treasure, Schultz 48 pp. $9.95
Looking Inside Telescopes and the Night Sky, Schultz 48 pp. $9.95
Looking Inside the Brain, Schultz 48 pages $9.95

Other Young Readers Titles
Habitats: Where the Wild Things Live, Hacker & Kaufman 48 pp. $9.95
The Indian Way: Learning to Communicate with Mother Earth, McLain 114 pp. $9.95

The Kids' Environment Book: What's Awry and Why, Pedersen 192 pp. $13.95
Kids Explore America's African-American Heritage, Westridge Young Writers Workshop 112 pp. $8.95
Kids Explore America's Hispanic Heritage, Westridge Young Writers Workshop 112 pp. $7.95
Rads, Ergs, and Cheeseburgers: The Kids' Guide to Energy and the Environment, Yanda 108 pp. $12.95

Automotive Titles
How to Keep Your VW Alive, 15th ed., 464 pp. $21.95
How to Keep Your Subaru Alive 480 pp. $21.95
How to Keep Your Toyota Pickup Alive 392 pp. $21.95
How to Keep Your Datsun/Nissan Alive 544 pp. $21.95
The Greaseless Guide to Car Care Confidence: Take the Terror Out of Talking to Your Mechanic, Jackson 224 pp. $14.95
Off-Road Emergency Repair & Survival, Ristow 160 pp. $9.95

Ordering Information
If you cannot find our books in your local bookstore, you can order directly from us. If you send us money for a book not yet available, we will hold your money until we can ship you the book. Your books will be sent to you via UPS (for U.S. destinations). UPS will not deliver to a P.O. Box; please give us a street address. Include $3.75 for the first item ordered and $.50 for each additional item to cover shipping and handling costs. For airmail within the U.S., enclose $4.00. All foreign orders will be shipped surface rate; please enclose $3.00 for the first item and $1.00 for each additional item. Please inquire about foreign airmail rates.

Method of Payment
Your order may be paid by check, money order, or credit card. We cannot be responsible for cash sent through the mail. All payments must be made in U.S. dollars drawn on a U.S. bank. Canadian postal money orders in U.S. dollars are acceptable. For VISA, MasterCard, or American Express orders, include your card number, expiration date, and your signature, or call (800) 888-7504. Books ordered on American Express cards can be shipped only to the billing address of the cardholder. Sorry, no C.O.D.'s. Residents of sunny New Mexico, add 5.875% tax to the total.
Address all orders and inquiries to:
  John Muir Publications
  P.O. Box 613
  Santa Fe, NM 87504
  (505) 982-4078
  (800) 888-7504